BOBBIE B.
THE UNTOLD STORY OF
A.A.'S "FANTASTIC COMMUNICATOR"

Other Books by Gary Neidhardt

Poseidon and the PC

King Charles of New York City

BOBBIE B.
THE UNTOLD STORY OF
A.A.'S "FANTASTIC COMMUNICATOR"

A Window Into the Alcoholic Foundation Office in the 1940s

GARY NEIDHARDT

ISBN: 979-8-88640-902-4 (sc)
ISBN: 979-8-88640-903-1 (hc)
ISBN: 979-8-88640-904-8 (e)

THE EWINGS
PUBLISHING

One Galleria Blvd., Suite 1900, Metairie, LA 70001
1-888-421-2397

For Lauren, Meg, and Lynda—Bobbie's grandchildren.
Their trust made this story possible.

CONTENTS

FOREWORD

How did it happen that one of the most devoted and loyal individuals in the formative years of Alcoholics Anonymous (AA) become an almost completely forgotten figure? Although probably best known for the role she played as National Secretary of the new organization that was forming its own identity, Bobbie B. essentially functioned as AA's unofficial director of communications in much of its formative years. During her tenure at the AA Central Office, she was the central nexus whose letters shaped autonomous groups across the country to become more unified by a common set of principles.

Bobbie's tireless replies to voluminous correspondence contributed immeasurably to the shaping of the Traditions, which took written form during her tenure. Notwithstanding the abundance of biographies that have been written about the founding fathers of AA, this story has never been fully told by anyone—until now. Had her letters throughout the fellowship ever been published, she would have arguably been one of AA's most prolific authors. In the pages that follow, historian Gary Neidhardt reveals the story of this pioneering woman whose guidance letters—at least in the thousands—would have filled more pages than the Big Book itself.

The history of any institution is filled with captivating characters, entertaining drama, and unsolved mysteries. The biographer's task of separating fact from fiction is not an easy one. Yet Neidhardt painstakingly explores uncharted territory with a balance of courage and scholarly vigor. In many instances this biography uses Bobbie's own words to tell her story. Compellingly writing with a combination of curiosity and compassion, Neidhardt provides an enlightening examination of roughly a thousand letters that have never been published. The result of this effort is a meticulously researched and densely packed account of the woman who was AA's most steadfast correspondent: her early life, her relationships, her countless letters, and her ideals that helped shape the evolving organization into what has become an enduring American institution that has reached across the entire globe.

Many mysteries continue to shroud the life—and untimely death—of the enigmatic Bobbie B, but *The Untold Story of A.A.'s Fantastic Communicator* provides a complete and engaging account of a fascinating chapter in the history of AA. Reading this book is like walking a trail with a guide who is a literary archeologist. Neidhardt has unearthed a wealth of archival materials, documents, and photographs that until now have been hidden away for almost seventy years. Like all great journeys this one begins with the first steps.

Willian F. Doverspike
Atlanta Counseling Center

NOTES ON THE MANUSCRIPT TEXT

I examined approximately a thousand letters Bobbie wrote while National Secretary, dictating them over three visits to the General Service Office (G.S.O.). The Photocopying Policy of the Archives of Alcoholics Anonymous allows for no direct copying or photographing of any unpublished personal letters. According to G.S.O. rules, I was allowed to take notes using a recording device. Their policies insist that anonymity is maintained for the living and the dead. Thus, the only last names used here are for non-alcoholics.[i]

I arrived at the Interchurch Center at 61 Claremont, New York City as close to 9am as possible, signed in at the front desk on the first floor, and took the elevator to the G.S.O. on the eleventh floor. Boxes of the original letters by the U.S. state I requested were brought to me by an archive office employee. All boxes contain copies, not originals. At the end of the day, When I was told my time was up (usually around 4:30pm – 4:45pm), I gave all the materials back to the office employee for return to the archives.

On occasion, I transcribed an additional letter that Bobbie did not write. Such a letter was either written to her or by someone else on a subject that applied to her. A better practice would have been to transcribe more of the words written to Bobbie that caused Bobbie to reply. Time constraints prohibited this. I hope future research can do a better job of documenting more of the letters written to her rather than only her responses. The omission of some of the words written to her diminishes the polemic nature of the correspondence occasionally sent to her.

The recordings were brought back to my home in Georgia where they were transcribed, which took a number of weeks after each of my three visits. The accuracy of this process has inherent flaws. Subtle errors may be present in the transcriptions. A claim that the letters were transcribed

---

[i] In cases of marriage and newspaper articles, last names can sometimes be deduced.

with 100% accuracy would be false. Thus, if any errors are someday discovered in my transcription process, accept my apology in advance.

Such transcription difficulties did not exist for other sources. "The Bobbie Family Collection" was in the possession of a son-in-law of Bobbie. The originals of these documents rest with the family as I received transmitted copies only. This collection has been unexamined for around 70 years and contains a number of Bill W.'s letters, some handwritten. What are being called "The Bobbie Daughter Collection" are copies of the original documents that were provided to the G.S.O. in 2013 by Bobbie's daughter Gloria, who has since passed away. There is a possibility that the G.S.O. may still have this collection, as it is unknown if it has been returned. The Georgia State Service Assembly (G.S.S.A.) archives contain letters both to and from the G.S.O. that are related to Georgia.

Automated grammar checking this manuscript is a nightmare. The grammar check interprets a period as the end of a sentence, not as an initial and period representing a last name. The question mark seems to have been either missing from most of the typewriters of the 1940s or was considered non-essential. A variety of awkward spellings were employed such as "thoroly" for "thoroughly." Quoted text has been left as close to the original as possible, though changes have been implemented for purposes of anonymity. The autocorrect capability of Microsoft Word at times corrected some of the spelling errors that were in the original text.

Lastly, the reader will find inconsistency between "A.A." vs "AA" present throughout this book, for which I apologize. Both are used interchangeably in quoted text and the inconsistency is further compounded by me.

ACKNOWLEDGEMENTS

'd like to give thanks to a long list of folks that have helped this book become a reality. First and foremost, my wife Mary; my cousin David Y. from Scottsdale, AZ, who familiarized me with NYC after many years away; Bobbie's three grandchildren Lauren, Meg and Lynda who very much wished this project to succeed. Their trust in me allowed the private side of Bobbie to be revealed such as I could never have conceived when this project started; the GSO Archives staff; the Stepping Stones staff; Gail L. who splits her time between Akron and Florida these days; Stephen R. from Tampa, FL; Karen R. from Tampa, FL; Joe U., from Boston, MA; Chris J. from Columbus, Ohio; Garth D. from Winnipeg, Manitoba, Canada; Anthony C. from Tampa, FL; David M. from Tampa, FL; Bill F. from Marietta, OH; Jackie B. from San Francisco, CA; Mike F. from Prescott, AZ; Drew H. from Atlanta, GA; John T. from Atlanta, GA; Kevin Hanlon from New York City; William S. from Connecticut; Roger W. from Vine Grove, KY; Ken B. from Akron, Ohio; Karlene S. from NSW Australia; Danny J. from Rome, GA; Carl B. from Columbia, Missouri; Thomas B. from Buffalo, NY; Bill T. from Detroit, MI; Jeff E. from Green Bay, Wisconsin; Joe G. from Wilmington, NC; Bill F. from Marietta, Ohio; Tom B. from Buffalo, NY; Cheri J. from Kansas City, Missouri; Rick F. from Tampa, Florida; Mark M. from Norman, Oklahoma; Roger S. from New Zealand. Special thanks to Greg J. of Pittsboro, NC for his efforts to edit the text.

FIGURES

All photographs used in the book originate with the Bobbie Family Collection with the following exceptions: Cover of Bill Wilson: source unknown; Figure 15 from Drew H.; Figure 16 from *Alcoholics Anonymous 1939-1942, The Archives of the General Service Board of Alcoholics Anonymous*; Figures 17 & 18 from *The Empty Jug*; Figure 20 from *The American Weekly*; Figure 25 from the credits of the film *One Too Many*; Figure 26 from the Chet Kirk Library at Brown University; Figure 28 source unknown.

A.A.'S FORGOTTEN FANTASTIC COMMUNICATOR

Many are familiar with the early beginnings of A.A. and the start of the little office in New York. Bill W. and Ruth Hock were the heart and soul of A.A. Headquarters, which became the General Service Office (G.S.O.).[1] During this pioneering time, there was a third significant contributor. Bill W. was said to have twelve-stepped her on September 24, 1940, though she claimed a March 1940 sobriety date. When she joined the small A.A. staff on Vesey Street isn't clear. Her first name was Margaret, but everybody knew her as "Bobbie." She would later become the National Secretary after Ruth was married and resigned in late February of 1942.

Bobbie B. worked some 11-12-hour days most likely at the 24th Street Clubhouse after the Jack Alexander *Saturday Evening Post* article was published in March 1941. Bobbie was one of the individuals, along with Lois W., who helped Ruth Hock, and possibly others, to answer as many as 6,000 requests for help that followed that ground-breaking article. Bobbie is believed to have been closely linked to Ruth by the time the Serenity Prayer was first read at the A.A. Headquarters office from a *New York Herald Tribune* obituary. It is certain that Bobbie helped circulate that prayer throughout the Fellowship in the years that followed.

Upon becoming National Secretary, she immediately began responding to a wide variety of correspondence written by the Fellowship in what Bill W. has referred to as "A.A.'s adolescent period." According to multiple sources, Bill was in the office at most two days of the week when he wasn't traveling (in some periods he traveled extensively). Bobbie was left in charge of responding to the prolific incoming correspondence, often without any supervision.

To call Bobbie a "secretary" is misleading. She might have been more appropriately called a "Communications Director." As her reputation increased, Bill considered her an "ex-officio" member of the A.A. Board of Trustees. She admitted to being a lousy typist, so she dictated most of her correspondence almost from the start. Most of her letters were typed by her subordinates.

During this first half of the 1940s there were no A.A. Traditions. Quite a few angry, unhappy, and sometimes insulting, letters were written to Bill but answered by Bobbie. Bill was to write later that it "was chiefly from this correspondence, and from our mounting public relations activity, that the basic ideas for the Traditions of Alcoholics Anonymous came." He also was to write in the foreword of the *Twelve Steps and Twelve Traditions* that "Everywhere there arose threatening questions of membership, money, personal relations, public relations, management of groups, clubs, and scores of other perplexities." Bobbie practiced "restraint of tongue and pen" long before that phrase became part of the wisdom of A.A. Some of these problems, according to Bill W., were "frightening beyond description." The unflappable Bobbie may not have liked the anger, frustration, and accusations made by some of the correspondents, but rarely did she respond in kind. She always wrote responses as if the yet-to-be-written Traditions were posted right in front of her. She knew her job was to reply to these requests by conveying the decisions already made by others, following a "trial and error" policy leaving local groups to decide most issues on their own. Whatever the local group would decide, in most of the cases, she asked to be informed so she could share the results with other groups who faced similar challenges.

Did she ever respond! No one knows how many letters she wrote for A.A. The number has to be in the many thousands over seven and a quarter years. Nobody knows how many letters she might have created in a day or how many days she worked in a row to answer the voluminous number of incoming requests. Many times she often wrote about being swamped— weeks behind in her responses and of the pressures of attempting to live up to the responsibilities placed on her. Despite the long hours on the job, Bill W. wrote that Bobbie never ceased to provide written examples filled with "never-failing sympathy, tolerance and understanding."

She was at the forefront of a wide variety of issues facing the emerging Fellowship in a period described by Bill W. as a time when the continued existence of the Alcoholics Anonymous was in jeopardy. Bobbie squarely addressed the issues of race and gender as a pioneer simply by responding with what she had learned through her correspondence with the Fellowship and her acquired wisdom from the co-founders. She made the announcement that due to the requirements of the War Production Board that the size and weight of the Big Book were going to be reduced. She took on the role of sponsoring many men through the exchange of letters without ever having met them – Dave B. was one of them as appears on Page 196 of the American fourth edition of *Alcoholics Anonymous*. She helped keep nearly three hundred soldiers serving in the Armed Forces connected to the Fellowship and sought to learn the addresses of more of them. She got Big Books to Australia and New Zealand at a time when almost the only material reaching those countries from the United States was military-related. No wonder that when one reads the history of how A.A. arrived in those two countries, Bobbie is honored for her efforts! A large percentage of the first 180 pages of the 2014 Australian conference approved book *One To Another* is a tribute to her. By the end of her tenure at A.A.'s Headquarters, roughly two dozen countries had been added to the Fellowship of A.A.

Bobbie wrote at the end of 1945 that "doctors took Bill away from active work about a year and a half ago and he seldom comes into the office." While Bobbie wrote or called Bill on the most important matters, there was no question that she was the one responding to most of the correspondence and functioning, as Nell Wing observed, as a "fantastic communicator." Bobbie had informed the Fellowship in May of 1945 that "Bill hopes to be with Bob [at the 10th-anniversary celebration of A.A.] if his health permits . . . The doctors have advised Bill not to do any traveling or Group-visiting for some time to come." Bobbie's role was truly that of a trusted servant to represent Bill in such a way. No wonder Nell Wing wrote later that "I can't tell you the number of people – all over the world who owe their sobriety to that woman." If we might consider the sponsorship chains of all those people who Bobbie helped, her legacy may include tens of thousands of sober alcoholics who are in her debt today and probably don't know it. Is it any wonder that the 1944 Christmas Greetings to the Fellowship written by Bill was signed from the Trustees, Bill, Lois, and Bobbie? This honor at Christmas was repeated in 1946 and 1948. Yes, she was held in that high of esteem!.

In 1945, the budget for A.A. Headquarters was around $9,000 for a six-month period for six full-time employees. This budget would quadruple in just four short years as the Fellowship rapidly grew. An assistant by the name of Charlotte L. was hired in 1946 to help with the enormous amount of correspondence, but by 1949, neither Bobbie nor Charlotte remained there.

How has this devoted, hard-working contributor been almost completely forgotten? Around May of 1948, her characteristic first and last name signature disappeared from the periodic A.A. bulletins. Was this a demotion? Though a signature of her first name appeared on occasion in the bulletins that were to follow, her first name only, with no last initial, was accompanied sometimes by as many as three other signatures or by the words "The Secretarial Staff."

By mid-1949, both Bobbie and her assistant Charlotte were said to have experienced "alcoholic slips" while employed at Headquarters, which led to them being "discharged." The sole source of this assertion has been Bob P.'s *Alcoholics Anonymous World History,* which was written no less than thirty-six years after the accusations of the slips took place. Bob P. wrote,

> "According to Nell Wing and Ann M., their relapses were partly caused by the enormous workload combined with the confusion of the early office . . . that poor woman (Bobbie) was just overwhelmed. The A.A. staff worked long hours all week and then sometimes went out to speak or to A.A. weekends, where they were 'Mrs. A.A.' and people showered them with affection and admiration. That ego inflation was hard to handle when they'd been sober just a few years . . . and they were exhausted too. Bobbie and Charlotte were apparently both on pills for some time before they returned to drinking."

Bobbie's last day of employment has recently been determined as June 13, 1949. Her office was declared vacant on July 25, 1949. Alcoholic Foundation Trustees met and she was provided with severance pay.

But what is the major shortcoming in Bill P.'s written history? He relied upon human memories, historically prone to be highly questionable especially if recounted decades later, and he quoted no primary documents. Until now, no one has documented what Bobbie wrote or what was written to her! Not even Bill W. himself left any article behind regarding the contents of what Bobbie composed on behalf of Alcoholic Anonymous. Bobbie worked for A.A. when letters were the primary means of communication. Her letters made a huge contribution to the formation of the Fellowship. She was the glue at A.A. Headquarters that held the Fellowship together in the 1940s when Bill was sometimes otherwise occupied!

Bobbie soon dropped out of view. After she left a psychiatrist's care in mid-July of 1949, little record was previously known of her activities that followed. Bobbie died on February 17, 1953. The cause of death in Manhattan was declared to have been from a heart ailment though she was only 49 years old. Documents regarding the last four years of her life reveal another story, told here for the first time. An accurate appraisal of her life can be told because Bobbie's grandchildren want it to be told. They have provided a wealth of documents and pictures that previously were hidden away for almost seventy years.

In Bill's brief memorial written in the March 1953 *Grapevine*, he wrote, ". . . upon our traditions her devoted labor set a mark which will endure as long as God will have our society last. Her pioneering work has proved an inspiring precedent for every Intergroup and Foundation secretary, and her departure creates in the heart of each of her friends a void which can only be filled by the memory of what she left us and the assurance that her destiny is happy and secure."

But has her destiny been appropriately "happy and secure" since her death? Despite those warm-hearted words, the many valuable contributions Bobbie made for the good of Alcoholics Anonymous have been all but forgotten. Similar "slippers" such as Hank P. and Ebby T. have been remembered and honored by the Fellowship despite their shortcomings. She deserves a place of honor throughout Alcoholics Anonymous. Her picture should be displayed today by A.A.s throughout the Fellowship and not only at Stepping Stones.[ii] Let us renew Bill W.'s pledge that her memory "will endure as long as God will have our society last." Let her full story be spread throughout A.A. so that this huge almost entirely untold story can see the light of day and this forgotten Fantastic Communicator be remembered as she should be: for her sacrifices, so that others could live.

If her full story becomes better known as part of the legacy of A.A. service, that accomplishment will fulfill the long overdue resolution of Panel 1 of the very first General Service Conference. During April 1951 they "unanimously resolved to go on formal record, by letter, declaring deep appreciation to Bobbie B for her years of faithful service as Secretary of the New York Office." Acknowledging her long overlooked contributions, which Panel 1 of the very first General Service Conference wished us to remember, is long overdue. This biography of Bobbie is not an ending. It is a beginning.

[ii]   Stepping Stones is the historic home of Bill W. and Lois, where Lois made a memorabilia "gallery." Today the home is a National Historic Landmark.

Dancing, Marriages, and Asylums

Bobbie was born Margaret Modelana Roberts in Detroit, Michigan on July 18, 1903. She was the first child of John Gillette and Emilie Roberts. The date her parents moved from Detroit to New York isn't known, but it is thought to be rather early in young Margaret's life. The only known address associated with her parents after their move back east was Dobbs Ferry, New York, twenty-one miles north of Times Square on the east shore of the Hudson River.

There was no previous history of alcoholism in her family. Her father, born in Illinois in 1872, was a patent attorney for Bell Labs. He was recognized as an authority in his field and as an inventor.[2] He was careful, methodical, and ambitious with a slow, analytical turn of mind.

FIGURE 1 - EMILIE AND JOHN GILLETTE ROBERTS

His attitude towards his daughter was always one of warmth and kindness. She had a strong respect for and attachment to him. For as long as she could remember, he and her mother had been on poor terms, quarreling openly and bitterly.[iii]

Margaret described her mother, born in Salt Lake City, Utah, 1878, as a cold woman who "made sacrifices for my sister and myself to the point of martyrdom." She would have fainting spells and complain of her heart whenever her authority was questioned, although her health was actually robust. She enjoyed the role of doting mother, but used it to dominate her children in every way. Margaret had never gotten along very well with her mother because she resented the constant subjugation. Her resentment, at times, amounted to a strong dislike. She felt that her mother was a neurotic and to blame for the disharmony in the family. Originally a Mormon, the mother never touched a drop of alcohol and was openly proud about this. The father occasionally took a drink.

FIGURE 2 - VARIOUS BALLET POSES

[iii]   Information regarding Bobbie's parents and her background heavily relies upon a psychological profile by the Department of Psychiatry, College of Physicians and Surgeons, Columbia University in 1945.

Margaret recalled having a very happy, active childhood. She played constantly with a group of children in her town and would be with them all day until their parents insisted that they come inside each evening. As a child, she was thin, "scrawny" and somewhat shy. She had a cheerful disposition and was seldom troubled, but she suffered agonies of embarrassment when her parents quarreled in front of other children. When the family was alone, she felt much less distress about the family dissension. She went to Sunday school as an Episcopalian[3] and enjoyed it, not so much because of the religious teaching but because there she could continue her association with her playmates, a group consisting of several boys and girls, in which she was an active member.

Her sister Ruth was born when she was eight years old on July 7, 1911, and for a time Bobbie was happy to take care of the new baby. She tired of this quickly though, for it lacked excitement, and turned to more active pursuits with her playmates. As the years went by, Margaret became very fond of her younger sister, describing her as a phlegmatic[iv] person, easy-going, happy and delightful. According to Margaret's grandchildren, Ruth would also suffer from alcoholism.

Margaret tended to think of herself as a "tom-boy," likely the origin of the nickname Bobbie, which followed her the rest of her life. At ten she suffered from measles, whooping cough and had an appendectomy. She did well in school, for she was brighter than most.[4] When she was twelve, she was sent away to a boarding school, and from this age on had little to do with the family. Menses began at fourteen, and her reaction was one of relief, as most of her companions had passed this stage some time before, making her feel inferior and immature. During her years in boarding school, she had a variety of boyfriends and crushes on a few of them. In 1919, at the age of sixteen, Bobbie was one of nineteen graduates from the Knox School of Tarrytown on the Hudson of New York. Though she passed examinations to enter college and was admitted to a woman's college, she preferred to study dramatics and take an occasional night course on the side. She continued to live with the family for a while, but stopped going to church with them. At this time, she had a retinue of boyfriends and was very active socially. She did no drinking, for at this time she thought it was frowned on for young people. She entered Columbia University in the fall of 1919, but it was not long until she gave up all her courses to concentrate

---

[iv]   Phlegmatic—unemotional and stolidly calm disposition

on her preparation for a stage career. She secured a small part in a comedy.[v] Her family accepted her choices. She lived with them for a short while longer, and then took an apartment with another young girl and an older woman who served as chaperone. During this time she had many men friends, one of whom, a writer of Bohemian nature, tried to seduce her, but met with no success. Now completely free of her family, her show went abroad, and after it closed, she toured Europe. She started touring with Donald Sawyer, who had been an accomplished professional dancer for a number of years. Exactly how and when they met is not known. Donald had lost his previous dance partner to marriage, so Bobbie took her place.

The twosome danced before royalty and the elite wealthy in some of the most elegant locations in Europe. Between tours, Bobbie performed in "Devlin's Revue" (July 1922), which was billed as "a gay, whirling bill of musical comedy, vaudeville, replete with lovely girls, brilliant costumes and scenic splendor and just jazzed full of rapid-fire pepe and humor."[5]

FIGURE 3 - VARIOUS POSES AS AN ACTRESS

---

[v]   Donald Sawyer, who was to become Bobbie's professional dance partner, may have met Bobbie in the comedy "Kissing Time," in which he had a named role. An ad appeared on October 3, 1920 for this comedy in which his name appeared in the *New York Herald.*

**FIGURE 4 - RETURNING FROM EUROPE
ON THE S.S. MAURETANIA**

FIGURE 5 - DONALD SAWYER & BOBBIE IN PUBLICITY POSES

The relationship between Bobbie and Donald, she recalled, was strictly professional, leaving her available for romance. During one of these trips, she fell in love with a wealthy Frenchman, but she felt that they were unsuited to each other and so she returned to America.[6]

In 1923, she spent three months in London as part of "The Music Box Revue" before departing for France.[7] In March 1924, Bobbie was part of a "delightful dance creation" at the Flatbush Theater in Brooklyn.[8] She then went to Europe once more with Donald Sawyer until November of 1924.

Shortly after she returned on the S.S. Mauretania with Donald on November 7, 1924, she fell severely ill with typhoid. Bobbie's poor health was the subject of a brief article in the *Yonkers Statesman* on January 17, 1925. She had "been confined in the New York Hospital for the past six weeks, suffering from the results of a dangerous attack of typhoid fever . . . [She] has recovered sufficiently to permit her being removed to the home of her parents."[9]

FIGURE 6 - PUBLICITY PICTURE KEPT IN HER SCRAPBOOK

**FIGURE 7 - IN THE "MUSIC BOX REVUE,"
LONDON, AUGUST 1923**

Norman Chapman Burger

"Miss Bobbie" likely was being courted by Norman Chapman Burger before 1921. He wrote her on August 22, 1921 in a manner which suggests they previously had become very fond of each other. One of his handwritten letters had fourteen pages. Another included these very affectionate words:

> Bobbie – I don't see why you should have such unhappy dreams – I dream about us, too, and everything has been just perfect. And why under the name of heaven should there be any suppressed fears? Freud's theory may be O.K. but for the love of Mike, Bobbie, there is no need for suppressed fears – they're out of the question . . . Bobbie – you're being a wonderful little correspondent and haven't failed me once. I may not sound my appreciation but if you know just what a letter from you did to me – well when one comes, I want to go out, blow the lake away, yank up the trees, and play golf with the stars.[10]

Apparently Norman was pursuing Bobbie—and with some success—whenever she was available, which must have been scarcely between dancing tours, plays, and overseas travel.

Her resume was highlighted when Bobbie's parents announced the upcoming wedding of their daughter in *The Yonkers Herald* on June 18, 1925. However, the wedding announcement seems to honor Bobbie's dance partner far more than her fiancé!

> Mr. and Mrs. John Gillette Roberts, Southlawn Avenue, Riverview Manor, have announced the engagement of their eldest daughter, Margaret Roberts, to Norman C. Burger of Brooklyn. The announcement was made at a dinner party given at the residence of the bride-to-be, on Sunday evening, June 14. Miss Roberts is a graduate of the Knox School, Cooperstown.[vi] During the past year Miss Roberts, together with her dancing partner, Donald Sawyer, have been appearing in the principle

---

vi   When Bobbie graduated from the Knox School, it was located in Tarrytown, NY. It relocated the year after Bobbie graduated.

theatres abroad. Also having danced before the King and Queen of England, the King and Queen of Spain, the King and Queen of Belgium, and the King and Queen of Italy.[vii] During the past three years both Miss Roberts and Mr. Sawyer have captivated lovers of terpsichore[viii] in the fashionable resorts of Paris, Deauville, Cannes, Vienna, Nice and London. During last November she appeared at the Hotel Ambassador, in New York for a brief engagement. Mr. Burger is a graduate of Williams College, Class of '21. The wedding will take place July 9.[11]

FIGURE 8 - ADDITIONAL DANCE POSES

Bobbie married Norman Chapman Burger just a few weeks later. She admired him as a straightforward, serious and honest person. A letter addressed to "My Darling Wife" from Norman dated the following December 11 mailed from New York to Boston still referred to her by her maiden name, which was how she was known professionally.[12] She and Donald were dancing at Copley Square at this time. Norman had a fair income and his family was well-to-do. Apparently he continued to trust implicitly in the strictly professional relationship between Bobbie and Donald. Norman was deeply in love with his wife when he wrote to her in March of 1926 while she and Donald were featured at the Egyptian Room at the Hotel Brunswick in Boston.

[vii]   Typed exactly as written.

[viii]   Terpisichore: a goddess of dance. As a proper name it is normally capitalized.

FIGURE 9 - MARRIAGE PICTURES OF BOBBIE TO NORMAN

FIGURE 10 - MR. & MRS. NORMAN C. BURGER

I miss you and want you horribly – more than anything else ever before or after. Now you're going to bawl me out for being a cry-baby – I'm not unhappy dear because I know you love me and miss me – as much as I do you? . . . I believe the trip will do you lots of good – you'll get some rest and a change of scenery which always help. And when you come home I'll be waiting at the G. C. terminal,[ix] the happiest person in the wide old world to see you again.[13]

FIGURE 11 - BOBBIE, SYBIL, AND GLORIA

She was later to recall in 1945 that she did not feel she had the passionate love for Norman that she had for her lover in Europe; yet she was very fond of him. He continued to write her for parts of 1926 as she continued her professional career. He wrote to her in February 1926 in Bermuda. Norman wrote four more letters to Bobbie at the Brunswick Hotel at Copley Plaza in Boston during March of 1926.

Bobbie's pregnancy later that year apparently put an end to her dancing career. Their first daughter Margaret Sybil (known simply as Sybil) was born on April 18, 1927 followed by Gloria Whitney on October 27, 1928. Tragically, Norman died suddenly, apparently from pneumonia on February 18, 1929 after only three and a half years of marriage.[14] The happiness of this union would elude Bobbie for the rest of her life. The one picture of the two of them together literally seems to exude the happiness shared between them.

[ix]   Grand Central Station in New York City.

After his death, she was supported by his family and her own for a time. Her reaction to his death was one of amazement and disbelief rather than depression. She felt that people thought she was harshly unemotional because of this. A former unnamed lover showed up before too long, and they had a series of intense and rather stormy affairs. The length of this episode remains unknown. At this time she was drinking, but supposedly only moderately.

Donald Sawyer had replaced Bobbie with a dancer named Joey Ray, but Joey Ray was eventually replaced by Donald's original dance partner— Florence Colebrook Powers. Together their success was highly publicized in the New York area. Donald Sawyer operated a Manhattan dance studio competitive with Arthur Murray in an era when ballroom dancing was very popular. Such was the prestige that Bobbie had left behind.

E. Shepard "Shep" Spink

Two years after her husband's death Bobbie began dating E. Shepard "Shep" Spink. Their relationship was volatile from the start. Before they were married, Shep pleaded for forgiveness in this early 1932 letter:

> I'm ashamed, humble, and apologetic. Please forgive me for everything – just one more chance – please . . . Of course I'm wrong to talk the way I did and hope I didn't ruin a good night's sleep for you . . . It positively won't happen again. I haven't any pride so far as you're concerned – just love, and you have it all.[15]

They lived together for a time with the idea of marrying if they found each other suitable. She had been working for Arthur Murray's Studio and Headquarters on 7 East 43rd Street in Manhattan as a dance instructor, which was quite a prestigious job.[16] At this time, Arthur Murray and his wife Kathryn would have been present often, though we have no record of the relationship Bobbie may have had with them. Quite a few Arthur Murray dance instructors married their customers.[17] She had every opportunity to be approached by many men, some of which would be wealthy members of high society. Shep may have been jealous of the male competition. No wonder she preferred the excitement of this arrangement, if we believe what Shep wrote her on March 21:

But about your suggestion, doesn't that include my making you free to play around all you want with others, without mentioning such dates, etc. to me? I think, now, that's part of what you were getting at – but you couldn't quite muster up the frankness to say so. If that is part of what you want – why hop to it – and I'll gladly (?) forget about your agreement to tell me about such affairs in advance. This brings up a point which I want to lecture you about. May I? Two people can't live together without perfect confidence in each other, and be happy and successful at it. [18]

Bobbie had been completely trusted by her late husband to remain loyal to him, despite the many opportunities she had with other men. Shep seems to have had other concerns. He looks to have demanded a surrogate wife. This requirement led to Shep's eventual demand for Bobbie to be just a housewife, which suited his role as an up and coming executive in the aggressive occupation of advertising. The seeds of conflict were planted from the very beginning.

FIGURE 12 - IN A BEAUTIFUL POSE

Bobbie's Psychological Profile

In Bobbie's psychological profile prepared for publication by the *Quarterly Journal of Studies on Alcohol* published by Columbia University (which guaranteed her anonymity), her psychiatrist summed up the events that followed the move to Detroit. The report continues as her symptoms worsened following a move to Cleveland as her ambitious husband's career advanced.[x]

> She went with him, and here started to drink regularly. Although he drank heavily, he seldom became intoxicated. They habitually had cocktails before dinner, and when he did not come home, she would drink all the cocktails she had prepared. As he came home less and less, claiming that he had to entertain his business associates with less respectable women, she drank more and more. She would drink the cocktails she had prepared for the two of them with the thought of him in mind, thinking resentfully, "See, if he can have a good time, so can I!" When she went out with him in the evening, she would insist on drinking as much as he did, and usually drank more. She would feel elated, but had no trouble in speaking or moving. She became increasingly unsatisfied with her relations with her husband. He was selfish and egocentric, wanting her and everything else, but willing to give nothing himself in return. Though he promised to mend his ways when she complained of his ignoring her, he never did.

FIGURE 13 - IN ANOTHER BEAUTIFUL POSE

---

[x]   3675 Traynham Road, Shaker Heights, Ohio, a wealthy suburb of Cleveland.

Soon after she started to drink when her husband failed to come home, she found herself looking forward to the prospect of drinking. At all times she would try to be with people she knew to be heavy drinkers, so that alcoholic evenings would be assured. She remained a social drinker however, and people did not seem to realize how heavy her drinking was becoming. Her need for it increased, and when she did not drink she would be miserable and restless. She began to drink very much to excess, although she managed to keep it hidden. During this time her arguments with her husband became more and more frequent, and she found that she was more able to answer his arguments with better ones of her own if she had been drinking. At times the quarrels would involve physical violence: he striking her and she throwing things at him. She was very unhappy, but still very much in love with him.

One morning she was unable to get out of bed, and the doctor who was summoned told her husband that she was drunk. Her excesses from then on were not so easy to conceal. Drinking then began to make her argumentative and depressed rather than elated as it had before. She began to think that she did not care to go on living, and decided that she wanted to get a divorce, although her love for her husband persisted. Before her drinking bouts she would feel definite anxiety and would then drink to pass out and drown these feelings in oblivion.

She took a trip to the South, and went on her first real alcoholic spree, one which lasted about ten days. Her husband and father came after her and put her into a hospital and this made her very angry.[19]

Hospitalizations Begin

The first hospital, according to the addresses found on the envelopes written by Shep to Bobbie, was Doctor's Hospital at 87th Street and East

End in New York City. This began a pattern: whenever professional help was deemed necessary for Bobbie to deal with her excessive drinking, the solution was to locate her in a psychological institution not far from New York City. In a letter dated February 29, 1936 from Cleveland, Ohio, Shep's motives appear admirable on the surface.[xi] Shep had arranged for Bobbie's two elementary-school-aged daughters to remain in Cleveland with him in hopes of Bobbie's quick return to the role Shep expected of her: to be a devoted housewife and mother to his two step-daughters.

> There isn't much I can say except that I hated so to leave you without taking you up in my arms and telling you how much I love you. No matter what you may think now, I hope you will soon realize that I love you with all my heart, and that what I have done was because I love you.[20]

On March 3, 1936, Bobbie's father "Pop" expressed his concern to Bobbie regarding her most recent binge.

> I know it is hard for you but am trusting that you are thinking more about your future health than present inconvenience. Just now it seems to me that nothing matters so much as keeping you well and happy. Of course one can never be certain about doctor and medicine but you and I agree Dr. Fisk[xii] is the one for you to put your faith in. Doubtless he can do more for you with your help than without it. I hope, therefore, you will find it possible to follow his advice.[21]

As many an alcoholic can identify, upon Bobbie being released from Doctor's Hospital on or about March 16, she really needed a drink! Shep arranged for the children to stay with Bobbie's parents, which allowed Bobbie and Shep to "do our recuperating together" by taking a vacation to Daytona Beach, Florida. He had written her that "we could stay longer

---

[xi]   A bill for a week ending March 4, 1936, in the amount of $125.36 ($2,348 in 2020) at Doctor's Hospital was addressed to Shep in Cleveland, thus Shep appears to have paid for at least part of this first hospitalization. (The Bobbie Family Collection)

[xii]   Dr. Fisk was employed by Doctor's Hospital.

and it would be fun getting all organized with you where we wouldn't have any interruptions or interference." However, there was no notion that she couldn't drink responsibly. So, before they left on the trip, she bought some scotch and before long she was drinking heavily again.

By no later than mid-May 1936, Bobbie registered as a patient at the Hartford Retreat – a sanitorium in Hartford, Connecticut with a robust history that dates back to 1824 when it was called the Hartford Retreat for the Insane.[22] She was to be there for around two months under the care of Dr. Burlingame.[23] This institution was the first Bobbie visited that featured elegant trees and gardens to provide a serene environment in which healing could take place.[xiii]

Meanwhile, Shep's career with Time-Life in Cleveland, Ohio, was prospering. He was fortunate enough to entertain Henry Luce,[24] "an American magazine magnate who was called the most influential private citizen of his day."[25] Soon afterwards he met the famous Clara Booth Luce, Henry's wife, an extraordinarily talented and famous woman of the times. Shep's career was blossoming. His letters were often filled with exciting news of the evening's entertainment: a jarring role—reversal compared to her previous marriage.

Shep's letters sounded sincere, but his demands seemed only reasonable to him. He wrote down his concept of their future together in a letter dated June 17, 1936:

> Dearest, of course I want you in Cleveland whenever your cure is complete. And of course I'm only anxious about your resorting to artificial courage in your differences and arguments with me. Anything you want to do at any time will be OK with me as long as you don't do that. And again of course I'll try my best to make you happy. Although I'm obliged to work hard anyhow. But as long as we tackle our differences in our normal state, I'm certain

---

[xiii] The gardens of this institution were designed by the prestigious landscape architect Frederick Law Olmsted. The Institute for Living, the present name for this facility, prominently features the rare trees that Olmsted planted on the grounds that come from all over the world. Olmsted's various landscape designs include Central Park in New York City, the Emerald Necklace in Boston, Massachusetts and very many others throughout the eastern half of the United States.

that we will be happy together. If only your ability to get mad without drinking is restored. No matter how unhappy you may be, or how angry you may be toward me, that must never happen again. That is the only reason you've been in Hartford, and it's the only reason your children & husband couldn't live with you.[26]

Bobbie emerged from the Hartford Retreat in late June, but she did not immediately return to Cleveland. On June 26, Shep wrote Bobbie who was staying with her parents and children in Dobbs Ferry. After ten days of staying away from the bottle, Bobbie started drinking as much as a quart a day. Events that followed aren't clear, but it seems Bobbie eventually made it back to Cleveland because Shep and Bobbie continued to have intense fights that summer. Shep tried to discipline her by abusing her through spanking and shaming her by exposing her alcoholic habits to other people, but this was to no avail. Memories relayed by Bobbie through her daughters and then to Bobbie's grandchildren many years later portrayed Shep as quite a "monster." Among other threats, Shep told her he wanted a divorce, but this made Bobbie more frantic and irrational since she wanted to stay married to him.

Bobbie's father, Pop, was deposed on February 8, 1937, by Bobbie's lawyer regarding what happened the previous August that led to a prolonged separation of Shep from Bobbie through her hospitalization:

> Pop told me [Bobbie's lawyer] that he was in Cleveland on August 25, of 1936 and at that time and in his presence, [Shep], claiming that he had been a failure as Bobbie's husband, told her he was through unless she would go to the hospital at White Plains. About 3 p.m. of that date Bobbie called her husband at his office and told him she would go to White Plains with her father and asked him to come out for dinner. It was agreed in Pop's presence that if Bobbie would go to White Plains at her own expense, he (her husband) would maintain the house and care of the children until she returned and after she returned, normal relations would be resumed. Love and affection between them was very much in evidence and both expressed themselves as being entirely satisfied; in short, it was

a practical plan and agreement between them by which to keep the home intact until Bobbie's return, after as long a period of hospitalization as the hospital authorities deemed sufficient.[27]

Furthermore, Bobbie agreed to pay for her third 1936 hospitalization herself. The bill for what turned out to be about a four-month stay away from Shep and her children turned out to be $1,767.87 (around $34,000 in 2022).[28]

Shep wrote of his frustrations to her soon after her voluntary admission to New York Hospital[xiv] in White Plains, New York in a letter dated August 30, 1936. The tone of the letter assumes he is blameless in their disagreements. In the merry-go-round of alcoholism, such beliefs by spouses of alcoholics, unfamiliar with the family disease of alcoholism, are all too typical. Shep wrote as if all the faults were hers:

[xiv] Bobbie, to our knowledge, left no record behind of the treatment she received while at New York Hospital, otherwise known to the locals as Bloomingdale's. However, Lillian Roth did when she was a patient there for six months ending in June, 1946. From her biography, *I'll Cry Tomorrow*, beginning on p. 223: "As I was to learn later, all an alcoholic receives in a hospital, or even a jail, is a cursory sobering up treatment. However in an institution like Bloomingdale's, which rarely takes alcoholics, the chronic drinker receives psychiatric and medical 'treatment' similar to that afforded regular mental patients . . . I had been without alcohol since my arrival. The paraldehyde, vitamin injections and other medication helped tide me over . . . A community therapeutic shower followed breakfast, to relax us. We sat in a line, naked but for a sheet, while nurses sprayed us with hot water, then tepid, then ice water needles. Gym and dancing followed (p. 226) . . . After a little fresh air, we were taken to mental therapy rooms. Some painted, some sanded boxes, some made leather goods . . . bedtime came swiftly enough. At eight o'clock, a bell rang – preparation for bath – and at nine o'clock, another, signaling lights out." Upon her release, she was provided seconal *[sic]* sleeping pills (p. 245) by her psychiatrist. "My bills at Bloomingdale's had run between $600 and $700 a month." (p. 247). Thus, if the bill in 1946 dollars was $3,900 for the six months in 2022 dollars, the amount was about $52,000. Lillian was drunk again within a very short time, a few weeks or a few days, which was identical to Bobbie's experiences in the mid-late1930s in such institutions.

Glad to learn from your letters that things are strict but that food is good and your doctor seems capable. Probably all this is for the best. If you get accustomed to a strict regime I am hopeful that it will help you be strict with yourself. Already in your letters I note you are placing part of the blame upon me. A strict accounting of yourself would not make this possible, and you are only kidding yourself when you say that you could have "come through" after I walked out on you last Sunday. Don't you remember what you did that night? Please stop kidding yourself – you are <u>not</u> kidding me. Probably the above will make you mad. But if your thinking is really honest you will know it's true and that you <u>must</u> face it.[29]

This was the first of thirty-two letters Shep wrote Bobbie while she was at the New York Hospital until Thanksgiving of that year. As the holiday approached, she asked her doctor if she would be allowed to travel to Cleveland to be with her two children for the holiday. Shep wrote to Bobbie that he had consulted with her doctor as well. Both Shep and her doctor said such a trip was out of the question. Shep's letter of November 23—three days before Thanksgiving—read, in part, as follows:

No, my dear, I cannot do what you wish. The very fact that part of your complete cure involves so-called practice week-ends to help you become readjusted indicates that there is a risk in getting your practice so far away from White Plains. I know only too well how hard it is to get you to go when you don't want to go – and I simply am unwilling to saddle myself ever again with the responsibility for your doing anything until all the practice is over. I attempted to make that clear in the beginning and it still stands.[30]

Two letters written by Shep to Pop shed additional light on these events. Shep received a message from Bobbie's doctor, which he shared with Pop in a letter dated November 27.

You probably think I'm a pretty heartless bird to put my foot down on the proposed trip to Cleveland for

Thanksgiving. But for your information about any plans for future trips, I want you to know just what the hospital wrote me. Here it is verbatim:

"I have your letter of November 20th in which you disapprove of your wife's contemplated visit to Cleveland for a week-end. I believe your judgment in this matter is wise and that she would not make such visits prior to the expiration of her hospital treatment. This matter was not suggested to her by her physician, but was proposed by her and discouraged by her physician."[31]

Shep proposed a compromise to Pop: Shep would bring the children to Dobbs Ferry—only ten miles from White Plains—for Christmas. Pop and his wife accepted the plan, but Pop discussed an additional matter with Shep. Shep had been punishing Bobbie for her heavy drinking by spanking her. Though Pop's letter to him is missing, Shep's reply to him survived:

I am much relieved that Xmas will be Dobbs Ferry – not Cleveland. And I shall do my best to make the days there pleasant for M. [Bobbie]. It is, of course, only for her sake that we are coming.

I know you are right when you say M. should not be spanked. While I do not intend to spank, I probably do so, and perhaps that is one reason why I feel she is better off for the time being seeing as little of me as possible.[32]

How hard it can be for a spouse or loved-one of an alcoholic to admit their part in the insanity: sometimes they fail to recognize the brutality of their own part in the dance of family alcoholism.

Divorced and Drunk

Bobbie celebrated Christmas 1936 at Dobbs Ferry with her husband and two children. Unbeknownst to her, Shep was concealing schemes hardly conducive of a Merry Christmas for him and his wife. Despite Bobbie having spent four months voluntarily hospitalized based on the promise of regaining "normal relations" with Shep, reconciliation was not to be. Quite the opposite. Instead, he wanted a divorce! Shep abruptly returned to Cleveland by December 28 and Bobbie was back at the New York Hospital in White Plains. He wrote her this observation:

> I do hope you have been happier today than you expected. It has been much on my mind that I should be the one to hurt you – and I hope the hurt is less than you thought. Believe me, it should be, for I'm simply not good enough or deep enough for that.[33]

Bobbie left the hospital on January 2, 1937 to return to what had been their home in Cleveland[xv]. By then Shep was living elsewhere. This missive from Shep on January 9 indicates they must have had some sort of verbal exchange regarding financial matters:

> Here's the check I thought I had with me – it was in my desk – sorry – Shall try to be prompt on the first of each month, – at least to the extent of what I think is fair, pending your wishes in the matter.

> Take care of yourself & let me know whenever there's anything I can do – I'll be seein' you.[34]

Bobbie believed, according to her 1945 psychological profile, "that her husband had been extensively unfaithful to her and was seeking a divorce behind her back."[xvi] Shep would express that he "had been particularly irritated by the efforts of his wife to uncover, by detective service, evidence of infidelity."[35] The divorce was uncontested and the separation agreement was dated April 7, 1937. It was reported in her psychological profile that sometime during "the divorce proceedings, and while sober, she took an overdose of a barbiturate in a sincere attempt to kill herself, but failed. She felt that if she died it would be better for her children."[36] No other details are known of the results, or the exact date.

[xv]   The address was 3675 Traynham Road, Shaker Heights, Ohio, a wealthy suburb of Cleveland, Ohio

[xvi]   Interestingly, Shep remarried on December 27, 1937, and a 1940 census lists one child born him and his wife Ethyl in 1939. (Ancestry.com)

The Columbia University psychological profile of Bobbie provided a glimpse of the next three years of chaos, out-of-control drinking and associated "whirlwinds" so typical of an alcoholic:

> Subsequent to the divorce her drinking increased and she went from one sanitorium to another. The process was always the same: she would become very inebriated, the family would have her committed, she would be discharged, and would start drinking again as soon as she left the hospital. She began to prefer alcohol to her children, though she tried to hide this fact from them. She drank heavily for three years, her longest period of abstinence being six weeks. On a few occasions when heavily intoxicated, she would think she heard people talking, when inspection showed that there was no one around her. She found herself lying as a matter of habit, even when there was nothing to be gained by it. She became engaged to an older man whose only attraction was that he would drink with her. While intoxicated, she would drink with anyone, male or female, but would never feel sexually stimulated. At times she would become unconscious and would forget what she had done. She never got into scrapes nor was she ever arrested, although she was frequently brought home by the police. Internally, she felt ashamed of herself, but in the presence of other people she would blame circumstances, situations, and persons for her predicament. When drinking she would have the feeling that "This is not I." At times she would set out to drink only moderately, at others she would definitely aim at drinking herself into a state of unconsciousness because she was so disgusted with herself. She never promised to give up drinking entirely, feeling that she could not live without it. At the same time, she was always sure that she could control her drinking.
>
> Her family criticized her strongly, and she accused them of driving her to drink and suicide. She felt that they were trying to have her put away, and in truth, they did want her

to be hospitalized. She became extremely angry, though
she never turned against her children.[37]

Letters written by Bobbie's two children, Sybil and Gloria, give
us the only information about where Bobbie was hospitalized during
these years. In September 1939 she was a patient at Stamford Hall in
Stamford, Connecticut, which was advertised as "New England's Largest
Private Sanitarium."[38] This may have been the sanitarium that the family
convinced Bobbie to attend for "a long term voluntary commitment." At
some time, most likely in the fall of 1939, she "spoke to a doctor to find if
this would be the best thing, and he advised her instead to contact A.A."
This apparently was her first introduction to A.A. and to a future Bobbie
could not have anticipated – a future that would "amaze her before she was
halfway through."

Inebriate to National Secretary

Bobbie likely became interested in Alcoholics Anonymous in the fall of 1939. Marty Mann attended a meeting in which she first saw Bobbie.[xvii] Marty learned a valuable lesson that day when she remembered her first impression of Bobbie.

> The Fall of 1939 continued to be a busy time for Marty and the AAs. Other meetings were springing up in various localities around New York. One evening two women appeared at Aeolian Hall.[xviii] The older one was the staff escort for the younger one, who had been sent to the meeting from a private mental institution in Westchester.[xix] Marty took one look at the patient and decided she wouldn't spend any effort on her –"didn't have one chance in a million." Marty was wrong. This woman did make it. Her name was Bobby *[sic]*. Bobby eventually became the secretary of AA's General Service Office, and her name was known to AAs all over the world.[39]

[xvii] *Mrs. Marty Mann*, Sally Brown and David R. Brown.

[xviii] Aeolian Hall in the Aeolian Building, which remains today, held a 1,100-seat auditorium on 29 West 42nd St in Manhattan. There is reason to doubt that A.A. could afford to rent the main auditorium, though it cannot be ruled out.

[xix] The hospital may have been the New York Hospital, sometimes called Bloomingdale's, located in Westchester County where Bobbie had been before.

Marty learned that one can't reliably predict what newcomer will get sober and who will not.

Little is known of Bobbie's activities in early 1940. Sometimes she required a nurse to accompany her, suggesting she was an inpatient at an institution. She maintained a close relationship with a boyfriend known only by the name of Mac. As part of Mac's evening business entertainment, he was dancing (and drinking) to the music of Guy Lombardo at the well-known Cocoanut Grove. He insisted that he was thinking of her constantly as he danced with a lady by the name of Elena who happened to compliment him on his dancing.[xx] Mac wrote:

> I told her I had been dancing for the last six months with a very charming girl who was formerly a professional dancer. Gee, how I was longing for you. You would love it. Dear I am counting the days until I head east. Will let you know just as soon as I know when I'm leaving for N.Y. and <u>you</u>. We are going through M.G.M. Studios Friday.[40]

Apparently Bobbie's relationship with Mac coincided roughly with the time she attended her first A.A. meetings. Since popular dancing and alcohol so often coexist, one may assume there was a strong temptation to drink when she was with Mac. They may have met at an Alcoholics Anonymous meeting. Chances are they did not meet at an Arthur Murray dance studio since Bobbie's frequent inebriation may have worn out her welcome at such places.

Bobbie asks Lois about Joining A.A.

We have no knowledge of how many A.A. meetings Bobbie attended after Marty first encountered her. Possibly a series of events, maybe with Mac, who proved to be much more than a heavy drinker, led her to conclude that she needed to take action to get and stay sober. Thus, Bobbie, using her own monogramed stationery, wrote to Lois Wilson on March 14, 1940, asking permission to attend an Alcoholics Anonymous meeting.

[xx]   This, incidentally, was the first time Bobbie's former career as a professional dancer was mentioned in a surviving letter since the death of her first husband Norman in 1929. Shep does not appear to have written about them dancing together.

> My dear Lois Wilson,
>
> Your name was given to me by Dr. Allen of White Plains (Bloomingdale's).[xxi]
>
> May I please attend your meeting on Tuesday, March 19 at Steinway Hall. I forgot to ask Dr. Allen what time.
>
> I would like to attend with the hope of coming a permanent member if I qualify.[41]

Why did Bobbie think it best to write Lois, who was not an alcoholic, regarding this matter? Could it have been because Lois often attended A.A. meetings with Bill during this time? It's plausible that Bobbie thought Lois was an A.A. member. Female A.A. members around then were in short supply. The date of her request suggests that Bobbie may have taken as many as six months to open her mind to the possibility of Alcoholics Anonymous as a solution. Stopping drinking had not been a problem. She had spent most of the last four years going to sanitariums where she could stop. Staying stopped had been far beyond her capability. She would drink soon after being discharged – terrifying her close relatives in the process.

[xxi] *New York Times*, October 16, 1994, 'Hospital Marking Its 100th Year" by Kate Stone Lombardi: "ONE hundred years ago Bloomingdale Hospital was open for public inspection here, and the *New York Times*, under the headline 'New Home for the Insane,' found 'everything was in the best of order, and the buildings and their management were praised by everyone.'

Tomorrow, the hospital, which is now formally known as the New York Hospital-Cornell Medical Center, Westchester Division (though still referred to among residents as Bloomingdale's) will again open its doors to the public, this time to celebrate the institution's centennial.

The medical center, a division of the Department of Psychiatry at New York Hospital in Manhattan, is now the largest long-term inpatient psychiatric unit in the county . . .

The hospital's location in White Plains was based on the concept that patients would benefit from the serene atmosphere of country surroundings . . ."

Bobbie's letter to Lois was passed on to Ruth Hock, National Secretary of Alcoholics Anonymous, who promptly replied on March 18, 1940:

> Thank you very much for your letter to Mrs. Wilson regarding Alcoholics Anonymous.
>
> The meetings are held on Tuesday evening, about 8:30 P. M. at Steinway Hall, 113 W. 57th St., New York City – (A.A. Society).
>
> We shall look forward with pleasure to seeing you there.[42]

Bobbie was repeatedly to claim a sobriety date of March, 1940 in upcoming years, though the exact day never seemed to have any importance to her.[xxii] The 30 Vesey Street office of Alcoholics Anonymous opened on March 16, 1940,[43] followed by the opening of the 24th Street Clubhouse on June 18,[44] just three miles away. Bobbie likely became familiar with both of these addresses around the time she got sober. It is probable that she met Bill W. sometime before June of 1940, but exactly when Bobbie first met him remains unknown. However, the two of them knew each other well enough to perform a Twelve-Step call on Bobbie's boyfriend Mac by the end of June.

[xxii] Embarrassment may have been the reason behind Bobbie's refusal to set a sobriety date because of her traffic accident as reported on March 30, 1940 in *The Herald Statesman* of Yonkers, NY, p. 3. This was about two weeks after she wrote Lois to attend the Manhattan A.A. meeting:

Dobbs Ferry Woman Faces Driving Charge.

Hastings-On-Hudson. Mrs. Margaret B—— of 50 Southlawn Avenue, Dobbs Ferry, has been summoned to appear on Monday April 8 before Police Judge Adolph W. Bevers to answer a reckless driving charge.

According to police, Mrs. B—— was driving an automobile on Warburton Avenue, mounted the curb and sidewalk and knocked down a pedestrian, Elliot Evans, twenty-two of 576 Warburton Avenue, Hastings. The reckless driving complaint was made by the owner of the parked car.

Mac wrote to Bobbie on June 24 from High Watch Farm in Kent, Connecticut after she and Bill had driven him there.[xxiii] By this time, Bobbie was approaching three months sober, but Mac's heavy drinking had apparently caught up with him.

> Just a note of gratitude for what you so willing done *[sic]* for me in seeing me to "Joy Farm"[xxiv] where I have met so many interesting people.
>
> It is the first step of a ladder which I feel reasonably sure will lead to the realization of things I have always wanted, but knew so little about securing.
>
> In the turmoil of things on the afternoon on which you & Bill drove me here, I forgot to remember my luggage which we placed in the rear of the car. I'd appreciate anything you might do in seeing that I have a clean shirt, etc.
>
> Thanks, & I'm looking forward to seeing you again.[45]

Bobbie Watched Bill in Action

Bobbie had a wonderful opportunity to see Bill in action early in her sobriety as documented in *Pass It On*. This event represented the earliest

---

[xxiii] High Watch Farm was by then a trusted location for new A.A. prospects to get sober as well as a retreat center for those already recovered.

[xxiv] Mac was actually at High Watch Farm, which exists to this day. "High Watch has a rich history connected to Alcoholics Anonymous. Inspired by A.A. co-founder Bill W., High Watch was established in 1939 as the world's first 12-Step treatment center. The debate over the role of Alcoholics Anonymous versus the role of professional treatment can be traced back to the first days of High Watch Farm. It was at that time, A.A.'s future was set to remain independent from the business of "treatment" for alcoholics. The colorful history of High Watch begins with Sister Francis, the woman who offered the farm to Bill W. in 1939." Taken from https://highwatchrecovery.org/history/. Before the name High Watch Farm was adopted by the summer of 1940, the location was called Joy Farm. Thus Mac was actually at High Watch Farm but was using the old name.

known encounter of an issue that would confront Alcoholics Anonymous with increasing frequency as the decade continued:

> As early as 1940, Bill had drawn fire for inviting two black alcoholics to attend meetings in the New York area. After hearing him speak at an institution, they asked him whether, on their release, they might join A.A. Bill said yes, and a few weeks later, they appeared at a local meeting.
>
> 'I remember it well because I was there,' Bobbie B. said. 'Immediately, a reaction started up within the group. We had some Southerners with us who strongly felt that Bill had overstepped in making this decision before consulting the group. They were ready to secede from A.A. and walk out. On the other hand, there were some Northerners who thought the Negroes should come in as full members with full privileges. And of course there were those who were on the fence.'
>
> Bill realized immediately that he had made a mistake. 'So he asked those who objected if they would agree that Negroes had the right to A.A. just the same as any other human being,' continued Bobbie. 'On the basic principle, there was complete agreement. So it was more or less decided then that Negroes should be invited to attend open or closed group meetings as visitors.'
>
> The compromise method of permitting blacks to come to meetings as 'observers' worked.[46]

No information is known regarding how long this "compromise method" supposedly "worked." This unfortunate outcome, typical for the times, is noted here for another reason: this text documents that Bobbie was active in an A.A. meeting with Bill some time in 1940.[xxv]

[xxv]   An exact date is not documented in *Pass It On*, nor does the book provide any source documentation for this event.

Mac on the Rebound

By early October, Mac was back to writing Bobbie rather regularly. She and her two children were living with her parents in Dobbs Ferry. On October 8, 1940 he wrote the first of fifteen letters in two months, suggesting that Bobbie "try not to look into the past but let's look to the future for what good we are assured is there."[47] Lois' October 10 diary entry records that she had supper with Bobbie and Mac.[48] The next few days found Mac packing for High Watch Farm. He wrote, "I believe you were right in your not being at the Farm at the same time I am." The same letter suggested that his drinking had cost him his job.[49]

In his next message on October 17, he had returned from High Watch Farm and was searching for a job. He expressed gratitude to Bobbie for sticking by him.

> Boy it is good to be sober. Thank God & my Bobbie for that. Honestly, I'm just beginning to recognize all the little things you did for me. I'll never be able to thank you enough for all the things but I would like you to know that I stand ready & willing to try. I have so much to be thankful for. I'd like to share it.[50]

Mac's letter of October 25 contained this rather interesting account of Bill, Lois, and Ruth Hock:

> Lois, Bill & Ruth just came in (2 P.M.) all filled with glee over their trip. They (B & L) are going out to country to-nite where Bert[xxvi] will pick them up tomorrow & continue on to Vermont.[51]

Mac wrote a twenty-page handwritten message to Bobbie on November 20—the first time he had written in three weeks. Unfortunately, almost all of the writing has faded beyond readability. However, the last few pages indicate that he had gone to High Watch Farm after another alcohol slip.[52]

His next letters were from the William Sloane House on West 34th Street in New York, which at that time was the largest YMCA in the

---

[xxvi]   Bert T., AA #69, according to the John B. *A.A. History Lover's* Message 8061. of the "First Hundred Sober in A.A."

country.[53] He was still writing Bobbie at her parent's home. Bobbie had to be commuting to Manhattan to attend the A.A. meetings at the 24th Street Clubhouse, but we have no record how often. Mac's November 22 letter included a prediction which was not to come true.

> You are going to make some man a wonderful wife one of these days. All the hell you have gone through hasn't been for naught & you are deserving of all the good that is due you. Claim it; demand it, it is yours. God intended that you should have it.[54]

Even though Bobbie was sober and enjoying fellowship previously missing from her life, Mac's letters indicate she carried a negative self-image. Mac wrote her on November 29 addressing how Bobbie considered herself to be a burden for Mac. One might mistake who was sober and who had been slipping.

> I regret very much what you say & feel about your being a hindrance to me & that you have concluded that it is for the best. I am deeply sorry for that & yet I cannot blame anyone or anything but myself for it. I am sorry that I caused you the unhappiness that I did. It is only my stupidity that hasn't brought this to my attention before now . . . Instead of your being a hindrance to me my dear you have been the most potent inspiration I have ever had in bolstering up my desire to attain my life's ambitions.[55]

Dick S. from Ohio

Bobbie and Mac were to soon go their separate ways. Dick S. from Akron, Ohio was to run into the "mess" called Mac in May of 1941, which strongly indicated Mac had been drinking to excess once more.[56] In May 1942, Dick sarcastically wrote Bobbie about her former boyfriend, asking if Mac's wife had a job! It was Dick's opinion that he had been unemployed for too long: "Was thinking about him the other night – got so mad I couldn't sleep. He has never tried to go the whole way – afraid he'd stop drinking."[57] His remark became the last news available about Mac.

It is believed that someone was hired by the Alcoholic Foundation, an assistant to Ruth Hock, in March of 1941 . Was it Bobbie? A paper that originated in Loyola University in Chicago has Bobbie being hired sometime in 1941 by the Foundation, but the month wasn't specified.[58] She definitely had existing responsibilities as secretary of meetings at the 24th St. Clubhouse, which likely made Bobbie a natural fit to assist Ruth.[59] However, even if she wasn't formally hired until February of 1942 as National Secretary at 30 Vesey Street, Bobbie was part of the team[xxvii] that responded to the overwhelming number of inquiries received after the explosive article in the *Saturday Evening Post* by Jack Alexander.[60] Bobbie's correspondence in later years was marked with experience about being a group secretary from her time at that first New York clubhouse.

Fifteen years after Ruth Hock left Headquarters, she verified that Bobbie began using what eventually became known as the Serenity Prayer almost from the moment it was brought to Headquarters by Jack C. "At this time, Bobbie B, who was terrifically impressed with it, undoubtedly used it in her work with the many she contacted daily at the 24th Street Clubhouse . . ."[61] Ruth indicated that Bobbie was probably not hired at HQ

[xxvii] Lois Wilson's memories in *Lois Remembers* ©*1979* as written on page 131 regarding the *Saturday Evening Post* March 1, 1941 article may actually give Bobbie (Lois refers to her with the common misspelling "Bobby") more credit than she deserves. Lois wrote: "Ruth Hock had left to be married to a member from Ohio, so Bobby B., the new secretary, and I worked out a plan to use volunteers to help answer all the inquiries that would flood in. I was to handle these AAs and their families, serve as liaison between them and the Foundation office, and use the 24th Street Clubhouse as Headquarters. That was a handy location, for Bill and I had just made one more move – our next-to-last, though we did not know it at the time." This confirms that Bobbie was heavily involved in answering some of the thousands of inquiries resulting from the article. Ruth, of course, remained National Secretary until a year after the article appeared. Therefore, Lois was mistaken that "Bobby" was National Secretary at that time. *Lois Remembers* ©1985 second printing removed Bobbie's name by rewording a sentence to give the credit to Ruth Hock on page 131. However, "Bobby's" name remains twice on page 132. Also, Francis Hartigan in his *Bill W.* on page 143 has Bobbie (with her last name misspelled) as a part of the responding team. On page 149 of *Language of The Heart*, Bill wrote "So volunteers with typewriters came to New York's old 24th Club," so even he remembered the inquiries being answered from where Bobbie was the secretary.

until later in 1941 or early 1942. The prayer concluded the A.A. Bulletin #3 dated June 30, 1941.[xxviii]

Even though Bobbie and Mac parted company, she was not without a male pursuer for long. Dick S., A.A. #27[xxix] from Akron, Ohio, author of the story "Car Smasher" in the First Edition of *Alcoholics Anonymous* quickly seemed to filled any void Mac left behind. Dick's personal business stationery boasted the prestigious address of 1149 Park Avenue, New York.[62] His many letters to Bobbie in this period carried return addresses of Chicago, Cleveland, Cuyahoga Falls, Boston, Akron and New York. Some of his mail to her was on Mainliner stationery as he often was flying in an era when most passenger planes carried no more than twelve passengers. Dick may have been divorced recently, which would have freed him to pursue Bobbie. She seemed very much a priority for him at this time.

Dick had to have been attending A.A. meetings with Bobbie in New York. He gave her advice regarding how she should manage her time while being a mother of two daughters. This April 7, 1941 letter was written to the 24th Street Clubhouse rather than 30 Vesey Street, suggesting that Bobbie had taken a paid position there by then. Dick knew the names of Bobbie's daughters. Other letters indicate that Dick had visited Dobbs Ferry and become familiar with the rest of Bobbie's family. He insisted that she was overdoing at her daughters' expense:

> Listen, Bobbie, I'm serious, when I tell you, you should
> make it a rule to go home every night except maybe two.
> You could pile up women for Monday nights and then
> stay in to one other meeting during the week, in addition
> to it being better for you. The girls want you – and in the
> past need you from what I've seen. You and they have a

[xxviii] Though Bobbie was to send out little cards containing the Serenity Prayer over the years, she did not refer to it using its commonly accepted name of today. Among her letters the only title for the prayer that she wrote came from the following: "I think you will appreciate it I am enclosing a little card that I have carried with us for over two years. This with "God Grant Me the Serenity" card are the two thoughts that help me more than anything else did." Written September 25, 1942, General Service Office Archives, Box 35, R17, File I.1, p 154.

[xxix] Dick was listed #27 in the John B. *A.A. History Lovers* Message #8061. "First One Hundred Sober in A.A."

very nice relationship, and don't laugh. There are lots of mothers & daughters who don't have that rather special comradeship & understanding confidence you have with Gloria & Sybil, and for the next five or six years it will be important as long as you are doing for A.A. surely. You can't be expected to stay down, night after night, and I know too – how you like to – it is hard not to go there but isn't that a little selfish – when they want you & maybe need you – not that they must eat & such – but those nights when they are full of chatter – which is important to them – and they should chatter with you.[63]

FIGURE 14 - BOBBIE - DATE OF PICTURE UNKNOWN

Dick may have had considerable influence with Bobbie being hired as a paid secretary for the 24th Street Clubhouse. Another letter, which, unfortunately, has no date associated with it,[xxx] concerns a club maintenance man by the name of Tom. The timing of this message must have been after the *Saturday Evening Post* article due to the references about being swamped with inquiries. The letter hints that this Tom was the

---

[xxx]   Dick often would only place the day of the week on the beginning of his letters, thus the only date associated with the letter was the date stamp on the envelope. With this particular letter, there is no envelope, no date, or first page.

only paid individual at the clubhouse besides a cook at this time,[xxxi] while Dick recognized the need for a paid secretary to offload a responsibility for which Tom was not qualified.

> No kidding – there has been over 200 inquiries – at least 75% from alcoholics themselves and Tom has just got more than he can attend to – and Bill says Foundation office is swamped already – so to have someone actually do detail of Tom's job – and to be at the club to answer phone, and to talk to people coming in – we did decide to try to get some one – and naturally you came to mind first. You are a natural for the job – only thing is can we afford it – we think that April should see enough coming in that we could double the money. The thought struck me that it would put you in New York – and in touch with other positions – and about pay actual expenses coming in each day. Think it over. The hours would have to be cockeyed. I suppose I hope we can have a chance to talk it over. I mean if you should feel so inclined.[64]

Several of Dick's letters suggested that their relationship had become very personal. Most of these affectionate communications were dated well before she became the National Secretary. Dick wrote this adoring note from the Congress Hotel in Chicago in April of 1941:

> Lord, Bobbie, you willing, I wouldn't leave you for a second while I'm there – and the second I have any assurance about when I'll be there, I'll let you know. And I don't have your private number, so I can call you. I wish I could come direct to you. Let no one know I'm there, and we could have oh hours & hours – to "dish" – maybe we'd both decide, I shouldn't come back here.[65]

Dick gives Bobbie a glimpse into what it was like for him to be at the 24th Street Clubhouse. It is progress, not perfection, for Dick since his need to take another's inventory seemed so appropriate at the time.

[xxxi] Tom almost assuredly was the janitor Bill wrote about on page 167 of *The Twelve Steps and the Twelve Traditions* in his essay on Tradition 8.

Called Tom, and he said he had a note about my seeing someone – so caught up with Bill, Lois, Herb, Shea, & Bussy (the nurse) then to [the] Club to find Bert wouldn't be there, and Gillingham talking to a very worthwhile person I'd met a few weeks ago – which didn't set too well. Hugh came about 8:45 – got meeting about 20 there – started about nine. Hugh spoke, and called on me so I could leave – and I think I was going "good" – you know. Like when you have a "warm" or cold audience. When a poor woman called, and talked 3 nickels worth (hers not mine) about her brother. When I came down stairs, Gill was well into his routine – and all I could see was a god damned old hypocrite – talking to a lot of trusting men – who were trying and left. I couldn't believe him if he said good morning.[66]

Dick concluded with some humor:

Good night Bobbie – remember a hundred years from now will laugh at us in 1941.[67]

Having only Dick's letters, it's impossible conclusively to determine just what kind of a relationship they had. He appears smitten with Bobbie, but, Bobbie, because of her disastrous marriage to Shep, must have considered Michigan and Ohio the dreary end of the earth. While Dick visited New York often, he was from Ohio. That may have discouraged her – and eventually him. Letters from Dick to Bobbie in later years are friendly, but strictly business. He was also a decade older than Bobbie.[68] Nonetheless, there's no question that he at one time had deep romantic feelings for her. Despite not feeling well one day, he had the strength to write like this for Bobbie:

I think I've never felt so low in my life – because – besides being half sick, I learned a little while ago that I missed you at the club. Lord, if I'd known you were there – everything would have seemed alright cause I'd have gone too. Then knowing I could go up to Dobbs Ferry tomorrow – only I'm going to have to call you & say I won't be able to – as

I will have told you, I'm going into Murray Hill Hospital tomorrow morning.[69]

It always seemed you looked nicer than I'd expected you to – and that seemed to give me the right to kick myself – for not really appreciating you – as I told you or tried to today. It isn't as tho I'd fallen in love with a "pretty face, and dear, I know you know what I mean – a "doll face" it has happened. Nor yet, was I like some I've known, in love with a "shape" something that was perfection – something to possess – but above all others, yours was the face and shape I wanted to see. When you'd come in late and I was where I couldn't see. Two steps in the hall and I'd know it was you, and was actually afraid others would notice, how it effected *[sic]* me, and here I was a dottering *[sic]* old grandfather. . . . I suppose I've written as tho *[sic]* I were going to jump off the bridge or some other foolish thing – which is not a fact. I am learning – knowing, that as you said tonight – this thing that has happened to me is nothing to be ashamed of – and as Bill said, is something over which I had no control (but had I had any, I wouldn't have used it). I've learned to love a woman, very deeply, honestly and sincerely, and am, I am sure, very much the better for it. I've a friend – I feel – that means so much – as a friend – I suppose that it will be a long time before I will stop thinking about what might have been.[70]

This letter from Dick was written as one of many during April—May. Bobbie kept many of Dick's letters, but most have faded. No letters dated after May 1941 have survived, so Bobbie's activities for the balance of the year are undocumented. It can be surmised that she gained quite a favorable reputation as secretary at the 24th Street Clubhouse as well as providing volunteer help to A.A. Headquarters when necessary.

In any case, by early 1942, Bobbie began a second career as A.A.'s second National Secretary: saving lives instead of entertaining them.

Bobbie Under Fire

The title "Secretary"—even preceded by the august adjective "National"—may be among the number of reasons Bobbie has been overlooked in A.A. history heretofore. Webster's defines "secretary" as "one employed to handle correspondence and manage routine and detail work for a superior." That definition sometimes matches the legend regarding the better-known secretary, Ruth Hock, who typed the Big Book while Bill dictated it to her. In reality, the secretarial image burned into the modern mind proves very misleading for both these formidable women. Ruth personally authored a good deal of A.A. correspondence as the first National Secretary while Bill was elsewhere.[xxxii] Bobbie was to do the same, but for a much longer period. Moreover, there were three different trips that kept Bill away for around ninety consecutive days during Bobbie's tenure. Another myth surrounding Bobbie's secretarial profession regarded taking dictation and simply typing. Bobbie was a self-professed lousy typist. Whenever possible, she dictated her letters to a subordinate. When an A.A. member had written her and apologized for their own sloppy typing, Bobbie replied:

[xxxii]   Among Ruth's strong ties to members of A.A. included her relationship with Clarence S. originally from Cleveland, Ohio. "Ruth Hock was extremely close to both Clarence and his wife Dorothy, and remained so even after they eventually got divorced. Ruth continued to correspond with, and visit both of them at their respective homes. She maintained this close relationship until each had passed on." *How It Worked*, Second Edition, Mitchel K., ©2014, Amazon Press, p. 177.

> Send along your helpful hints of what groups should not do even though you average many mistakes to the line. I make them too having picked up the art of typing after not touching a machine for 20 years. I dictate a lot of my letters except when the two girls in the office are busy. This is one of those times so I'm "pecking" myself these days.[71]

Before she celebrated her second anniversary of sobriety at the age of 38, she wrote this encouraging message to Wheeling, West Virginia dated February 18, 1942. Possibly Ruth Hock, who was soon to resign as National Secretary upon getting married the following February 28, was allowing Bobbie to get the feel of what was going to be her job for the next seven and a quarter years. The letter also addressed gasoline rationing. Traveling to help pick up newcomers and take them to Alcoholics Anonymous was going to be severely limited if only three gallons a week of gasoline were permitted per vehicle. New tires were also very difficult to find since rubber was rationed even before gasoline was.

> Here's hoping your tires last a while longer for I imagine the meetings in Pittsburg[xxxiii] *[sic]* are very helpful. Maybe later Mr. J and Mr. H. can journey over to your town to assist you in forming a group. We will help all we can from this end – to date we have no recent inquiries but will keep you in mind. Should any of our traveling members visit Wheeling we will ask them to get in touch with you. Please let us know how things are shaping up and we are reserving a very special "star" to put Wheeling on our A.A. Map. We have about 170 on it now and they are popping out so fast that the map takes on the appearance of a bad case of measles.[72]

In 1957, Bill recounted the transition of secretaries when he wrote *Alcoholics Anonymous Comes of Age*:

> [Ruth] was replaced by Bobbie B., who became A.A.'s National Secretary number two. Bobbie's complete loyalty

---

[xxxiii] Wheeling, WV is roughly 60 miles from Pittsburgh, PA, which might have taken two hours one way in those days.

and devotion and her unbelievable energy and capacity for hard work were priceless helps during the confused and hazardous years which now lay ahead of us.[73]

**FIGURE 15 - BOBBIE (LEFT) AND RUTH HOCK
IN AN UNDATED PHOTOGRAPH**

Confusion in Columbus, Ohio

Confusion and conflict arose before Bobbie could get settled into her new seat as national secretary. Columbus, Ohio A.A. provided quite a baptism of fire, requiring her to write three letters on the same day to reconcile contradictory claims disputing who was the appropriate A.A. contact. A.A. Headquarters had received a telegram insisting that Al B. was the only A.A. member "authorized to order and receive books, also that all correspondence is to be mailed to him. We are also advised that Mr. W. is no longer connected with the A.A. group in Columbus."[74] However, Mr. W. and Mr. S. of Columbus A.A. wrote to her with different instructions. Just the previous day, Bobbie had received and shipped an order for six books and pamphlets addressed to the attention of Mr. W. in Columbus, which posed a risk. It was the policy of A.A. Headquarters to send out books prior to them being paid for—on "consignment"-assuming the groups, many of which were broke, would eventually make good on the debt. The telegram introducing Mr. B. alarmed the new secretary: she may have sent the books to those who might not pay for them! Without taking sides in the local dispute, she wrote Mr. W., who ordered the books, asking for clarification. The policy of Headquarters in not taking sides in local disputes had already become established, which she followed despite not knowing who would pay for the six books.

> We have answered the telegram of Columbus A.A. and sent letters to Mr. S., Mr. B. and yourself. It is best to keep all of this in the open where it can be discussed freely. It is impossible for us to make any decision in matters like this and I am sure you realize the advisability of our standpoint.[75]

Bobbie wrote a third letter to Mr. S. on February 27 attempting to sort out the tangle, which today is probably rarely encountered by the New York General Service Office.[xxxiv] In these adolescent days of Alcoholics Anonymous, new groups evolved independently, without much knowledge of the challenges faced by other A.A. groups or the dilemmas being written to Headquarters. Often Bobbie could not afford the time or the effort to retype explanations she had already made. So, in this case, she referred to previous communication she had written to Columbus and asked that it be shared.

> To save me time, as this office is particularly busy right now, will you please ask Mr. B. to let you read our letter to him? We have also written to Mr. W. feeling it is wise to keep this situation in the open where it can be discussed freely by all sides. I am sure you can see the advisability of our not making decisions in matters of this kind – we really can only try to see everyone's viewpoint and hope that all of you will do the same. However, we are listing Mr. B. as acting secretary on the authorization of the Columbus A.A. Can you tell me if that is a committee chosen by the whole group or whether it means all the members?[76]

[xxxiv] Today, most conference-approved books published by Alcoholics Anonymous are purchased locally from area or central offices and not directly ordered from the G.S.O. "A.A.W.S. encourages ordering of literature and other items via your local groups, Intergroups and Central Offices." from https://onlineliterature.aa.org/. But in these days, all book ordering was centrally located in New York.

The real reason behind this conflict was that Mr. W. had been preaching Christian Science in the meetings he was leading. Mr. W. may not have read the book *Alcoholics Anonymous* himself yet, or if he had, was not using it. Bobbie provided an explanation of how A.A. members should stay away from preaching one particular brand of religion. Note that she wrote the following to Mr. W. around four years before Bill's landmark April 1946 *Grapevine* article "Twelve Suggested Points for A.A. Tradition" that included the "long form" of Tradition Ten, which stated, in part, "No A.A. group or member should ever, in such a way as to implicate A.A., express any opinion on outside controversial issues—particularly those of politics, alcohol reform, or sectarian religion."[77] She wrote the following as if Bill had already provided her many of the ideas that were to become the A.A. Traditions.

> At least some light seems to shine upon the Columbus situation. Thanks for writing me so fully in your two letters of March 3rd. As far as we can figure it out the main difficulties in Columbus in regard to A.A. seems to lie around religion. Perhaps it might be well for everyone to remember that in the A.A. program, as outlined in the book "Alcoholics Anonymous", religion is a personal matter and one that should be decided by each member for himself. We have in our groups all over the country Catholics, Protestants, Jews, Christian Scientists and members from all faiths. These people are free to interpret God as they see fit and according to their own personal desires. The only requirement for members in A.A. is a sincere desire to stop drinking and it does not matter much which road is taken – there are many different approaches which all ultimately arrive at the same end – sobriety with the help of a Higher Power. Perhaps your own recovery through the help of Christian Science has made you so grateful that you are anxious for others to benefit in the same way that you have. There is certainly nothing wrong in this as long as you realize that other people may care for an approach other than yours. Therefore, it might prove helpful if everyone will keep open minded on the other fellow's viewpoint on the subject of religion. I have written to Mr. B. and

made the same suggestions to him. For the time being, we understand that they are holding meetings in Columbus and you now tell me that you are too – so, we will be glad to cooperate with you both in any way we can.[78]

Bill Tries to Join the Army

Bobbie was getting a rapid introduction to "flying solo" as National Secretary. During much of March, 1942, Bill was in Washington D.C. alongside so many patriotic men trying to enlist in the Army. She wrote an A.A. in Buffalo on March 10: "[Bill is] in Washington D.C. most of the time trying to get into the Army. Think he will make it, too, and he certainly is happy. He is hoping to be affiliated in some way with the morale division."[79] A month later, on April 10, Bobbie reported, "No further news about Bill going into the Army. I am afraid that is all washed up as he failed to pass his physical. He's broken-hearted."[80] Might this failure of Bill represent as significant a milestone in A.A. history as his rejection of Charles Towns' job offer of the previous decade? After all, had he left New York Headquarters to join the Army, who would have filled his shoes? Bobbie, as the only other alcoholic employed at A.A. Headquarters, probably would have been left in charge, at least temporarily, of more than just A.A.'s day-to-day affairs. Where would A.A. be today had Bill been diverted from what really was his primary purpose, which in this period was to guide the movement through its adolescence? Bill's patriotism ran deep, but flunking his Army physical might have saved the lives of thousands of alcoholics. Shouldn't A.A.s be very grateful the Army turned him down? Here the Army was doing for A.A. what A.A.s could not do for themselves.

Bobbie's First A.A. Bulletin

Bobbie's first A.A. bulletin to the Fellowship, dated March 20, 1942, probably assisted by Bill, announced the rapid growth of A.A.

> Since the *Saturday Evening Post* article which appeared one year ago this month, Alcoholics Anonymous has become a national institution reaching country-wide – even to

foreign shores. We have come of age[xxxv] and are considered an indispensable part of American life. This time last year, we numbered 2000 in 50 communities while today there are 6000 of us in 175 localities.[xxxvi] While those figures are breath-taking, they can scarcely measure the universal devotion of our members to the A.A. principle of carrying the message to other alcoholics . . . The main purpose of our office is to carry out the 12 steps of the A.A. program. In doing so, we have answered almost 8000 requests for assistance from alcoholics or their families by personal letter usually enclosing a pamphlet and directions for contacting the nearest A.A. group. Many of these pleas were of a life and death character.[81]

The bulletin went on to describe the expenses for the past year starting in March 1941 of $6,721.64 of which $4,000 was covered by contributions and the balance covered by book sales. However, the book was still around $5,000 in debt and the Foundation was $3,000 in the red as well. The bulletin concluded with these encouraging words:

The Trustees again thank you all for your continued effort to support our central office – as Bill W. once said, "For much too long we alcoholics have stood in the public mind as weak individuals forever asking someone's help. How happy I am that A.A. is going to be self-supporting."[82]

[xxxv] Fascinating that these words "come of age" would be used as part of a title for a book *Alcoholics Anonymous Comes of Age* published 15 years later written by Bill W. There is the possibility that he authored most of this bulletin.

[xxxvi] Bobbie used "6000" or "over 6000" as the number of A.A. members in letters starting on March 20, 1942, and for the next six months. The first time she used 8000 members (according to her letters actually collected at the G.S.O.) was November 16, 1942. They should be treated with some skepticism as sometimes such numbers in A.A. aren't entirely accurate, but they do seem lower than as commonly reported as a result of the March 1941 *Saturday Evening Post* article.

Bobbie almost immediately began to take the role of a sponsor as A.A.s wrote with problems and questions. Following is a paragraph she wrote on March 25, 1942 to a fellow from San Diego that had recently written Headquarters seeking community with other alcoholics:

> May I give you a few thoughts to mull over that may help you a little until you make contact with Mr. K? One is an idea that most of our members live by and perhaps you have already begun it. We simply live for each day as it comes, asking for help in the morning and being thankful at night for whatever benefits that have come our way. It is surprising how the days mount into weeks and the weeks into years. None of us think of ourselves as "cured" for "once an alcoholic, always an alcoholic" - - we feel ourselves to be "arrested cases" but ones who need never have a reoccurrence of our illness as long as we keep the rules - - in other words - - the Twelve Steps are our safeguard. We seldom speak of being "on the wagon" and merely say that we have stopped drinking, putting no emphasis on any length of time.[83]

A Plan for A.A.s in the Armed Services

A world war rocked the country. Mail had begun to arrive from service personnel looking for A.A. meetings where they were stationed or writing to stay in contact with other alcoholics. Bobbie may have come up with this idea herself, or the mail she received made up her mind for her. In either case, on May 15, 1942 she wrote a bulletin to the Fellowship: "A Plan for A.A.s in the Armed Service."

> As we all know, many of our members are now in the service of the United States and we are justly proud of the work they are doing. We at home can do our part by helping these boys get in touch with each other. They will miss their group association as well as the understanding companionship of other A.A.s.[xxxvii]

[xxxvii] This book was intended to include letters Bobbie wrote to the military during World War II. Because of the pandemic, a full chapter on this had to be abandoned.

> With this thought in mind, we have started a file with the
> names and addresses of those who are serving our country
> in many parts of the world . . . Won't you add the names
> of your members who are similarly occupied, to our list?
> In this way, we will be able to have our boys contact each
> other no matter where they may be. Those of us who are
> civilians have no idea how much this may mean to them.[84]

Bobbie and other volunteers and staff members did their best to keep their address file current for soldiers in need. In June 1944, this responsibility was shared further. The very first *Grapevine* contained a *"Mail Call for All A.A.'s in the Armed Forces."* Parts of five letters from soldiers were in the first issue. The *Grapevine* introduced the need for this column this way:

> The records kept by our Central Office show approximately
> 300 A.A. members now in the Service . . . These figures,
> due to constant changes, are probably not complete . . .
> These men, and in a few cases, women, are as a rule cut off
> rather abruptly from any direct contacts with the Groups
> and are often subject to disturbing new influences and
> unusual temptations to take that fatal first drink. They,
> it would seem, face a harder battle in their recovery than
> most of us, benefiting, as many of us do, from almost daily
> association with our fellow members. Yet frequently they
> come through unscathed![85]

Bobbie appears to have been the one who got this started. She was the catalyst for managing the contact information and replying to some of the 300 soldiers well before the first issue of *The Grapevine* was published.

Bobbie and San Quentin Prison

Bobbie replied to letters from inmates in San Quentin Prison, California soon after she became National Secretary. Her reply to a prisoner named Ricard L. R. on May 15, 1942, is one example of the care she took when communicating with a prisoner there:[xxxviii]

Roger W. has documented Bobbie's activities in this area in far more detail.

[xxxviii] Her letter was addressed to "Ricard," but almost assuredly she was writing the prisoner known as "Ricardo" in later letters.

Thank you for your letter of May 4th regarding the work of Alcoholics Anonymous. In accordance with your request, we are enclosing a leaflet describing how the book *Alcoholics Anonymous* may be secured. I trust you will find it helpful. We, as alcoholics, have all had basically the same broad experiences. Then after "breaking down" and relating our problem to other AA members, we found that we were closely bound together in so many ways. We have found a solution to our problems in AA and know that you can also if you are really sincere in your desire to recover from alcoholism. Your own experiences have evidently proven to you that resolutions and your understanding of the matter in question will not keep you sober. In order to bring happiness to yourself and those close to you, you must first overcome the alcoholic problem or else you will never be able to have anything. Therefore, we trust the enclosed literature will give you a further insight into the AA program and what it has done for us.[86]

The date Bobbie began to correspond with Warden Clinton Duffy isn't known, but one thing is clear: she thought very highly of him. In an August 10, 1944 letter to Warren of the Kaiser Shipyards, Bobbie wrote that Warden Duffy "is a great man and one with a vision to see how worthwhile inmates can be with the proper help."[87] There is substantial evidence that Bobbie frequently exchanged views with the warden.[xxxix] In a March 17 letter to Frank in Los Angeles, Bobbie wrote that "we have written to Warden Duffy asking for permission [to make] copies of his piece to send only to wardens who write in for information." Another example was provided in November when Warden Sanford of Atlanta wrote Bobbie for assistance with an A.A. prison group formed there. She replied:

Thank you so much for your letter of November 20th telling us about the newly formed AA Group in Atlanta

---

[xxxix] There are only indirect references to Warden Duffy (occurring nine times) and Ricardo M. (eight times). The direct communications between the two men and Bobbie were not encountered for reasons unexplained. Included here are the indirect communications Bobbie wrote describing her exchanges with the two men.

Georgia Penitentiary. We now have several successful prison Groups namely in San Quentin, Folsom, Chino and Salem The first three are in California and the latter in Oregon. We are watching these Groups closely and over a two-year period find that many members who receive instruction in prisons make good citizens on their release. I personally correspond with several and hear of other through the Groups with which they affiliate after parole.

We are very happy to list this new Group and we will send your bulletins and data from this office as it comes out. As soon as an inmate secretary is selected to act for the Group, will you please ask him to get in touch with me. In the meantime we shall send all material to you.[88]

Warden Duffy traveled to New York in November 1945, prompting Bobbie to write to the San Quentin A.A. prisoners group.

This is just a note to tell you that Bill and I met your Warden Duffy early this week and we think he's one of the nicest people it has been our privilege to know. We can well understand after talking to him why he let A.A. into San Quentin three years ago. Bill and I sent personal messages to all of our San Quentin members by Warden Duffy.[89]

Ricardo M. was San Quentin A.A. group's first secretary. Her letter to Warren of Richmond, CA on April 9, 1943 that "Ricardo is quite a person and is very sincere and wrote a very sincere letter to us"[90] demonstrates he had gained Bobbie's respect. On August 2, 1943, she wrote the following about him:

I also believe that Ricardo has been a great inspiration and doesn't he write well. We have had many good letters from him but none lately. I'd love to see him make the group make the grade when he is released and I do believe he will.[91]

She continued to correspond with Ricardo up to the point of his parole. In a message to the group secretary that followed him, she wrote:

> Ricardo wrote that his release becomes effective tomorrow. Think he is one man who deserves it and I hope that all the AAs at San Quentin, who work as he has on AA, will soon have a chance to prove its worth on the outside.[92]

Columbus' Continued Communications

Mr. W. of Columbus, Ohio continued to write A.A. Headquarters with ideas and inquiries. Bobbie's April 9, 1942 response to him related how she, as the only other alcoholic in the 30 Vesey Street office, worked closely with Bill when he was available, mentioning the booklet they were working on together. If there was ever any product of this mutual effort, the results are not in extant.

> Very shortly Bill W. and I are going to set down some answers to the questions you wrote in on group activities and organization. We hoped to have the booklet I mentioned to you well on the way by now but on thinking that matter over we have decided to do it in a thorough manner and this will take time. So in the meantime I'll do what I can to get some temporary *[illegible]* to you – can't promise when I'm hoping to get at next week.[93]

The A.A.'s in Columbus continued to present challenges for Bobbie. They came up with an "Information Card for A.A. Applicants" for newcomers to fill out upon their attending their first meeting. Bobbie wrote to Mr. B. on April 27, 1942, to say that she knew of no other groups who had ever tried this kind of approach.

> The "Information Card for A.A. Applicants" is news to us and the first one we've seen. Where did it come from? I can't help but wonder if they're good for new people. It might tend to make the alkies feel we were registering them or putting them on-the-spot so to speak. Most of the ones I've talked to would not take kindly to such a

questionnaire in the beginning. I know of a few who would not even want any address or name placed on a membership list first. Of course most of us get over this feeling of sensitiveness and string along with any plan later on. Personally this kind of a card reminds me too vividly of information taken by doctors and sanitariums before a patient is admitted.[xl] How does it strike you? I just as soon answer it now but I would have hesitated at the idea of handing out this information to anyone when I first joined the group. And after all just what help does it give to know all the answers. These are all opinions "off the record" and until we know how it has worked out in several groups we would hesitate to pass on it one way or the other. However I seriously doubt if A.A. groups as a whole will take to a system like this.[94]

She did not assume any authority in the matter. Rather, she provided services to the groups, not instructions. Some of that came from what she learned from Bill, some from experiences shared by other groups. A.A. Headquarters had as its role to be a central point of communication rather than a source of instruction or authority.

A.A. Headquarters' Unlisted Phone Number

A.A. Headquarters was the hub of communication for this new and exciting organization. The cooperative and logistical challenges facing Bill, Bobbie and the small HQ staff were significant in their pre-digital era. "We are too few, at present to handle the overwhelming number of personal appeals which may result from this publication" are the words that appear in the foreword to the first edition of *Alcoholics Anonymous*.[95] Apparently the fear of being overwhelmed by incoming phone calls caused A.A. Headquarters to employ an unlisted phone number![xli] The phone number was CO7-3059. The number remained unlisted until at least October 20,

---

[xl]   Bobbie may have had extensive personal experience filling out medical intake forms when she was being admitted to sanitariums on a regular basis.

[xli]   The Wilson home also had an unlisted phone number. Lois wrote the following on p. 150 of *Lois Remembers*: "We loved to have our friends visit us, and we asked many to do so. For obvious reasons our phone was not

1943. Bobbie then provided the unlisted number to an A.A. member in Atlanta giving him permission to give the number to those who needed it.[96] Thus, often the only way for a new prospect or family member to contact with A.A. was to write New York. Regardless of whether it was written to Bill not, Bobbie opened the mail and, more likely than not, she was also the one to reply. Only as cities began to form their own central offices, such as Cleveland and Chicago, were there any other points of contact. Also, almost all magazine or newspaper articles written about Alcoholics Anonymous listed the mailing address as New York Headquarters. *Bobbie was the essential day-to-day conduit of communications for almost all of Alcoholics Anonymous domestically and internationally.*

All Hands on Deck

By July 1942, the United States' participation in the war intensified. Alcoholism was perceived to negatively impact the war because of absenteeism: too many civilians shirked even their civilian duties at a time when patriotism made the war effort a national responsibility. Bobbie responded to a fellow in San Diego, California on this issue on July 30.

> I was greatly interested in your news about the absentee list on Monday mornings at a nearby defense plant. We have been hearing much along similar lines and it is tragic to think of the wasted hours when we need everyone so badly to come out on top in this horrible struggle for freedom.[xlii] The head of the War Production Board heard about AA recently and Bill is to see him sometime in August. What will come of it I do not know but we have

---

listed, so other AA friends—some we already knew and some we were glad to meet–would drop in to see us unexpectedly, especially on weekends."

[xlii] Bill was to become very proud of the contribution Alcoholics Anonymous was making to the war effort. In an *Atlanta Constitution* article dated May 30, 1944, he was quoted as follows of A.A's contributions to victory: "Listing what he termed the 'byproducts' of Alcoholics Anonymous, Bill stated that 8,000 ex-drunks are in war industries, that over 1,000 A.A. members are in the armed forces, and that about $30,000,000 will be the earning power of the next 12 months of a group of men and women who once earned 'less than nothing.'" The source of Bill's figures remains unknown.

long realized that organization could be of tremendous help if we once could get the right entrée. Bill's efforts so far have run into stone walls but now the powers that be seem to be seeking us out.[97]

She mentioned the booklet project, which she was now calling a handbook, in a letter to Arnold of Buffalo, New York on September 11.

We will have to wait a little longer to have answers to your questions on rules, formations and functions of groups. All of this will be in the handbook – the first chapter of it has been written and it is good. When we first planned this book, Bill thought it could be dashed off in short order but the information that has come in from the groups demands a more carefully written book. Bill feels that it should be well done for once and for all.[98]

The handbook continued to be a point of interest with Bobbie as she wrote Brad of Stockton, California on October 1: "Bill and I are now deep in the business of writing this handbook and it is certainly a bigger job than we expected it to be – but with it all, loads of fun."[99]

Bobbie Substitutes for Bill

Bobbie served closely alongside Bill, assisting in his upcoming activities. A letter dated September 25, 1942 to Fay from Los Angeles shows how deeply Bobbie was involved in partnering with A.A.'s co-founder.

Your splendid invitation for Bill is gratefully acknowledged by him. He is coming but not until spring.[xliii] This seems a long time away at first and I will try to explain just why it has to be then and not now. None of the following reasons by themselves would stop him from taking the train right away, but accumulation seems to indicate that he should wait. First of all, the WORKS PUBLISHING INC. which publishes our book is now in the process of being taken

---

[xliii]   Bill and Lois did not arrive in Los Angeles until November 2, 1943.

over by the Alcoholic Foundation and it is necessary for Bill to be in on a lot of the meetings while this is going on inasmuch as he knows the back history better than anyone else. Also he cannot be away from here during the months that he lives up in Westchester in a home without too *[sic]* modern heating and water [that's] to be pumped from time to time into the storage tank. Bill does not feel he should leave Lois, his wife, up there during the winter to do this heavy work. He has also been ill for the past few years with a bronchial condition and the doctors have advised him to not let himself open to another attack in cold weather. These trips are often wearing and Bill came back from one last November in such a condition that he had to go to bed for weeks and take it easy for a couple of months. Before we thought of this trip at this time Bill was committed to speak before the Medical Research Council in New York and at the New York Academy of Medicine. These might be changed but Bill realizes the importance for contact with the medical profession and would not like to show disinterest. Both of us are going to be in Cleveland for the weekend of November 1st so if we went now he would have to make the trip short and hurry. This seems foolish for he wants to spend a long time with you when he gets there. We are blocking off the spring months beginning early March to be reserved for his traveling. If anything is certain you can count on him to get to the coast for the first trip of that series. With time, too, to plan an itinerary for him to follow while he was there we feel that more groups can be contacted. Perhaps you will help us out with that. It might be wise for him to make headquarters in several localities of California so that the nearby groups could come to join meetings. Say a week in Los Angeles, another week in north and one further south. How does that strike you.[xliv] With time you can make any arrangements that you like. He is an easy going person and can go with the plans the groups make. Perhaps too you

---

[xliv] The question mark was often omitted from Bobbie's letters.

had better put this up to the other California groups and see whether or not they want to get in on it as far as the railroad ticket is concerned. Several have written to me about it and I told them to get in touch with you. Just like me to give you another job when you already are doing the job of one or more men. It is a fact though that some people get all the jobs thrown at them. Could it be because they are so capable?[100]

Dinner Meeting Chaos

Not only were many of the groups throughout the country pioneering through their own difficulties, sometimes events in New York weren't running all that smoothly either. On November 20, Bobbie wrote her good friend Dick S. about the chaos of planning the annual Bill W. Sobriety Dinner in New York.

> What a week this has been. Ed W. had a lot of tickets printed up and sold over a hundred more than the restaurant can take care of. He is just surrendering the whole idea and going into the Coast Guard <u>before</u> the dinner, leaving everyone here to hold the bag. It is a mess. Bill and I are crashing the party and will probably not get fed. That doesn't bother me but Bill has asked a lot of important people (doctors etc.) and there is no place for them. We are going to a meeting of a hastily formed dinner committee this noon and see what can be done. Where else but in A.A. could such a thing happen – one member out of a clear sky printing up hundreds of tickets and then floating them around without anyone questioning how or where?[101]

Just a week later, she wrote about the Bill W. dinner of three days before, which had so troubled her. She wrote as if there had been no problem whatsoever! Somehow the volunteers put together an event which provided many pleasant memories.

The affiliated groups of New York ran off an A.A. dinner last Tuesday night. Harry Emerson Fosdick[xlv] was the principal speaker. Dr. Foster Kennedy[xlvi] who was to come too, was called out of town at the last minute but sent us a letter to be read at the meeting following the dinner. Enclosed is a copy. You and Alex W. might find it useful in seeing doctors from time to time as Foster Kennedy's name is known thruout *[sic]* the medical world. Did Alex mention in the spring some of the Cleveland members were going to try to interest outsiders in A.A. Sounds like a good idea thru these people we can reach more "prospects".[102]

Bobbie Continues to Assist on Various Matters

Publicity was a top priority for most new groups. Troubled alcoholics or their family members might only become aware there was help nearby if the group put an ad in the local newspaper. Sometimes that led to a newspaper article, but not every time. National publicity for A.A. was valuable but hard to get. National articles carried A.A.'s New York address

---

[xlv] Fosdick reviewed and approved the first edition of *Alcoholics Anonymous* in 1939. A.A.s continue to point to this review as significant in the development of the A.A. movement.

[xlvi] R. Foster Kennedy, neurologist, Bellevue Hospital. "Soon after World War I broke out in 1914, Dr. Kennedy went to France. He had many narrow escapes from death in the front line and he added much to his knowledge of nervous diseases. In 1918 he published a paper *'The Nature of Nervousness in Soldiers,'* an illuminating exposition of hysteria. Dr. Kennedy was the first to point out that shell shock is hysteria, and its various forms arise from the insoluble conflict between the soldier's instinct for self-preservation and his herd instinct. In this paper Dr. Kennedy took issue with Freud and said: "The tremendous mass of material made available by war demonstrates the general rightness of this principle (i.e., that neurotic symptoms may be produced by the antagonism of mutually incompatible emotional trends) but still more definitely proves the peculiar wrongness of the details with which the psychoanalysts have applied it and entirely invalidates their deduction – elaborate as a pontifical dogma – that the sexual instinct . . . is the only dynamic force possibly concerned." https://n.neurology.org/content/2/7-8/360.

if it was supplied, and Bobbie always desired to have included. On October 15, 1942 she updated Ray H. in San Francisco (Ray would later become a close friend and correspondent) on the matter:

> As far as we know there is no national publicity in the wind. The *Saturday Evening Post* would not be interested again so soon and we have been in *Liberty* before. *Readers Digest* has been dangled in front of us for years but something at the last minute always pops up to have them cut us out.[xlvii] There's one man at the head of it who will not listen as far as AA is concerned. He says there is no reader interest in such an article for their magazine – which is of course all wrong. There may be some other reason which he does not give but we have done our best to get in. I often thought that maybe inquiries to the *Readers Digest* from some of its readers might stimulate their interest. Want to try it? We always walk very warily in the matter of national publicity. Bill and I both realize that the time is ripe for some and you may be assured that we are not letting the grass grow under our feet when we get nibbles.[103]

The following month she asked Ray for an update on the San Francisco hospitalization plan. The membership had decided that they would attempt to provide paid hospital rooms to those alcoholics that wished to get sober. However, Bobbie knew of a similar plan that had been tried in Cleveland, Ohio, and relayed their experience with her typical, unassuming grace:

[xlvii] Alcoholics Anonymous first appeared in *Readers Digest* in the conclusion of a November 1944 article "Maybe I Can Do It Too," which featured the efforts of A.A. member Edward M. (who used his full last name) to help drunks in the Manhattan Bowery. A.A.'s chances of being published in the magazine increased when Fulton Oursler, the editor that accepted A.A. in the September, 1939 *Liberty Magazine* article, had become a senior editor at the *Readers Digest* by 1944. The first article featuring Alcoholics Anonymous (condensed from *The Grapevine*) appeared in the January 1946 issue with the title "My Return from the Half-World of Alcoholism – A letter to Alcoholics Anonymous saved the author's life."

Many thanks for keeping us up to date on what is going on in San Francisco. We are especially interested in your hospitalization plan. On the surface it sounds like a wonderful idea. Just one little thought creeps into my mind about providing a private room and all the trimmings for an alcoholic. Do you plan to have the alcoholics repay when they are on their feet again? Cleveland handled hospitalization in much the same way in the beginning I believe – that is paying the bills for the prospects that were put in the hospital. At the end of a period of time they found themselves very much in the red. I think your plan is a splendid one if the alky, benefitted by the contribution, is made to feel some responsibility. Otherwise, he might get in the habit of believing there would always be a paid up recuperation period after his benders. You doubtless have gone into this more thoroughly than you have told me and we will be glad to hear how it turns out.[104]

As 1942 neared an end, Bobbie had the opportunity to correspond with a woman from Hartford, Connecticut on the challenges of being the only alcoholic woman of her A.A. group. Many women throughout the country were having similar experiences. Among the reasons that closed meetings evolved in some locations were to remove the non-alcoholic wives from the meetings: they were prone to not trust their husbands around alcoholic women.[105] Thus, a new female A.A. faced double jeopardy: hostility from non-alcoholic women and being without female sponsorship. Fortunately, by the end of 1942, New York City had achieved substantial female participation. The following letter addresses this and also demonstrates that Bobbie and Bill functioned as a team.

A letter from Red W. tells us the good news that the Hartford Group has its first woman member in you. This really is grand for I have been slugging for them to put on an indirect campaign to get some of the gal alkies interested. Most groups shy away from the first one – I know – for Marty Mann and I have had that privilege in New York. Marty was first and I came shortly after. It was tough sledding for a while but am I glad I stuck. That was almost three years ago and since then we have picked up about forty good ones in the New York club. This is true all over the country. I rather envy you being the first girl in Hartford – you will have lots of fun and some headaches. But even the headaches can be useful. Bill and I hope to get up to Hartford early in February and we will meet you then. So welcome to A.A. – I know you can find the happiness that has been mine since I came in A.A. Good luck and if there is anything that I can do to help at any time just drop me a line.[106]

As 1942 ended, Bobbie's writing was marked by enthusiasm and determination. She wrote with the passion of being in the nucleic center of a solution for alcoholism. It almost seemed as if there was no challenge that could not be tackled as long as she could be a member of Alcoholics Anonymous and have Bill as her close confidant.

4

Settling In On Solutions

obbie became National Secretary less than three months after the United States entered World War II. Over 150,000 tons of Allied ships had been sunk by German U-boats off the Atlantic coast of the United States by February 6, 1942.[107] An air of patriotism engulfed the country, A.A.s included.[xlviii] Sobriety engendered a sense of personal and national duty and obligation as A.A.s "practiced these principles in all [their] affairs.[xlix] Bobbie's dedication to her own perceived duty seemed to be greatly increased by the crisis atmosphere surrounding her. when she took over from Ruth, who was married on February 28, 1942 and moved to Cleveland, Ohio.

Printed around the time Bobbie assumed Ruth's job was "An AA's Pledge for National Defense and Self-Preservation." It outlined the commitment and discipline expected from an A.A. when freedom itself was in jeopardy. It seems to represent the type of commitment Bobbie made when she took the job. Did taking on this sense of responsibility at the time, which no one asked her to do, lead to her long hours, even long after the war was won?

---

xlviii   This was before A.A. itself would dedicate itself to singleness of purpose and decline opinion on issues except those related to recovery from alcoholism.

xlix   Step Twelve.

AA's Pledge for National Defense and Self Preservation[1]

I will keep myself fit physically, mentally, spiritually—to be ready for any crisis, and to discipline myself for strength.

I will go about my business with a clear eye, a cool head and a stout heart, neither scared by wild rumors nor deluded by security.

I will do my particular job–in office, store, shop, mill or farm—better than it was ever done before, dedicating my skill to my country's service.

I will take an active interest in government—in town, school, district, county, state and nation—and make it my business to understand public affairs, laws and policies.

I will help build my town as a wholesome, balanced community, because if all the communities are sound, America will be sound.

I will vote in every election, appreciating the right of the ballot now denied in many lands.

---

[1] How much exposure the pledge received is not clear. It is not dated, but appears on page 38 of the first volume of A.A. newspaper clippings (1939-1942) kept at the G.S.O. Headquarters, which subscribed to a newspaper clipping service that regularly provided updates on where publicity was being generated. The pledge is surrounded by newspaper articles from February and March of 1942.

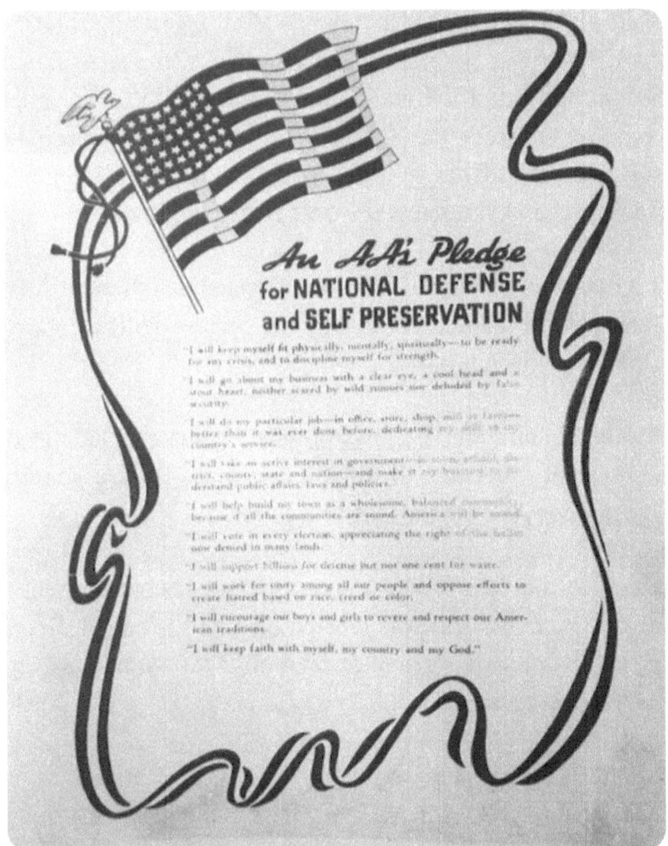

FIGURE 16 - AN A.A. PLEDGE FOR NATIONAL DEFENSE

I will support billions for defense but not one cent for waste.

I will work for unity among all our people and oppose efforts to create hatred based on race, creed or color.

I will encourage our boys and girls to revere and respect our American traditions.

I will keep faith with myself, my country and my God.[108]

An eye familiar with Alcoholics Anonymous literature will quickly notice many distinctive differences between the pledge and the Big Book.

One marked difference is that the pledge is all written in the first person singular while the Big Book is written mostly in the first person plural. The author and origin of the pledge are unknown. However, the spirit in which it was written resemble Bobbie's singleness of purpose in her career as National Secretary. Change a few words and Bobbie's behavior might be better comprehended (changed words underlined):

> I will do my particular job – in office, store, shop, mill or farm—better than it was ever done before, dedicating my skill to my <u>Headquarter's</u> service.

> I will help build my <u>Fellowship</u> as a wholesome, balanced community, because if all the communities are sound, <u>Alcoholics Anonymous</u> will be sound.

She decided that she should make a personal commitment to aid in the war effort. Mitchel Field was located on Long Island at that time. She volunteered to be part of a group of civilians that would stay on alert all night in case of an enemy attack.

> Spent last Tuesday night up all night watching the telephone . . . . We have the phone covered twenty four hours daily in order to get the "Yellow" signal for Mitchel Field[li] if an air-raid is on the way. I sure was tired yesterday and fell in bed last nite as soon as I got home.[109]

A Behavioral Imbalance Detected

Bobbie's first letters of 1943, written on January 5, indicate the presence of an imbalance in her recovery from alcoholism: "I seldom get up to go to the club at 24th street[lii] as all my time is spent down here now."[110] Her first priority continued to be her self-perceived duty to work long hours

---

[li] "Mitchel Air Force Base also known as Mitchel Field, was a <u>United States Air Force</u> base located on the <u>Hempstead Plains</u> of <u>Long Island</u>, <u>New York</u>, United States." (Wikipedia)

[lii] 30 Vesey Street, the location of A.A. Headquarters, was located 3 miles south of the 24th St. Clubhouse. Vesey Street borders near the site of what would become the World Trade Center.

at her job. Second was her role as mother of two teenagers, whom she loved but as a working mom. She firmly rejected the role of a housewife, which to her was routine and boring. Rarely did she share any benefits from her own personal experiences from attending regular A.A. meetings. She considered it vastly more important to communicate one-on-one or one-to-many through her correspondence. Her job as a communications conduit for A.A. became almost her entire focus. Bobbie acted as though she never read these words from the text of *Alcoholics Anonymous*: "None of us makes a sole vocation of this work, nor do we think its effectiveness would be increased if we did."[111] Her job became an obsession, her single-mindedness leading to severe personal consequences.

She was warned about the risks of overdoing it soon after she took the job by her very good friend, Dick S. who volunteered advice that she seemed to ignore.[liii]

> Don't overdo – oh hell, what's the use of arguing with a nit wit – I have, for a year now – and you do over do – and in doing it weaken yourself – we must as you say do everything you <u>can</u>, but you should also do it as <u>nice</u> as you can – and that don't mean in an overtired condition . . . [112]

Many a dry alcoholic, who was once extreme in the consumption of alcohol, can carry on their extreme habits in other ways. For Bobbie, it was losing herself in her work. As her 1945 psychological profile summarized:

> She shows impatience with detail, and with routine uninteresting tasks, but lends herself eagerly to problems which present a challenge to her . . . Her refusals are caused by her dislike of dull and monotonous work and her lack of patience . . . The subject is rigid in the goal which she sets for herself.[113]

[liii] Tom B. made the following observation to Bobbie in a letter dated June 15, year unknown: "I am glad to hear you say you are taking it easier. However, 'easier' with you would kill most others."

Warren T. and the Kaiser Shipyards

The Kaiser Shipyards were going to provide an important experiment for Alcoholics Anonymous: How should A.A. cooperate with private corporations in order to win the war? The Kaiser Shipyards were a historical phenomenon. Ships were produced there in record time. "The four Richmond Shipyards, located in the city of Richmond, California, United States, were run by Permanente Metals and part of the Kaiser Shipyards. During World War II, Richmond built more ships than any other shipyard, turning out as many as three ships in a single day."[liv]

Warren T. was employed by Kaiser and listed by the company as a member of Alcoholics Anonymous. His anonymity seemed secondary to the priority of making sure the thousands of workers at the shipyards were ready for work. The Richmond A.A. Group worked actively with the Kaiser Shipyards to help the workers to get sober or stay sober using Warren as the main coordinator. Bobbie and Warren wrote each other often as Bobbie worked hard to monitor these events. Bobbie wrote Warren on June 6, 1943:

> You have been hitting both the low and high spots in your work at Kaiser. Naturally in any experiment as big as the one you have tackled, you are bound to make a few backfiring decisions. On the whole, you have done a wonderful job and one I am sure will make AA history.[114]

Bobbie's approach, with the probable approval of Bill and knowledge of the Trustees, was to monitor this experiment to learn from it. She wrote Warren on May 8, 1944 that Kaiser was not the only private company associating itself with A.A. to help their employees staying sober. However, Kaiser was the only company they knew was openly communicating to its employees that a member of A.A. was employed by the company:

> I believe the Richmond Group is about the only one who has a known tie-up with industry—that is Kaiser employs an AA for that very reason. However, and this is not for

---

[liv] The shipyards are part of the Rosie the Riveter/World War II Home Front National Historical Park, whose Rosie the Riveter memorial sits on the former grounds of Shipyard #2. Shipyard #3 is listed on the National Register of Historic Places."

publication, DuPont has had an AA in its employee in the personnel division for over a year but our member is on the books not as an AA. The same is true in Akron in a couple of the tire companies. Both Bill and I anticipate a day when AAs will be employed as AAs in the major industries. Many large corporations in New York City now call us for help.[115]

This assertion suggests that A.A. "ought never endorse, finance or lend the A.A. name to any related facility or outside enterprise"[116] had not been conceived yet.

The efforts made by Warren T. of Kaiser Shipyards were reported to be quite fruitful, as Bobbie reported in a July 10 letter to Warren:

> The reports were finally sent on to me by *The Grapevine*. And they are marvelous. Grace Cultice[lv] is in here for this week from Chicago and she figured out that the man hours saved equals time one man would put in for 44 years of work. And that, my fellow AA, is a helluva lot of time. Wonder how many boats it might represent?[117]

The next month *The Grapevine* published the following on the Kaiser Shipyards.

AUGUST 1944
Lives and Man-hours Saved by Coast A.A.
***RICHMOND INDEPENDENT*, JUNE 21, 1944**

We all know that A.A. saves lives. But in war-time, and in the country that is "the arsenal of democracy," man-hours

---

[lv]   Grace Cultice was the first secretary of the Chicago A.A. Group. "The history of the Chicago central office, both the idea and the method of organizing it, will always bring to mind the memory of Grace Cultice. A non-alcoholic, her position in AA in Chicago was unique. She was the friendly helper of all in the new little group and at the time of her sudden death in January, 1948, this acquaintance was shared with countless AAs from New York to San Francisco." https://silkworth.net/wp-content/uploads/2020/07/Early-History-Sep-1951.pdf.

saved in war industries also save lives—soldiers' lives. And A.A. is saving man-hours, too—in big chunks. The Central Office has recently heard from an A.A. who is employed by the Maritime Commission in one of the largest Kaiser shipyards, to work with alcoholics. In other words, A.A., through this member, saves man-hours, to save lives, to win the war.

The leading newspaper of Richmond, Cal. ran an editorial about it: "Through the work of a little-known organization, thousands of man-hours and the abilities and self-respect and lives of many men and women employed at the Richmond shipyard are being saved. This organization, known as Alcoholics Anonymous, a non-profit organization composed of alcoholics who have conquered their desire for drink, has worked on 300 cases through and in conjunction with the Welfare Department of the Permanente Hospital. *Alcoholics Anonymous is credited with saving 600,000 man-hours in one year.*[lvi] One man, who was addicted to the use of intoxicants, who lost many hours from his job, called on Alcoholics Anonymous. He alone was responsible for the shipyards saving 8000 man-hours per ship in suggesting improved methods of doing work. There are alcoholics working in the Richmond shipyards today who are worth every minute and every cent—if it has cost anyone anything— that has been spent on them. They are holding down key jobs in a critical and highly essential industry. And through the foresight of the Kaiser Company and the work of Alcoholics Anonymous they are being given the opportunity that they have probably spent many months and years seeking."

Bobbie wrote to Warren around fifteen times during World War II. Her help and encouragement to Warren and the Richmond A.A. Group in California provided bountiful results in a pre-Tradition patriotic era.

[lvi]   Assuming a man worked 8 hours a day, 250 days a year, 600,000 man-hours represented 300 man-years.

A.A. at DuPont

Rather than ships, one of DuPont's main contributions to the war effort were ammunition.

> During 1940 and 1941 DuPont began making munitions for both Britain and the United States, now tentatively preparing for war. By the time of Pearl Harbor, DuPont workers in 14 states were helping supply TNT and other explosives for the Allies.[118]

DuPont's approach to handling their alcoholic workers differed from Kaiser. This relationship was created by the company – it was not an A.A. recommendation. The approach fit into the "trial and error" practice that was preferred by Bobbie and Bill: "Give it a try and tell us about the results" was generally recommended. Bobbie wrote the following to Warren of Kaiser in May of 1944 to explain an alternative at DuPont. DuPont was no stranger to the requirement for secrecy as well as anonymity.[lvii]

> DuPont (this is not for publication) in Wilmington, Delaware employs one of our members in a full time job. This man is simply listed as an employee in the personnel department.[lviii] However, all alcoholic and absentee cases come to his attention. AA's are paid masters at spotting alkies, so when our member finds one, he talks to him of AA more or less not as an employee of DuPont, but as a man who has recovered from alcoholism himself and can offer this new man the same chance. On the other

---

[lvii] "In November 1942, Brigadier Leslie Groves, director of the top-secret Manhattan Project, sat before a skeptical DuPont Executive Committee in Wilmington. A member of the Army Corps of Engineers, he had worked with DuPont on military projects before. In his mind, it was the only company in America for the job he had taken on – producing plutonium and uranium for atom bombs." *DuPont: From the Banks of the Brandywine to Miracles of Science*, Adrian Kinnane, "To DuPont Employees – Past Present and Future," ©2002, E.I du Pont de Nemours and Company, Wilmington, Delaware, 18989, p. 144.

[lviii] This man was probably Dave M. who in 1950, at the 15th Anniversary of A.A. in Cleveland, was one of three men that participated in the industrial meeting. See page 118 of *Language of the Heart*.

hand, if it were known that he is an AA, the employees coming before him might feel it would be advantageous for them to "yes" him on everything proposed. Now it can be that your way may work out better. As you know, all the success that has come to AA has found its way thru trial and error methods, some of them often painful, but nevertheless tried and true . . ."[119]

A.A. at Eastman Kodak

Bobbie's relationship with Warren T. of the Kaiser Shipyards was to continue for as long as she held her job as National Secretary. She wrote Warren on April 25, 1949 about the Eastman Kodak approach to handling troubled alcoholics. A.A.s were not employed for the purposes of helping new prospects get sober, but the personnel department did know which of their employees were in A.A.

> We are now closely watching the operation at Eastman Kodak. There, all alcoholic cases go straight to the medical department, where doctors, not AAs, do all the preliminary work. Of course, the doctors are well versed in the AA philosophy and what it can do for the alcoholic who wants to help himself. If after any length of time, the doctor believes the man can be helped by AA and desperately wants it, he then gets in touch with AAs working in Eastman. All of these men have been employees there for a long time; employees that turned alcoholic were helped in AA. But they are not on the Eastman payroll to do any AA work at all in any capacity. Their only function is to be called in for 5 or 10 minutes at the request of the medical department to invite the new man to a meeting or visit after hours. They then arrange an introduction to other members who take over the sponsorship of the new prospect.[120]

Thus, from the experiences at Kaiser Shipyards to those at DuPont to those at Eastman Kodak, a trend emerged.[lix] Where Kaiser used an A.A.,

---

[lix]   "Two prominent medical directors—Dr. John L. Norris (1903-1989) of Eastman Kodak and Dr. George Gehrmann (1890-1959) of DuPont—were pioneers

Eastman used a doctor not in A.A. A.A.s employed by Eastman were called in only when a doctor became convinced that the patient would benefit from the program. A.A.'s direct company responsibilities were greatly reduced, falling more in line with AA's Tradition Six: independence from "problems of money, property and prestige" that naturally occur in running a business.

Trip to Hartford, Connecticut

On January 5, 1943 Bobbie responded to Red, an A.A. organizing a dinner in Hartford, Connecticut that Bobbie and Bill were scheduled to attend. She had been asked what kind of food Bill might wish to have. Bobbie replied with what had become her characteristic familiarity with Bill. This comradeship would continue for most of this year as they often worked and sometimes traveled together.

> I am afraid that I won't be much of a help in deciding just what kind of a dinner to have for Bill in Hartford. I know his answers to such questions by heart. He always says that anything will be alright for him and he means just that. But let's discuss it just the same between the two of us. I feel that the plan that would please the most people would be the best one. If it can be arranged why not let everyone in on it. Bill gets around so seldomly *[sic]* that it seems a shame to leave anyone out. Don't worry about the time for this dinner – Bill and I will get up there as early as you want us. There is a train out of New York at 2:30 which

---

in using A.A.'s voluntary services to helping their companies' employees. Though non-alcoholics, they learned about A.A. and became enthusiastic supporters. Both doctors were introduced to the Fellowship by A.A. members in their own companies, and their success in helping alcoholic employees became a model for other companies in the 1940s." From Markings, Your Archives Interchange, Vol 25, No. 1, June-July 2005. Just how, or if, Bobbie was involved personally with these men as contacts for their companies is not yet documented. "Dr. Jack" Norris of Rochester, New York, as mentioned on p. 268 of *Pass It On*, was a non-alcoholic trustee for 27 years. Dr. Jack first heard Bill speak in Rochester in 1943, according to a 1949 *Grapevine* article "How Alcoholics Anonymous Can Help Doctors and Industry."

will get us up there around 5. If that is not early enough we can take the 1:30. We expect to go on to Boston and Worcester after seeing you.[121]

Later that month, she wrote Red again regarding a change in plans. Marty Mann would not be able to make it, so Bobbie would speak in her place. She used the term "drunken dames," showing her sense of humor regarding female alcoholics. She would repeat this lighthearted self-description quite a few times until 1945. She wrote:

> You have me on the spot since Marty Mann[lx] will not be able to come. I usually talk when I travel with Bill but as for being "outstanding" I'm afraid I cannot fill that bill. You know that I will do my best and in a town where they are not used to seeing too many women alkies maybe I can exhibit aid for the "drunken dames."[122]

Bobbie and Bill had every appearance of being a national A.A. road team.[lxi] The following was her final update to Red on January 26 prior to the twosome taking off on this three—day trip.

[lx]   As documented in the book *Mrs. Marty Mann* by Sally Brown and David R. Brown, Marty was already very interested in combating alcoholism by 1942, roughly two years before the founding of the National Council for Education on Alcoholism (NCEA, later NCA), which was greatly assisted by "E. M. Jellinek and Howard Haggard of the Yale Center of Alcohol Studies" and Dr. Ruth Fox, who lost her husband to alcoholism in 1943 (see p. 153 of *Mrs. Marty Mann*). The point here is that Marty in 1942 was already speaking about alcoholism, and according to Bobbie, was a much better speaker. While Bobbie had obvious talents as a professional dancer in her first career and as a "fantastic communicator" through her letter writing in her second career, public speaking did not seem to be her strength. To date, there is no transcript or recording known to exist of Bobbie. While Bill W. wrote on page 168 of the *Twelve Steps and Twelve Traditions* that hired workers such as Bobbie "weren't asked to speak at A.A. meetings" and "were actually shunned by fellow members," no complaints by Bobbie of such treatment have been discovered to date.

[lxi]   Marty was employed at ASCAP (American Society of Composers, Authors and Publishers) in this period, as relayed in the book *Mrs. Marty Mann*, thus she did not have the flexibility to travel with Bill that Bobbie did.

We leave Grand Central at 2:30 PM and arrive in Hartford
at 5:07. We have had a fine letter from Art N. asking us
to spend the nite with them but we have to push off in the
morning for Boston, stopping over in Springfield to have
a lunch with the surviving AAs there. We are planning
to take the 10:54 AM out of Hartford. How do you think
this will suit your group? We will have dinner with the
members, take in the meeting (darn you for making me an
outstanding woman member!) and then have some time to
"dish" afterwards informally. A couple of beds anyplace
will suit us fine.

This three day trip is being bunched together as the three
groups are on the same line in one round trip will allow
us to visit all three for the price of one. Must be the Scotch
coming out in us.[123]

While the results of that three-day trip remain undocumented, in
a February 12 letter she mentioned briefly that her traveling with Bill
probably would be over for a while. Furthermore, the completion date of the
handbook was postponed indefinitely despite the fact that on just January
29[124] she had projected March 1 as the completion date. Her words here
also implied that the project was a joint effort between the two of them.

Bill and I went on the road last week and finished the
travelling to be done until his writing jobs are caught up.
That may take six months at the rate we are going. We can
only write at nights and not too many of those as we have
found sleep is absolutely necessary once in a while . . . No
the handbook is not out yet and won't be for some time.[125]

Big Book Activities

March 1943 marked the fourth printing of the first edition of *Alcoholics
Anonymous*. There was a rumor that the Big Book was going to be revised
and shrunk. Bobbie dismissed the idea.

> It would be fun to know just to know how rumors over the
> "grapevine" start. There's no foundation for one that the
> book is being revised and its size cut. The fact is yours is
> the first suggestion we have had along that line in over a
> year. Most groups seem to like the complete volume.[126]

In a March 3 letter to Bill B. of San Diego, California she wrote that a thousand copies of the chapter "To Employers" had been printed and were ready for distribution. This chapter had been reprinted as part of the contribution of Alcoholics Anonymous to the war effort. Bobbie was pleased to relay progress A.A. was making to help achieve victory.

> The chapter 10 reprint of our Big Book is now available.
> At least we had a thousand copies printed up to see
> whether they would help interest employers and personnel
> managers. I'm writing to a few groups to find out if a
> further printing would be advisable. Inasmuch as your
> city is full of defense plants we thought you might be able
> to give us a good opinion on this. Do you want to check
> with the members and see whether they think the chapter
> 10 reprint would be helpful in opening the doors of the
> defense plants and business offices?[127]

Memories of the 24th Street Clubhouse

On March 8, 1943 Bobbie recalled the events at the 24th Street Clubhouse when the Jack Alexander *Saturday Evening Post* article on Alcoholics Anonymous appeared in the March 1941 issue. She relayed her memories regarding the thousands that admitted they were in need of help after reading the article. She wrote Dale A. in Seattle, Washington. Among other things, the letter indicated that Bobbie was already secretary at the clubhouse by March of 1941 when she had about one year of sobriety:

> It is an old story to me now but one that never fails to give
> me happiness. I happened to be contact and secretary
> of the then small New York Group when the *Saturday
> Evening Post* article bombshelled *[sic]* the country. In
> thirty days I saw several hundred men and women literally

crawl into A.A., some of them having gone all the way to the bottom because of alcoholism. Today many of these same people are now helpful citizens, all rehabilitated and back in their proper surroundings. It is hard to look back and believe my own memory of the early days. Out of our little New York Group have grown some 12 other Groups with a combined membership of over a thousand. So you see I can know just what thrills you are going to experience with the new Seattle Group. I rather envy you these first few years. There will be many headaches but so much happiness too. Disappointment will come but these will be overshadowed by the people who get well.[128]

A questionnaire was sent out by A.A. Headquarters early in 1943. A summary of the results was shared in a bulletin dated April 15.[lxii] Only one in twenty responses reported anything negative, Bobbie reported. Among the highlights of the bulletin:

A sharp increase in office costs is probable, as we expect within 90 days, to have two pieces of publicity in a national weekly of wide circulation – details later.[lxiii] This will

---

[lxii] This 1943 questionnaire is believed to have requested membership rules be sent in by the groups. In August 1946 Bill was to write "Who Is a Member of Alcoholics Anonymous?" in *The A.A. Grapevine*: "Two or three years ago the Central Office asked the groups to list their membership rules and send them in. After they arrived we set them all down. They took a great many sheets of paper. A little reflection upon these many rules brought us to an astonishing conclusion. If all of these edicts had been in force everywhere at once, it would have been practically impossible for any alcoholic to ever have joined Alcoholics Anonymous." At some future date, the sharing of these "many sheets of paper" might provide a fascinating glance at just what the introduction of the AA Traditions overcame. (See page 37, *Language of the Heart,* The AA. Grapevine, Inc., P.O. Box 1980, Grand Central Station, New York, NY, ©1988).

[lxiii] *The American Weekly,* a widely circulated Sunday newspaper supplement, ran a three-week series, July 11, 18, and 25, written by Genevieve Parkhurst (no relation to Hank) that resulted in up to 1,100 inquiries to New York, according to letters written by Bobbie. *Coronet Magazine* ran a November, 1943 article titled "Fraternity of the Water Wagon" (p. 104) by Clem Lane

surely mean more office space and another helper. We could, in fact, use those facilities right now. It does not seem clearly understood by all Group secretaries that every new prospect or inquirer writing the Alcoholic Foundation receives at once a personal letter and an AA pamphlet from the Central Office . . . [We] are now corresponding with about 300 A.A.'s in the armed services. Members in many camps have been brought together. More of this could be done if we had more names and addresses. So please announce this at meetings and send up the names. There must be hundreds more![129]

As *The Grapevine* would not be published until fourteen months later, it must have been an onerous burden that fell upon Bobbie to manage hundreds of military addresses, not to mention the additional work of contacting many of these individuals.[lxiv] Undaunted, her reaction was to ask for hundreds more!

Bobbie and Esther

Esther E., who came into A.A. originally in Houston in 1941, moved to Dallas in 1943.[lxv] Esther had lit up a very warm relationship with Ruth Hock through their correspondence. Similar affection developed between Bobbie and Esther as they corresponded no less than six times during 1943.[lxvi] Esther immediately wished to get an A.A. meeting started in Dallas. Bobbie enthusiastically encouraged her from the start: "Don't feel discouraged if the first few members are hard to get. They will be flocking

---

(From Wikipedia: "Clement 'Clem' Quirke Lane was the city editor for the *Chicago Daily News* from 1942 to 1958.") These two publications are possible candidates for the two pieces of publicity.

lxiv   Hopefully other authors have already covered at least part of this story. This topic was a planned research activity at the G.S.O. before it closed due to the pandemic.

lxv   Esther E. wrote the story "A Flower of the South" that appeared in the second and third editions of *Alcoholics Anonymous*.

lxvi   The six letters written by Bobbie in 1943 used as reference here were originally photographed at the N.A.A.A.W. event in Winnipeg in 2017 out of a Texas A.A. Archives book.

in soon."[130] That August, Bobbie expressed how she envied Esther for being part of a new group: "I envy you being in on the start of a new Group – don't know any greater thrill than watching new people thru their first joy in finding us. We can relive all our own first release and happiness."[131]

Of substantial interest is the personality snapshot of Bill that Bobbie shared with Esther in the same August letter, written right before Bill and Bobbie went to Yale. This lends confidence to the belief that Bill and Bobbie were traveling as a team at the time.

> Bill goes to Yale this week to lecture there in their summer school course on the Problems of Alcohol. It has been running for six weeks and we get the top billing by going in at the end when everyone else has shot their bolt. I'm going up with him too and wouldn't miss it for the world. Understand that all the WCTUs and the "wets" are marshalling their individual forces to try and pull A.A. over to their respective sides of the "wet and dry" fence. Bill is a past master at dodging and staying right in the middle. It will be fun to watch the maneuvering (is that the right spelling – I'm the world's worst) to trap him but I've never known him to be caught off base yet. This sitting on the middle of the fence in controversial subjects is so satisfactory. I used to be not only ready but willing to do battle at the drop of a hat – what a wealth of common sense and understanding I've had the privilege of learning thru Bill. Hope you know him someday – every [illegible] better and changed person just by saying "hello" to him.[132]

Bobbie's September 21 message to Esther mainly centered on planning for Bill and Lois' upcoming trip to the west coast, which included a return route that would take them through Houston and Dallas the following January. She concluded with a frank admission that she wished she could go on the trip, too: "I'm disappointed too that I can't go with Bill on the coast trip but I know you will love Lois and it is nice she can be with him – I usually get that break."[133] When Bill and Lois' actual departure became imminent, Bobbie wrote Esther on October 20, concluding with "Bill takes off Sunday – I'm lonesome already."[134] Esther and Bobbie's correspondence continued for years and they became very good friends through their letters.

Criticism from Cleveland, Ohio

Armchair historians know that on occasion A.A.s from Cleveland had a variety of comments and criticisms regarding mistakes or perceived shortcomings of Bill W., including accusations of making money off of A.A., among other things. Those remarks sometimes included Dr. Bob, and Bobbie was exposed to this fallout from time to time. Here is how Bobbie wrote to a member of the Cleveland Miles Avenue Group on April 22, 1943:

> Thought you would be happier having a firsthand letter from Bill about your suggestion about Dr. Bob. I don't know whether it can be worked out or not but you have made Bill very happy with the thought behind it. I know Bill has had some bad days about some of the returns out of Cleveland. Any feeling that comes now showing that people don't believe he and Doc were complete heels gives him a lift. I am happy to say that there are plenty of them so all will come out all right as it always does.[135]

Bobbie's Comments on Slips

Bobbie tackled a tough subject that persists today: relapse. Her comments about slips or "slippers" seem just as applicable today as it was on June 23, 1943:

> I don't guess any of the groups have found the answer for slippers. Like the poor they seem to be always with us. You may have been unable to find a way to warn those headed in the direction of Barleycorn even though this was apparent to everyone else. Perhaps the answer to the following questions may be at the bottom of so many slips. "Does each new prospect get a thorough and adequate presentation of the A.A. program?" When this is done we as propagators of A.A., have shot our bolt and if the man takes a big bite or small one it is entirely up to him. You

can show clearly the grim picture of alcoholism and you can also back it up with our experience the fact that the program only works in its complete form. A half-baked attitude towards it just does not bring results.[136]

She had additional thoughts about slips in a November 16 letter to Dr. Stephen Smith except she referred to a slip as a "tumble."

I can't help but be surprised when anyone takes a tumble – I've lost the faculty for predicting and guessing about such things. Perhaps I think so little about alcohol and have lost the emotional tie up with it, that it is hard to suppose anyone would want to take even one drink. I'm certainly glad I'm out of it if only for the reason of its terrific expense right now.[137]

Clubhouse Questions

Among the challenges facing the founding of a new A.A. group, questions would sometimes be sent to A.A. Headquarters regarding a suitable location for a meeting. Would locating a meeting in a church imply a relationship with that brand of religion? Would newcomers be reluctant to attend a meeting in a church if they were members of some other church? Bobbie attempted to provide some insight to the subject in a letter dated July 7, 1943 to a member in San Francisco, California.

There are many sides to look at when deciding about a meeting place that might be interpreted as being under the "umbrella" of a church or other organization. There will be a few Groupers who will feel apprehensive about it. But in the long run we must realize that anyone seriously seeking help will not let any little thing like a meeting place keep him from at least finding out what we AAs have to offer. As long as the church does not attempt to rule you in any way and if the meeting place they offer is better than you can get in another place, it would seem fairly "right" to try it. I know of one group that had the offer of a YMCA as a free meeting place. The members rose in a body and said thumbs down because of the implications. But look at Chicago, one of our strongest groups. They meet weekly in the central auditorium of the local Y right in the heart of Chicago. There is no "yes" or "no" on a question like you bring up. Best thing to do is to put it up to the majority for a vote and let them decide. If it turns out right, continue but if it seems wrong after a trial, then drop it for another. You might question some of your Catholic members to find out if they would object meeting in another church's rooms. I suppose the rooms you mention would be not in the church proper but in a vestry house or some such place. Now that we have run around the barn on the subject, I've left you right where you started – and that is in the lap of the group where the matter belongs.[138]

A.A. Pamphlets Not Produced by Headquarters

Just how much control could A.A. Headquarters expect to have over a group located in some distant location? Could there be a set of rules and could those rules be enforced in some way? Such questions were sent to New York as new groups continued to form. A.A.s in Miami, Florida introduced a pamphlet in 1943, which came to the attention of an A.A. in Akron, Ohio. The Ohio member was deeply offended by the Miami pamphlet and requested that Headquarters squelch it. Bobbie replied as follows:

We had not seen the Miami pamphlet until you sent in the copy. Where did you get it. I've wondered if they distribute them to all the groups as you people did with yours, forgetting us too. As to its contents, Bill and I can see where you would be upset about some of the material. I agree it is not my idea of A.A. thru out but it is another matter for us to write and try to stop publication. We have always stressed freedom for groups in local matters and personal freedom in speech, thought and, I suppose, action for members. We of A.A. have long seen the wisdom of making no demands for membership – the forward of the Big Book states "the only requirement for membership is a sincere desire to stop drinking".[lxvii] Now, suppose that we decided to try to control local situations and put brakes on individual's activity. We would be in hot water most of the time and actually accomplish nothing. There's no law in the world that can uphold us if we tried to inforce rules. On the other hand, I believe that our power and strength is based on friendly cooperation we now enjoy rather than any hard and fast rules we might have set up. How would the Akron members have felt if we had written you people to delete some of the material in your pamphlet.[lxviii] We had letters and calls from some members thru out the country asking us to do just that simply because they disagreed with you. Disagreement is healthy in fact. We learn much by them – tolerance among other virtues. Now I am not saying there is any comparison between the disagreement on the Akron pamphlet and the Miami one. I might be one to string along with you and say that Miami really took quite a detour from A.A. as the older people know and live it, but trying to suppress this pamphlet will not change the situation. I think the groups will do it themselves. I am willing to bet now that if those pamphlets were widely distributed that Mr. McC. has had a rise in his mail and much of the letters pointing out strongly where he has diverged from the true spirit of A.A. Why don't

---

[lxvii] The actual quote is "The only requirement for membership is an honest desire to stop drinking" (page xiv). She might have been too busy to stop and take time to get the quote exactly right.

[lxviii] *A Manual for Alcoholics Anonymous* is said to have been published in 1941. "This pamphlet was written and edited by members of Alcoholics Anonymous AA Group No. 1, popularly known as the King School Group. Akron Group No. 1 is the original chapter of Alcoholics Anonymous and includes in its active membership one of the organizations founders, the first person to accept the program, and a large number of other members whose sobriety dates back five, six and seven years. The text of this pamphlet has been approved by the membership." Akron's Intergroup sells other Evan W. pamphlets that were written during the 1940s. The exact dates that the pamphlets were written is in dispute. Some of these pamphlets may have existed at this time without Bobbie's knowledge.

you drop him a friendly note and point out how you feel about it. Honestly something from you and older members will carry more weight than an "order" from the Central Office.[139]

Rumors about Slips at A.A. Headquarters

On July 12, 1943, Bobbie reported on a rumor that would persist throughout much of her career at A.A. Headquarters – that someone, either Bill or herself, had suffered a recent alcohol slip. The fellow she was writing in Richmond, California was suffering from a similar accusation.

> Honestly it is a darn shame that you had to be ill and take in a hospital and on top of it be credited with a "slip". You have now joined the ranks of the famous in that Bill has been drunk from coast to coast and I hope I never have to actually go thru the bouts I have been accused of. Funny how some people enjoy putting the dry members on the rack. Just remember they are a lot sicker than you and I so not to be taken too seriously. Your good friends and contacts will easily see the truth.[140]

Bobbie issued a bulletin dated September 29 encouraging groups and individual members to make their contributions since money was so tight. The scheduled *Coronet Magazine* article for September had been postponed until November. Once again she was soliciting addresses of those in the Armed Forces so that every one of those soldiers could be sent Christmas greetings.[141]

Bobbie on Vacation in 1943

Bobbie opened up a rather active correspondence with Dr. Stephen Smith of Columbia, Missouri by April of 1942. The doctor, a non-alcoholic, was attempting to start an Alcoholics Anonymous fellowship there but was running into many obstacles. While he had been soliciting advice from Bobbie on A.A. practices, on September 15, 1943 she took the occasion to relay to him her aches and pains. She also reported that she and her daughters were lacking male companionship.

My vacation could have been better. I thoroly *[sic]* enjoyed the first week but contracted neuritis in my right arm and just agonized for the latter part. Was unable to sleep for more than a couple of hours at a time in spite of being doped up with codein *[sic]*. Came back to the office but had to leave again until the pain subsided. Now I am slowly getting rested again and falling in bed early at night. Nothing like loss of sleep to get one exhausted. Wish someone would invent a pill that would take the place of sleep and save all that wasted (?) time. So much for the vacation. The girls are both wonderful and having much fun as girls of that age can in almost a manless world. Most of their "puppy-loves" have gone to the wars. Even the seventeen year olds can't wait til *[sic]* that birthday to enlist in the Navy.[142]

Bobbie's Book Recommendations

Dr. Stephen Smith of Columbia, Missouri requested Bobbie to recommend books related to alcoholism, religion and spirituality. This interchange led Bobbie to relay a wide range of books with which she was familiar. In an April 4, 1942 letter, Bobbie wrote that the works of Glenn Clark "are fine though very heavy on religion."[lxix] In the same letter, she recommended *Alcohol, One Man's Meat* by Edward A. Strecker and Francis T. Chambers, Jr., which was a book she was to recommend a number of additional times. Once again in the same letter, she also favored *The Importance of Living* by Lin Yutang.[143] On June 9 she shared with the

---

[lxix]   Thriftbooks.com lists no less than twenty books authored by Glenn Clark (1882-1956). From the website http://glennclark.wwwhubs.com/: "A man who, without being himself a recognized New Thought leader, has been highly influential in introducing New Thought ideas and techniques into the churches, was Glenn Clark. A Presbyterian, reared in the church, teaching in a Presbyterian college, and teaching also a Sunday School class in his home church of St. Paul. For thirty years he was a professor of literature and athletic coach at Macalester College, a Presbyterian liberal arts college in St. Paul, Minnesota, where a Department of Creative Living was established for him. He was deeply religious and something of a mystic, a great believer in prayer."

doctor that she had enjoyed *Spirit: A Study in the Relation of Religion to Health* by Ethel P.S. Hoyt.[144] The next month she wrote the following to the doctor:

> Speaking of books and remembering your wish to hear about any new ones, you might enjoy reading Henry C. Link's "The Rediscovery of Man" – chapter 6 in this book is particularly good and the whole book is well worth reading. He is also the same Dr. Link who wrote "The Return to Religion" a few years back. Have you ever read "The Greatest Thing In The World" by Henry Drummond? It is one of my favorites.[145]

The book that received the most attention by far between Bobbie and the doctor was *Release* by Starr Daily. Prior to an April 19, 1943 letter from Stephen to Bobbie, he had learned that Bobbie (who he called Margaret) could not locate a copy of the book.[lxx] The doctor felt so strongly about the subject that he sent his copy of *Release* to New York so that both Bobbie and Bill could read it.[146] The doctor also inquired on Bobbie's opinion of Emmet Fox. Bobbie replied on April 20:

> Thank you so very much for the book "Release". Bill has heard several of the members talking about it recently. I'm hoping to get a chance to read it over the weekend. Just do not do any reading in the week. Try to get as much sleep a possible for the work here is tiring means constant watching – no let-ups.
>
> Emmet Fox has a great following not only at his Sundays meeting (some thousands attend in the largest hall in New York) but thru out the country with his writings. I especially like his "Sermon on the Mount" and his interpretation of "The Lord's Prayer." Bill says he thinks at one time, long ago, he [Fox] was interested in Christian

---

lxx   Starr Daily is believed to have been either Canadian or British, though no convincing biographical information has yet been located. His writing uses British spelling and not American, while his original heroes before his release were famous American criminals.

> Science, but his teachings no longer are similar. Several
> of our members are faithful followers of Fox. He is a great
> power for good whether one agrees with him in toto or not.
>
> Many thanks again for lending me your book. I shall take
> good care of it and return it as soon as it is read. Bill wants
> to read it too.

Apparently, both Bobbie and Bill read the book in the next ten days for she sent the book back to Stephen on April 30.

> Both Bill and I are so grateful for your lending it to us.
> It is so beautifully written and carries the convictions of
> certainty in the Power for Good. How lucky are the people
> who have found this. I suppose you noticed the similarity
> in Starr Daily's and any alcoholism down-path to the point
> where desperation demanded he go to God for release.[147]

Bill wrote the doctor on September 16 regarding his impressions of the Starr Daily book:

> Yes, that book RELEASE has made a profound impression
> on all who have read it. Daly *[sic]* is a very advanced spirit
> and his message is bound to be inspiring. Bobbie and I
> are both grateful that you brought him to our attention.[148]

The exchange of book ideas continued in Bobbie's letter to Stephen dated November 16:

> I'm trying to find time to read "The Prophet"[lxxi]. "The
> Robe"[lxxii] meant so much to me – I hope you have read it.
> Are you yet into "There Is A River"?[lxxiii] I missed hearing
> Edgar Cayce speak. Went to the lecture but could not get
> in. They had arranged for a hall to seat some 10 to 100

[lxxi] *The Prophet* by Kahlil Gibran first published in the United States in 1923.

[lxxii] *The Robe* by Lloyd C. Douglas was published in 1942.

[lxxiii] *There is a River* by Thomas Sugrue on the life of Edgar Cayce, an American clairvoyant.

people and about 500 showed up. Mr. Cayce offered to repeat his talk again at 10:30 but that would have kept me up too late. We are so very busy that I work long hours and feel the necessity of at least a good night's sleep each night in order to keep going. I'm trying hard to get more help in the office but help is as scarce as nylon stockings.[149]

A Letter to Dr. Bob

On September 30, she wrote Dr. Bob a regular quarterly letter that corresponded with her responsibility to ensure he received his royalty check from the sale of Big Books.[lxxiv]

> The enclosed check for $585.70 represents thirty-five cent royalty on 1674 books sold during the period June 30, 1943 to September 30, 1943. Ain't it something!
>
> I'm very disappointed that I couldn't see more of you and some of Anne which you were here on this visit. If you can ever figure out how a person can be in two places at once I wish you would let me know.
>
> It would be impossible to tell you (and not good for you anyway) how much the gang loved hearing you the other night. There's not a touch of Blarney in that, either.[150]

The Big Book in Braille

Bobbie received a request from Evan of San Diego on November 2, 1943 regarding the possibility of the Big Book in braille. Fortunately, she was close enough to the Fellowship to have an answer.

[lxxiv] These few letters are barely a sample of those likely to have been written by Bobbie to Dr. Bob. It's possible that, had the G.S.O. not closed in mid-March 2020, a more in-depth correspondence could have been documented. This omission was unavoidable. Hopefully, a future edition will reconcile this shortcoming.

> Your letter addressed to Bill about the blind man in Washington came in after he left. He arrives in Los Angeles today. I sent one copy of your letter to our contact in Washington and told him to get someone on the case right away. I have also sent the carbon copy (with a request for its return) to one of our grandest members in Youngstown. This man, Norman Y., of Youngstown lost his sight several years ago drinking bad liquor and has been in AA for over three years. He is one of the finest men I've been privileged to meet. His group thinks so much of him that they had our book *Alcoholics Anonymous* done in Braille for him. In the past he has been most helpful in writing to other blind AAs and prospects so I know he will do all he can for your member.[151]

Even if only the main program pages of *Alcoholics Anonymous*, which then were numbered from 1 to 179, were available without the stories, the fact that the Big Book was in braille only four and a half years after it was written reflected just how badly the book was needed by the physically blind as well as those spiritually blind.

The Integration Question

Bobbie first received a letter regarding racial integration as early as July of 1942. She replied with the words that some years later resemble the thoughts of "separate but equal." She encouraged the formation of a black group, but suggested that they be encouraged to form their own groups.[152] On October 5, 1943 she received news from Cleveland, Ohio that a black group was about to be formed there.[lxxv]

> I like the way you started out by saying nothing exciting is happening in Cleveland lately. And all that you have been doing is getting together with a nucleus of a Negro group. That's news and big news. I believe that such a group will be the forerunner of others in different sections of the

---

[lxxv]   The terms "colored" and "Negro" are used only in the quoted literature, representing the language of the times.

> country. Bill is very pleased and interested. . . . Do let me
> know how the Negro group progresses.[153]

However, apparently little resulted from these first efforts, as the first A.A. meetings for blacks would not form until early 1945.

In October 1944 Bobbie received an inquiry from Cincinnati, Ohio seeking A.A.'s position about blacks attending A.A. meetings. By this time, Pittsburgh, Pennsylvania was conducting an integrated meeting attended by a single black member. Bobbie performed her designated role—relay the experience of another A.A. group to the inquiring member. However, she expressed a belief that A.A. had to be concerned with "the greatest good for the greatest number." If racial integration of the A.A. meeting might cause the meeting to fail and the members to relapse, then the emphasis, so she wrote, would be for members of the established meeting to help blacks create their own meeting.[154]

Bill White, in his extensively researched book *Slaying The Dragon*, summarized the challenges facing Bobbie and the whole of A.A. in this uncertain time. By providing an accurate appraisal of how blacks and women were most often treated then, his presentation of their viewpoint should receive serious consideration. While White concentrated on the 1930s, much of the same reasoning can be applied to the 1940s and after until the culture changed – and A.A.s started paying more than just lip service to Tradition Three. Of course, the A.A. Traditions had not yet been composed. They would provide the essential wisdom that permitted A.A. to survive changing times regardless of "our race, creed, or color."[lxxvi]

> Indictments of A.A.'s response to women and people of
> color in the 1930s must be viewed with the historical
> and cultural context of this period of American history.
> It would be unfair to hold A.A. to a standard different
> than that of the whole culture of this period. Only a
> mere 15 years after women had won the right to vote,
> and at a time when "Whites Only" signs still decorated
> public accommodations in the South, it would have
> been unrealistic to expect a band of white alcoholic men
> struggling for their personal survival to respond more
> humanely to women and people of color than did white

[lxxvi] *Alcoholics Anonymous, Fourth Edition*, p. 28.

men within the larger culture. In A.A.'s early years, women and people of color encountered in A.A. exactly what they encountered within the culture as a whole, with one exception: there were several factors within A.A. (mutual identification as alcoholics, A.A.'s traditions, and the "group conscience" of A.A.) that slowly pushed this fellowship toward a higher standard.[155]

In the book *Mrs. Marty Mann*, the challenges that women faced were summarized realistically by authors Sally and David Brown:

> From [Marty's] writings and speeches, it is clear that she was painfully conscious of the stigma of being a woman alcoholic. It is also a matter of record that AA men were themselves victims of their culture, having the same prejudices and misconceptions as did the general populace regarding women alcoholics.[156]

Much of the "general populace" had the same "prejudices and misconceptions" about blacks as well.

First Black Meetings

Thanks to the extensive research performed by Glenn Chesnut in his work *Heroes of Early Black AA*, a few errors in A.A. history have been corrected. There were two A.A. meetings that preceded the one started by Jim S. in Washington D.C. in April of 1945, which was thought for many years to be the first black meeting.[lxxvii]

> The first black group created in the new Alcoholics Anonymous movement was formed in St. Louis on January 24, 1945 . . . St. Louis banned black people from coming to white A.A. meetings, but did allow them to form their own

---

[lxxvii] Jim was called "the originator of A.A.'s first black group" in the sub-title of his story in the second and third editions of *Alcoholics Anonymous*. This was changed to "one of the earliest members of A.A.'s first black group" in the 2001 fourth edition. In any case, the Washington D.C. Group turns out to be third oldest.

separate segregated black group . . . Howard W. from the St Louis black group had written Bobbie at the Alcoholic Foundation asking the New York office and the *A.A. Grapevine* to "withhold publicity about our group that may occasion controversial discussions of racial problems with A.A."[lxxviii] That is, sad to say, the very existence of the black A.A. group was kept almost totally secret, *at their request,* for fear that white racists would try to raise a public controversy about them.[157]

Around two months or so after the founding of the first black A.A. group in St. Louis, the second black group was formed in Chicago on March 20, 1945. This was the famous Evans Avenue Group, which is still active and going strong in Chicago today.[158]

Bobbie's letter to a Cleveland member in early June of 1945 spoke of a black group started there. She kept the St. Louis meeting a secret, as requested,[lxxix] and may not have known about the other two black meetings that had started by then.[lxxx]

[lxxviii] A paragraph taken from Harold W.'s letter to Bobbie dated September 26, 1945 (Box 45, R21, File Mo H.1, p.46) says: "In getting around to the matter of our discussion last week, I hope you can prevail upon *The Grapevine* to postpone any publicity about the activity here of our colored group. We are proud of what we are doing but feel that our colored group must be more firmly established and its membership increased before we have any publicity. We are pestered too with the current racial problems and prejudices that exist because of this problem. Until our internal affairs on this subject can be better defined and a more tolerant viewpoint is accepted by all we propose to shun publicity and handle this problem within our group."

[lxxix] When or if the black meeting in Chicago was recognized by A.A. Headquarters is not known. If the meeting was ever recognized in New York, the distinction that the meeting was older than the one in Washington D.C. apparently wasn't recognized.

[lxxx] Glenn Chesnut in *Heroes of Early Black AA* indicated the possibility of the fourth black meeting being founded in Valdosta, Georgia around September of 1945. Georgia State Service Assembly Archives (G.S.S.A.) contain a letter written from Valdosta by a Mrs. McKey to Bobbie that is dated January 25, 1946. Bobbie wrote Mrs. McKey in September, 1945 and in January, 1946. Mrs. McKey appears to be a volunteer nonalcoholic, almost

> Bill feels, as do we all, the Negro alcoholic should have their chance with AA but at the same time we realize racial prejudices make it impossible to accept them in mass into groups.[lxxxi] No matter how theoretically right it would be to accept them, you would nevertheless, cause more harm than good. If you do get a Negro group started ever, please let me know about it for it could be invaluable information for other groups facing the same problem.[159]

By October 10 Bobbie wrote to Los Angeles regarding "the hottest subject in A.A. today." She admitted to knowing of two black meetings by this time, but did not disclose their location. Consistent in the Headquarters approach, she suggested the local groups work out this solution themselves.

> When you start talking about the colored question you really are bringing up the hottest subject in AA today. We are closely watching the start of two Negro groups. I think in the final analysis that the answer to this question will have to be decided by each group locally. The feeling is too strong in different sections of the country to form an over-all national policy. Generally when a Negro inquiry comes in to the local groups arrange a meeting with him and if he is interested, offer to help him form an AA Group in his vicinity. This is about all I can give you on this question now. If you have any experience in California that will be of interest to us, I wish you would send it along.

A "national policy" was about to evolve. The third tradition of A.A. regarding membership requirements, which was going to be announced

---

assuredly white, trying to assist blacks with their alcohol problems. The lack of additional documentation suggests that if there was ever a sustained black meeting in Valdosta it did not continue. Bobbie also attempted to have the St. Louis meeting contact Valdosta, but despite an attempt, Valdosta never responded.

[lxxxi] Bobbie's original letters included "negro" rather than "Negro." Bobbie was corrected by the Secretary of the black group named Torrence C. in his letter to Bobbie dated September 20, 1945 (General Service Office Archives, Box 45, R21, File Mo H.5, p.9).

in the April 1946 *Grapevine*,[lxxxii] indirectly addressed the issue of race without using the word, though the "separate but equal" idea persisted without addressing integrated meetings for many years. The Twelve Traditions were not accepted by the Fellowship until 1950 in theory – and it took decades in some parts of the country for that acceptance to become a practice. Bobbie probably had not yet learned the simplicity of the Third Tradition from Bill. However, the text of *Alcoholics Anonymous* had stated a policy, as such, already when it was first published back in 1939 in the chapter "There Is A Solution."

> If what we have learned and felt and seen means anything at all, it means that all of us, whatever our race, creed, or color are the children of a living Creator with whom we may form a relationship upon simple and understandable terms as soon as we are willing and honest enough to try.[160]

As 1946 commenced, the whispers of black A.A. groups grew into a firm reality. Selections from three letters of Bobbie's letters follow:

> I think you will be interested to know that we now have two Colored Groups which have been successful for about a year. One is in Washington D.C. and the other in St. Louis. The start of another group is beginning in Newark, N.J. I feel sure these first Negro Groups will pave the way for others to come in more easily.[161]

> . . .

> We are just beginning to compile some solid information about our Negro Groups. Two have been in operation for about two years. These are in St. Louis, Mo., and

---

[lxxxii] Third Tradition (Long Form): "Our membership ought to include all who suffer from alcoholism. Hence we may refuse none who wish to recover. Nor ought A.A. membership ever depend upon money or conformity. Any two or three alcoholics gathered together for sobriety may call themselves an A.A. group, provided that, as a group, they have no other affiliation."

Washington D.C.[lxxxiii]. . . . In New York we now have a Negro Group meeting in Harlem and two in New Jersey. In none of these Groups are we attempting to solve any racial question. As you probably know, it is a very controversial one. Bill and all of us feel strongly that Negroes should have the benefits of A.A., but we also feel it would be unwise for us to set any direct policy about them. In some of our northern cities the Negroes do come to open meetings, but as a rule they prefer forming their own Groups. All they ask is that the regular members give them some help in starting. I know in Washington, St. Louis, New York and New Jersey, volunteer members of our established Groups have been helping the Negro Groups get started.[162]

. . .

I'm glad to hear that you in Cincinnati are thinking of a colored group. Quite a number have been started recently and we have had good reports from them. I imagine there are quite a number of candidates there in Cincinnati. Generally speaking, AA works best where the Negro members have their own groups. Usually the big groups cooperate with them, show them the way and start them off. It works out much like any other new group just beginning.[163]

Once again, the limitations of A.A. Headquarters to rule on this issue were clear. Their function was to be a conduit of communication, not a controlling body. Some years would pass before integrated A.A. meetings became common. In some places, such as Atlanta, Georgia, the change took a couple of decades.[164]

[lxxxiii] Why the Chicago A.A. meeting is not mentioned here isn't clear. Most likely they had not announced themselves to New York.

Bobbie Guides A.A. in Ireland

Richard P., born a Protestant in Catholic Ireland, developed a serious alcohol problem while a student at Trinity College, Oxford. His problem became so severe that he left without obtaining a degree, and eventually sunk into skid-row-type living in London. In late 1946, at the age of 44, he sought refuge at St. Patrick's Hospital in Dublin, Ireland, (a Protestant hospital), as a solution to his alcohol problem, but also to avoid the consequences of writing bad checks. There he was approached by Conor F., a native Irishman who had been living in Philadelphia. In the fall of 1946, Conor had about three years of sobriety and had come to introduce A.A. in Ireland. He had a number of failures dealing with the Catholic clergy: "they had no wish to waste time on the usual crazy and short-lived ideas thought up by Americans." Having found failure through approaching Catholic priests, Conor then tried to introduce A.A. to Ireland through sanitariums that treated alcoholics. After failure through that avenue, he encountered Richard P. at St. Patrick's, who warmed to the message of hope Conor brought him.

Since Conor was soon to return to America, Richard became the secretary of the new A.A. group. The group quickly grew to about fifteen members, Richard being the only Protestant. Since Richard was divorced and soon to remarry, he was not considered an ideal representative for A.A. publicity in a Catholic country where divorce was forbidden by the country's Constitution. So Richard wrote A.A. Headquarters seeking guidance. As documented in *Benign Anarchy: Alcoholics Anonymous in Ireland* by Shane Butler, Bobbie provided much needed wisdom.[165]

> Bobbie's response to these concerns about religious culture of Ireland and its potential impact on the fellowship reminded Richard explicitly that AA had no interest in engaging with, or bringing about change in, broader political or cultural issues. What was equally important perhaps was her tone, which implied that AA in Ireland could and would find solutions to its own difficulties, and that the New York 'headquarters' had no intention of prescribing or imposing solutions to problems experienced by the fellowship in other countries.

"I know that Ireland is steeped in rather hard and fast tradition and I am sure that AA, as you are now doing, will have to go along with existing conditions. We do not intend to, nor could we, change a basic mode of life, but rather fit ourselves into things as we find them."[166]

Additional suspicions about A.A. resulted from its former relationship to the Oxford Group, which was then known as Moral Rearmament. The Irish consensus was that America was known as "the land of freak religions" and A.A. might be just one more. A question was posed to Bobbie asking her what she thought of American religious figures endorsing A.A. for the benefit of Irish skeptics. Bobbie was "disinclined to offer an American solution to what appeared to be an Irish problem. She did not think that endorsement of AA by American Catholic authorities would necessarily be of any help to its members in Ireland . . . " The eventual solution was for Richard to be replaced by Catholic alcoholic Sackville M., who eventually built the bridges to the Catholic community, allowing A.A. to become a permanent fixture there.[167]

Bobbie's experiences shared from A.A. Headquarters were validated by events in Ireland that she confidently predicted would take place eventually. Her focus was strictly on the recovery from alcoholism. Social change supported by A.A.s, while highly desirable, would have to follow. Each A.A. would then be free to pursue needed social changes as their conscience dictated, but not insist that Irish A.A. change until the group conscience, as stated in Tradition Two, changed as well.

The Directory

From the earliest years, Alcoholics Anonymous has tenaciously attempted to keep up to date with the contact information of A.A. groups and key people temporarily in positions of responsibility. This essential but unrewarding task to help maintain unity was accomplished through most of the 1940s by updating the member directory every six months until 1949, when one directory per year was considered adequate.[168] Directory update cards were sent to the name and address of the group secretary on file at A.A. Headquarters. Typically they would be mailed with a cover letter signed by Bobbie's more formal name Margaret along with her last name. However, often the address of the group, if it was a group and not a single individual, soon became obsolete and the secretary's name changed sometimes almost randomly.[lxxxiv] Bobbie would advise groups to rent a PO Box to substantially diminish the changing address problem. She also recommended that the terms of a secretary should not expire until it was time for the next directory. However, her requests were often as futile as they were frustrating when her recommendations were not followed.

> The June 25, 1947 directory update card requested the following: City; Name of Group, membership. P.O. Box; Secretary's Name, Address, Telephone number; Clubhouse address and Telephone number; Affiliation with a Central Office and Contributions for the past period.[169]

Her update request for the August 1947 directory stated the purpose of the effort.

> These Lists are primarily made up to facilitate intergroup correspondence, for referral of members from one group to another and for the benefit of our army traveling AAs. Therefore we do not list institutional, hospital, or prison groups. However we have a large number of these groups in our master file and are happy to furnish information about them on request.[170]

While this task may appear trivial, the growing pains of Alcoholics Anonymous across the country were not. All too often when a group was founded in a city, the founders often behaved as if they had been granted an exclusive franchise. Any outsider who did not obey them might be treated with suspicion if not outright hostility. The 1942 dispute in Columbus, Ohio mentioned previously included instructions that a secretary had been replaced while simultaneously the alleged replaced secretary insisted that he was still the primary contact! As early as 1941, Denver "attempted to use a Central Committee as a spiritual 'neutral' zone between two warring A.A. factions." The dispute continued through most of 1942 about who was eligible to be an A.A.[171] Politics plagued A.A. meetings in New York City in 1944.

[lxxxiv] Single individuals were tracked by A.A. Headquarters when that individual was the only A.A. in an area.

> The Clubhouse "Corporation" decided to separate itself from the Manhattan Group by allowing only outside groups to conduct meetings at the [41st Street] Club on a rotating basis. This arrangement didn't go over too well with the Manhattan Group. A lot of harsh words and threats were exchanged between the Manhattan Group, the Clubhouse "Corporation," and other Groups in the area.
>
> The "Corporation" resigned over this controversy, and a new Board of Directors was elected. All sides tried to drag Bill W. into this controversy, but Bill refused to take sides. He let the parties involved resolve the "New York Clubhouse riots" by themselves.[172]

What applied to Bill W. appeared to have applied to Bobbie as well. If she attended the Manhattan Group during these times is not known. Her attendance likely would have been interpreted as her siding with one group over another. Chances are she followed Bill's lead and stayed away. However, her perceived necessity to stay out of local disputes by not attending meetings will prove to be a very significant detriment to her own recovery.

Women Alcoholics Have a Tougher Fight

Marty Mann addressed a previously untouched subject for Alcoholics Anonymous when she wrote a *Grapevine* article "Women Alcoholics Have a Tougher Fight" in May 1945 before the magazine celebrated its first birthday. Some of Marty's observations in the article follow:

> [A] great many women alcoholics learn the last retreat from possible exposure: they discover that sedatives are easily hidden, can be taken almost unobserved, and leave no smell. And that they produce the same effect as quantities of liquor . . . with ten times the danger . . .
>
> We'd been away from reality so long—we'd twisted and turned so adroitly in our speech, our actions, and in our very thoughts—could we come back? And if we tried,

would they let us? Would we be acceptable? Or would the double standard work here too?

The return to honesty is hard for all alcoholics, but for most women it is harder than for men. Everything in the pattern of a woman alcoholic has conspired to make her dishonest. It hasn't been entirely her fault; the world and its ways are much to blame.

Those of us who are already well and happy members of A.A. have a great responsibility in the battle against stigma. If we can freely and proudly admit our A.A. membership when there is an opportunity to do so, if we will speak at meetings whenever we can and work with other women, we can win that battle.[173]

Just how much did Bobbie have a "tougher fight?" Inevitably, her first few years in A.A. were dominated primarily by men. Fortunately, by mid-October 1942, she reported that, "You wouldn't know the New York Group. I understand they have about 40 women members, 25 of whom have had no trouble since coming in."[174] Perhaps she experienced substantial female program camaraderie from this date forward? There's no record that she took advantage of the opportunity. Did she trust other women? How often did she "admit our A.A. membership" by simply attending New York A.A. meetings? Little was left behind that recorded any efforts regarding her personal recovery from alcoholism or fellowship with other women. In a letter to Esther of Dallas written in November of 1943, she said, "I wish I could get to meetings – should be ashamed to admit that I make only about three a year in my own Group."[175] To her, Alcoholics Anonymous mainly seemed to represent more of a vocation. No evidence has been found that she personally sponsored anyone in New York; her role resembling a sponsor was done almost entirely through correspondence. It seemed to be a responsibility of her job. She didn't write about anyone sponsoring her, though she probably would have claimed Bill as her sponsor until her last months working at Headquarters. One wonders just how many female friends in or out of the program she had in New York. After all, why should she attend regular meetings when she could be in the presence of a co-founder, or even better, represent him?

Bobbie and Sedatives

Bobbie received a letter from Alice B. of Minneapolis, Minnesota on July 23, 1946, which she could not answer until August 8 due to a heavy workload. Alice reported that an increasing number of women were using sedatives to the degree that they were "staggering around the clubhouse." Since nothing was written in *Alcoholics Anonymous* on the subject, Alice and other sober female members were holding back any action until some words of wisdom could be received from Headquarters. The letter asked for the thoughts of Bill or Dr. Bob, so Bobbie did her best to direct them to what had been written on the subject already.

> Perhaps by now you have received the October[lxxxv] and November 1945[lxxxvi] issues of the A.A. GRAPEVINE which I asked them to mail you last week. In these issues there are many articles about pills and sedatives. I think the reading of both these papers on the subject will do much to clear up your questions.
>
> Personally, and I did a little playing with pills in my pre-AA days, I consider all sedatives, Benzedrine etc. is the same class as the bottle of beer or a glass of wiskey *[sic]*. They just aren't for us alcoholics and they do affect us differently. Why I don't know. I have been told that about 50% of the people coming into AA have had some experience with sedatives. I do not think you would be amiss in pointing out everything you read in THE GRAPEVINE and my small personal feelings to all the members of your group. Actually I can spot anyone who's had a few pills a mile away because I've used them myself and know what symptoms to look for.
>
> To alcoholics who use pills do so for the same reason that we drink, to get high or to gloss over reality. We think we are getting away with a "sedative" drunk because no one can smell liquor on our breaths. Actually we are just

---

[lxxxv] "Evidence on the Sleeping Pill Menace."

[lxxxvi] "Those 'Goof Balls'" by Bill W.

following out one of the symptoms of alcoholism, that of kidding ourselves.

The Tenth A.A. Anniversary Celebration

The Tenth Anniversary Celebration was held in Cleveland, Ohio, June 9th and 10th of 1945. The formal program in Cleveland listed both Bill and Dr. Bob, and it appeared to be a predominantly male event—with one exception. To provide women a place to congregate, a tea was organized from 3:00pm to 5:00pm on Saturday, the 9th. The *Cleveland Central Bulletin* reported on the event, which included a rare historical gem: Bobbie and Lois were reported to be together in the same sentence:

TENTH ANNIVERSARY TEA

The pre-formal opening of the Tenth Anniversary was a tea given by the Cleveland Women AA's for their out-of-town guests in the Spanish Room at Hotel Carter on Saturday, June 9th.

What a bright-eyed vivacious crowd turned out— members from almost every State in the Union from California to Vermont. Lois W. and Bobby *[sic]* B. of New York were enthusiastically welcomed, and charmed everyone with their ability to be at ease with the constant demands on their attention. We were able to renew our old acquaintances and add many new ones to our growing list of out-of-town friends.

The attendance far surpassed our timid estimate of a few weeks back; in fact, it grew to such proportions that the adjoining dining room was opened so we could circulate more freely. Popular guesses placed the number at about 250—a record turnout for a "manless" tea.[176]

Female Frailties as Described in *The Grapevine*

Among the obstacles women faced entering A.A. included thinking promoted by other women. Grace O. from Manhattan documented her thoughts in the October 1946 *A.A. Grapevine* regarding the eleven alleged shortcomings that plagued women entering Alcoholics Anonymous.[lxxxvii] She called them "female frailties" in an article titled "Women's Meetings". One wonders what A.A. meetings Grace attended and for how long which led her to assemble the female alcoholic stereotypes written here.

1) The percentage of women who stay with A.A. is low. Too many of them drop out after the novelty wears off; a few months to a year and a half.

2) Many women form attachments too intense—bordering on the emotional. Best-friends, crushes, hero-worship cause strained relationships.

3) So many women want to run things. To boss, manage, supervise, regulate and change things. Twenty want to decorate; one will scrub or mend what is already around.

4) Too many women don't like women.

5) Women talk too much. Gossip is a cancer to all A.A. groups and must be constantly watched. Men gossip far too much, too. But few men use it for punishment, or revenge, or cutting someone down to size. Once the news value has been absorbed, men generally drop a topic. But women worry the same dead mouse until it's unrecognizable.

6) Women are a questionable help working with men and vice versa. In 12th Step work, the intimate confidences often lead to the pity

---

[lxxxvii] Grace was the second wife of Fulton Oursler. Alcoholics Anonymous was very much in debt to him for his previous assistance. As editor of *Liberty Magazine* when Charles Towns approached him on behalf of Alcoholics Anonymous, the September 1939 article "Alcoholics and God" resulted in the first substantial publicity so desired by A.A. at the time. Fulton authored the warm-hearted article "Charming is the Word for Alcoholics" in the July 1944 issue of *The Grapevine*. Note that this article has an additional twist when one realizes his wife was (or was soon to become) an alcoholic. Fulton Oursler, who converted to Catholicism in 1943, was to author the book *The Greatest Story Ever Told* in 1949.

that's akin to love, and is often mistaken for same. The protective, the maternal, the inspirational interest often lands one or both in a broadside slip—and sometimes in extra-marital experiments, which, however clothed in the glory of "honesty," are disillusioning to many others, and frequently present a troubling question to those who are actually trying to live the 12 Steps.

7) Sooner or later, a woman-on-the-make sallies into a group, on the prowl for phone numbers and dates. Oddly enough, perhaps, she does not wear a placard and is not always easily recognized. Results of her operations can cause havoc.

8) A lot of women are attention demanders. Spotlight sisters. They want to be spoon fed, coaxed, babied, encouraged, teased, praised and personally conducted into recovery.

9) Few women can think in the abstract. Everything must be taken personally. Universal truths, to many women, are meaningless generalities. These women are impatient of philosophy, meditation and discussion. This is the kind of woman who figures "Just let's have this bargain; we'll pay so much faith down and the rest in installments." Which is a deceiving deal, for such buyers are generally the ones who have to watch the collector come and take the piano back.

10) Women's feelings get hurt too often. They rapidly and frequently are misunderstood.

11) Far too many women A.A.s cannot get along with the non-alcoholic wives of A.A. members. They feel ashamed or defiant, and they show it. Often they unwittingly forbid overtures—and then feel snubbed! Lots of A.A. women feel they attend a meeting to be *helped*—and concentrate to the point of rudeness on non-A.A. contacts. If they behave superciliously toward the non-alcoholic wives of members, they should hardly complain of being treated coolly in return.[177]

Many of these observations appear patently absurd, if not entirely offensive, to women today. Did any of them apply to Bobbie? Item 4 seems likely since there's little evidence that Bobbie liked to be with most other women. Most of her warm-hearted female relationships all seemed the result of correspondence, which sometimes resulted in occasional visits, but there remains little evidence of long-term, face-to-face female friends.

The only other item that may have been applicable could have been 11. In this case, Bobbie may not have gotten along with non-alcoholic wives very well and vice versa. Her high IQ coupled with her intense and repeated sanitarium experiences may have contributed to a boredom with subjects that the "normal" non-alcoholic women enjoyed.

Thus, the alcoholic women of the times had one more additional hazard to navigate: not only did they have to endure the prejudices of male alcoholics and their wives, but prejudices against each other as well.

Bobbie on Vacation in 1944

Bobbie's single status provided her certain freedoms. She enjoyed the game of golf, probably from growing up in Dobbs Ferry with her affluent family. She wrote the following on April 29, 1944 after returning from vacation.

> Played hooky last week and took time out for a short ten days in Pinehurst, North Carolina. I've needed a rest for some time for the pressure here has been terrific. Finally went voluntarily before I was forced to give up. Had a marvelous time and loved every minute of the golf and sunshine – now I feel ready for anything without batting an eyelash.[178]

There's no record of who accompanied her on this vacation. Her daughters may have been with her—they were taught the game of golf.[179] She may have played with some people she knew previously. Her time off appeared to be more than necessary. She had written that "every once and so often I must take a couple of weeks completely away from the office – the pressure is such that I'd end up wackier than I am if these vacations weren't possible."[180]

The subject of golf also caused Bobbie to write a paragraph that ended with one of her most accurate predictions. She wrote the following to Vic in Sacramento, California on January 11, 1944:

> Remember the "log" you wrote about Bill and Lois' visit –the one where Maloney tied him with 103 in golf? Can I please have another if you have a copy. Ours is lost.

It was such a fine piece of description and gave such a nice background of the visit that I sent it to one of the trustees. He in turn liked it so well that he sent it to Dr. Harry Emerson Fosdick. Now he liked it so well that he took it home to show his wife and promptly got taken ill with the flu. When he arose from this session the letter was gone in the confusion. He has hunted high and low and is feeling pretty badly at the loss. I would very much like to keep the letter in our files. Someday in the future the story of AA and Bill's life will be written. It will be from our files that much of the personal and intimate sidelights on Bill and AA will come forth.[181]

How to Sponsor a Country: Australia

Australia's Alcoholics Anonymous General Service Board published the book *One To Another* in 2014. The majority of the first 180 pages of the book include about forty letters exchanged between Bobbie and Dr. Sylvester M. of Sydney, Australia between December 7, 1942 and May 17, 1949.[182] While the majority of members of A.A. today in the United States do not know who Bobbie was, Australia has been ahead of the curve. When Australia published its 1995 Commemorative Edition of *Alcoholics Anonymous*, Bobbie's name—not Bill's—appeared in the preface.[183]

Dr. M. was the medical superintendent of a psychiatric hospital in Rydalmere, Sydney when he read about Alcoholics Anonymous in *The American Journal of Psychiatry*. He wrote to the publication for information exactly one year after the attack on Pearl Harbor. The magazine forwarded his letter to A.A., which did not arrive on Bobbie's desk until January 26, 1943. As World War II in the Pacific was well underway by then, civilian correspondence between the two countries was understandably slow and irregular.

Bobbie's Eloquent A.A. Introduction

Bobbie replied on February 2. She wrote an eloquent nine- paragraph introduction that should make any seasoned A.A. member of today grateful that she was there to write such an appropriate synopsis of Alcoholics Anonymous. Here is a sample of her 820-word response:

> Our members come from all walks of life. Our spiritual
> concepts are broad – our members are Catholics, Protestants

> and Jews and most nationalities are represented. In round figures we believe that we have about one woman member to seven men. Alcoholism is no respecter of race, color, creed or sex – any may become alcoholic but all can recover if they wish and have no additional psychoses. Many groups in this country have started from scratch with nothing but our book and some correspondence with this Central Office. We realize the difficulties of rapid mail service between here and Australia so I shall write, at length in this letter. Bill W., who wrote the text of the book *Alcoholics Anonymous* and I are now editing a compilation of group experiences over the past five years. This may be out this summer and we will be glad to send you a copy if you are interested.[184]

At the time Bobbie wrote this, she was the only other alcoholic that worked at Headquarters. Note that she claimed that Bill and she were together "editing a compilation of group experiences." One wonders: to what degree did Bobbie participate in providing thoughts and/or feedback to Bill's writings of this era? Her writings of this period often suggest an almost peer-to-peer relationship with him.

She decided to donate a copy of *Alcoholics Anonymous*[lxxxviii] to Dr. Sylvester M., which, following standard procedure had to be sent separately due to cost considerations. She described how prospective members, or "prospects," could be found just about anywhere. She stressed how any A.A. group should be self-supporting. Though she knew she was talking to a professional psychiatrist, she asserted that much of her writing involving A.A. was mainly "avocational." The Alcoholic Foundation was briefly described. She concluded by recommending that Dr. M. should feel free to write at any time: she wished to help in any way she could.

Dr. M. replied with a general description of how little success he had witnessed as a professional over a twenty-year period of dealing with alcoholics. His words included an alphabet of failure, relapses, grudges, tragedies, and rescues. He also wished for an American member of

---

[lxxxviii] Most likely it was a first edition, third printing. When Bobbie decided to hand out copies of the Big Book, she never seemed to have to ask permission of anyone.

Alcoholics Anonymous to help get the program started in his hometown of Sydney.

Religion Says—Medicine Says

Bobbie's May 4, 1943 response contained a section which closely resembled the "Religion Says – Medicine Says" speech that Bill W. made a year later to the Medical Society of the State of New York.[185] Bobbie presented how medicine had treated alcoholics in comparison to religion in five different facets of recovery. While she had to have borrowed these ideas from Bill, her knowledge suggests she was very familiar with these ideas around a year before they were published.[186] She wrote that both professions "have been unable to build a strong bridge of mutual understanding and confidence between themselves and their patients," something that often rings true today. She stressed that a newcomer to A.A. most often required a "new compelling interest" to stay sober, a solution professionals could not provide but that Alcoholics Anonymous could. She further described how agnostics should be handled: "Remind him that alcoholism is as fatal as cancer . . . If he had cancer he would not think he could cure it by himself." She concluded with the encouraging words that if Dr. M. persisted in helping start A.A. there, he could not fail.

Fourteen Months Later

There was a fourteen-month gap before Dr. M. wrote again. He reported that an American A.A. had visited recently, intending to return next time to help the doctor start an A.A. meeting in Sydney. Dr. M. thought that Australian alcoholics faced some challenges that weren't often present in the United States: "Australians tend to be rather reserved and do not accept a new thing with the enthusiasm and spontaneity of Americans. I think that this fact has been our main difficulty in starting AA here." Nevertheless, he stressed that "there is an urgent necessity for AA in Australia. Once started the movement will grow like a snowball."[187]

Bobbie replied on August 17, 1944 — the day after she received Dr. M.'s letter. She surmised that A.A.s in the American military could be of assistance to him, and she would try to arrange introductions. She wrote these encouraging words, "I know we will one day have groups in Australia and you may be sure we will do everything we can from this end to bring AA to your country as quickly as possible."[188]

Archie McKinnon

As with Dr. M., Archie McKinnon[lxxxix] first learned about Alcoholics Anonymous in *The American Journal of Psychiatry*. He read *The Therapeutic Mechanism of Alcoholics Anonymous* (1944) by Dr. Harry M. Tiebout. [189] In late November—early December 1944, a copy of *Alcoholics Anonymous* sent by Bobbie arrived. For some time McKinnon thought this was the first copy received in Australia. He would later learn that Dr. M. had received one almost eighteen months earlier from Bobbie. Archie previously received a letter from her on September 15, introducing him to Dr. M. and suggesting the two of them combine their efforts. This was one more example of the valuable role she performed during these times. Even though these two men were fourteen time zones ahead of New York, they were put together by an A.A. secretary on the other side of the world during a world war; even though the men were practically neighbors![xc]

Archie replied on December 18 to thank Bobbie for the book and accompanying literature. This book was eventually given to Rex A., who "was to become the cornerstone of Australia's first AA Group."[190] He also reported that he had communicated with Dr. M. and that he believed that they shortly would be starting an A.A. group.

[lxxxix] McKinnon was a psychiatric nurse.

[xc] An article, authored by an Australian Ted C., appeared in May 1978 titled "How AA Came to Australia" in the New South Wales publication called *The Reviver*, which credits a Father Murphy as introducing Dr. M to Archie McKinnon in 1945. Obviously, Bobbie could not be physically present to do the introduction, but she did write Archie about Dr. M. in a letter dated September 15, 1944, which precedes the reported introduction by the Father by many months. The article has a significant error. In light of the documentation of *One To Another* published in 2014 and Conference Approved in Australia, the letters exchanged between Dr. M. and Bobbie spanned seven years and not just two.

Australia's First A.A. "Branch"

Dr. M. reported on March 21, 1945 that an A.A. "branch" of four former "inebriates" had been formed in Sydney, Australia. Since they had only two A.A. books to share, Dr. M. asked for more. Archie McKinnon sought additional "recruits." They met at Dr. M.'s house once or twice a week, though many of the newcomers required hospitalization. Dr. M. also had good news: the group was growing and Rex A. was the secretary. Dr. M. assured Bobbie he would continue to lend his support: "I will take a keen interest in the branch and will advise them professionally until it is on its feet."[191]

Rex A. wrote Bobbie on March 26 responding to Bobbie's letter of August 17, 1944. He reported that the material she sent was now in his possession. He named three non-alcoholics as co-founders: Dr. M., Archie McKinnon, and Father Tom D., a Roman Catholic priest. Rex reported that the "branch" had grown to 7-8 members.

Bobbie wrote a short reply of congratulations to Dr. M. on April 27 and wrote that we "fully realize that without you an A.A. Group in Sydney would not have been possible." Bobbie also wrote she would be replying to Rex very soon.[192]

Australian Uniqueness Claimed

About this time Dr. M.'s letters lengthened significantly as a wide variety of problems confronted this fledgling group of recovering alcoholics. A May 24, 1945 letter said cultural differences between Americans and Australians made their circumstances more difficult. Australians were dominated by "respectability:"

> Quite unlike Americans we tend to boast of our family connections and not of our achievements. In such a community any skeleton in a family, such as alcoholism in one of its members, must be kept hidden from the world and the offending member cast into oblivion.[193]

Dr. M. observed that the shame and guilt of Australian alcoholics were beyond the range of comparable experiences in the United States. Many of the newcomers were veterans fresh from horrific memories of the war—memories they wished to drown in alcohol. "Backsliders" (slippers) plagued the group. Destitute, homeless members sought shelter in Dr. M.'s hospital. However, as they left Dr. M.'s supervision, they would relapse. Father Tom volunteered to make a home for them to ease the burden on the hospital, but they seemed to be stuck, going nowhere fast.

Dr. M. sought help from more experienced A.A. members in the United States. He believed that "a stranger from a foreign land is an ambassador, to whom so many people will listen and for whom many barriers, erected against the native born, will be lowered."[194] Dr. M. learned the hard way a slice of wisdom heard in A.A. today: "You can tell an alcoholic anything, but you cannot tell him much." The newcomers didn't seem to be listening to him or following any program.

In her early July 1945 response, Bobbie attempted to be most comforting. She suggested that "some of the disappointments you write of are not as serious as they seem to you people right on the spot." She assured him that American experiences had been just as intense and frustrating. She claimed, possibly referring to the Bowery of New York, that about half of the American A.A. newcomers were homeless and penniless. To help ease their shortage of books, she announced that six copies of *Alcoholics Anonymous* would be shipped to him the next day.[195]

Dr. M.'s August 10th response was much more favorable than before. "We feel that we are at last on our feet and more confident of the future." He was glad to know that the frustrations of recent times resembled those of American experiences. Dr. M. wrote that he was being asked to speak rather frequently about his experiences with A.A. "Your letter has given us the lead we should follow, that is, we must try and educate the public that alcoholism is a disease and not a crime." Dr. M. was actively making inroads with prison officials to raise awareness and, hopefully, see that inebriate violators were treated as patients rather than criminals.

He also reported that 40% of the returning soldiers who were suicidal were inebriates.

> But in a land where psychiatry is still in its infancy, and where inebriety is a crime, the job to convince people of these facts will be slow and difficult. For this reason we are using 'blitz' methods hoping that by wide publicity, we can interest sufficient people in the shortest period of time in a scientific study of alcoholism and its problems.[196]

Dr. M. was also beginning to realize that the words written by Bobbie contained not only wisdom but experience. What follows is the first of many times this professional psychiatrist expressed his appreciation for the kind encouragement Bobbie had been providing him:

> We are ever grateful to you for your interest in us, and for your advice and for your kindly thought in our welfare. For months past we have had periods of great optimism followed by period *[sic]* of black despair, when things seemed to be going hopelessly wrong. Periods of despair still come, but the fact that they are less frequent and not so dark shows we are making progress. With very many thanks for your interest in us.[197]

On October 26 Bobbie replied to Dr. M.'s August 10th letter, advising him that American A.A. had never employed a publicity director, an idea Dr. M. had been considering. Bobbie's eloquent words would form a portion of Tradition Eleven of Alcoholics Anonymous when it was published for the first time six months later.

> You speak of the necessity of having a publicity man become a member and I can imagine this could be a big help in directing news items into the right channels. However, it might interest you to know that we have never had a publicity director in our National Headquarters in these eleven years. One news-paper man said that we had had over a million dollars' worth of publicity absolutely free and all of it came to us by the method of 'attraction' rather than 'promotion'. I know of no time when we have deliberately gone out after publicity from a national viewpoint.[198]

In addition, Bobbie provided Dr. M. with news that two States,—New Jersey and Alabama—had passed legislation that treated alcoholism as a disease rather than a crime, and that many returning veterans were experiencing challenges as they returned from war. Bobbie closed, as she often did, with encouragement: "you can count on us to do everything in our power to give you the advantage of our now eleven years of experience."[199]

Australians Learning the Hard Way

Dr. M. wrote again on December 10 observing that the events of last year had convinced him that Australian professionals knew almost nothing about treating alcoholism. Their naïve good will had produced little other than prolonged alcoholic binges from their patients: well-meaning gifts of money and shelter simply enabled drunks to stay drunk. He had discovered he needed to unlearn most of the last twenty years of frustrating experiences.

> We are learning the hard way because we are so far away from you all to send out an SOS. But in a way we are grateful for having to battle on our own. Bitter experience is the best teacher of all, and it has taught us to understand why the progress of AA in the first four years was so slow. We admire more and more the vision, courage and perseverance of the founders of the Society.[200]

He concluded with the words "We are ever grateful to you for your help and encouragements and wish you the best."

Dr. M.'s next letter, written on November 25, but not received in New York until January 8, 1946, was among his most controversial:

> We are glad to know that inebriates are the same the World over. I do think, however, that the technique, but certainly not the principles of AA may have to be modified to suit different countries and races. For example, the Americans are much more extroverted and religious than we are. This was further impressed on us by American soldiers in Australia. What appealed to them did not always appeal to us and vice versa.[201]

He further surmised that "we may have to modify AA technique to suit Australians," but admitted that future experience would reveal the validity of that assertion. He mentioned that he had heard from Marty M. and that he was using the literature Bobbie had provided. Though his little A.A. group had been experiencing long periods of stagnation, progress was now underway because "we now unconsciously are 'Australianising' AA principles [so] that our progress has been more rapid." He concluded with conciliatory words of appreciation for Bobbie stating, "Assuring you always of our feelings of deep gratitude to you for your help and encouragement at all times, and wishing AA every success."[202]

Three days later, on January 11, Bobbie received a second Dr. M. letter written the previous November 27. An outside issue, a clinic, was about to be opened under the sponsorship of Dr. M. and A.A., which was intended to help offload wet drunks from crowding their club room. "The whole clinic is in the lap of the Gods, the first of its kind in the British Empire, a virginal field and we enter it not knowing in the least what to expect." He admitted the clinic experiment was a gamble. Recent newspaper publicity was favorable. He expressed gratitude for what he claimed to be Bobbie's A.A. motto: "Hope for the Best and Never fear the Worst."[xci] While expressing determination to pursue their courses of action, he wished to express that this was not "disloyalty to AA:"

> It is not. All we are thinking is that as we are the first branch away from America our experiences will be a very useful guide to AA and to those forming branches in other parts of the British Empire and in other parts of the world.[203]

A Convalescent Home for Inebriates was to be opened in the very near future with a capacity of six patients. Finally, he mentioned that a search was on to find a female inebriate. "Women inebriates have an infinitely worse time here than the men and their history is kept hush-hush by relatives. Family pride reigns supreme."[204]

"A.A. is a Little Like a Cafeteria"

Paper letters as the means of communication over great distances presents some problems. Bobbie sent an airmail message dated December 11, 1945, a month before Dr. M.'s November 25 and November 27 letters

---

[xci]   280 A.A. slogans are listed in *Stepping Stones to Recovery*, on pages 221-252, authored by Bill Pittman, copyright 1999 by the Hazelden Foundation. Interestingly enough, the slogan attributed to Bobbie by Dr. M. is not among the 280 slogans contained in the book. No exact matches found on the Internet through searches, though there are close matches.

were received in New York. She wished everyone in Australia a Merry Christmas, reporting that "the members of our country have come to the conclusion that financial help seldom stops a man from drinking." She recommended that the best approach of working with a newcomer was to "give him a clear and concise picture of alcoholism." She then made this analogy:

> We explain AA is a little like a cafeteria. (Do you have them in Australia?) Our plan for recovery is set out for people to take as little or as much of as they choose but it is not served to them as in a regular restaurant. It is there for the asking, but one must ask."

She closed with good wishes and that both Bill W. and she were "extremely grateful for all you are doing."[205]

Bobbie received the two most recent Dr. M. letters on January 8 and 11 and replied on January 15, 1946. She did not accept that Australian A.A., over the long haul, was going to be any different than American A.A. She believed that in five years the meetings were going to be functionally identical. She provided an example of the Seaman's A.A. Group in New York City that had tried what Dr. M. had seemed to be advocating. After six months, none of the seamen were sober. Those that could eventually came back and used the Twelve Steps just as they were written. Her hunch would be true for Australia, though she hadn't yet been informed how right she was going to be!

Dr. M.'s Mea Culpa

Dr. M.'s January 5, 1946 letter covers nine pages in *One To Another* and is the first of what was to become his first lengthy report of a number of "mea culpa"[xcii] learning experiences. "We are simply in a stage when enthusiasm has to overcome common sense," he wrote.

> I would take it that we are nothing else but troublesome children who want to do the right thing but with our inexperience, our enthusiasm, we unmindingly *[sic]* cause

---

[xcii]   Mea culpa - an acknowledgment of one's fault or error.

> worry and anxiety to you in America to whom we owe
> all. All we require at times is a gentle rebuke and we will
> come to heel.[206]

He admitted that both the hospital and the convalescent home had become dismal failures—the wet drunks simply used them to stay drunk. He further observed that the only successes were when all Twelve Steps of the program were being followed. He had abandoned all attempts to modify the program for Australians. "It is so easy to speak with the dogmatism of ignorance. It takes the bitterness of experience to teach one the truth."[207] He admitted that they had tried to mix outside funding with A.A.'s spiritual principles and "this was where we grievously offended you." He fervently hoped that someone from the United States could visit and provide guidance in everyday matters. Still, learning was taking place and the branch was growing, however haphazardly.

Dr. M.'s January 5 letter did not arrive in New York until May 22. Bobbie immediately expressed her concern:

> In some way or other I sense that you feel we have been
> acting like the parent to a disobedient child and this worries
> me a little . . . I have tried in all of my letters since the
> very early ones to suggest ways and means of helping you
> based on the experience we have had in America. If you
> will check back on my letters you will see that we realized
> from the very beginning how alcoholics fundamentally
> are the same in spite of nationality differences.[208]

She reassured Dr. M. that similar mistakes had been made in the United States: "Your story could easily have been ours – we all went through the same organizational difficulties, differences of opinion, over-conservatism and over-promotionalism." Then she took on a characteristic resembling Bill! She stretched numbers or dates to make a point, which appeared from time to time throughout her writing. With regards to making sure A.A. avoided getting involved in the wet-dry controversy, Bobbie wrote, "We have completely steered clear of this with our neutral attitude for twelve years . . ."[209] Of course, twelve years previous to May 22, 1946, Bill was still drinking and A.A. didn't exist. The name Alcoholics Anonymous itself didn't exist either. But surely Bobbie can be forgiven for occasionally stretching numbers to make a point!

She once again tried to be encouraging. "You people are pioneers and I hope I can convince you that we are in complete sympathy and accord with all you are trying to do . . . Let me reiterate that we want to help in any way we can and that no matter how busy we get, your letters will always take precedence over others."[210]

Dr. M. was most gracious in his June 17 letter after receiving Bobbie's May 22 response:

> In all our many trials and difficulties, when we thought that we knew everything, your letters have shown us the way we should go. The fact that we have caused you worry was quite inadvertent and we apologize sincerely for it. Let us assure you at all times of our gratitude, loyalty and our sincerest desire to co-operate with you all in New York.[211]

The general tone of the rest of Dr. M.'s thirty-one paragraph letter was upbeat and positive. The letter was so long that the postscript was an six additional paragraphs. Highlights included over thirty people attending their last Friday meeting and they were about to decide if they should split into two smaller groups. He very much liked the idea of having future meetings in members' homes, which he attributed to Bill W. The management of housing alcoholics was now separate and distinct from A.A. There were still problems, such as finding places for the wet alcoholic to dry out. He felt as if his requirement to be a supervisor of A.A. events had diminished to the point that he probably wasn't required any longer. He continued, "During the past 18 months our mistakes have been legion. We have learned by bitter trial and error. One lesson we have learnt, and one you repeatedly warned us about, is to not force AA on patients. We now follow your advice – tell them about AA and if they want help at any time it will be given"[212]

Bobbie congratulated Dr. M. for the progress that was being reported:

> I'm just delighted to see you working out everything so well, that after making mistakes you rectify them. If you remember, one of the things I tried to tell you was not

to clothe, feed and give money to alcoholics or less you would be flooded with a lot of panhandlers and those who do not want to stop drinking but want other kinds of help.[213]

She was pleased to hear that there was a movement to split into smaller groups. But she advised, "Small groups are splendid and very necessary but many small groups cooperating all together are even stronger." She realized, however, that her observation was for the future and not an immediate requirement. Included in this letter is some of what would become Tradition Nine: "I think you will eventually find that a minimum of organization and only the smallest amount of money to keep going will eventually answer many of the problems that come up."[214]

Dr. M.'s Step One and His Praise for Bobbie

There was no communication between them until Dr. M wrote on March 8, 1947. He admitted that he had not been well and that alcohol had been involved: "It now seems to be that even though I never became an inebriate, I must have had leanings that way."[215] In other words, as can be said in many an A.A. meeting today, an alcoholic can be described as being on an elevator going down; he can get off on any floor, before he hits bottom. Dr. M. was himself an alcoholic. "Unconsciously, being a psychiatrist, I must have known that I was an inebriate; it was a big blow to my conscious pride to admit it." Upon admitting his alcoholism, he realized the life-saving contribution Bobbie had made for Australia and him personally. Over the next couple of years, here are the many expressions of gratitude that Australian A.A. co-founder Dr. M. made in praise of Bobbie. No wonder the Australians knew of their debt to Bobbie long before most of the rest of the A.A. world discovered their own debts to her.

> March 8, 1947: We previously had no idea how vast your organization is and what a busy woman you are. We now feel very proud that you have taken such a great interest in us. Being the first non-American branch we felt very proud and expected to be waited on hand and foot. That you have done so has spoilt us. But truth to say we have enjoyed

being spoilt, even though we did show our enjoyment by being petulant at times.[216]

March 8, 1947: And we feel that you, with your correspondents from all parts of the world, are the acme of tact, sympathy and understanding.[217]

March 8, 1947: Your flock now extends to many parts of the world. I know your time for reading such long and rambling letters becomes less and less. But we assure you that once we are firmly on our feet, we will 'pull our weight' more with American branches and will no longer be so dependent on you for help and advice.[218]

June 24, 1947: No one knows more than I do the debt of gratitude we owe to you. Your eternal patience with us in the days of our pride and arrogance; your gentle rebukes, your words of encouragement when we were in the doldrums all tided us over very difficult times. All we hope now is that someday, please God, some of us will be in New York and will be able to thank you personally for your eternal goodness to us.[219]

November, 1947: No one knows but the early AAs in Sydney how much the movement owes to your tolerance, patience, and endurance with us, when we had our 'feet firmly planted in mid-air," to use your own expression. Now that we have come down to earth we take all these things and crises, true to your training and advice, in our stride.[220]

November 14, 1947: We are indeed grateful to you for your unfailing interest in us . . . When we followed the teachings of AA and not our own in rearing it, it became a strong healthy child. Now it has brothers in all states of Australia . . . We will have our ups and downs, but since we have learned tolerance, we face the future with calm and confidence keeping always to the 24 hour program . . . We send to all of you our most cordial greetings and express to you our most heartfelt thanks for being always our true guide, philosopher and friend . . . God willing some of us will be able to thank you personally in New York, we hope within the next three years.[221]

February 2, 1948: We pray that a Bobby B will be sent to us here and all our difficulties will be solved.[222]

June 3, 1948: To all in the Central Office we send all greetings and all good wishes for the future. Our thanks to you personally can never be adequately expressed.[223]

August 8, 1948: But we do recognize that we must have a secretary – unfortunately we have not yet found a Bobbie B – we await patiently her advent.[224]

January 10, 1949: I know that I have changed completely, for the better I hope, and it has all been due to your help, encouragement, tolerance, advice and infinite patience with us, and I now know how difficult and arrogant we were. You taught us everything and now when we meet crises, as we do very often, we are as patient as you have taught us to be and everything comes out alright.[225]

April 15, 1949: You have been my 'Patron Saint' in AA and I have taken up too much of your time . . . "[226]

6

The Stubbornist,
Most Closed-Minded AA

midst answering overwhelming piles of mail, advising newly-formed groups and collaborating with Bill, Bobbie became embroiled in the Carl K. episode that could have divided, if not destroyed, Alcoholics Anonymous had the controversy not abruptly ended.

Carl K. was a Chattanooga newspaperman who had lost his job due to his drinking. Six weeks after getting sober on July 18, 1944 (including some false starts), Carl did what came naturally: he founded his own A.A. newspaper entitled *The Empty Jug*! Through Carl's considerable promotional talents, what started as a one-man, four-page journal eventually boasted no less than 600 paid subscribers in 44 states, Mexico and Canada.[227] The fact that he was a newcomer to Alcoholics Anonymous never seemed to curb his belief that others deserved and desired to hear his opinions. If he ever had a local A.A. advisor or sponsor, he never found it necessary to share who that was. Consequently, as an example of why the A.A. Traditions became so very necessary, the Carl episode seems to have very few known rivals in the history of Alcoholics Anonymous.

To fully piece together this intense two-year episode, letters written by people other than Bobbie must be included. Combining Carl's letters with Bobbie's suggests that many of her letters to him are either missing from the A.A. General Service Office Archives or lost.[228] Carl's letters written to New York may not be complete either. Letters exchanged between Carl and Bill W. have been included, since Carl continued unrestrained despite Bobbie's attempts to guide him. In addition, letters to and from Rev.

Sam D., then of Rome, Georgia, are referenced to fully document Carl's sensationalism and desire to stir up controversy.

Carl wrote "Miss B." a most positive introduction on August 22, 1944 when he had just six weeks of sobriety. He reported that ten people had attended a meeting the previous Friday and that twenty were expected the next Sunday. One newcomer, who allegedly had almost died just seven days prior as a result of his last drunk, was leading three new men to attend the next meeting. Carl observed that his group was "the talkingest group in AA." One of the members was not worried about his anonymity: everybody in town supposedly knew what a loud-mouthed drunk he had been. Another new member, Bob, had taken eight quarts of liquor to a convention in Atlantic City and somehow survived his blackout drinking to arrive back to Chattanooga. However, upon his return home, his terrified wife called the police and had the violent and irrational drunk arrested. Someone, whom Carl called a "senior AA member," and might have had a few months sober, had bailed the husband out of jail and taken him to a sanitarium to dry out. This wild man was to be at the meeting the next evening, so Carl observed, "I have had one of these hunches which, at times, are uncannily accurate, that Bob is through drinking for good." His ego well nourished, he decided to share his literature with Headquarters:

> As a former newspaperman I had to write something for AA besides letters so I have started a little paper a copy of which I am enclosing. It is poorly mimeographed and the text might not be startling in its value, but it will improve.[229]

Such was Bobbie's first introduction to *The Empty Jug*. Her September 1, 1944 reaction described the little newspaper as being "wonderful." She wrote that she was aware of roughly twenty similar publications that had sprung up around the country, and asked to be put down as a subscriber. She then introduced Carl to *The Grapevine* (which had premiered the previous June) as "the paper originally intended for the New York group members in which were quickly subscribed to by A.A.s all over the country." She suggested that he should become a subscriber himself. Her conclusion contained a very upbeat message: "Hope your next letter will contain much more good news about the Chattanooga Chapter. Both Bill and I are so happy to have this AA representation in your city."[230]

Carl seemed to almost bubble with enthusiasm in his next message written three weeks later on September 22: "You can tell Bill W. that the Chattanooga Group is out of the bush leagues." As Secretary of the Chattanooga Group, Carl was going to make things happen:

> If you will pardon the lack of modesty, they made the wrong man secretary if they think they are just going to sit around and talk about AA. It may be wrong, but I am going to do something. The cuss me and yell at me calling me in the middle of the night to go and get some drunk— but they honestly like it.

He then issued an invitation:

> Now regarding the open meeting October 13 which is referred to in the enclosed clipping, we want Bill W. to come if it is possible – if not we would like to have someone else from the New York office. Meeting will be held in the main ballroom of the Reed House, Chattanooga's best hotel, which seats about 500 people . . . Please let me know by return mail if we can count on anyone from there.

Carl encouraged the alcoholics' wives to get involved in helping prepare for A.A. events in Chattanooga. There was every evidence that this A.A. group was becoming a healthy, rapidly-growing pocket of enthusiasm.[231]

Bobbie replied on September 26. "I'll have to tell you it will be impossible to get Bill W. Perhaps you don't know that he hasn't been well and been under doctor's orders to remain inactive until the first of the year, so we are not making any speaking engagements for him." She recommended that Carl get a speaker from either Birmingham or Atlanta. She sent her condolences on being unable to attend by saying "I can only wish it was possible for Bill and I to visit every group when they have these get togethers."[232]

Principles Before Personalities

Bobbie wrote again on October 24th answering an October 16 response from Carl[xciii]. She had read Carl's most recent issue of *The Empty Jug*, and promptly sent a "suggestion:"

> I presume you have seen *The Grapevine* and have noticed in it that nicknames and last initials are only used. Actually our anonymity among ourselves means nothing, in the group most of all its disregarded entirely, but with the general public with anything in print we do try to adhere to the policy that Bill and the Trustees established years ago . . . I know of several cases where people have definitely stayed away because the anonymity of a member was broken. Another reason Bill felt so long ago that we remain anonymous, at least to the public, is that he realized our strength lay in publicizing the principles and not personalities.

Bobbie concluded one of her paragraphs with the words "principles" and "personalities" a full year and a half before Bill W. introduced those words in what became the concluding words of Tradition Twelve. Throughout the letters of this period, she, as the only other alcoholic in the Headquarters Office, had been working together with Bill. Sometimes, she reported, they worked alone after hours because the interruptions of office activity during regular business hours made such work too difficult. This is one of many examples that Bobbie had much exposure to Bill's thoughts long before they were shared with the Fellowship through his written articles.

Unfortunately, an October 27 message from Carl, and a likely response from Bobbie, is missing. The next letter included in this exchange was from Carl dated November 26. Among Carl's self-appointed responsibilities as leader of this Chattanooga meeting, was to provide a status of the current members.

> My roster now shows 28 active members, 8 of them not slipped since becoming members, 9 have slipped once – 5 of them only for a day – 4 have slipped twice, 4 have

---

[xciii]   Unfortunately, this letter is missing.

continued to drink but have shown improvement, and three haven't been in a month yet. There are 4 in bad standing and are not included in the 28.[233]

He reported that he earned $103 because he had gone into advertising. The idea that such a practice might be an outside issue did not seem to occur to him. Generally speaking, his mood was positive and upbeat.

Carl Gets the Blues

Four months transpire before Carl wrote Bobbie on March 18, 1945, which suggests that more letters are missing. He announced that he now had eight months of sobriety, but otherwise, there was very little good news to report:

> I also know that so long as I practice all twelve of the steps I will be OK. Bobbie, what am I writing about is our Chattanooga group. It isn't going anyplace at all in so far as the real purpose is concerned, and I just want to tell you a few things and see if you can put your finger on the trouble. Oh, we will get the house if we want it, and we can do other things of a similar nature, but the group isn't worth a damn as a unit . . . with 85% of the members their hearts are not in it . . . Here is what I'm talking about. We elect or appoint a program committee. There won't be a single member on the committee who can tell you he is even on a committee thirty minutes later. The membership committee, the welfare committee, or any other kind of committee . . . . it is the same thing. If I don't get a speaker or arrange the program there won't be any program . . . The national batting average is 50% great as soon as they get active in AA; 25% slip once or twice then quit for good; and the remaining 25% continue to drink but show improvement. Our batting average based on members of more than a month standing is about 20, 20 and 60, with those who have continued to drink getting worse if anything. We have had a lot of bad slips this past month.[234]

He concluded with a postscript:

> In your last letter you said "You can, catch more flies with
> honey than you can with vinegar" . . . true, lady, but we
> have too many flies now . . . bar flies . . . we would like to
> have a queen bee or two.[235]

A Thoughtful Response

Bobbie replied almost immediately to Carl's disheartened message.
Her March 22 reply is so full of mature experience, strength and hope: her
contributions rarely more obvious. It is arguable that Bill himself could not
have composed a more thoughtful and encouraging thousand-word reply
to Carl, who was so badly in need of help. She had listened to the wisdom
of Bill for around five years by now and her written words proved she had
been absorbing much of his insight. Therefore, this letter will be included
in its entirety.

> First of all, congratulations on your 8 months in A.A. –
> no matter what else happens that period of happiness can
> never be taken away from you. And, from what you write
> I have a very strong feeling that these 8 months will grow
> into many, many more. I wonder when you reread your
> long letter to me about the difficulties in Chattanooga, you
> realize you have found several answers. I believe every
> new member, and the same goes for new groups, must
> go through a period of "wet-nursing" in order to come
> to the conclusion that instead of helping the alcoholic we
> often retard his recovery. Please, keep in mind, however,
> anything I say should not be made into an iron-clad rule.
> I have seen several members go through 2 or 3 years
> of the so called "wet-nursing" first by one and then by
> succeeding members – and I have seen these people
> eventually become solid good A.A.'s. But on the whole if
> we make things too easy for the alcoholic we are actually
> simplifying the results of his drinking and giving him
> extra crutches to lean on. I don't know of any groups so
> far who have found it profitable to help new members

financially. By "profitable" I do not mean from a money angle but from the standpoint of giving real help to the alcoholic. "First things first" seems to come in right here and the first thing for an alcoholic to do is to seriously consider an honest desire to stop drinking. Don't ask him to explain why but I know from our experience that once an alky clears up his drinking problem most of his other problems are taken care of automatically. On the other hand by putting the cart before the horse and trying to straighten him out financially or otherwise, he rarely stops drinking.

I agree with you in that you have taken too much upon your own shoulders for the good of the group. I certainly believe it was necessary in the beginning but now even with your small nucleus of dry members why don't you drop some of the work in their laps. I think the simplest ways to do this is to call the whole group together, for a business meeting in fact. You tell them you realize the Chattanooga Group is becoming your responsibility of just a few instead of the cooperative venture of everyone. Toss the problem right into the laps of the members instead of trying to solve it yourself. Ask them what they think should be done about it. You might suggest temporarily after they have talked the matter over, that a rotating committee be formed of your five members. Start the committee off based on seniority. In order to give everyone a chance the oldest member (based on sobriety) go off this committee after one month and a new member come on. It might be wise to keep a secretary for about six months and have all the rest rotating on a monthly basis. This committee could plan meetings, take care of new inquiries and handle all incidental problems that come up. With a rotating system which is used in many groups you will find that all members get a chance to serve in a fairly short period. And it is surprising to see how much being on a committee stimulates interest in a group.

I wouldn't worry too much about better club rooms right now – they'll come naturally. Until you have an adequate membership that can support one, a clubroom can mean only a headache.

As for more interesting meetings, there are several suggestions I can offer. Why not try different kinds of meetings? Invite nearby groups to exchange good speakers. Will you, or have two or three of the Chattanooga members volunteer each time to take ten minutes to tell their stories or assign one of the 12 Steps for each to discuss. Every other week you might have what we call a discussion meeting. Have questions thrown out by both new and old members be answered by volunteers. You would be surprised what interesting meetings you can make out of just two or three good questions, everyday questions that pop up especially for the new men.

I think it is unfair to compare the Chattanooga Group with the Nashville or any other group. You may have been unfortunate in getting a lot of people in A.A. who have as of yet really not wanted to have stopped drinking. On the other hand Nashville may have been dealt prospects from the top of the deck, meaning those that honestly were looking for a solution to their problem. Let me tell you right here of Bill's experiences in his first two years of A.A. work. Last year he and his wife listed what they called their first 75 failures. These 75 were men that Bill had worked with, taking care of, "wet-nurse" and generally given everything he knew. At the end of the two years not one was dry or even in A.A. They in checking up have found 64 of them members of good standing, some coming back 2, 3, and as long as 8 years after he first contacted them.[xciv]All admitted when he questioned them that they really had not wanted to stop drinking, that they

---

[xciv]   Bill W. presented the "75 Failures" to the New York State Medical Society in May 1944. Bobbie would refer to the "75 Failures" repeatedly in 1943-1945.

also said when the time came they were up against that final stonewall they realized A.A. had the answer. So that work of Bill's which he thought at the time was useless proved to be very worthwhile.

I probably have tied you up in circles by now and keep in mind that you have the right to disagree with anything that I have suggested. But I do strongly urge you to keep right on in your merry way as far as you are personally are concerned. It is a terrific challenge to others to see their members stay dry through all the ups and downs. When the going gets toughest it is a good idea to fall back on "Easy Does It". In as much as I never practice it I am a good one to preach.

Lots of luck to all of you – I am sure everything will work out with tact, a little time and a lot of patience.[236]

These are not the words of a simple secretary taking dictation from a superior or copying a form letter. These are the words of a senior member of Alcoholics Anonymous dictating a letter containing "experience, strength and hope" to a typist. Her message speaks for itself and holds up remarkably well today. Her letter reveals someone performing an excellent job who is knowledgeable in multiple facets of what was making Alcoholics Anonymous an attractive solution. Notice how softly she wished to guide Carl. She was careful to remind him as well that he had the right to disagree with anything she suggested. For those familiar with how Bill composed his letters, could her writing easily be mistaken for being his?

Carl responded around April 20, 1945[xcv] to update Bobbie on their progress in obtaining a clubhouse in which as many as seven A.A. members could live. The eleven-room clubhouse would be run by a board separate and distinct from A.A. He claimed that soon there would be some A.A. females joining the group as well. He concluded by reporting that "he got along OK" with his recent talk to the W.C.T.U. (Women's Christian Temperance Union). "I refused to answer three questions and made it plain

---

[xcv]   April 20, 1945 is approximate. The source appears to be a second page without a G.S.O. catalogue number.

that we do not take sides."[237] Before long, however, Carl was going to take sides on the "wet-dry" controversy that he said he avoided this time. Bill and Bobbie consistently tried to avoid any association with the wet-dry controversy whenever it arose.

The G.S.O. Archives appears to be missing a letter Bobbie wrote to Carl. His July 18 message celebrating his 1st sobriety birthday began "It is coincidental that I should receive this letter from you this morning," But the collection does not include what Bobbie wrote, which must have questioned Carl's use of first and last names in *The Empty Jug.* Carl appeared most apologetic and conciliatory: "Please believe that I am motivated by the interest of AA as a whole. It has never been otherwise. I may have been cockeyed in some of my viewpoints, but I shall always subordinate my personal feelings to the good of AA." Very soon he was to behave as if he never wrote those words. He also revealed that he cared very little about maintaining his own anonymity.

> As for myself I still don't give a damn who know I am in AA, but I realize that has nothing to do with the concensus *[sic]* opinion. All my life has been public . . . newspaper reporter, etc. When I got drunk nothing would satisfy me but the main street ... and now that I am sober I am sure as hell am not going to hide ... and when people see me sober and ask me how come I am going to tell 'em why.[238]

Carl Protests *The Grapevine*

In October 1945, Bill W. declared *The Grapevine* the national periodical for Alcoholics Anonymous. This announcement went out to six hundred groups and appeared in the magazine the next month.[239] Carl objected—and drew the attention of the co-founder himself!

We have only the second page of Carl's argumentative letter, but Bill's reply dated October 23 places it before then.

> I have just received a copy of THE EYE-OPENER[xcvi].
> I guess you have seen it. The mast-head is swell. And

[xcvi] Understood to be a "can-opener," otherwise known as a local A.A. publication.

there are others, such as THE TOSS-POT[xcvii] that will graduate into printing formats. I hope we have a thousand. We are going to have a lot of fun with these papers – with the attendant result that everybody will get to know everybody else – and some day not so far distant THE PRESS ROW at a national AA convention will be a table of a half a block long – all of them kidding each other but THE GRAPEVINE will have an atmosphere all of its own – the official sponsorship of Bill W.

We do not want any official sponsorship for THE EMPTY JUG. We could have gotten that at The Birmingham Convention.[xcviii] It was mentioned and urged a number of times for The South. We may be screwy on a lot of subjects, but the other papers will be screwy too, too – UNLESS THEY GET SOME POOR, BENIGHTED NORMAL PEOPLE ON THEIR STAFFS – so what?

If you think you have seen some screwballs, just wait until you have the opportunity to gaze upon about 50 or 60 alcoholic newspaper men jawing about this and that at an AA convention –BUT, BILL, DO I FEEL SORRY FOR ANY OUTSIDERS THAT TAKES A POT SHOT AT ANY OF THOSE SCREWBALLS OR HIS PAPER—and you will see some real writing from time to time.

I just love the prospects.

No, Bill, I do not agree with you on the subject of anonymity, but we probably misunderstand each other on that question, too. I do not think I have the right to divulge the identify of another person unless I have his permission, but I think the biggest fault with the policy of

---

[xcvii] ibid.

[xcviii] Birmingham, Alabama was the site of the first Southeast A.A. Regional Convention. While Bill did not attend, he did write a message dated September 25, 1945 to be read to the attendees. The event is believed to have taken place on October 8, 1945.

personal anonymity is that the individual has to cover-up for himself in almost daily contacts . . . . but we will go into that when I see you.[xcix] Anyway, I have surrendered officially on that topic. Neither do I believe in passivity. Following the AA program rehabilitates a person and reestablishes him as a component part in the picture of citizenship. Through my status of normalcy I have regained views on subjects and obtained new views, that are inseparably intertwined with AA.

Another thing I do not agree on, the statement that my SOLE purpose NOW in being in AA is to keep myself sober. That is the FIRST purpose but if AA have made of me an instrument to help other people I think I am required to keep that instrument clean for the sake of other people I will learn to love just as much as the fact that I like clean utensils in my own house. In other words, I do not believe I was put in this world, finally got AA, just to produce a respectable life for myself, without considering others.[240]

Bill Weighs In

Bobbie likely opened this letter first but recognized that with regards to such a multi-faceted communication as this, she needed to forward this letter directly to Bill. He responded in a humble, conciliatory manner. There appear to be certain similarities to the yet- to-be-published Traditions in some of his words. There seems to be no adequate way to summarize what he wrote. Thus, here is his first reply to Carl in full dated October 23, 1945:

Thank you for your long letter. My first thought about it is that you and Bobbie and I ought to be better acquainted personally. If that had been the case I doubt you would find any reason to write as you did. I can see you were hurt and that makes me feel rather badly, too. That time may show that the choice of *The Grapevine* as our national medium was a mistaken one is a perfectly real possibility.

[xcix]   There is no evidence that Bill or Bobbie ever met Carl.

In fact, if you knew me better you could see I'm not what you think I am. You would see that I, like yourself, am just one more fallible alcoholic trying to get along. You might see yourself as an able newspaperman with almost no A.A. experience. You would see me as a person with no newspaper experience but nevertheless one who knows the national pulse of A.A. – that is, of course, if anybody knows it.

Truly your idea that *The Empty Jug* is a competitive medium had never occurred to any of us here. That you regarded it as a competitor in circulation, prestige or authority came as a surprise. Another thought comes to mind: have you ever made an effort to put yourself in the place of a national organization? As the experienced newspaperman that you are, you must see the desirability of having a recognized national medium. You can see that we have reached the point of our development where we have to have a periodical which will reflect our national conscience, art and mine. Newspapers such as yours which largely reflect your viewpoint after one years' A.A. experience could hardly be expected to accomplish these objectives, especially with you in Chattanooga and our Headquarters here in New York. We cannot make the selection upon the sole consideration of a newspaper experience alone. And it was almost imperative that the national organ be closely linked with our national Headquarters here in New York being geographically as well as personally. I am sure that on a second thought you will agree with this reasoning.

When I sent out the bulletin expressing the hope that *The Grapevine* would become our national medium, I was merely declaring something that had already become a fact. For months we have been receiving letters containing this as a suggestion. We have also been receiving many letters taking exceptions to some of the policies of *The Empty Jug.* For example: The tradition of anonymity right or wrong means a great deal to the vast majority A.A.'s.

Barring a few justifiable exceptions, groups would like to see this tradition preserved.

It is also a powerful tradition that the A.A. groups have one aim only, "to help the sick alcoholic." It is felt that we should never express an opinion on any controversial matter such as politics, religion, prohibition, etc. There is an intense conviction that our safety lies in minding our own business. And strictly. Therefore, it was no surprise when we received scores of complaints about *The Empty Jug* when it began to run counter to these well founded policies. The letters also expressed concern that *The Empty Jug* would create mistaken ideas in the minds of the newer groups about these vital matters. People agreed that as a newspaper enterprise it was good but that as an A.A. function, a reflector of A.A. opinion, it was not so good.

Under these circumstances, you can well see why the groups did not regard *The Empty Jug* as a national medium, its circulation not withstanding. So, what am I giving you, Carl is not my opinion. It is what I feel is the collective reaction to what *The Empty Jug* actually is. But above all means, please do not feel discouraged. I like your ability as a newspaperman and I hope you will continue to put out *The Empty Jug*. I hope a lot more such enterprises spring up each with their own flavor and slant. The more the merrier. But surely there does seem to have to be some agreement among these sheets on matters of traditions and policies. And some one of these new newspapers had to be chosen as the "Bell-Cow.[c]" Personally I think the choice of *The Grapevine* was logical, all things considered. And I am sure that one day you will agree.

But please remember that no one is a prophet. The rest of us may be wrong and you may be right, but meanwhile, we

---

[c]   The lead cow in the herd.

> shall have to be guided by a collective sense of tradition
> that has evolved up to date.[241]

The Conflict Escalates

While Bill wrote in a conciliatory manner in this previous letter, that tone was soon to change. Carl re-published a June 1945 editorial in his October newspaper under the section titled "The Editor's Personal Column." The title of the article included in this section was "Let's Get Untangled." Carl's complaint was "that the liquor interests are guilty of misrepresentation in advertising and that they are not putting up a fair fight."

> Through the power of suggestion in attractive settings, the liquor interests are influencing the subconscious minds of children into forming opinions that are disastrously incomplete – in this instance a malicious ulterior and purposeful practice no less contemptible than Japan's stab in the back at Pearl Harbor.[242]

The tone of Bill's next response to Carl, written on November 14, was no longer conciliatory. Rather, he identified multiple threats Carl's publication posed to A.A.'s future. Just selected paragraphs of Bill's message follow:

> But I feel deeply concerned about your unexplained insistence upon publishing controversial material. While I would be the first to defend your legal right to print what you please, I nevertheless question very seriously the usefulness of your attacks on the liquor people and your general disposition to "blast away" on topics that are not the least concern of A.A. as a whole . . . You describe yourself as an A.A., talking to A.A.'s. Your meeting has an attendance of many hundreds, including wives and friends that expect A.A. but you disappoint them by burying your perfectly good A.A. discourse with a powerful denunciation of something or somebody. By all means, Carl, keep up your good A.A. work. Go on with your paper. <u>But I beg of you, please don't use *The Empty Jug* to fight anybody or</u>

<u>anything</u>. That is not A.A. It is a hell's broth that will only burn you and the rest of us in the end.

And can I somehow convince you that this strong letter is not just "one man's opinion". I am sure that practically all the A.A. membership would agree with it in principle. Another point. The trustees of the Alcoholic Foundation are becoming concerned. They would like, at all costs, to keep A.A. out of the "wet-dry" controversy and they do not wish to see you, even with your best of intention, doing things with *The Empty Jug* which could land us in the middle of that endless conflict.[243]

Reverend Sam D. of Rome, Georgia Gets Involved

In hopes of reaching Carl through another channel, Bill contacted Reverend Sam D. of Rome, Georgia on the very same day he wrote Carl.[ci] Sam had been given the title of Associate Editor to *The Empty Jug* and wrote the column "Some Sense by Sam." Sam was well— known to both Bobbie and Bill as co-founder of A.A. in Atlanta in 1941 before his move to Rome, Georgia in 1944 to serve as a reverend.

Bill confided in Sam his deep concerns about the *Jug's* reflection on A.A. and his reluctance to confront Carl. Circumstances, Bill believed, had given him no other choice.

Bobbie and others have been pleading with him to bring his paper into line on the matter of anonymity and the discussion of controversial questions outside the province

---

[ci] This is the same Sam D. that Bill W. referred to in *Alcoholics Anonymous Comes of Age* written in 1957 beginning on page 25. "Shortly after the beginning of A.A. in Atlanta, that shaky group was sparked by the appearance of Sam, a high-powered Yankee preacher, temporarily minus frock and salary. Sam spoke with great effect from both pulpit and A.A. platform. He created a sort of 'Chautauqua' brand of A.A.' which was mildly deprecated by some members but cheered on by others. Sam has since passed away, but his work is remembered gratefully." Sam's biography is *The Pulpit and the Bottle* written in 2005 written by a son and granddaughter. Sam D. is credited as being a co-founder of A.A. in Atlanta, Georgia.

of A.A. Rather reluctantly, we thought, he adopted the policy of anonymity, but in his last issue he has certainly evened matters up by engaging in another 50 round bout with the demons of the liquor industry. Fulminations of this sort are common to all of us in our first years of A.A. If *The Empty Jug* did not already have considerable circulation I would count the matter a passing phenomenon. I can still smile when I see your column "Sam Talks Sense" completely surrounded by a whole page of hate. For that's what it is, no matter how much some people might feel it justified. It really isn't funny at all.[244]

Bill then tried to enlist Sam in reaching Carl to convince him to stay away from "angry denunciations" and to stop indulging "in controversy on non A.A. matters.[245] In a reply by Sam to Bill dated November 24, Sam said that he had discussed the issues with Carl. Sam's tone was generally favorable while indicating that Carl was reluctantly going to obey anonymity in future newspaper articles.[246] Unfortunately, Carl seemed to quickly forget any promises he made to Sam that day.

The Empty Jug, March, 1946 – Carl Publishes a Rumor

There is almost a five-month gap until the next letter concerning Carl and his magazine. Carl's March 1946 issue contained a wild rumor on the front page about A.A. Headquarters:

Rumors! We place little credence in the rumor that the Twelve Steps are being rewritten in New York. We do place credence in the rumor that New York is preparing a manual for group organization—and if they do this you can trace it to non-alcoholic influence in the Foundation. Some people are nuts on the subject of organization. But such a manual will not bother anybody—we've as many "walking organizational manuals" now as there are members—and a few printed tomes will just make us all screwier—and happier.[247]

On the editorial page, he assumed he could speak for Alcoholics Anonymous regarding the definition of an alcoholic:

> This statement is contrary to the AA definition of the "alcoholic." To us, the "alcoholic" is known as the person who has never grown up and who obtains escape from reality of the adult world in which he is unable to acclimate himself through the avenue of intoxication.[248]

He also identified a pictured female on the front page as, using her first and last name.

Bobbie Writes Rev. Sam D. to Try to Reach Carl

Bobbie had repeatedly tried to reach Carl on avoiding controversy and practicing anonymity, but her efforts were obviously unsuccessful. Bobbie tried a flank attack. She wrote Rev. Sam that he should influence Carl. She wrote him repeatedly. The first of these was written on April 10, 1946:

> I'm writing this letter at Bill's suggestion and it has to do with Carl K. I don't need to tell you that Carl differs very strongly with the majority of groups and individual AA members on AA traditions and policy. The recent March 1946 issue of *The Empty Jug* openly flaunts many of these traditions and we are beginning to get an abundance of mail from "irate" AAs to do something about Carl. You know how reluctant Bill of this office is to interfere in such matters, especially if they are confined to just a local situation. Carl and his paper are now taking on a national impact and Bill felt, perhaps, that you can unofficially be of help. We hesitate to hurt Carl in any way for we believe him to be fundamentally a fine person. He is yet too new in AA to take a stand against the whole of AA which is composed of many older members. . . . It's unpleasant for us to have to write you as I have and Bill doesn't like it either. We just hope that someone, somewhere can reach Carl and make him understand that he as one AA member

should not decide the policies for AA as a whole as no one has that right including Bill or anyone else.[249]

Sam wrote back immediately to Bobbie on April 13. He had just written to Bill (unfortunately, we don't have that letter). Sam said he was trying to reign in Carl as best he could.[250] The Reverend enclosed a copy of what he had written to Carl also dated April 13. Reverend Sam asked for feedback from Bobbie and Bill regarding his letter to Carl, in which he attempted to be as friendly but firm as possible. Sam wrote that there had been

> too much of intolerance, irrelevant matters discussed, and controversial issues included in *The Empty Jug*. In my opinion, whether it is worth anything or not, this is not good AA policy. So far AA has been free from fanaticism and intolerance, the two things that have wrecked so many other worthy movements. We must keep it so.

Otherwise, Sam wrote with restraint and tried to be as friendly as possible under the circumstances.[251]

Carl replied to Sam two days later in a rather petulant telegram dated April 15:

> I will get out of AA and I will abandon THE EMPTY JUG but I will not compromise with my honest convictions. I do not have two sets of opinions one for my private conscience and one for public display as to the burr under the New York saddle. I will post a certified check for $500 and if for every letter of criticism of my editorials I fail to produce ten in praise of them they can have the money.[252]

On April 17, Bobbie replied to Sam's April 13 response. Rarely did she ever speak so bluntly by taking somebody's inventory like this! She ended with a positive forecast, but it was not to come true.

> Thank you so much for your letter of April 13th and the copy of your letter to Carl. This was a very fine letter but from past experience I doubt very much that anything any of us say can change Carl's attitude. I personally like

him immensely and so do many of the members who have met him. Without doubt, though, he is the stubbornist *[sic]*, most closed-minded AA I've come across. He even borders on being unreasonable. I think when Carl has been in AA for about five years, he will mellow and become a very valuable part of our great cooperative venture.[253]

Reverend Sam sent a copy of Carl's April 15 telegram to Bobbie, to which she replied on April 24. She had all but given up writing to Carl; she and Bill had tried every way they could to have Carl understand the necessity for anonymity and avoiding issues outside of A.A., but without success.

> All of us hesitate to land on Carl in a body for I don't think it will do any good in any way. He would be righteously indignant and feel that we were ganging up on him and could assume the pose of a martyr. I wish to goodness he would come up here for I am sure if he knew us and understood clearly a little more of the great AA picture that he would become sweetly reasonable. Everyone likes Carl so much as a person – It's hard to get mad at anyone who is so genuinely fine.[254]

The Empty Jug, June, 1946

Two months transpired without any known exchanges regarding Carl. But then a firestorm erupted. In a June 26 letter to Bill, Sam warned Bill of oncoming trouble.

> I have discussed policies with Carl but he disagrees with me on practically every point. Sunday he called me and indicated that the next issue would contain material of a controversial nature and in my opinion wholly foreign to AA. I want you to know I am in no sense responsible for it nor do I approve of it. As much as I think of Carl personally, it may be advisable for me to sever my connection with the paper.[255]

PUBLISHED MONTHLY BY THE CHATTANOOGA GROUP OF ALCOHOLICS ANONYMOUS

Volume 2   CHATTANOOGA, TENNESSEE, MARCH, 1946   Number 6

MARY LADDY IN CHATTANOOGA APRIL 12

A STATEMENT

At a recent series of lectures at the First Presbyterian Church of Chattanooga, Dr. Donald G. Barnhouse, noted Bible scholar, teacher and publisher of the magazine, "Revelation," is reported to have replied flatly in answer to a question from the audience that alcoholism is not a disease.

Our contention that alcoholism IS a disease is supported unequivocally by Mayo's Clinic, United States Public Health Service, Yale University Clinic, the Rockefeller Foundation, and others.

We did not hear Dr. Barnhouse, and we are writing him to ascertain the exact phrasing of his answer, after which we will do some replying ourselves.

In the meantime, it might be well to remember that Dr. Barnhouse, when considering his glib denial that alcoholism is a disease is neither a doctor or medicine nor an alcoholic.

Attention!

The next issue of The EMPTY JUG, April, will be the 12th number published since we began printing it.

During the last 11 months we have sent out a large number of sample copies, especially to groups, with a view to obtaining subscribers who really liked the paper!

We now have more than 600 paid subscribers in 44 states, Mexico and Canada—and beginning with the May, 1946 issues, the paper will be sent only to those persons and groups who have sent one dollar for a year's subscription.

There will be no more samples.

We know that a large number of AA's have never seen The EMPTY JUG.

Mr. Secretary, that is your fault. You have received copies — and will receive copies of this and next month's issues.

Kindly give the members of your group an opportunity to see The EMPTY JUG, the "DOWN-TO-EARTH" AA paper.

GRACIOUSLY DISTRIBUTES HOPE

Lovely and capable Mary Laddy, member of AA, secretary to State of Alabama Commission on Education with Respect to Alcoholism, with offices at Birmingham, will tell of her work in disseminating information about the disease of alcoholism the evening of April 12 at The Read House to a selected audience.

The motion picture of the book, "The Lost Week-End" is an excellent portrayal of the typical alcoholic's physical and mental tortures.

It should be impressive stuff for holics all alcoholics—but the non-alcoholic does not have the slightest notion what it is all about. The audience reactions show this—the most grimly tragic sequences are (Continued on Page 4, Col. 4)

Charming AA to Tell of Work in Information Centre

Educational Program Progressing Rapidly in Alabama Under Feminine Direction

The Non - Alcoholic Advisory Committee of the Chattanooga Group is sponsoring another in its series of public meetings intended to make information on alcoholism available to all who are interested. Miss Mary Laddy, secretary to the Commission on Education with Respect to Alcoholism of the state of Alabama, will be the speaker at this meeting which is to be held at 8 p.m., Friday, April 12 at the Read House. Special invitations are being sent out by the Committee to leaders of civic groups and organizations, clergymen and doctors; the general public will be informed of the meeting through newspaper publicity.

Miss Laddy started her work with the Alabama organization recently. This commission is the first state-sponsored and state-supported effort to place the facts about alcoholism as a public problem and a public responsibility before people generally. As a part of her duties Miss Laddy is appearing before service (Continued on Page 3, Col. 3)

Rumors!

We place little credence in the rumor that The Twelve Steps are being rewritten in New York.

We do place credence in the rumor that New York is preparing a manual for group organization—and if they do this you can trace it to non-alcoholic influence in the foundation.

Some people are nuts on the subject of organization. But, such a manual will not bother anybody — we've as many "walking organization - manuals" now as there are members—and a few printed tomes will just make us all screwier—and happier.

FIGURE 17 - *THE EMPTY JUG*, MARCH, 1946, PAGE 1

In the June 1946 issue of *The Empty Jug*, Carl went to new extremes in his opposition to A.A. Headquarters – predominantly Bobbie and Bill, whom he criticized as "smug" and whom he said "wrist-slapped" him. He published a temper tantrum that may be without competition for the most vitriolic outburst in the history of Alcoholics Anonymous by one who claimed to be a member. Because there was nothing in the Steps that said otherwise, he believed he should not have to "submerge" his identity; it was more than appropriate for his arguments to appear in his newspaper. He considered the accusations of Headquarters to be unfair harassment. Never mind that he was constantly breaking his own anonymity and the anonymity of other alcoholics; he wrote that "atheists are fools and idiots;" he wished to use a machine gun on liquor company executives whom he compared to a "nest of snakes;" he accused A.A. Headquarters of believing that "the Garden of Eden and the Throne of God [were] both located on Manhattan Island;" he expected to be "ex-communicated" from A.A.; he wished the return of Prohibition; he thought liquor executives were guilty of a conspiracy to take over the country by turning the population into "human derelicts;" he demonized the motion picture industry; he accused a motion picture executive of being guilty of murder because of a movie he produced; finally, he condemned A.A. for favoring the liquor industry over the W.C.T.U.[cii] [256]

Unforeseen Consequences

Carl's opinions resulted in unforeseen consequences. Sam resigned as associate editor of the newspaper on July 5.[257] Six days later Sam wrote Bobbie that he had had a phone call with Carl who was in Memphis, Tennessee. Carl was described as having "a pretty bad case of the dry jitters and a very clear indication of remorse." He seemed to have realized that he had gone too far. He confessed to having been entirely "too cocky."[258] He was admitted to a hospital that night "showing every evidence of deep mental and emotional distress," according to Sam.[259]

Two days later, on July 13, Carl died reportedly of a cerebral hemorrhage five days short of his 2nd sobriety anniversary. He is believed to have been just 42 years old.[ciii] While death by cerebral hemorrhage was

---

[cii]   Carl's opinion piece is in the Appendix.

[ciii]   www.ancestry.com.and www.Find A Grave.com

the listed cause of death, his behavior in the months and days before his hospitalization could point to an alcoholic cause of death.

Bobbie wrote these words to Sam in Carl's memory on July 15:

> I'm happy for Carl's sake that he felt he might have been over-stepping before he died and no one can take away the demonstration he made these last two years in sobriety. I have sensed for a long time that Carl was a very sick man – there could be no other explanation. I'm shocked at his death but my beliefs give me assurance that we will all one day meet again in a happier world.[260]

PUBLISHED MONTHLY BY THE CHATTANOOGA GROUP OF ALCOHOLICS ANONYMOUS

Vol. 2   CHATTANOOGA, TENNESSEE, JUNE, 1946   No. 8

AN OPEN LETTER TO SUBSCRIBERS, MEMBERS OF A.A.

Since its inception some twenty-one months ago, THE EMPTY JUG, because of its definite and vigorously expressed convictions, has met with the disfavor of the New York office.

Of eleven letters of criticism that have been received by the editor of THE EMPTY JUG, nine of them have come from the New York office.

We have been wrist-slapped for our stand on anonymity, but we still don't like it, and we are able to withstand the accusations that we are going in for personal glorification.

We have been scolded for our statement that "atheists are fools and idiots," but in that assertion we do not back-track an inch. We believe in God as The Supreme Being and as our Creator, and we do not apologetically refer to Him as "the man upstairs."

We have been denounced for our attacks on the liquor industry, but we could still turn a machine gun on the whole kaboodle with no more compunction than we would have exterminating a nest of snakes.

And, in every instance, the New York office has blamed us because WE TOOK SIDES AT ALL.

"Members of Alcoholics Anonymous," they smugly inform us, "do not take sides on anything, do not argue, do not enter controversies."

There is nothing in THE TWELVE STEPS that says whether a member of AA should argue or not, in print or out.

There is nothing in THE TWELVE STEPS that says a member of AA has to be a fence-straddler, in print or out.

There is nothing in THE TWELVE STEPS that says a member of A.A. has to submerge his identity in a program of namby-pamby, wishy-washy, middle-of-the-road tactics on questions affecting his life and the lives of persons he loves.

THE TWELVE STEPS are the principles or precepts of AA. We have followed them to the best of our ability for the two years we have been in the organization, and we shall continue to practice them to the best of our ability.

Everything else pertaining to A.A. is METHOD, and to adopt methods which fit our conscience and our convictions, we do not find it necessary to accept those issued by the New York office as being acts of Providence which we are supposed to swallow as if they were so many pills. We have tried this a good while . . . and a number of times we have had acute indigestion.

The Alcoholic Foundation is made up of seven persons, all of whom

EMPTY JUG STAFF

In all humility, but for the information of persons who may be interested, the editor and two associate editors of THE EMPTY JUG have a combined, uninterrupted total period of sobriety in A.A. of more than ten years—the associate editors six years and 26 months, and the editor, 23 months.

This statement is not made in a spirit of braggadocio, but as a statement of fact.

What growth of character the editors may have attained in A.A. is directly and solely attributable to a simple and sincere effort to live by THE TWELVE STEPS, and not by applying a veritable "Roberts Rules of Order" to their personal lives concerning the application of those steps.

These men are not cocky. They are not putting themselves up as examples. But, on the basis of their records—all creditable—they are sick of having "official" interpretations of this, that and the other in A.A. thrown down their throats.

To neither of them—or all of them—is there anything "official" in A.A. Instead, to them, it is what it was intended to be, an informal organization in which men and women help themselves by helping each other, and in which freedom of opinion and expression is an integral essential to keeping alive the lovable and interesting individualism so characteristic of the typical alcoholic.

A Hobo On AA Special

(The writer of this article, as it will be seen, is not an alcoholic, but a person who solved his problem also through the A.A. program. He was voted a full membership at Rome some two years ago. —The Editor.)

Perhaps you might think I am in the "right church but the wrong pew"—maybe you will think I am encroaching on Alcoholic Anonymous—or maybe you will smile and know that your organization is helping someone who could not otherwise help himself. Having been associated with A.A.'s for the past two years, I have grown to understand them in many ways. Never have I met such a wonderful lovely and finer class of people, filled with as much cussidness, hard-headiness and sincere people living "right." These creatures (and I am proud to class myself as one of them) are better known in our fraternity as "screw-balls."

I am not an alcoholic from the standpoint of beverage alcohol. Tonight I can drink or leave it alone. Alcohol is no problem in my life. However, I realize that it is possible to awake in the morning a confirmed alcoholic. If I should become affected with this disease of diseases, thank God, I was taught the answer in advance — and, having been given the answer in advance—seen the patients at their lowest—witnessed the individuals pain and suffering and the pain and suffering of their loved ones—may I say that I shall not fly in the face of God to the point of gambling on my chances of leading a non-alcoholic's life.

Did I say "gambling on my chances—"? Well, that's where I

have the typically-New York notion that the Garden of Eden and The Throne of God are both located on Manhattan Island.

Why isn't Cleveland represented on the Foundation? Or Chicago? Or Los Angeles? Or New Orleans? Or Memphis?

Not that such an adjustment of the personnel of the Foundation would alter the weight of the repercussions that will come in response to this open letter, but it would give a more equitable inter-

(Continued on Page 3, Col. 1)

(Continued on Page 4, Col. 1)

FIGURE 18 - *THE EMPTY JUG*, JUNE, 1946, PAGE 1

Bill W. wrote Sam on July 25 comments which reflected the aftermath of Carl's controversial editorial on top of his previous history of being outspoken:

> The death of Carl came as a very sudden shock. Children that we alcoholics are, I am fearful that those letters of protest about the last printing of *The Empty Jug* might have hurt him cruelly and so hastened his end. Or, as I must hasten to say, the beginning of his new life across the Great Divide.
>
> This terrific outburst from the groups clearly shows with what emotional dynamite we deal in A.A. Also, how well some of our traditions are already established, however sound or unsound they may be.[261]

When Alcoholics Anonymous was involved, Bill W. almost always seemed to practice principles before personalities. Were these words, near the conclusion of Tradition Twelve in *The Twelve Steps and Twelve Traditions*, written with the personality of Carl in mind?

> We simply couldn't afford to take the chance of letting self-appointed members present themselves as messiahs representing A.A. before the whole public.[262]

In a January 1955 *Grapevine* article "Why Alcoholics Anonymous is Anonymous," Bill revisited the Carl K. affair in this manner without mentioning his name.

> Presently an AA member began to publish a crusading magazine devoted to the cause of Prohibition. He thought Alcoholics Anonymous ought to help make the world bone dry. He disclosed himself to an A.A. member and freely used the AA name to attack the evils of whiskey and those who made it and drank it. He pointed out that he too was an "educator," and that brand of education was the "right kind." As for putting AA into public controversy, he thought that was exactly where we should be. So he busily

used AA's name to do just that. Of course, he broke his anonymity to help his cherished cause along.[263]

Bobbie provided a summary of her two years of intense controversial experiences with Carl when she wrote to an A.A. in Chattanooga on August 7 who was also trying to deal with the firestorm that Carl had instigated:

> Personally I always had a soft spot in my heart for Carl although we did disagree on principles as applied to A.A. There was never a doubt in my mind but what Carl was a sincere person and I cannot help but feel that he was a very sick man during his last six months. I have a complete file of his letters to me and mine to him. It was about six months ago that I noticed a strange change taking place. I am happy with you that Carl did not see the letters sent to him after the June issue of *The Empty Jug*.[264]

For two years Bobbie had been on the front lines attempting to restrain a wild, unsponsored newcomer who had much energy and enthusiasm but very little wisdom regarding the overall issues facing Alcoholics Anonymous. Bill got involved during the last eight months out of necessity but could not reach Carl either. Bill was to summarize episodes like this one in a 1962 *A.A. Grapevine* article:

> In this remarkable and now rather amusing era of our affairs, any number of us commenced playing God all over again. For some years AA power-drivers ran hog-wild. But out of this fearsome situation, The Twelve Steps and Twelve Traditions of AA were formulated. Mainly these were principles designed for ego reduction, and therefore for the reduction of our fears. These were the principles which we hoped would hold us in unity and increased love for each other and for God.[265]

The last wild confusion instigated by Carl broke out soon after the *Twelve Suggested Points for AA Tradition* appeared in *The Grapevine* in April 1946. Subscribers to *The Empty Jug* may have had a head start in recognizing just how these Traditions filled a great need. However, *The*

Empty Jug is believed to have had only 600 subscribers out of a membership that was to number 29,000 by the end of 1946. It is likely that relatively few A.A. members knew of Carl's efforts to influence the membership. If more active A.A. members had known about Carl's insistence upon controversial, outside issues, might the Traditions been accepted by the Fellowship more willingly?

The Twelfth Tradition clearly states that principles should be practiced before personalities. The need for such principles becomes epitomized when examples of the personalities behind the principles are revealed. The need for several A.A. Traditions comes to mind through this unfortunate episode. In Carl's defense, there was no one in Chattanooga to sponsor or advise him. How a newcomer with just six weeks of sobriety could start an A.A. newspaper, which ended up having national distribution, sounds impossible today. Nevertheless, that's why it seems so wise to employ "rarely" rather than "never" in a study of A.A. history. As more is remembered, the more stories are encountered that initially sound like fiction, but prove to be true. Are there more significant, as of yet untold, episodes that await discovery? No one can say at this time. Keep in mind that the majority of letters Bobbie authored as National Secretary remain undocumented. Add to them the subjects to which she responded. Who knows what letters written by others that would reveal other reasons for gratitude that A.A. survived their ideas?

7

Press, Radio and Film

Questions regarding how Alcoholics Anonymous should be portrayed through radio programs confronted Bobbie soon after she became National Secretary. She wrote a response to Fay from Los Angeles on April 17, 1942 regarding this issue. Both Bill and Bobbie seemed to fear a potential catastrophic verbal slip over a nationwide hookup that could severely damage the future of Alcoholics Anonymous.

> Bill and I read your letter with your very well thought suggestion about radio publicity. This has been in our minds for some time but we purposely held off for several reasons. To begin with we feel the large growth since The *Saturday Evening Post* article should be better coordinated and stabilized before we let ourselves in for the massive inquiries that will result from a national broadcast . . . There are also so many dangers in radio broadcasting that should be avoided before we go into it. Written publicity can be censored to some extent and we always try to see proofs of magazine writings in order to keep the articles on the "party line". On the radio especially with semi-routined *[sic]* program you can see the pitfalls that we might fall into. A thoroughly organized program would do us much good but a slip or misstatement on one could sink us temporarily, as far as new people are concerned.[266]

One should keep in mind that at this time A.A. Headquarters carried an unlisted phone number. They were quite intimidated by the belief that a national radio program could generate such a massive amount of inquiries that they'd never be able to respond to them all. This intimidation was to continue to some extent throughout the decade. There is no known record of any national radio program sponsored by Alcoholics Anonymous in the 1940s. All of the radio programs were local–most notably Hartford, Connecticut and Detroit, Michigan.

On June 24, 1942 Bobbie responded to Sam D. of Atlanta regarding the radio programs coming out of Jacksonville, Florida. Bruce H. had achieved some substantial success promoting A.A. over a local Jacksonville radio station. However, his enthusiasm was leading him to dream of accomplishing nationally what he was doing for his local city. Bobbie wrote:

> Bruce H. seems motivated right but pointed in the wrong direction. He wants to broadcast nationally for the whole A.A. and if not with the Trustees permission then without it. Something will have to be done because it is dangerous for the good of all to have one man go on record and speak without permission. All national publicity should be agreed upon by all. A good radio broadcast would do us much good while a bad one might hurt us temporarily.[267]

Previous accounts have Bill traveling to Jacksonville to meet with the local A.A. founder Tom S. in "early 1942,"[civ] however Bobbie's letter was

---

[civ] "Bill W's first trip to Jacksonville was in early 1942. A most important reason for his trip was to visit the Jacksonville Group and speak with one of its early members Bruce H. Bruce was a promoter who had Gulf Life Insurance Company provide him 10 radio spots 3 to 4 minutes in length to promote AA. His spots were very successful and many people became attracted. He wanted to expand the radio program nationally and was in process of receiving backing from Prudential and Metropolitan Life Insurance Companies. He wrote many letters to The Foundation stating his intent and his answer resulted in a visit from Bill W. Tom S met Bill at the train station and they went to meet Bruce. Bruce never did another radio spot for AA in Jacksonville. After the meeting Bill spoke for the first time in Jacksonville at the Seminole Hotel for 20 to 25 people. Dinner cost $1.25. This was the first of many times Bill spoke in Jacksonville." AADistrict28. org/history/Scott 75 Year Fl Script.pdf.

written on June 24 with the clear indication that Bill hadn't yet begun the trip south. On July 8 Bobbie responded to a Bob in Atlanta news that Bill would come to Jacksonville soon to deal with the issue. Further, Bill was going to visit Atlanta on his return north.[cv] Bobbie had hopes that this national radio matter would be resolved soon.

> There will be ways to handle this situation and I hope it can all be done amicably. All to whom we have spoken about such a broadcast are definitely against any one man getting up and speaking for them without their permission. It just isn't right and in keeping with our policy. All national matters are very carefully gone over by the Trustees and at the time of the SEP article we had Jack Alexander spend six weeks talking to members from various groups thruout *[sic]* the country. We do not stand in the way of any local matters—leaving such entirely up to the groups themselves but in national affairs it is a different story.

> Here is some news that I know will be welcome. Bill W. is going to be visiting you soon—sometime after the 15th of the month. So shine up the clubhouse (not that he would notice any specks of dust but I know you'll want some advance information). I'll let you good people know just when to expect him.[268]

As the rest of 1942 went by, there was a consideration of some sort of national radio program, but nothing came of it. "War news is taking all space in the papers and on the radio," she wrote to Dick S. of Ohio on November 20.[269] San Francisco had arranged for a radio presentation in early 1943, which led Bobbie to respond to Ray there on February 17. The need for someone to fulfill a role that Marty Mann was to begin to represent the next year was implied in Bobbie's response: "You know half

---

of our job is educating the public about what alcoholism really is – this will do much to open the way for untold prospects."[270]

A gentleman in the Army[cvi] made several talks on the radio in the later part of 1943, sparking an outcry about anonymity. As concerned A.A.s flooded Bobbie's desk she wrote to Dan in Seattle, Washington regarding the issue with some quotes from Bill.

> Just before Bill left for the coast he dictated a few paragraphs on the anonymity angle. Back of this was the fact that one of our members in public office (Army) made a series of talks to the papers and over the radio and used his own story as a foundation. Had he done this in the third person it would have been all right, but he used the "I" method. Many letters came in here asking why our anonymity, which is our biggest selling point to the new guy, was broken. I believe he did it in enthusiasm but perhaps he has made it harder from some people to take up A.A. now. Anyway here is what Bill said on the subject. We will probably put this out in bulletin form some day. I quote:
>
>> "There is a growing tendency among A.A.s to forget their Anonymity. In one way it is very healthy that we no longer regard our alcoholism as a shameful sickness to be hidden from all save other alcoholics. But, there is another aspect of the matter which isn't, perhaps, so good. Numbers of us are being asked to speak and write on behalf of A.A. for public consumption. Here, I feel, some of us could be more discreet about the use of our names in print. If A.A.s commence giving personal interviews with names, they can scare off new prospects who are newspaper shy while some may feel that these people are seeking personal publicity. Of course, any of us should be able to sign any kind of piece even about A.A., if it does not

---

[cvi]   Despite a number of searches, the identity of this Army individual remains unknown.

appear that the writer is an A.A. himself. And, when speaking, an audience will in most cases be told the name of the speaker but newspaper men present will, with suggestion, respect our wish for anonymity."

"One more thought – it is surely wise to avoid being publicly quoted on any controversial subject in such a way as to spread the impression that the A.A. Groups as a whole have fixed beliefs on such matters as religion, prohibition, etc."

None of the above is one bit a personal feeling. Most of us oldsters have told our business and personal friends all about A.A. The anonymity policy is for the good of all the new people yet to come. Bill honestly feels this policy to be right for A.A. and so far it has proved him right.[271]

The Lost Weekend

It was through the radio that Bobbie became aware of Charles Jackson and the book he was writing that was to become the well-known *The Lost Weekend* book in 1944 followed by the movie released on November 16, 1945.[cvii] She wrote the following to Frank from Los Angeles on March 17, 1944:

> Isn't *The Lost Weekend* a honey? We were sent three publication copies to criticize before it hit the bookstores. We think it is a "must" on alcoholic's bookshelves. The man Charles Jackson is an alkie who dried up seven or eight years ago via the Peabody method – sort of a lay psychological approach – but he added principles somewhat similar to ours.[272]

[cvii]   A fourth printing of *The Lost Weekend* measures only 5½" by 7½" due World War II paper rationing.

Radio Fears Materialize

Early in 1945 some of Bill's and Bobbie's fears of a harmful radio program became a reality. A Los Angeles radio station KRJ broadcast a largely bogus history of Alcoholics Anonymous. Even though the policy of A.A. Headquarters was to allow local A.A. radio presentations to take place without any interference, the historical errors were so egregious that they could not be tolerated without an attempt to correct them. Bobbie's letter to Phil LaV. from Los Angeles dated January 26 resulted. While Bobbie's corrections, revealed later, were close to the truth, some were not altogether accurate. Bobbie's understandings, after all, were second-hand and probably provided to her orally. Anyone familiar with the hazards of second-hand witnessing should be able to forgive Bobbie for any inaccuracies written here.

> It has just come to our attention through a radio report manuscript service that a program went on the air over station KRJ in Los Angeles on January 9th at 1:15 PM. The commentator's name was Lee Shippey. I am enclosing a copy of the report where you can see is inaccurate on many facts which pertain to the Alcoholic Foundation and the connection Mr. John D. Rockefeller, Jr. has with it.

> In the first paragraph it states that in 1940 we had 60 members, actually we had 400. This of course, is incidental but I thought you would like to know for the record.

> Two, Mr. Rockefeller is said to have invited 60 AAs to his home for dinner, offering to finance a campaign which the AAs turned down. Actually, what happened is that Mr. Rockefeller gave a dinner early in 1940 in one of his clubs[cviii] to which he invited many of his personal and business friends,[cix] together with a few available AAs from New York, Cleveland and Akron. Mr. Rockefeller, instead of the AAs, was the one who saw that AA might be spoiled

---

[cviii]   The meeting was held at the Union Club at Park Avenue and 69th Street in Manhattan.

[cix]   61 notable Rockefeller guests attended, 197 invitations were sent out.

with money,[cx] and with rare foresight felt that the prestige that he gave us by acknowledging AA would be worth much more than financial aid. I might add that at the time, AAs were thoroughly discouraged when they felt money was needed to launch Alcoholics Anonymous. So Mr. Rockefeller did give the dinner and many of his influential friends found out what AA could do for the alcoholic.[cxi] He, and also others, did contribute small sums of money, just enough to keep the organization going. Today, Bill W. and all of us realize that Mr. Rockefeller's foresight and wisdom was the greatest contribution he could have made to AA.

In the third paragraph it states that Mr. Rockefeller advanced the money for publishing the book Alcoholics Anonymous. This book was entirely financed by subscriptions from a handful of AAs from New York, Cleveland and Akron.[cxii] This money has been returned to the original contributors. Last year Mr. Rockefeller and others did loan us some money to buy in the stock of our book company so that the Alcoholic Foundation could have complete control it. I am happy to say that

---

[cx] True for the 1940 meeting in which J.D. Rockefeller, Jr. donated just $1,000. However, it was Albert Scott in the December 1937 meeting who was most concerned about professionalism and that high finance might be dangerous for A.A. The source for this correction, and all the others involving Bobbie's letter, are derived from *Alcoholics Anonymous and the Rockefeller Connection*, Jay D. Moore, Shut Up and Get in the Car Publishing, ©2015.

[cxi] The dinner was J. D. Rockefeller, Jr.'s idea, but he became ill. His son Nelson Rockefeller substituted for his father. Albert Scott ran the majority of the meeting after dinner. Speakers included Bill W., Dr. Foster Kennedy and Dr. Harry Emerson Fosdick.

[cxii] Bobbie omitted that Charles Towns loaned $4,194 over a thirteen-month period to the Big Book project as documented on p. 293 of *King Charles of New York City* (Westwood Book version ©2018). An additional $1,000 loan was made by Bert T. in the summer of 1939. According to Bill Schaberg's *Writing the Big Book*, 179 shares of stock were sold (p. 304). Schaberg also documented (p. 304) no one in Ohio was involved in financing the project. All of the stock subscribers were eventually paid back.

the Alcoholic Foundation, Inc. was able to return half of
this to him with gratitude. Although we were ready to
clear up the whole amount, Mr. Rockefeller insisted on
contributing the balance.

In the last paragraph there is certainly a misquote about the
central office maintained as headquarters for Alcoholics
Anonymous by the Alcoholic Foundation. When it was
first opened, it was financed by small profits from the
book, together with some help from Mr. Rockefeller.
Today you people know that groups support this office
entirely.[cxiii] It is a service office for the groups and members
as a national headquarters. I am sure the members would
have every reason to question what is being done with
the generous contributions they send in for this office if
Mr. Rockefeller was the one that was responsible for it
financially.[273]

California Temperance Federation Inquiry

Time Magazine published a brief article on Detroit A.A. radio on March
5, 1945. The radio program featured an A.A. member who had "hit bottom"
calling "alcoholism . . . a disease . . . an obsession . . . an allergy . . ." WWJ
radio ran the 15-minute A.A. program every other Saturday at the rather
late hour of 11:15 p.m.[274]

Bobbie received a request from the director of the California Temperance
Federation on March 13. They wished to link up their organization with
A.A. after reading the March 5 *Time Magazine* article about the Detroit
AA radio program. Bobbie delivered the substance of what would become
A.A.'s Tradition Six about a year before Bill W. introduced the wisdom to
the Fellowship.

Thank you for your letter of March 13th inquiring about our
policy on local radio broadcasts. The Detroit broadcasts

[cxiii]   Not always true in this era. Group contributions to the Alcoholic Foundation
did not always cover expenses, thus, book profits were sometimes used to
subsidize the operations of the Headquarters office. Additional contributions
were made by Rockefeller dinner attendees until 1945.

which were referred to in *Time Magazine* are a project of the Detroit Groups, broadcast over Station WWJ on sustaining time. It is not sponsored in the usual sense of the word. Actually the broadcast you proposed over Station KPASS in Los Angeles would also be local and, therefore, if put on, under the sanction of and cooperation with the local Los Angeles Group. However, we see a difference between what is proposed by you and what is being done in Detroit, namely the sponsorship which touches on another policy.

Alcoholics Anonymous, both nationally and locally takes no stand on the controversial questions such as the "wet-dry" issue. Our one main purpose is to help alcoholics recover if they wish. We feel we can be much more effective by not entering into the pros and cons of prohibition or temperance. A program based on AA under the sponsorship of any temperance or liquor industry might imply opinions which we do not have. Therefore, although we actually have no jurisdiction over what local groups wish to do, we feel the Los Angeles Group will agree with us that any program sponsored by an organization with strong "wet or dry" issues involved, would be unwise and out of line with our policy.[275]

Bobbie was clearly up-to-date with Bill's thinking regarding any kind of affiliation with an outside group as well as avoiding the "wet-dry" issue. She understood that an "A.A. group ought never endorse, finance or lend the A.A. name to any related facility or outside enterprise . . ."[276]

A.A.'s policy on local radio programs began to evolve. She wrote on March 27 to Ed in New Haven, Connecticut that the "Trustees, Bill, and I are carefully watching and compiling all local experience in this field." As with many other matters, Headquarter's strategy centered on learning "by trial and error" about the successes and shortcomings of local radio broadcasts. She advised Ed to avoid controversial matters, and added:

From the little we have seen so far we feel it is advisable to let the radio station take the responsibility for the broadcast. By that I mean instead of saying "AA of New Haven presents," rather say "Station X presents its views on AA" or something like that. Bill is beginning to think a policy of publicity by "attraction" rather than "promotion" may be more helpful to us.[277]

Here is another example of Bobbie using words and phrases that have been attributed to Bill W., but she was employing them before they became commonly presented to A.A. members – in this case, a year before they were announced in the April 1946 *Grapevine*. "Attraction rather than promotion" became common words associated with Tradition Eleven.[278] Though A.A. wished to avoid any formal association with an outside group, Bobbie and Bill thought it wise to have some outside voice introduce A.A. to the general public rather than A.A. attempting to promote itself.

San Quentin's Plans for a Radio Program

The decision to avoid A.A. promoting itself on the radio seemed to become particularly astute when Bobbie learned that A.A. in San Quentin Prison was organizing a radio program with the help of the local San Francisco A.A. group. For the second time in three days, she espoused the elements of Tradition Eleven.

> We are coming to believe that publicity via radio is more advantageous to AA thru the "attraction" rather than the "promotion' angle. By this I mean we wonder if it is not better to have other people talk about us than to have us sponsor our own broadcasts. In those places where broadcasts have been given by the AA groups the general public usually feels that all AAs are speaking and it does give a somewhat official sanction to whatever is used in the script.

> If a broadcast is to come out of San Quentin we believe it would be wise to have it sponsored by either by Warden Duffy or the prison officials themselves. And inasmuch when word as this is a new idea on which we have had no previous experience I think the San Francisco group might

wish not to be tied up with it. I am sure it would be just as effective if Warden Duffy or someone from the prison gave his views on just the progress AA has made on the inmate members. It might even be possible to interview one or two of them but the project would be under the sponsorship of the prison.[279]

Bobbie received requests for template scripts for local groups to create their own radio program, but no such scripts existed. She replied to Dave of Colorado Springs, Colorado, "We haven't any local radio scripts and as in all publicity we handle and arrange only for that which has a national aspect. Most local groups write these with the help of the station themselves."[280]

Since Headquarters was not experimenting with radio broadcasts, Bobbie thought it best to recommend that radio program inquiries be directed to those who had successful experiences: Hartford, Connecticut that broadcast over WTIC or a group in Detroit, Michigan that broadcast over WWJ.[281]

Bill W.'s Involuntary Anonymity Break

Maintaining Bill's anonymity was always problematic. Often before an A.A. event began in which he was in attendance, anonymity was insisted upon from the podium. However, on occasion, events took place that made Bill look as if he used his last name during a meeting in which reporters were present. Such was the case when Bill visited Iowa in October of 1948. Bobbie reported on this event in a letter she wrote to Harry from Cleveland on December 22.

> Recently Bill went out to two large conferences in the Middle West, one in Iowa[cxiv] and the other in Minnesota.[cxv] Because Bill believes so thoroughly in this anonymity, before he accepts any invitations to talk he asks for assurance that his name will not appear in any public media. You can imagine how he felt after having this assurance from Iowa when he and Lois woke up the

---

[cxiv]   October 24, 1948.

[cxv]   October 30-31, 1948.

morning after the talk in the hotel, switched on the radio, and the first thing they heard "Bill W——[cxvi]—- said" etc., "last night". Then, with a slight touch of apprehension they opened the morning papers and there he was in the headlines full name and all.[cxvii] All this happened after Bill had also had a press conference with the groups and the papers before the meeting [in] which he explained the reason for anonymity. But, it just happened that an alcoholic reporter, who was mad at AA because AA had not dried him up, took his resentment out on Bill. So I guess he ran around the town explaining how Mr. W—— was the one exception and even got on the radio.[282]

"Problem Drinkers"

The March of Time was an American short film series sponsored by Time, Inc. shown in movie theaters from 1935 to 1951.[283] On June 14, 1946, the nineteen-minute short, Volume 12 – Number 11 entitled *Problem Drinkers*, was released to the movie theaters. After a skit featuring a drunk ending up in jail, the first solution to alcoholism offered is a psychiatric approach featuring Dr. Jellinek and the Yale Clinic. About nine minutes into the film, the "voluntary organization" Alcoholics Anonymous is featured. After packets of letters are shown being picked up, four women are featured busily moving about in an office diligently pursuing their duty of answering this correspondence. The announcer is heard saying, "And though not a religious organization, its twelve step program calls for belief in some power outside the individual." Before a picture of a woman seated at a desk concentrating on correspondence in front of her, the commentator states, "Direct contact with those for whom help is asked is made only by A.A. members who themselves have gone the long road from alcoholism to sobriety."[284] Since Bobbie and Charlotte, Bobbie's assistant, were the

---

[cxvi]   W— is Bill Wilson

[cxvii]   "Men and women are turning to Alcoholics Anonymous for help at the rate of nearly 10,000 a month, Founder Bill W—— of New York, N.Y., told 3,000 persons Sunday afternoon at KRNT Radio Theater. W——, who along with most A.A. members usually remains anonymous to the public, was introduced by name when he talked at the open meeting . . ." *The Des Moines Register*, De Moines, Iowa, October 25, 1948.

only two alcoholic women working in the office in mid-1946, they had to be among the real women being portrayed in this movie.

In mid-July, Bobbie fielded a complaint from an Atlanta A.A. member that the film was not being shown in local theaters. Her response documents that A.A. Headquarters was very involved with the dialogue used in the film and that they were quite happy with the results.

> THE MARCH OF TIME headquarters here tells me today that they do not think any pressure group is keeping the film from Atlanta. They think it is a matter of local theatre policy. They suggest that you see [the] District Manager or [the], Branch Manager, for the local office of the 20th Century Fox at 127 Walton Street N.W., Atlanta 3 (MARCH OF TIME distributes their films thru 20th Century Fox). Perhaps these men may be able to help you on how to get the MOT film, Problem Drinkers, into an Atlanta theatre. It is worth a try anyway. I certainly hope you see it – it has been well received by the groups so far. Naturally we think it is pretty good but we could be prejudiced having worked on the parts dealing with AA for many long months.[285]

Bobbie's Trip to California

A highlight of Bobbie's tenure as National Secretary was her trip to the west coast in October 1946. This trip seemed to be personal in nature – more of an opportunity to meet the A.A. members with whom she'd corresponded in recent years and some Hollywood producers that had been attempting to acquire the rights to create a full-length movie about Alcoholics Anonymous.

From hand written notes she wrote while on the trip, a rough outline of her journey can be approximated. Bobbie arrived in Los Angeles no later than October 3. She attended a committee meeting on that day with Ed A., followed by a "general meeting" the following day. On October 5, her activities included a Hollywood Women's meeting with Rene & Jenn followed by another meeting she named the Central Hollywood meeting that she attended with Bob R. The next day she either watched a motion picture or attended a motion picture studio then she attended a "Bob Smith" dinner. She met with the Hollywood personality Bob Smith as well.[cxviii]

On or about October 7, she met the very well-known movie producer Hal Wallis at his home. The meeting sparked the following rumors to appear in the Louella Parsons[cxix] gossip column, which printed Bobbie's first name and misspelled her last name along with referring to her as "Miss," also inaccurate.[cxx]

> HERE IN OUR town is Margaret B., secretary of the National Alcoholics Anonymous. She came to close a deal with Hal Wallis for putting Alcoholics Anonymous on the screen. But the deal will not be actually closed until she approves the script.
>
> When one of our well known agents offered $50,000 to buy it for Leo McCarey,[cxxi] and later for Monogram, Miss B. replied, "We're not interested in money. We represent half the wealth of the country. We're just interested in helping people. The only reason for putting the story on the screen now is the belief that someone who is cursed with a craving for drink can be encouraged to overcome it."[286]

[cxviii]   This dinner was not to honor Dr. Bob but was either hosted by or in honor of a Hollywood personality who shared this very common name with the A.A. co-founder. This Bob Smith was "Robert Cecil Smith" who was an American actor of the stage, television, and film. (Wikipedia)

[cxix]   Louella Parsons (born Louella Rose Oettinger; August 6, 1881 – December 9, 1972) was the "Queen of Hollywood gossip" and first American movie columnist and a screenwriter. She was retained by William Randolph Hearst because she had championed Hearst's mistress Marion Davies and subsequently became an influential figure in Hollywood. At her peak, her columns were read by 20 million people in 400 newspapers worldwide. She remained the unchallenged "Queen of Hollywood gossip" until the arrival of the flamboyant Hedda Hopper, with whom she feuded for years. (Wikipedia)

[cxx]   The text has been edited to maintain anonymity.

[cxxi]   Thomas Leo McCarey (October 3, 1898 – July 5, 1969) was an American film director, screenwriter, and producer. He was involved in nearly 200 movies. (Wikipedia)

Bobbie would later recall this gossip column in February 1949 when A.A. was once again approached by Walter Kane,[cxxii] who had been aggressively pursuing a movie deal with Alcoholics Anonymous for some time. Bobbie believed it was Walter Kane who learned of Bobbie's 1946 visit to Hal Wallis and leaked the bogus rumor to the very popular Louella Parsons resulting in the gossip column. She recalled this encounter with Walter Kane:

> Incidentally, I did see him when I was in Hollywood more than two years ago and he pulled a very pretty trick by calling Louella Parsons and telling her that I was in that city negotiating for a picture about Alcoholics Anonymous. She printed it in the paper with my name on a lot of unfactual *[sic]* data, not a word of which was true. Then Mr. Kane came back and tried to collect $5,000 from us saying that we had discussed this matter with him the previous year and any plans we had wanted "in". It is necessary to tell you that Mr. Kane did not get either $5,000 or $1. It was all sheer bluff.[287]

Grace Cultice of Chicago wrote Bobbie an undated note following all the gossip. It read in part,

> Now it really comes out! So you went to Calif. to sign the control, eh! And if we have half the wealth in the country, why don't you and I get some of it? That story made me mad – no one could ever tell me that it was authentic (I mean the interview) but some people are so ready to believe what they read! . . . Our people here know such

---

[cxxii] From the UPI Archives: https://www.upi.com/Archives/1983/05/28/Obituaries/5533422942400/: "Walter Kane [was] director of entertainment for Howard Hughes' Las Vegas gambling resorts . . . and one of the late billionaire's closest friends for more than half a century . . . discovered such stars as Wayne Newton, Foster Brooks, Juliet Prowse and Rich Little, went into vaudeville in New York with partner Roscoe 'Fatty' Arbuckle and they became one of the most popular acts on the Keith and Orpheum Circuit."

things aren't true, and if they have any doubts, I'll 'larn *[sic]* them.[cxxiii]

She then left for San Francisco. On October 8, she attended a meeting in Oakland with a Dr. H., Russ R., and Peggy Y. She apparently returned to San Francisco on the same day to attend an open house. On October 9, she reported that she attended a large San Francisco meeting preceded by a dinner with Anne C., Ray H. and a number of others. The next day she attended another large meeting and a dinner in Sacramento with Dr. Rog P. and Vic M. On Friday, October 11 she attended a secretary's meeting. She spent Saturday with a married couple in Pasadena. The next day she traveled to 219 Abalone, Balboa Island where she was with a Mr. and Mrs. Harry C. On the next day, she left by rail on The Chief for her trip back to New York.

While Bobbie was on this trip, Charlotte L., recently hired to be Bobbie's assistant, traveled to Asheville, North Carolina. She was quick to learn just what Bobbie meant to the people there. Charlotte wrote Bobbie that the trip would have been easier if she could have become Bobbie.

> You know how interested AA's and the public are in women alkies. For my money, you're No. 1 from every standpoint, a point of view which seemed to be shared by all in attendance at Asheville. They were wonderful to me, and the only thing which would have made things easier would have been being YOU. So I'll know you'll be a big hit.[288]

"I Am an Alcoholic"

Early in the history of Alcoholics Anonymous, the practice of introducing oneself with one's name followed by the words "I Am an Alcoholic" was not nearly as common as it is today.[cxxiv] A Box 459 article reprinted by Cleveland A.A. in 2012 documented a movie that gave a

---

[cxxiii]   The Bobbie Family Collection.

[cxxiv]   The book *September Remember* by Eliot Taintor, (a pseudonym for Ruth Finch Boyd and Gregory Mason) published in 1945, which probably was the first novel to feature Alcoholics Anonymous, has a female alcoholic named Sylvia introducing herself as "I am an alcoholic."

significant boost to this practice: RKO's 15-minute short film *I Am an Alcoholic* released in mid-1947.

> At small meetings, the members knew one another and didn't need to identify themselves. But in the large *"public"* meetings, where there was *"witnessing"* along the lines of an A.A. talk today, personal identification became necessary. Chances are that someone at some time said, *"I am an alcoholic"* . . . One early New York A.A. does recall hearing the expression, however, sometime after World War II, in 1945 or 1946; and it is a matter of record that in 1947 a documentary film entitled *"I Am an Alcoholic"* was produced by RKO Pathe, lending further credence to the notion that the phrase was recognizable in recovery circles even then.[289]

A website "Big Book Sponsorship" investigated this practice of announcing oneself as "I Am an Alcoholic" and came to the following conclusion:

> How did the early members of A.A. introduce themselves when gathered together? If you <u>listen to recordings of the original A.A. pioneers</u>, none of them identify themselves in this manner. If you listen to recordings of Bill W. and Dr. Bob, you will hear that they never used this approach to introducing themselves.[290]

Bobbie announced the upcoming release of the RKO picture in a bulletin dated June 5, 1947.

> Pathe Pictures, makers of "This Is America" movie series, has completed a 15-minute "short" about Alcoholics Anonymous which will be distributed through RKO. They tell us that this film will be shown soon in neighborhood theatres. Pathe suggests that you check with your local theatre for its release date – we cannot supply it. The film is called "I Am an Alcoholic." It not only shows how one man recovered through AA, but portrays a reasonable

> facsimile of the founding of AA in Akron by Bill and Dr. Bob. Because of our former agreement with Hal Wallis on the Paramount project, we were unable to cooperate with the makers when the story was filmed. When the Paramount deal was terminated, however, we were able to assist a little with the narration at the very end. So if all sequences are not completely satisfactory to AAs, it is not the fault of either Pathe or the AA Movie Committee. Bill and others saw a preview of this film last week, and they hope you will like it.[291]

As Bobbie documented, A.A. had very little to do with the creation of this film due to previous contractual restraints with Hal Wallis of Paramount Pictures. One wonders what the title might have been had A.A. been involved from the beginning. If the title of this movie short had been "I'm an A.A. Member," as suggested in the foreword to first edition of *Alcoholics Anonymous*, would A.A.'s today be introducing themselves that way rather than as "I Am An Alcoholic?" The movie, which appeared in hundreds of movie theatres across the country, may have been a most important influence towards how alcoholics have introduced themselves throughout the country ever since.[cxxv]

[cxxv] Internet searches can provide a variety of additional information on the subject. AA.org has a section "Alcoholics Anonymous – Frequently Asked Questions About A.A. History. The question is asked "What is the origin of introducing oneself with the statement "I am an alcoholic" at A.A. meetings?" The answer: "As with the origins of other customs of A.A., this is something of a mystery." Henrietta Seiberling is quoted as saying that the tradition dates back to the Oxford Group. In small meetings, the phrase was not required, but in larger meetings where everyone did not know each other, the phrase was used. But at the end of the explanation, the RKO Pathe picture "I am an Alcoholic" is mentioned.

Bill and Bobbie

The date when Bobbie was first introduced to Bill remains a mystery. It's probable she had been in an A.A. meeting with him while she was still an inpatient. Possibly they became better acquainted after she got sober—New York A.A. was still a pretty small world in 1940. She was very attractive and just 36 years old. She soon became a very visible secretary at the 24th St. Clubhouse when there weren't many women in the Fellowship.

Yet, Bobbie has never achieved the most complimentary designation of "Bill's Secretary." Both Ruth Hock, who preceded Bobbie, and Nell Wing, who followed Bobbie, have received a widely accepted place in A.A. history with that familial designation. But not Bobbie! One significant difference between those two women and her: she was an alcoholic and they weren't. There were well-documented prejudices against alcoholic women in that era and for years following. Such prejudices may be among the reasons she has been overlooked for so long. A possible answer for why she has been all but forgotten evolved as this book was close to completion. That theory, which will become clear near the conclusion of this book, explains why Bobbie has yet to achieve the flattering status of the other two women. Bill's letters to her, some of which are documented here for the first time, show his opinions about her contributions to A.A. and what her loyalty meant to him.

Bobbie referred to meeting Bill "long, long, ago" when she wrote to an A.A. member on November 17, 1943. Her admiration for Bill was evident when she wrote to the Californian A.A. who had just met Bill:

> That was a very beautiful letter you wrote me early in the morning of the 14th. Somehow I know exactly how

you feel. I went thru much of the same experience long, long ago when I first met Bill. Don't know whether I'll show Bill that letter on his return. He would do a lot of squirming. He is such a naïve person that hasn't the slightest idea how truly great he is. But someday when he has a big disappointment (they happen to him, too) out will come your letter and make the stars shine again for him.

That feeling of inner happiness need never leave you. Religion calls it "rebirth" but to me it is more an awakening of a sixth sense in us. The things we are now seeing and feeling were always around but we were asleep to them. It takes a Bill to turn on the lights, so to speak. I know from experience that the sensation of which you speak of cannot be explained by any of our five senses – hence my attempting to clarify it as much of a sixth sense . . . I am a very lucky person – lucky and fortunate like you to have the privilege of knowing and working with Bill.[292]

She must have had her crystal ball out that day, for she was seeing a remarkably accurate future for Bill. In November of 1943 she recalled Bill's inability to get anybody sober in New York after he achieved permanent sobriety in December of 1934:

For six months he worked trying to get other alkies interested but no go until one day when he was on the verge of going overboard he realized that he could only help himself if he could find another alky to help. He did dig one up and it was Dr. Bob S. of Akron. He and Dr. Bob have worked tirelessly and without thought of themselves ever since. Bill gives Bob such credit for AA and always refers to him as "co-founder." Someday all this early history will be written, I suppose in Bill's biography for I can see that coming even if he can't.[293]

Among her responsibilities were making necessary travel arrangements for Bill's trips and helping manage his appointment calendar. In the summer of 1942 she became aware of a possible trip by Bill to the west coast. To an A.A. in San Francisco she wrote how such a trip would benefit the west coast A.A. members who had yet to meet him in person.

> Bill is playing with the idea of going out to see the coast groups and we will let you know if the plan goes thru. I feel sure he will want to meet with all the groups and I have an idea that they might be glad to know him. In my opinion everyone he talks to is a little better after that experience but don't ever tell him I said so – he would wring my neck.[294]

Bobbie and Bill Travel the Midwest

Nine months after Bobbie became National Secretary she wrote that she was going to accompany Bill on a trip to the Midwest. In these days, she was the only alcoholic employed at Headquarters.[cxxvi] She provided a living example that a woman could get sober too. To Wally G. of Akron, Ohio dated October 29, 1942, she wrote, "I am looking forward to meeting you when I am in Akron on our trip west.[295] Thus began her first documented out-of-state trip with Bill to Pittsburgh, Akron, Cleveland, Toledo, Detroit and Buffalo. After the trip, in a letter dated November 16, she recalled their mutual experience: "On our return today after two weeks of so-called 'grouping' leaves us both rather awed at the wonderful spirit of all the groups."[296]

[cxxvi] Just to be clear, Bobbie was the only alcoholic paid staff member. Bill, of course, while receiving royalties from the sale of the Big Book, was not receiving a pay check as a staff member.

FIGURE 19 - LOVELY PICTURE OF BOBBIE - UNDATED

The next day she wrote Bill H. reminiscing about their journey:

There are many reasons why our trip to Cleveland was such a wonderful experience. As Bill says "We were privileged to witness a wholesale miracle on this trip" – no small part of this was in Cleveland. I had the opportunity to not only see the crowd at the dinner but also to meet many individual members. In this way I came to know and talk with some fine people. The true A.A. spirit runs very high in Cleveland.

It was indeed a privilege to be at the dinner. I was astounded at the ease and simplicity with which it ran off. The whole dinner committee deserves much credit for the job they did. And I'm sure they felt that the long and hard hours of preparation were worth the result. A.A. dinners will come and go but it will be a long time before another even ties the splendid record setup in all ways by the Cleveland Groups on Sunday, November 8th.[297]

Bill and Bobbie wrote thank you notes to the group or individual that had invited them. One of her thank you notes was written to Buffalo, which they had visited on November 13. Buffalo had been the sixth city, and the last city they visited during the trip.

> We would like to ask you as chairman of the committee to thank all the members of the Buffalo Group for the perfectly wonderful time you planned for us while we were in your city. Bill feels that, on the whole trip, that we were privileged to witness a "wholesale miracle" and much of it was right in the Buffalo Group.
>
> From the moment we arrived and were met at the station until we were waved goodbye the next morning we felt a warm welcome. You have a grand crowd of A.A.s. It made us very happy to be with all of you.
>
> Please tell each and every member how grateful we are for the part they took in making our visit such a memorable one. Our warmest regards to all.[298]

Their next known trip together was a brief three-day trip to New England. The pair visited Hartford, Connecticut on February 2, 1943 and then traveled on to Springfield, Massachusetts and then Boston, intending to spend one day at each location.[299]

The Handbook

From 1942-1943, Bobbie repeatedly mentioned creating a handbook, a guide for A.A.s and groups.[300] Bill and Bobbie apparently worked together on this project – a markedly different arrangement than Bill dictating *Alcoholics Anonymous* to Ruth Hock. When Bobbie wrote Dr. M. of

Australia about the project on February 2, 1943, she hoped to have a finished product soon:

> Bill W., who wrote the text of the book *Alcoholics Anonymous*, and I are now editing a compilation of group experiences over the past five years. This may be out this summer and we will be glad to send you a copy if you are interested.[301]

On March 2 she wrote to Wally G. in Ohio using the term "we," suggesting she was an active contributor to the handbook.

> The handbook is progressing slowly. I doubt very much that we will finish even the rough draft for several months. This kind of writing must be checked and rechecked very carefully inasmuch as it is a compilation of the experience of all of our groups. As to price, I haven't the slightest idea. That will depend upon the amount of copy and cost of material at the time of printing.[302]

Yet there is some room for confusion regarding what exactly was her role in the project. In a March 3 letter, she wrote that "Bill is now working on a hand-book," but then in the same paragraph she wrote that "Bill and I must do this writing. . ."

> Bill is now working on a hand-book which will be a compilation of group experience and also we hope to revise the AA pamphlet at some future date. However all this writing takes a lot of time so do not expect to see a finished copy for some months to come. Bill and I must do this writing at night when all is quiet . . . . . hence it is slow work.[303]

However, as documented in a letter to Wally G. of Akron, Ohio dated March 28, 1944, she wrote that we "had an idea once of making up an AA handbook of experience but after going into the matter more thoroly *[sic]* decided it would not be particularly useful or advantageous."[304] Obviously this decision did not last as a *Handbook for the Secretary* was published in

1949. One might assume that Bobbie's seven years of on-the-job experience by 1949 would be heavily referenced in this handbook. To what degree this project contributed to the development of the Traditions remains unknown.

Visiting Columbus, Ohio and Charleston, West Virginia

By March 18, 1943, Bobbie wrote to Charleston, West Virginia about an upcoming visit for herself and Bill. They were to take the train to Columbus, Ohio and arrive on March 26. Parts of three days were to follow in Charleston beginning on Saturday, March 27.[305]

Bobbie wrote this lovely thank you letter to the Charleston Group afterward on April 1.

> It is the hardest thing to find words to tell the members of the Charleston Group of our appreciation for the reception and plans made during our stay with you. From the moment we stepped off the train till Monday night as we waved goodbye, everything possible was done for our comfort. All your plans fairly shouted "consideration".
>
> I knew we were going to see a grand bunch of members but they far exceeded our expectations. Solid is the word for the Charleston Group and we know that no matter what comes up from now on that you all are on your way towards establishing one of the best groups in the A.A. picture.
>
> We are grateful for the opportunity made to know so many members—we just hope you enjoyed the visit as much as we did.
>
> Will you as secretary please convey our thanks to each and every member for making our stay with the Charleston Group as enjoyable and worth while.[306]

The Need for Three Bills

By now, Bobbie was pretty used to opening Bill's mail, holding the important matters for his eyes only, but often answering letters regarding subjects where she felt qualified to share applicable experiences of other A.A. groups. She was sensitive to some A.A. members' disappointment to hear from her and not Bill. In one case, an A.A. member was angry because he did not get a written response rapidly enough from Bill. Bobbie responded with her diagnosis of the problem: there needed to be three Bills. "I often dreamt up a combination of Bills; one to stay in this office and write letters (also help me), one to take care of the public relation work, and one to travel among the groups."[307] In any case, Bobbie strived to be a worthy substitute. Reducing his workload represented an outstanding, yet little noticed contribution, allowing him to pursue other valuable activities.

There is no question that this pair developed a close working relationship. Personal letters from Bill to Bobbie, revealed here from a recently discovered private collection, undeniably portray an association filled with mutual respect and love for each other's talents and dedication. Here is a private note written by Bill:

Bobbie dear,

Just a word of my confidence and love.

There are but a few for whom I would go anywhere anytime and to any length. You must know that you are "kept among first" options.

I wish I could tell you how much you mean to so many people – many, many. Bobbie, I shall speak for myself. I've done that already – you so under estimate yourself.

The trial of the desert has come again for you. But you suppose are alone. Cling to the greenness of the trees. They are green you know and can be rectified. That by it you can find little purpose for I so change as to make you more released.[308]

The symbolism of "the trial of the desert" and the "greenness of the trees" appears to have had great significance between them.

Bill and Bobbie's Second Trip to the Midwest

Bobbie wrote a hurried letter on June 5, 1943 to an A.A. member that she and Bill were leaving for the Midwest the next day.

> Bill and I leave tomorrow for a two week's jaunt thru the Middle West. We want to get as much of this traveling done as possible so as to leave him free to get to the coast this fall. Whether I come or not is in the hands of the gods. But I do know that Bill is going to make every effort to be out there before the year is out.[309]

A partial itinerary for this trip began with Chicago on June 8. The following day, an article featuring Bobbie ran in the *Chicago Tribune*. Journalists mentioning Bobbie on one of these trips was a relatively rare event; most of the newspaper articles concentrated on Bill. In this case, Bobbie's presence provided an unmistakable example that A.A. was for women, too. The article had the title "OLD TOPERS ASK LADIES TO JOIN THEM ON THE WAGON – Alcoholics Anonymous, Aid Erring Sisters."[cxxvii] The newspaper article wasn't very accurate, but such were the risks when publicity was written by a journalist not entirely familiar with A.A.

> Alcoholics Anonymous, for years an exclusively male organization[cxxviii] of reformed drunkards and those in

---

[cxxvii] A June 8, 1943 article in the *Chicago Tribune*, page 22, "Nameless Band to Meet Bill in Nameless Spot" documented the visit.

[cxxviii] "Women's groups were probably the first special groups to form. The first women's group in the world is believed to be in Cleveland, Ohio, in June 1941. The following year, Ruth B. wrote G.S.O. from Minneapolis, 'There has been some discussion here of having the women alcoholics meet in a separate group. We have heard that women do meet in separate groups in Chicago and Cleveland...We have less than a dozen women alcoholics in Minneapolis, only four of whom are very active...' Bobbie B. replied, 'I suggest you write directly to Marion R., 12214 Detroit Ave., Cleveland, Ohio. Marion is the secretary of a women's group out there who recently celebrated their first anniversary. New York who has about 40 women alcoholics on their lists, 25 of whom have been dry since contacting A.A., holds a meeting once every two weeks for women only...' At about the same

process of climbing on the water wagon, has set out to salvage women inebriates.

This national group, nearly nine years old, has a membership of more than 10,000 persons, of whom about 500 live in Chicago. Membership has never been denied to women – the only requirement is an honest desire to quit drinking – but only within the last year or so have there been more than a few ladies enrolled.[cxxix]

How to gather more unfortunate sisters into the fold was explained last night at a meeting in the loop of 400 members, including perhaps a hundred women, by Miss Margaret Roe (to let the cloak of anonymity shelter the identity of a charming new national secretary.) Miss Roe, a New Yorker, said the problem of how to lend a Samaritan hand to matrons is the most puzzling question the organization has before it. The quickened pace of war time living, it was agreed, has spread the habit of feminine drinking from the night club belts to the suburbs and the smaller communities.

Both Miss Roe and Bill Doe (they are anonymous only to the public, not to their fellow members), who founded the movement and who is its national leader, declared that the established method of overcoming alcoholism by

---

time, Bobbie received a similar query from Harrisburg, PA, and replied in part, 'There are over 60 in the New York [women's] group. This is remarkable, because when I first met the group a little over two years ago, there were only 2, and some thought that perhaps this program just wouldn't work for women.'" From *AA History Lovers* Message 711, Jim B., 12/1/2002.

[cxxix] The statement is not accurate. On June 4, 1943, just five days previous to the newspaper article, Bobbie wrote Cincinnati the following: "I'm anxious to meet your woman members. Naturally I have a soft spot in my heart for the "drunken dames". We are now so many that it is hard to believe that about three and a half years ago when I came in there were about three women who had made the grade in the whole country." General Service Office Archives, Box 43, R23 File Ohio – N, p. 40.

example of members and spiritual reawakening of victims, probably is the best way to reach the ladies.

<u>Women Harder to Convince</u>.

Women, Miss Roe said, are more difficult than men to convince, because they have stronger inhibitions and wear a mask of reserve that is hard to penetrate, even when the need for rehabilitation is greatest. Unlike men, they do not care to talk about their bad habits, she said, and so are slower to admit they are in need of help, which is the first step on the road to beating the liquor habit.

Their trip continued on to Milwaukee on June 9 and Minneapolis on June 10.[cxxx] The A.A. newspaper article in the *Minneapolis Star* dated June 10 mentioned Bill only, and it was repeated in the *Star Tribune* article of the next day. Bill and Bobbie then traveled on to Kansas City, Missouri, arriving the evening of June 11. Landon Laird in his "About Town" column in the *Kansas City Times* wrote a very rare piece of journalism when he featured Bobbie rather than Bill. His article picked up the "Miss Roe" name that she had recently been called in the Chicago newspapers.

MIGHTILY interested were the members of Alcoholics Anonymous in Greater Kansas City to read in *The Star* Wednesday night an interview in Chicago with Miss Margaret Roe, new national secretary of the organization, telling how women were joining it in numbers. Miss Roe will arrive in Kansas City tomorrow to visit the local groups of Alcoholics Anonymous. She will be accompanied by Mr. Anonymous, the founder (or co-founder, as he prefers to be called) of Alcoholics Anonymous . . . The report of Miss Roe (that name cloaks anonymity, too) on the number of women climbing on the Alcoholics Anonymous "wagon"

[cxxx] According to Bob P.'s *Alcoholics Anonymous World History*, Lois was present in Milwaukee. "A visit by Bill W. and Lois, with Bobbie B. from the New York office, gave the Milwaukee group a shot in the arm in October 1942." (p. 42 of the hardcopy, p. 47 of the PDF). Thus, in any of the trips Bobbie and Bill took together, Lois may have been traveling along too.

> in New York, Chicago and elsewhere in the country, was
> greeted by the A.A.'s here with the information that there
> have been women A.A.'s in Kansas City for a considerable
> time, and the local women A.A.'s have been doing good
> work in winning women drinkers to the A.A. battle cry,
> "Liquor's quit us!"

How did the columnist come to believe that "Liquor's quit us" was the battle cry of A.A.? Such observations often resulted from columnists that approached Alcoholics Anonymous with little more than their first impressions.

Their trip continued to St. Louis, Missouri, where on June 14, a dinner was held at the Congress Hotel in honor of Bill W. William Dee Becker, mayor of St. Louis, and the Reverend Edward Dowling, S. J. were among four speakers that preceded Bill as listed in the program. Dr. Stephen Smith of Columbia, Missouri, who had become a valued correspondent with Bobbie, attended the event.[cxxxi] He was very pleased to meet both Bill and Bobbie. In a letter to Bobbie following the event, Stephen observed that "I can see the tremendous responsibility on your shoulders."[310]

The last city on their itinerary was Indianapolis, Indiana, concluding on June 17. Before they left on the six-city tour that covered roughly 3,000 miles by train, she had written, "It will be a tiring trip as is with all (or most of) our sleeping done on trains."[311] Leisure time for the two of them obviously was a very low priority!

The American Weekly Articles

Bobbie's strong commitment to Alcoholics Anonymous was very clear. She observed that she was going to have to stay close to Headquarters if Bill left for the west coast in the fall. She believed they both couldn't be gone from Headquarters at the same time for too long. The large numbers of

---

[cxxxi] Bill had apparently discussed having an ulcer with the doctor during this visit. He was to write Bill about his ulcer later on September 16, 1943: "Bill, how is your stomach ulcer doing since I saw you? Are you able to get the Aluminum Hydroxide tablets (Wyeth). They are off the market here. However, I have found a tablet put up by Geo. A. Brown & Co. that I like better than I did Wyeth's." General Service Office Archives, Box 44, R21, File Mo C., p 76 (Area 38 Archives).

inquiries requiring her attention were the result of three consecutive Sunday feature articles. They started on July 11, 1943 when *The American Weekly* published quite extensive articles on A.A by Genevieve Parkhurst.[cxxxii][312] Bobbie wrote the following in an August 12 letter to a Tennessee A.A.:

> Our recent publicity produced over 1300 inquiries and we have just been swamped trying to get them answered together with all the other necessary work. I'm off for a long vacation tomorrow and I need it after working 11-12 hours a day for over three weeks. Guess you people will just have to come up here. Don't see how Bill and I can get away. He and Lois are going to the coast in October for a six week visit in California and far western groups. None of these have ever seen Bill and have been after him for years to make the trip. I'm dying to go too but both of us can't leave this office for that long so you people plan a trip up here in September and we will love seeing you again.[313]

On pages 15 and 19 of *The American Weekly* article, a story is told about an alcoholic lady by the name of Enid. Enid strongly resembles Bobbie. In particular, her marriage to Shep, which suggests Parkhurst wrote at least part of Bobbie's story giving her another name.

> Enid's husband became more and more absorbed in his business. Then he began staying out night after night. He told Enid that he was out with his business friends. At first, she believed him. Then she became suspicious and jealous . . . 'I began,' she told me, 'by drinking double instead of single cocktails . . . But when I found out that my husband was in love with another woman, I was filled with revenge and self-pity. All I could think of was myself and my troubles.' It took seven years of drinking to make an inebriate of Enid . . . Enid did try Alcoholics Anonymous. 'I don't know what it was,' she will tell you, 'but I went out of the first meeting with the most exalted

---

[cxxxii] No relation to Hank Parkhurst.

feeling I have ever had.' Three years have gone by. Enid is now a leader in the A.A. movement.

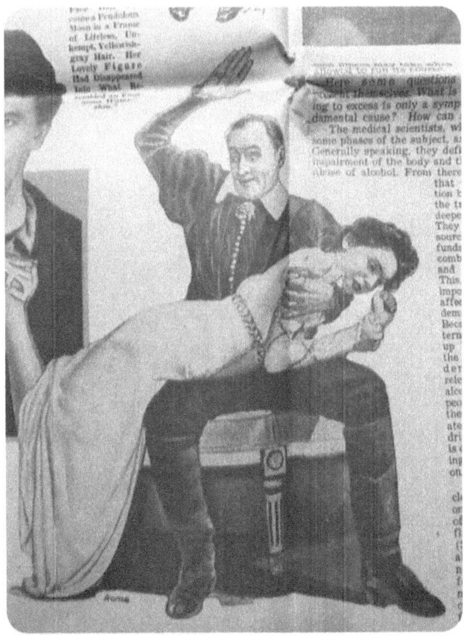

FIGURE 20 - "ENID" BEING SPANKED AS BOBBIE WAS

Similarities abound. Bobbie had three years of sobriety when the article was written. Bobbie was married in 1932, her first year of marriage was satisfactory, but she started drinking heavily in 1933. By December of 1936, Shep admitted to Bobbie's father that he should stop spanking her.[314] Bobbie drank as an inebriate for seven years. Thus, the portrait of a woman being spanked, which was featured dead center in the first of three Sunday articles in *The American Weekly*, and the story about Enid — was all about Bobbie.

Bill's 1943 Letter to Bobbie on Vacation

There is no question that a female alcoholic with more than three years sober in '43 was a rare individual. Bobbie had continued to work intensely on behalf of Alcoholics Anonymous. That Bill would praise her determination and discipline in flattering terms is certainly understandable. In this letter he also apologized for some of his dark moods. Bill composed these words on the morning commuter train into work in his own handwriting a couple of days after Bobbie had left for vacation.

> Enroute to NY
>
> Bobbie dear –
>
> Perhaps this is a time to say some things which I hope you will like. But first an apology for these last few days of my fumbling. Nothing can be such a brake on the joy of living as to have one around in a black mood whose pall covers everybody in reach. And specially with you so very tired. It was a really mean exhibition of childishness for which I'm very very sorry. Doubly so, for I did not think I could be so self-centered. And, as I'm sure you know, my better self would rather be concerned with making you content, joyful and secure.
>
> Now to something more appropriate — and cheerful – I wish I might be endowed with the words to tell you <u>just</u> how deeply and affectionately I regard you as "Bobbie", my dear partner of our fabulous enterprise; of the sheer joy of being with you and working together in rapport; of these glimpses of that incredible future in which I pray that we may both contribute what the Master expects. You have been doing just that, so loyally, so beautifully. Bobbie dear, that I know I shall be inspired to follow your example. Forgive me – I have so often been dead weight to be carried.
>
> I'm so prodigal with words, to everyone that I hope you will not discount these to you. They spring, dear partner, from my better self, from the finest and the best there is in me.
>
> Affectionately,
> B—[315]

There are very few letters written by Bobbie directly to Bill that are known to exist at this time. However, observations made by Bobbie written to other A.A. members reflect her feelings regarding him. One of those letters was written to Dale in Seattle on October 20 regarding his upcoming trip to the west coast with Lois.

> He starts out this Sunday and the first leg of the trip and I'm starting to miss him already. I'm so very happy you people will get to know him for he is truly a great person – something he doesn't know himself which is probably one reason he is so fine. From this you might gather I think he is "tops" and I do.[316]

Bobbie wrote to Dr. Stephen Smith on November 16 that "I believe that Bill has the power you speak of – that of loving all people. He is genuinely fond of everyone and never sees anything but good in anyone. Wish I could say the same."[317]

Bill and Lois Travel West for Three Months

Most of Bill's travels during the 1940s don't seem to have been very well documented regarding all of the dates or exact itineraries.[318] One of the better documented trips was the West Coast trip Bill made with Lois that began by train on October 24, 1943 that lasted roughly three months. Chapter seventeen of *Pass It On* provides a some details. They traveled through Chicago to Omaha to Denver where they stayed for a couple of days.[319] While in Denver, Bill hand-wrote Bobbie the following dated Friday, October 29.

> Bobbie Dear –
>
> Able to snatch a minute for you – aren't I the good boy about writing?
>
> Your letters are so inflationary.[cxxxiii] You make me think the whole AA – even you Bobbie dear—verge of collapse now that I am no longer in New York.

[cxxxiii] After many attempts in deciphering Bill's handwriting, this is the best guess.

> Last night's meeting went off handsomely – it was quite packed with townsfolk, judges, doctors, preachers and "red" lily are the groups which *[faded beyond recognition]* in the clear. Chuck is such a powerhouse. He and wife and daughter, swell girls both, drove us to the mountains all day yesterday. *[Rest of letter illegible]*
>
> Entre-Vous
>
> Bill[320]

Lois recalled that next they visited the Grand Canyon, which they had never seen before. They took army mules down to the Colorado River for a picnic lunch.[321] They arrived in Los Angeles on November 2, 1943 where they were to stay for three weeks.[cxxxiv] *Pass It On* provides a summary of what a typical visit was like.

> With minor variations, the procedures on all these stopovers was very similar. Bill and Lois were met at the station and taken to their lodgings – sometimes a hotel, sometimes a private home. Then, they met local A.A.'s for a meal. If the meal was lunch, the afternoon was often spent touring the local sights. If the meal was dinner, it was invariably followed by an A.A. meeting, at which Bill always spoke . . . All the A.A.'s were anxious to tell Bill their own stories and to hear his. If the visit was a one-night stopover, Bill and Lois would board their train sometime the next afternoon. From one stop, the journey to their next destination would last overnight; from another, only a few hours; In places where stay was longer, they might get a chance to catch their breath and perhaps a few hours of sleep.[322]

[cxxxiv] In a November 22, 1943 letter from Bobbie to Pat C. of Minneapolis, Minnesota, Bobbie revealed a surprise regarding Bill, though the surprise was probably only temporary: "Bill is fine and keeping rested. He stopped smoking a month before he left so he would have added vitality and it's working. Hope that doesn't mean I'll have to – smoking is the one vice I'm hanging onto.

Their stay in Los Angeles was filled with variety of activities which filled their days. The day after Bill and Lois arrived in LA, Bobbie wrote to an A.A. associated with the Chino Prison regarding her opinion of Bill, which was being discovered by Californians in person as the trip continued. "I'm certainly missing Bill but at the same time so happy that you people are getting to know him. He's tops in my book and there never was nor never will be another Bill W."[323] Very soon after their arrival they began to be accompanied by Bill's mother Emily Strobel. According to Lois, they stayed a number of days at a "monastery-like retreat in the desert at Trabuco."

> Dave D. from Palo Alto, California, introduced us to Gerald Heard, a nonalcoholic, who was a great philosopher, writer and student of both Eastern and Western religions. He became a lifelong personal friend and admirer of A.A. and soon introduced us to the famous writer Aldous Huxley, who became another lifelong friend and admirer of A.A. It was Aldous who wrote that Bill was "the greatest social architect of the century."[324]

They left for San Francisco on November 23 to spend about ten days. No letter was written by Bill W. to Bobbie during the stay in Los Angeles, but he found the time to handwrite a couple of times from San Francisco. The first was written on November 27 from the Clift Hotel.

> Thank you so much for remembering my birthday. How did you know – forty eight and not grown up yet – sentimental as eighteen! May God give me the serenity to accept things I cannot change – I don't want to be different anyhow and here's hoping you won't want me to grow up too much –
>
> I'm astounded at what you say about all the inquiries – We must be entering the "big business stage." A grand thanksgiving at the D————s. They are a swell couple – then the Palo Alto meeting last night after a drive among the redwoods. They made one feel young too as they are the world's oldest living things. Many

were respectable trees when Christ was on earth – Oh that role – what a book. I can understand your feeling about it.

Warren T. has done a pretty good job at the shipyards but manages to stay in the outs with the groups.[cxxxv] Actually he doesn't know the older people here well and they dismiss him as commercial, which is far from the case. The poor guy is so sincere and hard working. But he borders on the mental. Still in the fixing stage he feels quite persecuted when people disagree or criticize – I've built him up with the older ones. Maybe they will be able to cooperate better now. I hope – I hope.

Enclosed two letters which Lois wishes you would address. One to the Tuly girl the other to Tom and Lois – We have their phone no., but not the White Plains address.

Am writing this with a new Sheaffer – a birthday gift from the groups. There was a cake too! The people here are cordial but not so articulate as in L.A.

Still not too tired – Digestion much improved. Perhaps these spooks do know their stuff – And if so right about one thing why not another![325]

Five days later, on December 2, Bill followed up with a second letter to Bobbie from the Clift Hotel. He had just learned about the impact her letters had made to various west coast groups—how she helped guide them through their growing pains. The trip helped Bill learn what a difference Bobbie's letters were making. People at the Headquarters weren't reading what Bobbie produced – only the recipients of her letters really knew. Now Bill was receiving letters from her. While her letters to Bill are missing, his reactions show he was quite pleased to receive them.

How very happy your grand letters make me. How you find time is a mystery. I'm getting really concerned about

---

[cxxxv] This is the same Warren T. of the Kaiser Shipyards of covered in Chapter 4.

the lack of help down there. Please don't get too tired for I'll need you such a long time!

What a wonderful experience this has been here in California – It is truly miraculous how the groups have sprung up and have felt their way along to the right conclusions – I'm more convinced than ever that AA is automatic – foolproof. This speech making of mine is a pleasant luxury for people here but no necessity, thank Heaven. It is, on the contrary, you who is needed. More and more I see what you mean to them – they tell me![326]

Before Bill and Lois left for San Francisco, they also visited Sacramento and a variety of other meetings and locations. Bill also visited San Quentin and Folsom prisons around this time.[327] From San Francisco they went north to Portland and then to Seattle, then they turned around and went south all the way to San Diego where they spent Christmas with Bill's mother Emily Strobel. A.A. activities may have been temporarily suspended or reduced while there. At the beginning of the New Year, "they went back to Los Angeles, to Tucson, to Houston, to New Orleans, back to Houston, to Dallas, to Little Rock, to Oklahoma City, and back to Little Rock."[328]

Back at Headquarters, Bobbie had written the following about Bill on December 2. Since so few personal letters written by Bobbie to Bill are known to have been examined to date or known to have survived, Bobbie's A.A. correspondence to others has been the only way to find out her opinions about him. Here is one more example of how great she thought he was when she wrote a Californian who had recently met Bill:

I know exactly how you feel, down here we describe it as the "pink cloud" feeling. That letter of yours made me recapture some of the thrill of nearly four years ago when I first met Bill. Any time you want to start an "admiration society for Bill W." put me down as a charter member. Probably one of the nicest things about him is that he doesn't realize how truly great he is.[329]

Bill had to have written this January 11, 1944 thank you letter to the "avalanche" of Christmas cards some time during the west coast trip.

Since he and Lois did not return home until January 22,[330] he must have relied upon Bobbie to tell him just how many cards had been received at Headquarters. Of particular note is how Bobbie is included as a member of a three-person A.A. team. What a wonderful compliment! To be included like this was the first known warm-hearted tribute she received during her tenure as National Secretary.

January 11, 1944

TO ALL AA GROUPS

The Christmas mails have brought Lois and Bobbie and me a veritable avalanche of cards and letters of affectionate greetings. There are so many that we cannot hope to acknowledge each one.

Each of us exclaims "Is it possible, that I, once so much alone, can now have so many wonderful friends?"

Truly, we sometimes think, that with so many friends like you, we three must be the richest people on earth.

So now – Happy New Year.

As Ever,

Lois and Bill W. and Bobbie B.[331]

While Bill and Lois were on their west coast trip, the annual celebration of Bill attaining sobriety was held in New York City at the end of November 1943. According to Bobbie, there were 800 people present. The main speaker was the well-known minister and radio preacher Norman Vincent Peale of the Marble Collegiate Church in lower Manhattan. Bobbie quoted him as saying that "Bill was the greatest spiritual force on the earth today"[332] in a letter she wrote on December 1 followed by a second letter the next day when she wrote that Peale had said "Bill was the greatest living spiritual force in the world today."[333] Apparently Bobbie got carried away in her praise. Other sources reported Peale's words differently.

Alcoholics Anonymous was being praised by Peale rather than just Bill. Jay D. Moore, in his masterful book *Alcoholics Anonymous and the Rockefeller Connection* credited Peale as having said that A.A. was "the greatest spiritual force in the world today."[334] Lois quoted the exact words by Peale in *Lois Remembers* about A.A. as well that were quoted by Moore.[335] Thus, Peale's actual words were almost assuredly about A.A. rather than just Bill, but Bobbie's admiration for the co-founder probably led her to exaggerate.

Bobbie's Last Trip with Bill as a Team

Bobbie and Bill left for a trip at the beginning of March 1944. They visited Cincinnati on March 2; they were together in Dayton on March 6 followed by Louisville, Kentucky on March 7. Their last stop on this trip is believed to have been Parkersburg, West Virginia on March 11. Bobbie relayed her experiences in a letter to an A.A. in Portland, Oregon upon her return. She also lamented being three weeks behind in her correspondence.

> Your letter came in while I was out on the road with Bill for a 10 day visit to some groups. We took in a group a day with only two exceptions, traveling most of the early morning and being up all night "talking" to members. So we are plenty tired. The rush awaiting me on our return is something. This AA is spreading faster than we anticipated. Our inquiries are running three weeks behind in the answering and my mail is piled a mile high. My able assistant did get the formal acknowledgement to you for the contribution and please know how much we appreciate this showing of confidence in the Central office.[336]

This was the last extended trip Bobbie took with Bill. There are hints that Bobbie wished to travel with Bill when he departed in May for his next trip that took him all the way south to Miami, Florida.[337] But the days of Bobbie traveling with Bill were over.

Instead, Bobbie went on a spring vacation. She had favorite locations in Connecticut and New Hampshire that she visited from time to time. Bill wrote her the following letter on April 11 that contained all the images of spring. His fondness for Bobbie is unmistakable. In addition, he felt that sharing some of his "spook" experiences with her were appropriate.

How really overjoyed I was to get your letter of Saturday nite. I wish you could guess. For in it I could see the Spring coming in you as you told me of looking at the countryside. The cold of winter giving way to warmth and life budding again – No more loneliness, perhaps. Yes, "everything is rather wonderful isn't it"?

For a man resolved to withdraw from life to ponder the nature of things, I still seem fairly busy. This week I have several evenings out – I have to "fix" the "club corporation", the new newspaper, the Ourslers[338] and a lot of things besides. Oh yes, there is a trip to Stamford to see that medium, who can float the trumpets (5 at a time) and make them all talk while his own mouth is glued. J——— has seen it a dozen times and swears it's on the level – I want to get him over to Chappaqua to take some pictures and make some records –

Not too busy here – Punk[cxxxvi] & I have sworn to have you up to date on your return – And Lord, how we miss you!

Bill[339]

Despite the warmth expressed in these letters, as the summer of 1944 approached, more intense storm clouds were intensifying on occasion within Bill. He periodically suffered signs of plunging into long, deep depressions. Since Bill's emotions had taken a turn for the worse, Bobbie's self-imposed job requirements expanded: she felt it was her clear duty to protect the man she admired so much.

[cxxxvi] It is assumed the name "Punk" was a nickname for one of the employees at Headquarters.

Steady As He Goes

ill W.'s episodes of deep depression experienced over a dozen years are beyond dispute and very well documented.[cxxxvii] While the actual causes of these depressions remain beyond the scope of this book, one fact remains: Bill suffered intensely during these episodes, though the duration of the individual encounters seem to be a mystery. He was to write to Mel B. years later in 1956: "In the last twelve years of my life, despite all my blessings and opportunities, I have spent eight in depression, sometimes very severe ones."[340] In mid-1944, for two sessions with a psychiatrist per week, "Bill drove the fifteen miles from his home in Bedford Hills to [Dr.] Tiebout's office in Greenwich, Connecticut"[341] By 1945 or 1947, Bill met weekly with psychotherapist Dr. Frances Weekes. These sessions were to last until 1949.[342]

The book *Pass It On* devotes an entire chapter to the serious nature of Bill's depressions. After his January 1944 return from the three-month tour of the west coast, "Bill was plunged into a depression so black that its effect on him was more debilitating than a physical assault."[cxxxviii] It was not

---

[cxxxvii] "I had a neurotic depression that lasted from 1943 until 1955, one from which I never fully surfaced. About three years of this was suicidal. But the release from alcohol had been so thorough that I was never tempted during this long siege to resort to drink." *The Language of the Heart*, "Where Willpower Comes In," May 1962, p. 274.

[cxxxviii] Despite the onset of his depression upon his return from the west coast in late January 1944, he was able to take two more trips. A March 1944 trip with Bobbie included Cincinnati, Dayton, Louisville, and Parkersburg, WV. A May-June 1944 trip followed to the south that included Miami, Daytona, Tampa, Atlanta, Birmingham, Chattanooga, and Knoxville. Soon after this

unusual "for him to spend a day or more in bed with no clear diagnosis of what was ailing him . . . The first two years, 1944-1946, were apparently the worst." Marty Mann was quoted in these pages: "There are long periods of time when he couldn't get out of bed. He just stayed in bed and Lois would see that he ate. An awful lot of people believed he was drinking. That was one of the worst rumors we had within A.A."[343]

As bad as his bouts with depression were, he was often able to experience very productive periods when he made numerous long-lasting accomplishments. Many of his most valuable contributions to A.A., after authoring *Alcoholics Anonymous*, took place when he experienced relief from these self-professed periods of depression. He wrote regularly for *The Grapevine* magazine, rarely missing a month. Starting in July 1945 until the end of 1948, a period covering forty-two months, he only missed having an article included seven times. But that was only one of his activities. Years later Nell Wing[cxxxix] described the decade of 1945—1955 this way:

> Yet that decade also saw an incredible outpouring of
> creativity and some of the greatest achievements of his life;
> the conference plan, acceptance of the Twelve Traditions,
> improvements in the service structure, assistance to the
> *Grapevine* and many of his important writings.[344]

Bobbie accompanied Bill on a two-week trip to four cities in the Midwest in early March 1944. For whatever reason, that trip was the last documented time when Bill and Bobbie toured out of New York state

---

  second trip, announcements followed that he was done traveling at least for a while.

[cxxxix] Additional remarks involving Bill's depression from Nell Wing were found on *AA History Lovers*, message 164, where a member of *The Grapevine* magazine interviewed Nell in 1994. "Most times you didn't know he was going through it. His depressions came and went. Sometimes, not often, but occasionally, when he was dictating to me in the office, he would just put his head in his hands and weep for a bit. The worst of these depressive bouts were between 1945 and 1955. What he accomplished, AA-wise, despite his depressions, is a miracle. So many people wanted Bill's advice - not just AA and Al-Anon friends, but nearby neighbors at Bedford Hills. They'd ask if they could come over to Stepping Stones, and Bill always said yes to everyone."

together as a team of recovered alcoholics. When Bill left two months later on a trip which took him as far south as Miami, then over to Tampa, up to Atlanta and then west to Birmingham, Bobbie was not able to accompany him. A possible reason was that one of Bobbie's roles as a mother required her to remain with her daughters.[345] In Bill's absence from the office, standard practice was for her to continue to open his mail, per his instructions. She would either send items to his attention or hold them until his return. Often she would answer much of his mail with his implied permission. Sometimes she would speak for him, with phrases such as "Bill thinks" or "Bill feels." She would elaborate on his thoughts as Bill had explained them to her. Due to the sheer increase in volume of mail coming into the New York office, an arrangement like this had to evolve. Bill never had a chance to keep up with the mail addressed to him without at least one office secretary handling the majority of the volume of correspondence. In the four post-war years from 1945 to 1949, A.A. was to grow by an average per year of nearly two-thirds. There had never been a time in A.A. like this before. Rather than annual growth in the hundreds or thousands of members, A.A. was growing by no less than five figures of members and by two-thirds every year.[346]

The summer of 1944 was the beginning of a long period during which Bobbie responded to letters from A.A.s concerned about Bill's health. She attempted to protect Bill whenever there was any concern about his mental or physical condition. On June 30, in a letter to a Cleveland A.A. she wrote that Bill "is being forced into taking a vacation – he has overdone it for the last ten years and his doctor is now telling him to stop for a while so he can stop under his own steam."[347] By July 25, she wrote that the duration of the vacation would be two months because he "was run down from overwork and is now taking a two month vacation on doctor's orders . . . I am afraid that all traveling will be out for some months to come."[348]

There is every possibility that Bobbie, on her own authority, decided to protect Bill from the increasing cacophony of rumors regarding his health and strength. Implying that Bill was under doctor's orders conveyed that matters were under control and there was nothing to worry about. She initiated a protective shield of calm regarding Bill's health, which she exercised for most of the rest of her career at Headquarters. Repeatedly she would dampen rumors, put out fires, and reassure concerned A.A.s that everything was alright. She did this without ever naming the type of doctor that was treating him—she was not found to ever have used the term "psychiatrist." She wrote that Bill was overtired or overworked. He had been dedicating his entire life to A.A. for the last ten years and deserved a rest. The thought of Bill being depressed was not even a remote possibility. She behaved almost as if she was appointed to be Bill's office guardian angel.

Bobbie treated Albert Scott, Chairman of the Board of Trustees of the Riverside Church and trusted Rockefeller confidant, no differently than anyone else when the subject of Bill's health was involved:

> Thank you for your letter of July 31st addressed to Bill W. Bill has been away from this office for over a month and is not expected back until the middle of September. He had not been feeling well for the last few months so the doctor suggested a prolonged vacation. We all feel this is a good idea inasmuch as Bill has given us his last ten years without any thought of himself.[349]

By mid-August, Bobbie explained that Bill "has not been feeling well for the past six months . . . he is being very sensible in doing what the doctor ordered . . . We hope he will come into the office around the middle of September for a day or so a week."[350] In another letter written the same day, she wrote that his "condition is not alarming but could be serious if he did not take care of his health now. For ten years Bill has devoted all of his time to AA and this concentrated continued pressure work finally took its toll." She ended this last letter with a most unexpected short paragraph: "The doctor has asked that Bill not receive any so-called 'business' mail so I'm holding your letter until he returns. I'm sure you will understand and agree that we must think of Bill's health first – so long he thought only of us."[351]

How can this be? Could Bobbie have been in communication with Dr. Tiebout, or some other professional, on Bill's behalf? Wasn't it more likely that Bill would have relayed this request to Bobbie about the time when he first started seeking professional help?[cxl] Not only was Bill on vacation,

---

[cxl]   Robert Thomsen in his book *Bill W.* addressed Bill seeking professional help as a courageous choice: "[Bill] knew he was not the same man he had been in 1935, but if he was still being immobilized by spells of depression, if he was still burdened by ancient guilts—of the sort which he knew in other cases had started in childhood and so often were the last to let go—then he was still a man hanging on to 'old ideas' and possibly even displaying the typical

according to Bobbie, but his mail was on vacation too! Bobbie was in charge! If she was being supervised in this period of Bill's occasional intense depressions, no documentation has been found to point out who would have been supervising her in place of Bill.

A week later, Bobbie directly addressed an incoming letter containing a startling rumor. Had Bill experienced a nervous breakdown? Bobbie answered:

> Right now he is taking part of his rest cure up in Massachusetts and I haven't his address. Bill's condition is definitely not serious and no one should be alarmed. He's simply tired out and by following the doctor's orders to take things easy for a few months, we know he'll be back in good condition shortly.[352]

That was a prediction that did not come true right away. On September 1, she was back to firefighting a rumor that Bill had had an alcoholic relapse:

> Rumors and even facts do grow on our intangible grapevine. Bill has not had a breakdown and he has not gone into a hospital. Late in June several of us pushed Bill into going to a doctor for he didn't seem too well. The doctor checked him carefully and said that he had better take several months out now while he could still do it under his own steam. So since July 1st Bill has been "on vacation" which means he is getting lots of outside exercise, plenty of sleep and eating properly . . . All sorts of stories drift back to us and one is that Bill has had a slip. Where do people get such vivid imaginations? Perhaps because the doctor felt Bill should not see too many people (in fact none of us drop in at his home at all without

---

alcoholic's desire to go on nursing and clinging to his guilts. But however Bill viewed his problem, at this point, just before his fiftieth birthday, and with all the ego-flattering prestige of being considered a spiritual leader, to stop, take a look and admit he needed professional help was more than open-mindedness; it was an act of courage." Hazelden, Center City, Minnesota 55012-0176, ©1975, p. 301.

invitation) some may imagine he is worse than we say. Taint so at all – Bill is just plain pooed *[sic]* out after his ten concentrated years helping other people to get well. I, for one, am so glad that something forced him to take it easy for a while.[353]

Was Bobbie really one of a group of concerned members and friends that "pushed" Bill into arranging for medical and/or psychological help? Who else might have helped convince him? Her words suggested that he was pushed into seeking help. Yet, once again, Bobbie was calming the rumors and protecting him as best she could by writing that his mental and physical health remained stable and he was being carefully monitored. Notice also that some curious A.A. members had confused his mood swings with those of an alcoholic slip. Bobbie would be accused similarly in years to come. Accusations of Bobbie suffering a slip on the job and being discharged were to persist for decades.

Numerous additional examples of Bobbie exercising damage control followed during the balance of 1944. As the requests for Bill to speak or travel came in, Bobbie discreetly answered them by saying that there were no immediate plans for any A.A. trips or talks for him. She made an observation that times had changed. He would no longer travel to individual meetings: "With the immense growth in groups, it now looks as though he will have to cut out traveling entirely at least to separate groups. For one man could not possibly cover over 370 and it certainly would not be fair to visit some and not the others."[354] This dilemma of saying yes to one group and not another would be a significant future dilemma not only for Bill but for Bobbie as well.[355]

Bill "Came Out of his Temporary Retirement"

Bobbie was rather frank about Bill's absence from Headquarters in a letter to Barry C. of the Nicollet Group in Minneapolis, Minnesota. She wrote him a November 11 letter about an A.A. celebration that previously had taken place in New York: . At this time she was considering Bill's sobriety date as being worthy of being called "A.A.'s tenth birthday."

I am just about back to earth after the thrill of this last week. The New York Groups celebrated AA's tenth birthday with a big dinner and meeting at the Hotel Commodore. We filled the Grand Ballroom with about a 1000 and words leave me when I try to describe the wonder of it all. Bill came out of his temporary retirement for this one night and spoke. I suppose you know that he is really trying to follow the doctors *[sic]* orders and completely rest for these six months. Perhaps after the first of next year he will be more active again. He did come in town every day this week to greet the out of town members who journeyed so far to the dinner. We had eight in from Cleveland, eleven from Youngstown and ever so many from nearer out of town Groups. Each day saw 20 or 30 of us lunching together – it was simply a wonderful week and I wish that more of our friends could have been with us. Today I am in (and it is 7:30 PM now) trying to create some order out of the chaos I let accumulate. I haven't read much less answered any of my correspondence for the last four days.[356]

The 1944 Christmas Message

As 1944 concluded, Bill wrote this lovely Christmas Message" to the Fellowship. His words did not contain the slightest clue, as he wrote in later years, that he was battling depression.

Greetings. On our 10th Christmas – 1944. Yes, it's in the air! The spirit of Christmas once more warms this poor distraught world. Over the whole globe millions are looking forward to that one day when strife can be forgotten, when it will be remembered that all human beings – even the least – are loved by God, when men will hope for the coming of the Prince of Peace as they never hoped before.

But there is another world which is not poor. Neither is it distraught. It is the world of Alcoholics Anonymous, where thousands dwell happily and secure. Secure because each of us, in his own way, knows a greater power who is love, who is just, and who can be trusted.

Nor can men and women of AA ever forget that only through suffering did they find enough humility to enter the portals of that New World. How privileged we are to understand so well the divine paradox that strength rises from weakness, that humiliation goes before resurrection; that pain is not only the price but the very touchstone of spiritual rebirth. Knowing it's full worth and purpose, we can no longer fear adversity, we have found prosperity where there was poverty, peace and joy have sprung out of the very midst of chaos. Great indeed are our blessings! And so, — Merry Christmas to you all – from the Trustees, from Bobbie and from Lois and me.

Bill.[357]

Could there be any finer proof of the central role Bobbie was performing for Alcoholics Anonymous? What an honor for her name to be included as part of this Christmas greeting! How many other A.A.s were part of a similar salutation written by Bill?

1945 was a period in which some of modern Alcoholics Anonymous was forged on anvils of disputes, accusations and hurt feelings. As Bill later relayed, "This period, 1945 to 1950, was one of immense strain and test."[358] Nell Wing would later speak of these years as "the most turbulent, exciting, and innovative era in the history of Alcoholics Anonymous."[359] Robert Thomsen described it as follows:

It was an absurd situation and one that took on an alarming urgency as more and more members understood what was at stake. Not only did the thousands of new prospects have to be answered; some method had to be devised to unify AA. If it could hold together, everything would be right; if it fell apart—which at times it showed every sign of doing—all would be lost; after this brief flurry there would be chaos, they would disband and pass from the scene.[360]

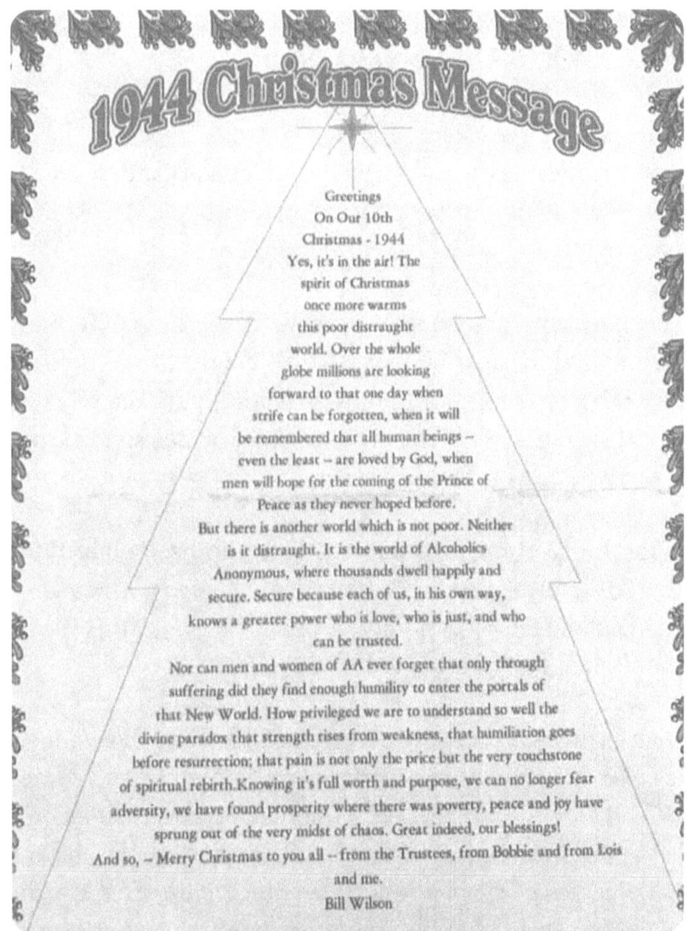

FIGURE 21 - 1944 CHRISTMAS MESSAGE

A War Time Edition Big Book

For whatever reason, it was Bobbie and not Bill who made the announcement to the groups that the new printing of the Big Book would be reduced in both size and weight. Paper was rationed. Books were allowed a quota by the War Production Board that was measured not by numbers of copies but instead by the ton of paper. The per-copy requirement for paper per book had to be reduced or the supply of Big Books might not match the anticipated demand. Bobbie wrote the following announcement dated February 12, 1945:

NEW WAR TIME EDITION OF THE BOOK
ALCOHOLICS ANONYMOUS

Because of the acute shortage of book paper we have repeatedly, on order of the War Production Board, reduced the weight of the paper used in the book Alcoholics Anonymous.

We have now arrived at the point where because of further reductions in paper we must sharply cut the overall size of the book by trimming margins to a minimum. Happily we shall still be able to use the same book plates so the type face will be as readable as ever.

Practically every publisher has long ago been obliged to make these changes so we hope that AAs everywhere will understand the necessity for them and be glad of this small additional contribution to the war effort.

Our printers are a badly overworked firm and though this new edition was arranged for many months ago, we are told there will be some delay on delivery. We will be out of books by February 15th and will probably not be able to ship copies of the new war time edition until after March first, how long after we do not yet know.

I hope you will all be patient if your orders are delayed somewhat. Please be sure we shall make shipments the moment we can.[361]

The dedication and discipline behind her letter should be readily apparent. Bobbie meant what she wrote. Big Books were going to be shipped absolutely as soon as possible. There was a war on, and for some, part of that war was a battle to stay sober no matter what.

Increased Health Concerns

By April of 1945, the tone of Bobbie's explanations regarding Bill's health changed significantly. Gone were the references to a vacation. Instead there was more concern regarding his health overall. On May 3 she wrote, "Bill is taking a long leave from active work in this office due to his health. For a year now he has been trying to come in part time but finds it hard to stick to this schedule. Once in the office things pile up and the next we know he is snowed under again."[362] The key phrase here: "in this office." There is every indication that he rarely was making the hour trip from Bedford Hills by train into the New York office. Twelve days later, Bobbie published a bulletin to the Fellowship regarding the planned 10th Anniversary celebration upcoming in Ohio the next month:

> Bill hopes to be with Bob at these meetings if his health permits but has asked me to tell you how much he regrets not being able to accept the many invitations coming in from other nearby Groups. The doctors have advised Bill not to do any traveling or Group-visiting for some time to come. However, he wants to be with Bob and the Tenth Anniversary meeting knowing so well that without Bob AA could never have been. Let me assure everyone that Bill's condition is not serious and we should not be alarmed as long as he practices "Easy Does It."

Additional significant topics included a movie about Alcoholics Anonymous, *The March of Time,* which had recently hit the movie theaters without any advance notice to the Fellowship. A.A. members were writing New York asking why they had not been warned. Bobbie replied that since the movie short "was taken from material out of a book about us but not connected with us, officially, *The March of Time* editors did not think of notifying us." Then she commented about a similar incident with the *LOOK Magazine* article to be published the next month: Headquarters had had no other choice than to accept the article as it was written due to time constraints. Last, she relayed the anonymity challenges over envelopes and stationery displaying the name "Alcoholics Anonymous" indiscriminately. People were complaining throughout the Fellowship that their anonymity was being violated through the mail.

Bill's Possible Resignation from A.A.

There are many clear examples of Bobbie providing leadership for A.A. Among them: Bill had delegated the task of explaining his lack of visibility to the membership, so she did the explaining for him. Bill's varying moods of these times were being carefully shielded from almost all the Fellowship, as the reality would have been far too disturbing for A.A. members. He was so troubled that he considered resigning from office activities altogether but remained extremely concerned about the risks to A.A.'s future! Here are excerpts taken from his extraordinary 3,877-word letter to trustee Leonard Harrison on May 2, 1945, explaining just how much he thought the position of National Secretary meant to the future of Alcoholics Anonymous (Bobbie is referred to here as Mrs. B——):

> At the last meeting of the Foundation there was discussion of my personal situation and of the possibility that I might retire from active participation in the affairs of our Central Office and Works Publishing Inc. . . .

> It can be fairly said that the Central Office, under the guidance of the Trustees, myself and two excellent National Secretaries we have had, has been the keystone of the arch under which thousands of alcoholics have found their way to a new life. As the movement made the book financially, so did the book and the Central Office make AA what it is today . . .

> But the point I am trying hard to make is this: in these matters which vitally touch the spread of A.A., personal relationships with out of town groups, preparation of literature, public relations, and daily supervision of office routine – in these matters practically every decision has always been taken by the National Secretary and myself. It had to be that way because the Board of Trustees, busy with their own personal responsibilities, could not be expected to evolve the necessary principles and relationships, much less actually follow through. So this side of the activity of

our Central Office is naturally the least understood by the Board. That will always, to some degree, be true.

When we address ourselves to the present situation it becomes perfectly clear that if I now relinquish my activities or should suddenly pass out of the picture, there would be no one left in all A.A., excepting Mrs. B——, who has anything like an adequate comprehension of our Central Office. Should she sicken or leave we would be in a serious predicament indeed. Obviously this is a weak state of affairs. The whole continuity of the Central Office is still depending on the good health and continued attention of Mrs. B—— and myself.

While the business mechanism of the Office are well understood by most of the Trustees, the intricate maze of personal relationship between the National Secretary and hundreds of outlying groups is scarcely understood at all. It is upon these very relationships that the success of the Central Office absolutely depends. They are vital to the spread of the work, vital to the field of public relations. Upon them the Board of Trustees must place their entire reliance for the group money contributions which support the Office. I wish every Trustee had the time to read half a dozen of our correspondence files. They tell the story. It is the National Secretary who actually personifies the Alcoholic Foundation. Hundreds of groups regard her almost as a parent.

Perhaps too much preoccupied with other phases of A.A., I am afraid I have never made this picture clear enough to the Trustees. So long as I have been at the Central Office it has been natural for the Trustees to suppose that these vital relationships, policies and traditions were matters which concerned me, rather than Miss Hock or Mrs. B——. Actually we have always shared these responsibilities and relationships together. At no time has either acted as an ordinary private secretary or head clerk to me or to the Foundation.

Realizing that I could not forever maintain this relation to all National Secretaries yet to come I have been, of late, deliberately withdrawing – partly because of my health and partly because I wished to see how the setup would function by itself.

For the past year and a half, I have made few decisions, nor have been much at the Central Office. I am happy to say that Mrs. B——, occasionally consulting the Trustees on the detail side of the Office, has done an excellent job. She has operated Work Publishing Inc. recently turning out a large new edition of books without any assistance from me whatever. Two or three new public relations matters come across her desk each week, many of them requiring an intimate knowledge of personalities out in the groups as well as a thorough understanding of our public relations policies. I have encouraged her to make these decisions herself excepting upon issues involving some new or large problem. She has done very well indeed . . . We might be faced any time with the problem of finding a new National Secretary. Someone would have to train the new Secretary. That would be about a two year job, assuming we were lucky enough to find the right one. Consequently it seems of prime importance that we assure a thoroughly qualified understudy as soon as possible.

In an offhand way I have already discussed this matter with some of the Trustees. There are differences of opinion. It has been suggested, for example, that we secure a non-alcoholic for the job, making the non-alcoholic the National Secretary over Mrs. B——. It seems to me that such a plan entirely discounts Mrs. B——'s invaluable experience, and what nearly every A.A. group in the United States would declare to be her great competence – plus the probability that no non-alcoholic would be received by the groups in any case.

The suggestion has been made that we hire a man alcoholic, either as Mrs. B——'s assistant or as National Secretary. The chance that we shall find one having the qualifications seems remote. If we engaged one as an assistant we could not begin to pay him enough to attract the right person. If we put up a man as National Secretary, I am positive he would soon be suspected by the groups of trying to assume the role of national leader. This may seem ridiculous to you. But it is probably true – that's the way the alcoholic mind is.

So that dwindles our choice to alcoholic women. And the field is mighty narrow there too. If good on business detail they may lack personality and caliber. If strong on personality they usually have nothing resembling the energy, discipline or business ability required. If they happen to have all these qualities they are mostly career women making two or three times what we could possibly pay. Or they are married.

It is to be hoped that the Trustees may have a suggestion about some A.A. member of National Secretary caliber who might become Mrs. B——'s assistant . . .

In this connection I am positive that New York is the last place in America to inquire how effective the Central Office is, and just what it does for the National picture. Marty Mann, who has now travelled widely among the A.A. groups, came to me the other day telling enthusiastically of what was being said all over the country about the strength of our National Headquarters and the personal esteem in which our National Secretary is held.

Tom B—— recently came in from Atlanta with the same impressions. Taking such satisfaction in the

> accomplishments of the Central Office, I suppose my
> own opinion may be biased. But I am sure it is not
> overstatement to say that few have contributed more to
> our success, nationally speaking, than Ruth Hock and
> Margaret B———. May their kind continue as National
> Secretaries forever."[363]

Had Bill ever followed through and resigned at this time, Bobbie would have been left as the only sober A.A. associated with the New York Central Office! That fact best portrays just how thin the ranks at Headquarters were back then. How important Bobbie was to A.A. at this time! Bill's words written to Leonard Harrison recognized how dependent A.A. was on their first two National Secretaries. Both wished to stand behind Bill and support him by putting the spotlight on him at every opportunity. Yet, Bill, in his own words, wrote that it was "the National Secretary who actually personified the Alcoholic Foundation." First Ruth Hock, then Bobbie, provided the cohesive spiritual energy to guide A.A. through some of its most turbulent growth. Somehow the title "secretary" never has seemed to adequately convey what these two women truly contributed, as Ernest Kurtz wrote, to Alcoholics Anonymous "attaining maturity."[364] Bobbie today has remained unknown to a majority of the Fellowship despite the fact that she served as National Secretary for more years than Ruth and was in communication with a much larger number of A.A.s with the additional valuable capability: she communicated as an alcoholic with experience.

As 1945 continued, Bobbie continued to downplay the seriousness of Bill's physical condition. On August 8, she once again passed the responsibility of Bill making no trips and few appearances for the last year to "doctor's orders."[365] With Bill visiting the office so infrequently, she felt her place was to continue to communicate with the Fellowship. As such, she also turned down opportunities for herself to travel and speak.[366] As 1945 ended, Bobbie had become very accustomed to answering letters for Bill that communicated that he was unavailable for speaking engagements or to travel very far from home. Here is but one example:

> Thank you so much for your letter of December 12th and
> I'm sorry to disappoint you by sending an answer from me
> instead of Bill. Perhaps you have not heard that the doctors
> took Bill away from active work about a year and a half

ago and he seldom comes into the office. All the work having to do with new groups and, in fact, practically all correspondence now clear through my desk. However, you may be sure I shall call your letter to his attention when he does next drop in and I know he will be happy to hear from you again.[367]

Bobbie's Expanded Responsibilities

By early 1946, Bobbie's responsibilities had expanded so much she was opening all of the mail addressed to Bill: "In as much as Bill comes in the office so seldom, he's left orders for me to open all of his mail, to sort out that which is important to forward him and to handle what I can myself if it is of a purely business nature."[368] Thus, she had achieved a role of being implicitly trusted by Bill to screen his mail and provide to his eyes only what she thought he needed to see. This was not the role of anything less than what many would call the responsibilities of an executive if the job wasn't working for Alcoholics Anonymous. Bill had delegated a huge amount of responsibility to her. On February 26 she finally mentioned a possible reason for Bill's absence with a word she had previously avoided: depression. "Bill must get away from all the AA activity for a while - - his doctors say so. He is definitely not well. About the best name we can give his condition is mental exhaustion but it takes the form of depressions."[369]

Bill handwrote this extraordinary letter the very next day.

Bedford Hills
February 27, 1946

Bobbie dear,

Yesterdays *[sic]* experience in town has convinced me that I shall have to hasten my parting with our national activities. It was so alarmingly severe that I dare not ride many more – worse than the time I left for Florida two years ago – worse because a hundred such experiences have worn any lingering hope that I shall ever be better under present conditions. The power of my obsession has finally dispelled the illusion that it could ever basically improve as things are now. It was a previous illusion <u>but</u>, like others in which I have taken comfort, I guess it will have to go. I need to make a decision like yours of two years ago. You had to see clearly what was impossible for you. You then declared it, acted upon it, and stuck to your course without a hair breaths deviation. Because, for you, there was no other way. May God grant you that same firmness of purpose and the wisdom to quit a situation where neither time nor exhaustive effort has made the slightest difference. A new life – elsewhere – has to be the hope. There is no other that I can see. Sometimes you do not seem to understand the need of mine. Yet I'm sure you must, for a new life, <u>elsewhere</u>, was <u>precisely</u> the answer you found for yourself. After several years, even chance reminders of your past life could shock you deeply. Surely, Bobbie dear, <u>you</u> understand.

All last year, I wanted a thousand times to make a decision. But I could not. I would hope something might turn up a remedy, diversion, or maybe a fresh experience that would bring release. And I did not want to disturb your truly beautiful faith that all, one of these days, would be well. I didn't want to throw the full burden of our national affairs on you and the others. I could not leave unfinished tasks undone, for whose completion I felt terribly responsible. So I continued my misleading course without a rudder – And for these same reasons I'm still on that same course, yawing badly, heeling over dangerously. Shall I keep on like this? And if so, for what good end? And with what? The resources to stay with the ship in this course seem to be gone. I cannot seem to surrender my obsessing nor drive it away, nor has anyone been able to take it away. Even God in his wisdom has seen fit not to intervene.

When I wrote R—- about Chicago and after I had told you and Chrys that I was coming to end of the AA road, I experienced some relief. It wasn't all osteopathy, I'm sure. I think it was that near decision which brought the release that enabled me to talk so freely and do that long *Grapevine* piece. Then when I read R——'s reply, I felt that perhaps I must always stay on year after year; that, after all, I lived on borrowed time and feel I belonged to AA: that I had no right to make this new bid for personal freedom. Feeling no ability to decide that conflict, I collapsed. It's the same way about coming to New York. When here, I'm irresistibly drawn there. When there, I soon must fly back here. That deadlock can't continue too much longer without serious consequences. There has to be a decision. And I don't see how it can be the decision to stay on. We've given that one a two year trial. Nor can one stand forever the whipsaw of indecision.

It might be if I could decide these things as firmly and finally as you did in the matter of our other "impossibility," that I would be released enough to do some part of the remaining writing job. Perhaps that would offer a hope. Thoroly *[sic]* for me a grim one. Whether I shall ever marshal the courage to really give up so much I love, I don't know. I might for the ultimate good of everyone. I can now see no other course.

Above all, Bobbie dear, don't take any of these thoughts to heart. For your loyalty to me and to AA through these dark times is its brightest page; a really sublime outpouring of the kind of love which I so admire, but of which I seem to know so little in myself.

It's so hard for me to talk nowadays – Yet I felt I should tell you. Were I not so weak I would tear this up. You should not be asked to carry any of the load – it was surely none of your doing. But, dear God, how hard it is to be alone with such emotions! Please forgive me.

Affectionately,

Bill[370]

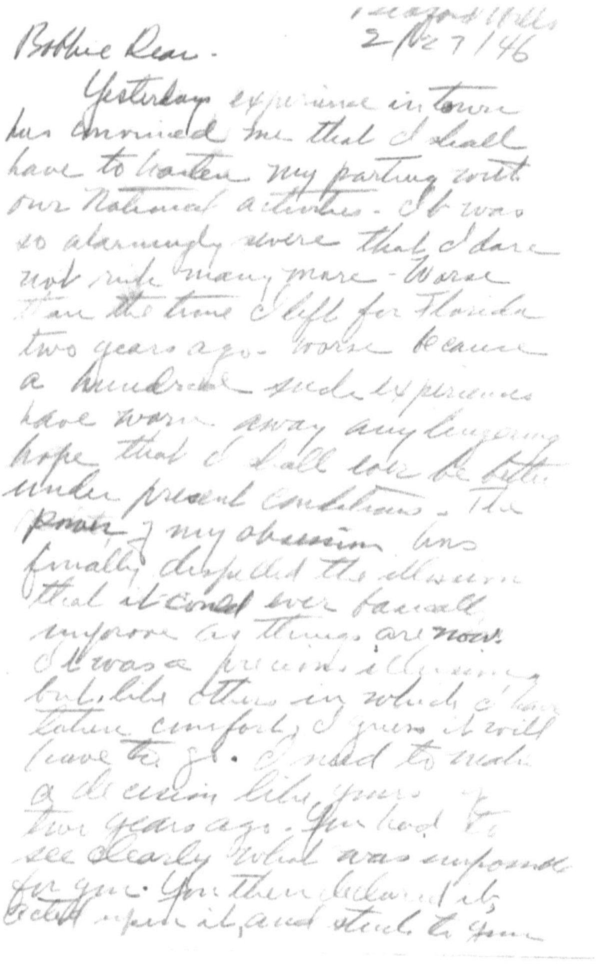

[illegible]
2/27/46

Bobbie Dear -

Yesterday experience in town has convinced me that I shall have to hasten my parting with our National activities. It was so alarmingly severe that I dare not risk many more - Worse than the time I left for Florida two years ago - worse because a hundred such experiences have worn away any lingering hope that I shall ever be better under present conditions. The power of my obsession has finally dispelled the illusion that it could ever basically improve as things are now. It was a precious illusion but like others in which I have taken comfort, I guess it will have to go. I need to make a decision like yours of two years ago. You had to see clearly what was imposed for you. You then declared it, acted upon it, and stuck to your

FIGURE 22 - PAGE 1 OF BILL'S FEBRUARY 27, 1946 LETTER TO BOBBIE

Bill had been considering walking away from Alcoholics Anonymous since at least the May 1945 letter to Leonard Harrison, but had remained. He persevered despite being in a severe disturbance worse than the depths experienced before his trip to Florida in May of 1944. He appeared determined to continue despite his agony. He could not visualize walking away from A.A. Headquarters and leaving Bobbie, still the only alcoholic employed there, to hold more of the responsibility of representing the future of Alcoholics Anonymous than she had already. The article "Twelve Suggested Points for A.A. Tradition"—a huge milestone to ensure the future of Alcoholics Anonymous—may have been composed by then, though it was still some weeks before it was published in the April 1946 issue of *The Grapevine*. That article was just one of the unfinished tasks he visualized that hung in the balance. If ever there was any doubt of the personal price Bill was paying for pursuing his vision of what he hoped Alcoholics Anonymous would become, this letter provides a glimpse of how his human emotions had been stretched by criticism and adversity. Bobbie, a confidant, an alcoholic, his colleague, and a loyal National Secretary was in a position to witness and comprehend Bill's emotional challenges. She treated this matter with utmost confidentiality throughout her life.

The letter also raises more questions. What exactly was Bobbie's decision "of two years ago?" Was it a coincidence that Bobbie had stopped traveling with Bill roughly about then? Such speculation may not result in a firm conclusion, but at a minimum, his writing made it clear that Bobbie had been experiencing substantial emotional challenges as well. Bill's mood swings in her presence had to have had a significant impact on her.

On April 11, 1946, she wrote to an A.A. member:

> Bill is still not feeling too well and has retired to Bedford Hills to do some writing for the *Grapevine*. When he finishes this, he and Lois plan to take a long vacation. His doctor suggests they all get away from all AA activities for a few months and we are all hoping Bill will follow this advice. I know if they get as far as the coast that they will want to stop in and see the groups unofficially.[371]

Charlotte L. was hired as an assistant to Bobbie, who was suffering under the strain of a heavy workload and prolonged defense of Bill.[372] She was to be a very heartfelt colleague of Bobbie for the next two and a half years. Charlotte's sobriety dated far enough back for her to have conversed with Ruth Hock.[373]

Bobbie wrote to Dr. Bob on April 26 regarding Bill's depression. She expressed "deep concern over its severity" – strong words she otherwise seemed to avoid when writing the Fellowship.[374] On August 9, Charlotte wrote, "The letter addressed to Bobbie and Bill has arrived in the absence of both from the office. As you will know, Bill has left for a three months non-AA vacation. Working with Bobbie's doctor, all of us have been able to persuade her to take a much needed rest and she will return in about a month."[375] Here was clear evidence of how the strain on Bobbie was weighing very heavily on her. The name of her doctor remains unknown.[cxli]

Bill himself relayed to Rev. Sam D. in Rome, Georgia that he was following doctor's orders in a letter dated July 25, 1946:

> The doctor insists on keeping me under his thumb for the balance of the year. Though I am much improved I feel I could attempt almost anything. Last Spring I cancelled several major speaking engagements and announced my intention of doing nothing more until 1947.[376]

In a September 17 letter from Bill in Victoria, B.C. to Bobbie, he clued her in on what he thought had been contributing to his misery:

> I suddenly realized the extent to which I have been trying to dominate . . . others; also the extent to which I have been indulging in fruitless self-accusation . . . everything swinging in the direction of control of something or somebody.[377]

Note the level of trust expressed by Bill to Bobbie here. Though Bill clearly admitted to some personality defects, Bobbie held these words in confidence. There is no record of her ever sharing Bill's personal explanations with the Fellowship. One of her most honorable attributes as National Secretary is the way she handled herself in these times. While the preservation of these personal letters from Bill reveals a personal side of him not often seen, his letters to her elevate them both: him for admitting the true depths of his feelings from all the challenges he faced, her for practicing restraint of tongue and pen.

Farther along in 1946, Bobbie seemed void of any concern regarding Bill's health. Part of the reason may have been that Lois and Bill had simply left New York for substantial periods. Bill wrote Dr. Tiebout about his status on June 1:

[cxli]   The doctor may have been Dr. Tiebout, but Bobbie had previously visited several credentialed professionals regarding her various challenges.

Until recently, there has been almost no relief from depression for two years. And when I used to feel better, it was only that I had less of the blues than usual.

About six weeks ago, I cancelled every single speaking engagement and completely withdrew from the office situation. We then went to Vermont. Regime: sleeping, eating, walking, fishing, reading. Lois and me alone at an old farmhouse near Brattleboro.[cxlii] One morning, after about ten days of this, while she was reading to me in the living room, I suddenly went 'quiet.' No elation, nor was there any special sensation of peace. I just became very quiet inside. . .[378]

By August, Lois and Bill began a three-month trip.[cxliii] Lois wrote about their adventures in *Lois Remembers*:

In the summer of 1946 we drove our new Desoto to many of the beauty spots of the West and North. The trip included a visit to Bill's dad and his wife, Christine, in Marblehead, British Columbia. It was not all vacation, however as things at the AA office in New York began to pile up. Bill received several frantic wires, so he had to take time to write a bulletin about anonymity to be sent to all the groups. We also stopped In Hollywood to see how a script was progressing for a movie about AA to be produced by Hal Wallis.[379]

At least some of the "frantic wires" had to do with Marty Mann and the fundraising letter of the National Council for Education on Alcoholism

---

cxlii   Brattleboro, Vermont is located 160 miles north in southernmost Vermont on the Connecticut River.

cxliii   Ernest Kurtz in *Not God* referred to this west coast trip as follows: "It was an extended vacation at the low point of the depression that haunted him through most of this decade, . . ." Hazelden, Center City, Minnesota, 55012, Copyright 1979 by Ernest Kurtz, p. 119.

(NCEA).[cxliv] Bill and Dr. Bob's names had been used in a letter soliciting funds for Mann's organization. An unacceptable anonymity violation was declared due to the NCEA being considered an outside issue to A.A., thus contradicting the recently published Twelve Traditions. This controversy took place in mid-September and seemed to end Bobbie writing about or publicizing Marty to the Fellowship. Bobbie knew Bill and Lois' itinerary, so she could wire updates to Bill on matters only he could handle. Many years later Nell Wing would observe that this crisis had quite an impact and the fallout of which was to last four years,[cxlv] which would have been one more source of tension for Bobbie. Two years later, Bobbie reluctantly commented on this tension that remained regarding what Bobbie refers to as "the national committee" when she once again wrote Warren T. of the Richmond Shipyards.

[cxliv] There is some confusion regarding the names NCEA and NCA. While some sources declare Marty founded the NCA in 1944, that abbreviation was NCEA in 1944. From Wikipedia: "Marty Mann . . . organized the National Committee for Education on Alcoholism (NCEA) in 1944, which later became the National Council on Alcoholism (NCA) in 1950 and then NCADD in 1990 to address concern with other drugs."

[cxlv] From a 1994 interview by the *Grapevine* of Nell Wing, message 164 in AA History Lovers: "Well, for one thing, when Marty M. was soliciting for the new National Committee for Education on Alcoholism (later the National Council on Alcoholism), she made a big error in 1946. She said that whoever contributed to the NCEA would also be contributing to AA, or that AA would benefit from it. Well, that created some explosion! Bill was traveling and speaking out West and AAs were bombarding him with questions: "What's going on? What is this woman saying?" The Trustees of the Alcoholic Foundation had their first press conference because of this, explaining that what Marty said was not endorsed by AA, and that the Trustees had nothing to do with the solicitation announcement. Bill and Dr. Bob had earlier let their names be put on the NCEA letterhead because Bill was very supportive of what Marty was doing in the field of alcoholism. Bill never believed that AA had all the answers for every alcoholic. He always said that whatever worked for the individual was what was needed. Anyway, the Marty M. controversy lasted four years - it was a fast and furious business at the time. But it helped galvanize acceptance of the short form of the Traditions, which were later accepted in 1950 at the Cleveland Conference."

> Bob G. wrote me about Sybil T.[cxlvi] and thanks for the additional information. I wrote Bob that we did not have any plans for her in this office, but that we would be happy to do anything we could. You know, the usual service and we will be really glad to meet her. If she already plans to see Marty, then we will keep out of any discussion on that. In fact, it is much better for this office not to discuss the national committee, pro or con. I don't know any subject that is more controversial, even the prohibition one.[380]

Bill and Lois were back by the beginning of October. As 1946 came to a conclusion, Bill had been away from the office for at least six weeks during one trip and three months for another. Bobbie, by default, had been in charge at the A.A. office regarding most day-to-day matters involving the Fellowship. For the time being, concerns about Bill's health seemed to diminish. Among Bobbie's letters written during the remainder of 1946, she was not found to have written on the subject.

Once again, Bobbie received the distinct honor of being included in Bill's Christmas message to the Fellowship. This was in a bulletin dated December 5. The final paragraph of the message was:

> So, Merry Christmas to you all; from Dr. Bob and Ann,[cxlvii] from the Trustees, from Bobbie and the Central Office, from Tom Y. and the Grapeviners – and from Lois and me.[381]

Among her activities she wrote about in 1947, Bill's health was not a topic. Bill may have been feeling better, but there was another possibility. Bobbie and Bill simply may not have seen much of each other. His trips into the office may have been infrequent. There's no record of her visiting Bill and Lois at their home at this time.

Bill and Lois left for a three-month trip to the west coast via Canada on February 7, 1948. Bobbie wished that she could have accompanied them on the trip, but those days had been over for years. Bobbie wrote that

---

[cxlvi]   Sybil T. should not be confused with Sybil C., the first female A.A sober west of the Mississippi.

[cxlvii]   An unfortunate misspelling as Dr. Bob's wife was Anne, not Ann.

the itinerary had been planned carefully to make sure they didn't get too exhausted, suggesting an almost maternal concern for them.

> On this trip, we are scheduling some breaks for Bill and Lois. They will drop out of AA existence every once in a while for a few days and take a short rest. In this way, we hope they can come through this trip without being too exhausted. Of course, if Bill tried to cover all of the individual groups or even some of the larger ones in one city, he would get very tired, and that is one thing that none of us want.[382]

Bobbie laid out the plans for the trip and in the same letter reported that Bill was still "struggling." She also showed support for the concept of an A.A. Annual Conference long before the idea was well-known.

> Bill is still struggling and underneath all my agreement I realize his wisdom. AAs must one day learn to operate without Bill and he hopes to see that structure go into effect while he is around. He simply cannot answer every letter that comes in, and usually tosses his mail to either Charlotte or me for answering. Bill is spending all of his time on writing and on working out the Traditions. Incidentally, the Traditions will be the subject of his talks on this trip now being planned.[383]

Bill and Lois went west by train visiting quite a few cities in Canada: first Toronto, followed by Winnipeg and Calgary.

> "Crossing the vast Canadian land, they were awakened in Regina, Saskatchewan, at 4.00 a.m. by the lone A.A. there . . . In British Columbia, they made a stop to visit Bill's father . . . Bill and Lois stayed at Marblehead for a week . . . They left Marblehead on February 21 . . . Two days later, Bill and Lois arrived in Vancouver."[384]

Then they would head south through Seattle, Portland, attend a conference in San Francisco, and arrive in Los Angeles by March 18.

Phoenix held a convention coinciding with Bill's visit. Bobbie reported on April 14 that Bill had "dictated a letter to his Audiograph Machine while in Mexico," which had been sent by him to Headquarters for transcription.[385] Members from San Diego had financed a trip, for a "few weeks," according to Bobbie, at Ensenada, Baja California, Mexico, where Lois and Bill were able to rest.[386] By April 17, they were as far east as Lubbock, Texas[387] and by April 22 they had arrived in St. Louis.[388] Their last city on this tour was Chicago. They arrived back home on April 30.

The information regarding the next six months of Bill's activities is hard to follow. Bill initially announced that he intended to drop all plans to travel for most of the rest of the year. In a letter dated May 7, barely a week after the end of the west coast trip, Bobbie reported:

> Bill dictated the following paragraph to me which I have been sending out to so many.
>
> 'Since returning home I realized that considerations of health and other unforeseen circumstances, will make it impossible for me to meet any summer or fall engagements with the groups. It is only with great reluctance and regret that I've been obliged to come to this decision."
>
> There it is and we are all so sorry. At least you people won't be the only ones disappointed if there is any consolation in that.[389]

However, a month later Bill's travel plans changed, according to a letter Bobbie wrote on June 4 to an A.A. in Buffalo, New York:

> I had better let you in on some sad news right away. Bill has been back for more than a month now and I have discussed invitations for the future for conferences with him. He has asked me to write all of you in the area that right now he looks as though he should not commit himself for any more conference visits, with the exceptions of four already set for this year. His health and other unforeseen circumstances have convinced him it is wise not to make any future plans along these lines.[390]

Those four conferences were as follows: He was in Austin, Texas from June 18 through June 20 for the third annual Texas Conference and Southwest Convention.[391] Next, he traveled to Jacksonville, Florida on September 3 and 4 for the Southeast Regional Convention.[392] That was followed by a trip to an A.A. convention in Des Moines, Iowa as reported on October 23.[393] Lastly, he spoke in front of as many as 3,000 people at the Upper Midwest Club in Minneapolis, Minnesota the following day.[394] There is not the slightest hint that Bobbie was ever considered to accompany him on any of these trips. Bill continued to be enthusiastic and determined to promote the acceptance of the A.A. Traditions.

Bill's mood swings persisted into 1949. In a reply to a telegram from Little Rock, Arkansas addressed to Bill, Bobbie apologized that she had to answer instead. Apparently Bill needed a break from the correspondence from the membership: "Please forgive me for answering your telegram instead of Bill. He is honestly trying to stay out of everything for as long as it takes him to regain his health completely."[395]

Frank Amos, formerly a Rockefeller associate in New York and long-time supporter of Alcoholics Anonymous, knew who to write to get an accurate assessment of the atmosphere at Headquarters as well as a report on Bill's health when he wrote Bobbie on February 4. Frank wrote from Cambridge, Ohio where he was the general manager of *The Daily Jeffersonian* newspaper. His letter makes clear just how much he trusted Bobbie as a source of accurate information.

> This letter is confidential, and if you do not feel justified in answering any or all of it I will understand.

> You may or may not know that on January 24 the Foundation trustees elected me to their Board. I believe you know me well enough to pass unbiased judgement as to whether you believe I can render real worthwhile service on that Board, living out here and probably getting over there at most not more than four or five times a year but spending four or five days to a week each time I go over.

> The second thing is I learned from Chipman that Marty Mann has been in the hospital. Chip has taken for granted that I know all about it for he merely says that her situation

is not as serious as was anticipated. I had learned nothing whatever regarding her until receiving this note.

The third thing has to do with Bill himself. Is his retirement for the time being because of disagreement with the trustees, or has it to do with almost entirely with the condition of his health? If you cannot answer this, just pass it up until I have a chance to see you personally which may be in April.[396]

Bobbie's reply has not been uncovered.

On April 13, the subject of Bill's health dominated Bobbie's reply to a request from Denver for him to attend an event there:

He intended to visit Denver and some of the larger centers late last year but his health gave out. He did go to Des Moines, Iowa and Minneapolis, Minnesota because he had definite commitments and larger conferences had been planned. But, his doctor would not let him take on anything more. He has been very inactive in all AA affairs for some time. Perhaps you did not know that he has been off and on the sick list for four years. Early last year he began to feel better and took a fling around the country to Canada, down to the west coast and back via Texas, Chicago to home. This lasted three months and just about floored him.[397]

A week later, on April 20, she wrote to an A.A. in Huntington, West Virginia that Bill wasn't feeling well and was not making any visits except for an upcoming trip to Montreal, Canada, where he was presenting a paper to the American Psychiatric Association's 105th annual meeting on Tuesday, May 24. This event happened to be preceded by the three-day North Eastern Regional A.A. Conference that began on May 20. A May 23 newspaper article documented Bill's presentation. The article reported that a "small group of people who built A.A. from an idea into world-wide organization" were guests of honor.[398] Bobbie most likely was one of those guests. Actually, she may have been much more than a guest as she may have been involved in helping organize the event. However, soon after the trip ended, Bobbie's life was going to change forever.

10

Rotating Leadership is the Best

The principle of rotation was first practiced by Clevelanders in either 1939 or 1941 depending upon the source accessed. The idea has been credited to either Abby G. or Clarence S., both from Cleveland, Ohio.[399] This sensible practice is almost taken for granted in Alcoholics Anonymous today to ensure, as Tradition Two states: "Our leaders are but trusted servants, they do not govern." However, the awkward manner in how rotation was to apply to Bobbie's job as National Secretary would ultimately determine much of her fate at A.A. Headquarters. Rotation also would intentionally limit the potential of Bobbie's successors to achieve the personal recognition that she, a female, gained domestically and overseas, with one notable exception. Nell Wing did not rotate as either "Bill's Secretary" or as A.A.'s first archivist. The title of National Secretary (or General Secretary) was to become obsolete.

Early in Bobbie's A.A. secretarial career, rotation seemed to have been only an occasional topic. On December 9, 1942, she responded favorably to the idea when she wrote, "Think you are wise to keep up the rotating plan and change committee members every once in a while. Besides you probably need a rest. The job of secretary can be a demanding one but at the same time very satisfying."[400] In a letter to California six months later, she wrote quite positively while noting that most groups started out with "a few individuals assuming leadership because of necessity." Rotation would evolve naturally once the A.A. group gathered more members and periodically changed leaders. She cautioned that what was right for other groups might be wrong for California. Bobbie was always careful to report experience rather than attempting to advise or instruct.[401] On January 19, 1944, she was pleased to respond to a group from Seattle, Washington on the subject: "Glad to hear that you are trying out Bill's ideas for a rotating committee. Let me know how it turns out. It does seem the fairest and best way to avoid politics and keep the Group on an even keel without jealousies etc."[402] When Carl K. of Chattanooga complained that if he didn't do the work for his group it wouldn't get done, she made the following recommendation: "With a rotating system which is used in many groups you will find that all members get a chance to serve in a fairly short period. And it is surprising to see how much being on a committee stimulates interest in a group."[403]

Rotation requires that there are enough participants to share the responsibilities. As 1945 unfolded, the Headquarters personnel consisted of just six people. Bobbie probably was the only alcoholic staff member until Charlotte L. was hired in April, 1946. Until then, Bobbie alone among the staff could write to alcoholics with experience in the language of the heart. As some of her writings already proved, her letters sometimes reflected phrases that closely resembled ideas that ended up in the A.A. Traditions long before they were published.[404] While there is no direct evidence that Bobbie helped Bill compose the long form of the Traditions, there is direct evidence that the correspondence received by A.A. Headquarters, most of which was first received by her, was among the most significant factors in shaping the Traditions. Bill validated this history in a 1955 *Grapevine* article:

> As early as 1945, from the correspondence, and from our mounting public relations activity, that the basic ideas for the Traditions of Alcoholics Anonymous came . . . Such a traditional code could not, of course, ever become rule or law. But it could act as a sure guide for our trustees, Headquarters people and, most especially, for AA groups with bad growing pains. Being at the center of things, we of the Headquarters would have to do the job. Aided by my helpers there, I set to work. The Traditions of Alcoholics Anonymous which resulted were first published in the so-called "long form" in the *A.A. Grapevine* of April 1946.[405]

Who were the helpers? Horace "Chrys" C., Dick S., and Bert T. represent a threesome of alcoholics that could have been among those used by Bill as sounding boards. These three trusted servants, all of whom served as Trustees, seemed relatively close to Headquarters according to the many times they appeared in Bobbie's letters around then. There had to be others, too, but one of those helpers was likely Bobbie. She was one that could be counted upon to be a confidant when the chips were down. She also was the only alcoholic you could count on being there most every day during regular working hours – and many additional hours after.

Tradition Nine as originally published in April 1946 directly addressed rotation. The long form of Tradition Nine reads, in part, as follows:

> Each A.A. group needs the least possible organization. Rotating leadership is the best. The small group may elect its secretary, the large group its rotating committee, and the groups of a large metropolitan area their central or intergroup committee, which often employs a full-time secretary . . . All such representatives are to be guided in the spirit of service, for true leaders in A.A. are but trusted and experienced servants of the whole. They derive no real authority from their titles; they do not govern. Universal respect is the key to their usefulness.[406]

With a Headquarters office of just six full-time employees and a budget of roughly $20,000 in 1945,[407] Bobbie seemed unaware that the principle of rotation eventually would apply to her job. She may have continued to recommend the practice to correspondents, but any potential impact on Headquarters seemed out of the picture. However, who could have predicted that the next four years would see such a significant growth spurt of A.A.? By 1949, the Headquarters budget would be nearly four times larger at $76,000 with nearly twenty employees.[408]

Nor did the idea of rotation at Headquarters seem to occur to Bill at first. In April 1947, he included Bobbie's name in an important document directed to the Trustees, advocating the formation of an annual conference to be held consisting of delegates selected by popular vote of their geographic areas. As part of his advocacy of the functions performed by Headquarters, he wrote: "Popularly known to thousands as 'Bobbie', our A.A. General Secretary now serves world A.A."[409] In the same document, he declared that Bobbie was an ex officio member of the A.A. Board of Trustees, a title he also used to describe the editor of *The Grapevine*. He wrote of these two that each were "alcoholic of note, and hard workers. Dr. Bob and I know these as our close associates; we recommend them to you all."[410] Would he have written about Bobbie in that manner had he been anticipating that he would eventually lament that the principles of rotation hadn't applied for her job and that Headquarters had become too dependent upon her?

Bill Praises A.A. Headquarter's Two Secretaries

Bill seemed very pleased with the "special workers" of Headquarters and believed they deserved salaries worthy of their contributions.

> There must be few societies or organizations in the whole world whose General Service expenses are as modest as ours: One dollar a member a year of voluntary contributions. We therefore think that our necessary Headquarters services should be the very best – that our few full time workers should be paid, not by charity standards but by business standards; that since more of us, thanks to A.A. earn excellent livings at business, we should not ask our special workers to do with less.[411]

Furthermore, he was very pleased with two secretaries at Headquarters. In 1947, they were Bobbie and her very trusted colleague and dear friend Charlotte L. Together they handled the vast majority of responses to the voluminous amount of incoming mail.

> At the General Office the vast outcome of nine years exciting experience reposes in our files and in the heads of our two Secretaries. Because of their station at the heart of A.A. they are bound to have a broader view than most of us. Out of strenuous experience they have developed effective ways of handling the multitude of problems and situations that press for answers. They have an immense personal acquaintance that stretches all over the globe. With them a "crisis a day" is routine. We are coming to see that a permanently successful operation of the General Office will depend on the preservation of these accumulated experiences and contacts. Lest these immense assets be someday lost, we shall always need several assistant

secretaries in training. And may we always remember that these secretarial servants of A.A. have a most strenuous vocation. They are entitled to our fullest appreciation and backing – theirs is no sinecure.[412] [cxlviii]

By mid-1946, the office had grown from six employees to twelve. The expenses of Headquarters almost doubled from $20,000 to $36,000 in less than two years.[413] Just how many of the twelve directly worked for Bobbie is not clear. One of those employees was originally Nell Wing, who was hired to be Charlotte L.'s assistant on March 3, 1947.[414] According to Nell:

> The second staff member, Charlotte, on the other hand, was a good businesswoman. She lent stability and a lot of practical know-how to the whole office operation. From the advertising agency where they both had worked, Charlotte had brought in Marian W—— to be office manager. When Marian proceeded to introduce some needed office reform and discipline, most of the employees quit or were let go. I was the first of the "new breed."[415]

Thus, from Nell's words here, Bobbie was not at all opposed to bringing good talent into the office as long as the new hire was willing to work for a small salary in a job where hours were long and the spiritual rewards "great."[416] In any case, things were changing at Headquarters. The ability to manage comes from either talent or training. Bobbie, once a professional ballroom dancer and occasional actress, didn't seem to have the managerial talent and she was not known to ever receive any comparable training.

Bill wrote more in the October 1947 *Grapevine* on the necessity for rotation.

> Times have changed. As everyone knows, AA has since exceeded our wildest expectations. Speaking for Dr. Bob and myself, we feel that we oldsters need not take the prominent roles we once did. AA leadership is becoming, happily and healthily, a rotating matter.[417]

[cxlviii] Sinecure: a position requiring little or no work but giving the holder status or financial benefit.

In a second *Grapevine* article published in October 1947 titled "Why Can't We Join A.A., Too?" Bill continued to promote his strong preference for principles above personalities:

> In actuality, AA has a score of "founders," men and women without whose special contributions AA might never have been. But somehow the title of "founder" seems to have attached itself almost solely to Dr. Bob and me—a phenomenon due perhaps to the general lack of information about our early days . . . AA may be able to function upon the power of its own fundamental principles rather than upon the prestige or inspiration of a highly personalized leadership. Thus the whole can become of transcending importance over any part; continued unity and success can then mostly depend upon God as we understand him working vitally in thousands of hearts rather than a few.[418]

Bill continued advocating for rotation in the January 1948 *Grapevine*:

> The group conscience will, in the end, prove a far more infallible guide for group affairs than the decision of any individual member, however good or wise he may be. This is a striking and almost unbelievable fact about Alcoholics Anonymous. Hence we can safely dispense with those exhortations and punishments seemingly so necessary to other societies. And we need not depend overmuch on inspired leaders. Because our active leadership of service can be truly rotating, we enjoy a kind of democracy rarely possible elsewhere. In this respect, we may be, to a large degree, unique.[419]

Tom Y.'s Letter to Bill with a Cover Letter to Bobbie

On April 20, 1948, Tom Y., editor of *The Grapevine* and author of the A.A. Preamble,[420] wrote a letter to Bill W. He also provided a cover letter addressed to Bobbie knowing that she would see the letter before Bill did. His cover letter was apologetic in tone to her as he felt compelled to practice principles before personalities.

> I am enclosing a copy of a letter to Bill because I hope it will underline the fact that there is certainly nothing personal in my feelings on this whole subject.

> If I hadn't happened to be on the *Grapevine* when the thing brewed up, I probably never would have been in the unhappy position of having to express views that may differ with yours and those of Bill. Yet, I can't help feeling that everyone involved directly is working for the same ends, though by different methods.

> Anyway, let's hope it comes out with friendships intact, and A.A. in one piece.[421]

The "whole subject" had to do with anonymity and rotation. Since *The Grapevine* was originally published in June 1944, the volunteer editors had carefully guarded their anonymity in print. They also soon began to rotate job responsibilities as seemed suitable for volunteers. In his letter, Tom was addressing the fact that Headquarters was not operating under the principles outlined in Bill's writings. Evidently, there was some event in which Tom Y. was involved in which "the thing brewed up." Since he was about to embark on a business trip, he thought it timely to write Bill directly regarding this rather sensitive subject. Bobbie had been neither anonymous nor part of a rotating team since she started work as National Secretary. Tom's first page was confined specifically to the status of *The Grapevine*. However, by the sixth paragraph, his focus changed to cover all those associated with Headquarters:

> My conclusions regarding the *Grapevine* undoubtedly reflect my personal opinion that making careers out of A.A. can be dangerous to both the individuals and to A.A. While some people might be able to do this without harm to themselves and while performing great service to A.A., the greater number who could not do so suggests the need for the establishment of this policy as a further safeguard.

I know that you have sought through your reorganization plans to prevent the development of a bureaucracy in A.A. and the creation of positions of personal power. The fact that your plans have encountered disagreement as to whether they would accomplish those aims or defeat them does not discount their importance. The *Grapevine*, of course, as a periodical going direct to increasing numbers of members, represents great potential power and a likely place for the growth of one bureaucracy unless every check possible is applied, now.

As the *Grapevine's* editor of the moment,[cxlix] I feel obligated to adhere even more strictly than in the past to the above policies and principles. As an individual A.A., I also think that the more widely the policies of anonymity in office, rotation of office, principle over person, and service over career, can be applied to all A.A. activities, the safer the future of the movement will be.

I know you will agree that since the question was put to me, I was obligated to express my convictions no matter with whom they might disagree.[422]

The "making careers out of A.A. can be dangerous to both individuals and A.A." statement directly focused on Bobbie! She had to have recognized it! Why else would Tom have provided her the cover letter? His message suggested that Bill already had some reorganization plans that included rotation for Bobbie's job. An example of a rotating group was already nearby: *The Grapevine* had a volunteer editor until 1964.[423] It had begun as an anonymous volunteer organization consisting of six alcoholic members of the New York Group.[424] Tom's letter advocated for the good of A.A. that these principles should not be postponed or ignored any longer.

Bobbie responded two days later on April 22 with an uncharacteristic, apparently hurried, emotional response. While she normally preferred

---

[cxlix] Message 8194 of *AA History Lovers* lists Tom Y. as editor of *The Grapevine* from 1944-1946. However, in this letter, he claims to be "the *Grapevine's* editor of the moment" in April 1948 when Al S. is listed as *The Grapevine* Editor in message 8194. No answer to this difference has been found.

to dictate her letters, she typed this one herself. No one proofread it. Otherwise, the obvious errors might have been corrected. Sadly, this letter was simply not representative of the reasoned quality of most of her correspondence. Here was a time for restraint of tongue and pen, but she didn't seem to have the power, or a sponsor, to advise her to possibly tear this letter up. (For readability, the misspellings are included below in brackets after the corrected word.)

> I do want you to know how much I appreciate your letter of April 20th and especially your thoughtfulness in sending it to me.
>
> Perhaps I'm dumb but I can't see anything in the letter you wrote to Bill (on or between the lines) that I do not agree with. Somehow or other, I've been "lined up" as for or against certain people and their ideas. I spout off too much about things that do not concern me and forget them quickly. Healthy difference of opinion is good and it is too bad that all such differences can't be kept on that way.
>
> My belief has always been that no employee of this office should be as important as the whole. I do believe this office is important from a useful standpoint. Its [It's] responsibility is to AA and its direction should come from the Trustees. Consultation has never seemed out of order to me but a "club" or "stick" held in a voting power would never solve anything and only bring about harm. I've always felt cooperation in working together was the only way. I guess my unfortunate contribution [contirbation] to this [illegible] "brewed up" as you put it, came because of a desire to get things done. Actually I don't give a hoot how they are done.
>
> Decisions one has to make which involve loyalties [loyaltitles] and reason are often painful. And any I make are for me alone.
>
> What is best for AA and my personal friendships are important to me. Thank [Thanks] God I haven't any vote but if I had one, that's where it would go.[425]

Perhaps she is "dumb" and has been "lined up?" She "spouts off too much?" "Actually I don't give a hoot how they are done?" If she had regularly written letters such as this one, she would never have gained the respect and love of so many with whom she corresponded. She was obviously disturbed! Surely as the office expanded, possible personality conflicts arose. If office politics were involved, to what degree we'll never know. Did Bill reply to Tom? Did Bill soften Tom's words to Bobbie? No answers have yet been found, but one fact remained clear: after this exchange of letters between Tom and Bobbie, her job at Headquarters was never quite the same. She recognized that she did not have a voice on "what is best for A.A." or even if her contributions were appropriately appreciated.

Evolution or Demotion?

Since Bobbie took over as National Secretary, she wrote almost every bulletin to the membership or groups. Most were signed by Bobbie with her first, middle initial and last name. Charlotte shared that honor with her on a bulletin dated June 5, 1947. But those days were soon to be over. The next bulletins were signed "SECRETARIAL STAFF, General Service Office," or used the first names of all the employed corresponding secretaries. The following explanation was provided in a bulletin to the membership on May 14, 1948 without documenting how the decision was made:

> To carry out the spirit of anonymity in general mail we plan from now on to sign our bulletins simply "Secretarial Staff". Behind that signature will be the cooperative efforts of the secretaries here now and others who will follow us.[426]

The December 1948 Bulletin contained the names of Ann, Bobbie, and Virginia. Charlotte's name was conspicuously missing as she had left at the end of October when she and her husband Joe moved to Ohio for him to assume a new job.[427] The April 1949 Bulletin carried four first names with Bobbie's listed second behind Ann's, with additional names being Jinny and Lucy.

Bobbie signed her last letter with her first name, middle initial, and last name on or about May 7, 1948. In letters that followed until she left

Headquarters, they were signed with her first initial, middle initial and last name followed by a "/" and two letters such as "dt" or "gm" signifying who typed the letter. The days of her warmly writing "Sincerely, Bobbie" to end her letters were soon to be a relic of the past.

Charlotte apparently worked just as long and hard at her job as Bobbie did. In the late part of the summer of 1948, Charlotte went on vacation. Bobbie wrote encouraging her to not hurry back.

> I also wanted to see you Sunday to try to put some pressure on you not to come back to work on Monday, but to just take a little more time off . . . I'd like to see you stay in bed late in the mornings, have coffee in bed, served by Joe of course, and then lunch with somebody and go to a movie. Won't you please try that just for a few days? . . . Everything's going along smoothly in the office and the work is getting done. You've had quite a lot of mail, but between the two of us, Ann and I are answering it. All the carbon copies will be saved so you will know what we've been saying behind your back. Ann is really doing a wonderful job and yesterday we had a long talk and she is about to start signing some of her own letters. I feel now it's the time to begin this.[428]

When Ann was hired isn't clear, but it's important to note that she was beginning to take on a similar role to that of Bobbie and Charlotte in September of 1948. This fact will have significance in the interpretation of events that were to come.

Regardless of any increased distance between Bobbie and Bill, she was still a close senior member of the Headquarters family as Christmas 1948 approached. Bill wrote Christmas greetings to the Fellowship, with a copy of it being included in the *Cleveland Central Bulletin* December issue:

> To nearly everyone Christmas brings thoughts of warm ties to be renewed, gifts to be given and received. Fresh and wondrous is the vision of him who shines down the centuries to all who will look up and behold.

To us of AA, the Christmas experience is sure to be doubly meaningful. We know ties more precious than any we had dreamed; we have received the gift of life itself and may freely pass that on; each of us has seen and felt a redeeming radiance which he knows to be the Grace of God. What more could we ask; what more could we receive?

Yes, it's a Merry Christmas—a Merry Christmas indeed!

The Trustees, the Grapeviners, Dr. Bob, Anne, Bobbie, Lois and I wish you the happiest of New Years—

As Ever

BILL[429]

Indispensable Bobbie

Bobbie dictated this letter over a weekend but it was typed on Valentine's Day, which was a Monday, by an office assistant. Because her letters were almost always typed by someone else on regular work days, the ability to document how many weekends she worked has not been determined reliably. She was offered a speaking engagement in Binghamton, New York, roughly 180 miles from Bobbie's apartment. She flatly turned down the invitation because she wasn't "feeling too good." She also observed that if she accepted the invitation, she would feel obligated to accept others. She mentioned that her doctor had her "on a pretty rigid schedule." The doctor at this time was likely to have been Dr. Tiebout, but that has not been proven. Events that followed make that guess probable.

Much as I would like to visit Binghamton some Saturday evening, I will have to take a rain-check as I have in many other similar invitations. Believe me I appreciate you wanting me but I just cannot leave the office for any length of time. And, it follows, if I do accept one invitation, I must accept many. Also I haven't been feeling too good for the last few months so the doctor has me on a pretty rigid schedule – complete rest except while I'm in the office. Today is one exception for I brought my dictating machine[cl] home to help get caught up and I am in my own apartment with about five hours of correspondence for dictation ahead of me.[430]

By 1949 voice recordings were becoming more common. Her decision to avoid such invitations, whatever the reasons, may have contributed to her lack of recognition in years that followed. There are no known voice recordings of her.

The Salary Review of March 1949

By March of 1949, Bobbie performed a salary review for herself and the three people she supervised. She wrote an internal memo to the Finance Committee dated March 3rd titled "PROPOSED MATTERS FOR DISCUSSION AND APPROVAL AT THE MEETING OF THE FINANCE COMMITTEE OF THE ALCOHOLIC FOUNDATION." She first dealt with the need for additional rental space along with associated costs per square foot. Then she directed her attention to the recommended salaries for Ann and the two newer hires Virginia and Lucy:

> I would like at this time to recommend a salary adjustment for Ann L. as stated on the attached form. This seems fair in line with the salaries of our two new AA Secretaries, Virginia T. at $3600 and Lucy P. at $3000. It would place Ann L. on the same salary basis as Virginia T. who deserves this amount because of her experience as an Intergroup Secretary. Ann L. has shown her ability and value to us especially since Charlotte L.'s resignation. She and Virginia T. should complement each other in acting [actin] as co-assistant secretaries with Lucy P. as Junior Secretary.[431]

These salaries she recommended were approved almost as written when the Board of Trustees acted on salary recommendations some months

---

[cl]   Might any of these dictations have survived and possibly be in the Archives at the G.S.O.? If we are to ever hear the sound of her voice that may be the only possibility.

later on July 25, 1949. An additional person, Polly F., was included by then.[432]

The notes that follow are Bobbie's exhibit to the Finance Committee regarding her own employment at Headquarters. Some were especially appropriate considering Bill's criticisms of her in later years. She knew that times had changed. Losing Charlotte was a big hit to the office and to Bobbie, since she considered Charlotte to be an equal to her in almost every way and very good friend. Bobbie realized that the three people now working for her had to become fully qualified to assume the capabilities and contacts that Bobbie had once handled by singlehandedly. So she wrote these notes in preparation for her meeting with the Finance Committee.

In requesting a review for an adjustment of my own salary, I do this entirely on three counts. 1. Responsibility of position, 2. Record for seven years, 3. Current salary scale for similar position elsewhere.

1. Although it has been necessary to put in many extra hours of work in the past few months, this is not a sound reason for an increase in itself. The responsibility of a job is to get as much work as possible accomplished to the best of one's ability and with whatever help is available. There has always been overtime work to some degree since my employment here and I doubt that this condition will ever change. The addition of Virginia T. and Lucy P. will not lessen but increase the responsibility of my job. With their help we should be able to take care of the main projects pending such as the "Secretaries Manual", various translations of the AA Pamphlet, AA Group visits and more detailed attention to all correspondence. In as much as my experience has been longer in this office and I report to the Trustees on office and AA matters, the direction and planning of all aspects of work here falls on me. I plan to arrange the secretarial duties so that each specialized service will eventually be covered by two members of our AA Staff. This should cover us in emergency absences, vacations, resignations and Group visiting trips. With this sounder set up I hope to have time to become better acquainted with other services in the general office, thus discharging my over-all responsibility on a more detailed basis.

2. My record for the past seven years in this office will have to stand or fall of itself.

3. It is difficult to compare my job in this office with a similar one in another business. Although a large part of the eligibility for being in charge here rests on the plus value of my being an AA member, never the less other qualifications of a business nature are necessary. Perhaps these may be rated at what I might make if employed elsewhere. In each of three definite offers made me, the salaries have been greater than mine here with the opportunity for more advancement in a financial way. I have chosen always to remain in this office and should like to continue as long as the Trustees wish me to remain. In my early days of employment here, the cost of living was much lower, my outside income was greater so the necessity for a larger salary was not too important. Also I knew that it was not possible with our financial condition. Today the cost of living is much higher, my personal income is reduced to practically nothing and our financial prospects of meeting the 1949 budget through Group contributions is most promising. It seems possible now to set salaries here in line with job-requirements and present day conditions.

Therefore, based on points 1, 2, and 3 may I ask consideration for an annual salary $7500.

I should like to add a few thoughts on the future AA Secretarial Staff department as I now visualize it. In a year or two, one of the three assistant secretaries will naturally show more adaptability and capability for second place on the staff, the position so ably filled by Charlotte L. I would hesitate to predict who this might be and think it will come about automatically. As I view the three secretaries today, each has specialized value to us based on personal and business background plus AA experience of diversified kinds. In my opinion, each secretary should be given an equal opportunity to learn all phases of our work and find her own place with us.[433]

Just two years before, Bobbie was considered by Bill to be an ex-officio member of the Board of Trustees. In 1948, she was listed as the Secretary-Treasurer of Works Publishing, Inc. and also held the title of director.[434] She identified herself as a functioning executive since "the direction and planning of all aspects of work here falls on me." She claimed to have received three recent job offers at a higher salary, with more "opportunity for advancement in a financial way."

Bobbie's salary request of $7,500 likely was an immense figure relative to other staff salaries in 1949. Regular A.A. General Service Conference Reports only started in 1951 (reporting on the financial activity in 1950). Thus, the complete financial information for 1949 remains difficult to ascertain. From a May 5, 1949 Bulletin #4, the 1949 budget figure of $75,000 was clearly visible in the lower left-hand corner.[435] Bobbie was asking for a salary equivalent to a full 10% of the total Headquarters budget for all of 1949, or the equivalent of 15% of the amount budgeted for salaries, $50,000, as documented in 1949 Bulletin #2. With as many as 16-18 other employees, and the associated expenses of running the office, the $7,500 salary request seems quite ambitious. Could the 1949 financial year contributions have started out so well that she thought Headquarters could afford her increase? Bobbie considered the contribution trend "promising," but the contributions actually received according to the May 5 Bulletin—$20,865—represented a rate that would result in a little more than $60,000 by the end of 1949, or a $15,000 shortfall against the budget expenses. Why Bobbie seemed so optimistic about her salary expectations remains unclear. The December 1949 A.A. Bulletin #12, roughly eight months after Bobbie's March personal salary proposal, reported a $20,775 deficit. (Her previous salary, most likely, was printed in previous Trustees' minutes but remains unknown). The raise percentage may have been a big surprise to the Finance Committee! Problems of money, property and prestige do divert people from their primary purpose, to paraphrase Tradition Six. How was her proposal treated? No definite answer has been determined.

Adding to the pressures at Headquarters was an ongoing dispute between Bill and the Trustees regarding the potential for an annual conference. When *Alcoholics Anonymous Comes of Age* was later published in 1957, Bill wrote how this conflict negatively affected Bobbie in 1949: "At the office Bobbie, caught squarely in the middle of this fracas about the Conference, was already exhausted to the cracking point."[436]

Finally, the significance of Bobbie's final paragraph should not be overlooked. While the word "rotation" does not appear in her words, she wrote that each of her three secretaries "has specialized value to us based on personal and business background plus AA experience of diversified kinds. In my opinion, each secretary should be given an equal opportunity to learn all phases of our work and find her own place with us." Bobbie wanted to educate her three secretaries in all the phases of the job, which could only have been accomplished by rotating responsibilities. This fact should be remembered in the future when she becomes accused of hiring only those inferior to her.

The Trip to Montreal, Canada

Montreal, Canada held the 1949 Northeastern Regional A.A. Conference the weekend of Friday, May 20. Bobbie probably was intricately involved in a variety of ways with this event. Esther E. from Dallas, Texas wrote a letter to Bobbie after the conference, "Hope the Montreal Conference came off without a snag."[437] A May 23 article followed in the Montreal newspaper, *The Gazette*, which reported on the event:

> The small group of people who built A.A. from an idea into this world-wide organization of more than 100,000 members were guests of honor at A.A.'s three-day North Eastern Regional Conference which ended in Plateau Hall last night . . . Bill W., anonymous founder of the organization and a former alcoholic, was the guest speaker at a luncheon in the Mount Royal Hotel Saturday and at two meetings in Plateau Hall yesterday. He and his wife, Lois, described the beginnings of A.A., which is founded in a spirit of fellowship, with emphasis on religion as a guiding force in the rehabilitation of the alcoholic.[438]

There is no mention of Bobbie, which was not unusual since the spotlight was almost always on Bill and sometimes Lois. A letter written by her to Lucy P. further documented that Bobbie had traveled to the conference in Montreal.[439] The following Tuesday, May 24, Bill addressed the American Psychiatric Association (APA) in Montreal.[440] There is no evidence that she actually attended this event and heard Bill's presentation, but her dates away from the office suggest she did stay in Montreal to hear him. Was she ever acknowledged by Bill during the trip as a member of his team? In any case, her journey to Montreal was the last she took as an employee of A.A. Headquarters. Could something have taken place, or not taken place, during this trip that impacted Bobbie, such as possibly being ignored or not being considered as she once was during her golden traveling days with Bill that ended in 1944? Or was a subject introduced at the American Psychiatric Association that instigated a cataclysm of emotions within Bobbie that could not be suppressed for long? Could Bobbie have realized that her sober life had been ruled by an addiction? Had her work and long hours taken the place of alcohol? Had she recognized herself as a workaholic?

> According to the *Oxford English Dictionary* (2014), the term *workaholic* first appeared in Canada as a satirical reference in April 5, 1947 edition of *The Toronto Daily Star*; "If you are cursed with an unconquerable craving for work, call Workaholics Synonymous, and a reformed worker will aid you back to happy idleness."

Was this topic of overworking introduced at that May 24, 1949 APA conference that Bobbie attended? If not, might there possibly have been "state-of-the-art" literature at the conference, which Bobbie thought had defined her? She had been warned about over-working even back in the days when she was a secretary at the 24th Street Clubhouse[441] in 1941 and again soon after she succeeded Ruth Hock in 1942.[442]

Bobbie's June 1, 1949 letter to Ebby T., who was staying at High Watch Farm in Kent, Connecticut, held no hint of any upcoming changes in her life. She reported the death of Anne Smith to Ebby,[443] which came as somewhat of a surprise to Bobbie since most of the previous concern had been on Dr. Bob's health.[444] She wrote a letter to Clarence P. dated June 6 to say that his *Grapevine* article was submitted too late to be included in the June issue. Again, she reported the recent death of Dr. Bob's wife, Anne. Then she wrote, "But, isn't it fun and isn't it grand we are able to put so many constructive working hours a day into each 24."[445] The next day A.A. Bulletin #5, regarding the status of the Headquarters secretaries, reported that "Ann is now on vacation, Jinny goes shortly, Lucy follows her and Bobbie will be away most of August."[446] Everything seemed as it should be.

Within a week she quit without notice! She simply got up and left! Her dream diary later revealed the date to be Monday, June 13 at 6:30 pm. She drove herself to Blythewood in Connecticut to be treated by Dr. Tiebout just as rapidly as she could get there.

Bob P.'s Version of Events Regarding Bobbie and Charlotte

"Bob joined A.A. in New York City in 1961, probably never dreaming one day he would be the manager of A.A.'s G.S.O."[447] Bob P.'s story appears in the third and fourth editions of *Alcoholics Anonymous*: "A.A. Taught Him to Handle Sobriety." After he retired as general manager in 1984, he introduced an informal history of the Fellowship titled *Alcoholics Anonymous World History*. Bobbie's name appears in the text twenty-eight times, including a variety of Bobbie's correspondence not included in this book. It contains the only currently known account of Bobbie's exit from her job until now. His writing about her is almost always favorable, but he alleged that Bobbie had been on pills for some time before she returned to drinking while still employed. Then her relapse was exposed and she was discharged. The full text of his allegation follows:

> The appointment of the General Service Committee coincided with (and was perhaps prompted by) the discharge of Bobbie B – and soon afterward, of Charlotte L. as well because of alcoholic slips. According to Nell and Ann M., their relapses were partly caused by the enormous workload combined with confusion of the early office. Nell says, "The four or five movie companies and all the press they had to deal with, and the groups proliferating and the prisons and hospitals starting, and the internationalists, and all – that poor woman (Bobbie) was just overwhelmed. The AA staff worked long hours all week and then sometimes went out to speak or to AA weekends, where they were 'Mrs. AA' and people showered them with affection and admiration.[cli] That ego inflation was hard

---

[cli]   Contrast the assertion of how "people showered them with affection" with the words Bill W. wrote in *The Twelve Steps and Twelve Traditions* regarding the accusations of professionalism pertaining to the alcoholics employed at the Alcoholic Foundation (G.S.O. today). The following appears

to handle when they'd been sober just a few years, as they had in those days. And they were exhausted too." Bobbie and Charlotte were apparently both on pills for some time before they returned to drinking.[448]

The published date of Bob P.'s A.A. history is 1985 or 1986. Thus, his account describes events that took place around 36 years before. Any memories, without written backup, over three decades old may be cloudy and inaccurate even by the best intentioned. How does Bob P.'s summary stand the test of time? Evidence presented here tells a much different story.

The A.A. Bulletin dated November 10, 1948, a full eight months prior to Bobbie's departure, announced that Charlotte had left Headquarters.[449] No hint of any alcohol relapse by Charlotte before she left was mentioned.

Nell Wing and Ann M.[clii] were used as references to justify Bob P.'s assertions, but there are no supporting quotes of Ann M. in the text, so using her as a source should be dismissed. Nell, on the other hand, mentioned the heavy workload on Bobbie and Charlotte, which has been fully narrated beyond doubt. Nell was quoted as saying that Bobbie and Charlotte fell for "ego inflation" from being overly praised while they had been sober "just a few years." Yet, Nell herself was not an alcoholic and a relative newcomer during these times, thus her observations very well may have been inconclusive. At this time, she was a non-alcoholic receptionist relatively new to everything happening around her. At no time, not in her autobiography or in any other known literature, did Nell ever document such behavior by the two secretaries as an eyewitness. By June 1949, Bobbie had nine years of sobriety. Charlotte was believed to have had five years of sobriety when she first started work at Headquarters in 1946, thus, by the time she left in 1948 she would have had around seven years

---

on page 168 in the essay on Tradition 8: "At one period the status of these faithful servants was almost unbearable. They weren't asked to speak at A.A. meetings because they were 'making money out of A.A.' At times they were actually shunned by fellow members. Even the charitably disposed described them as 'a necessary evil.' Committees took full advantage of the attitude to depress their salaries. They could regain some measure of virtue, it was thought, if they worked for A.A. real cheap."

[clii]   Ann L. appears while she was working for Bobbie. Ann L. was her married name according to Bob P. She was to be Ann M. for most of her 35-year career working for A.A.

of sobriety. For the 1940s, nine years and seven years of sobriety were not "just a few years." Very few women of the times could claim that amount of sobriety! The "few years" observation undermines the accuracy of Nell's memory on this issue, however well intentioned.

Furthermore, note how the Bob P. paragraph is constructed. He accused Bobbie and Charlotte as having "alcoholic slips," but Nell's quotes did not directly support those words. Yes, Nell reported Bobbie and Charlotte "being overwhelmed," then suffering "ego inflation" and being "exhausted." All were reasonable remarks. However, Nell's own observations do not document an alcoholic slip as an eyewitness. Ann M.'s name appeared as well, but she wasn't quoted at all.

An Accurate Interpretation of Bobbie's Summer of 1949

There is a very plausible explanation of the events surrounding Charlotte's return and quick departure. Charlotte and her husband returned from Ohio to New York on or about the time Bobbie quit her job. Charlotte apparently had become jobless, and her husband Joe was quitting his job.[450] Though the exact dates aren't available, evidence exists that Charlotte was rehired, at least temporarily, at Headquarters. She appeared to have attempted to fill the gap left by Bobbie's abrupt departure. Charlotte and her husband briefly stayed at Bobbie's Manhattan apartment while Bobbie was at Blythewood.[451] Charlotte had an alcohol relapse either before or during her rehire – the relapse may have taken place while still in Ohio—proven in a letter written by Charlotte to Bobbie sometime in late June or early July when Bobbie was still seeing Dr. Tiebout and staying in Connecticut.

> I can't think of anything more wonderful than a chance to see you, to talk this thing out, to try to think of something that can be salvaged from the muddle. But I can't let you do more than you've already done, Bobbie, and I'll try as never before to start making some sense. Unless I'm actually crazy – and there's a certain amount of evidence that I am, God knows – something ought to take hold if I can just get a period of sobriety behind me.[452]

Thus, the probable sequence of events was as follows: Bobbie quit her job on Monday, June 13, 1949[453] followed by Charlotte's reappearance at

Headquarters. How long Charlotte was present there is not known, but her drinking was soon discovered, justifying Bob P.'s observation that she had slipped. However, all available evidence argues that Bobbie was not "discharged" for a slip. No! She quit! The fact that Charlotte's relapse was so quickly associated with Bobbie's exit led to an understandable misrepresentation of events over time. Thirty-six years later Bob P. incorrectly reported that Bobbie was discharged first and then Charlotte followed.

"Bobbie and Charlotte were apparently both on pills for some time before they returned to drinking," according to Bob P.'s history. Stereotypes typical of the times for females may have also influenced his assertion. As noted by Marty Mann in her 1945 *Grapevine* article "Women Alcoholics Have a Tougher Fight," the stereotype of the times alleged that alcoholic women were more likely to employ sedatives, which Bob P. may have been referencing when he wrote "little white pills." Marty's observations are worth considering:

> Women alcoholics *do* have special problems. To begin
> with, the double standard works overtime for them. Even
> before they become alcoholic they're in a different position
> from men who drink. They are expected to handle it if
> they drink at all . . . And finally, a great many women
> alcoholics learn the last retreat from possible exposure:
> they discover that sedatives are easily hidden, can be taken
> almost unobserved, and leave no smell. And that they
> produce the same effect as quantities of liquor. . . with ten
> times the danger.[454]

No conclusive evidence regarding Bobbie or Charlotte having employed sedatives or "little white pills" has been uncovered. Bob P.'s assertion should be best interpreted as no more than hearsay.

Bobbie's abrupt collapse seems best understood as the result of workaholism – a burn out – the consequence of a life out of balance. She could no longer withstand the compulsive desire to overwork and exhausted herself with self-imposed standards.[cliii] Alcoholics Anonymous for her had

---

[cliii]   "Miserable and unhappy as the breakdown progresses, the workaholic
      shuts down and no longer knows what he would like to do, where she

become all duty, obligation, and compulsion. She had ignored her own personal recovery! She had invested seven and a quarter years into a job that was being functionally eliminated by the upcoming requirement for staff rotation. What kind of "thank you" was that? Feelings of emptiness, thanklessness and puzzlement seemed to be her lot. After a few weeks of near emotional paralysis, she wrote the following to herself at Blythewood on or about June 28, 1949.

> Work in the past has only meant violent action – determination – do the job in spite of anything else – make oneself – discipline in its most self-propelled sense. So thinking of "work" as used by Dr. T. in connection with "silver platter". I must work for what I am to receive – "peace and quiet". Work in this sense is passive – being open – ready and willing to learn – seems to have no action – is passively positive. This new meaning is not connected with job or getting <u>things done</u>.
>
> "Friendship" before was action taken – doing things for others but always action. Now groping for truer meaning – one must be worthy to receive friendship before one can give it – have to be loved for yourself and in turn then can love others not on your own standards but on understanding theirs. (This seems sound but I don't feel it).[455]

Ann L. recalled the reasons for Bobbie's exit on June 27, 1949. Here is a firsthand account writing her version of events to an AA member within the same month they took place – a very credible memory.

> This will acknowledge, belatedly, your letter of June 11 addressed to Bobbie. I know you will be sorry to learn

---

would like to go. Sense of self is lost as the work persona becomes a fuzzy and confused image." *Workaholics, The Respectable Addicts – A Family Survival Guide*, by Barbara Killinger, Ph.D., FIRESIDE, Simon & Shuster Building, Rockefeller Center, 1230 Avenue of the Americas, New York, NY, 10020, ©1991, p. 91. Bobbie shut down – other descriptions are that she "collapsed." For more information about the affliction of workaholism, go to https://workaholics-anonymous.org/.

> that she is a sick gal - nervous exhaustion, the doctor says.
> And he urges a long rest, as well as medical treatment, to
> put her back in the pink. Of course, no one is particularly
> surprised, in view of the fact that she has spent long years
> in the center of an emotional volcano! We all hope and
> pray she'll take the doctor's advice.[456]

This Ann L. is the very same female used in Bob P.'s paragraph that is referred to as Ann M. (Ann must have been married sometime after the cataclysmic events of June, 1949). Had she thought Bobbie had relapsed and as a result discharged, wouldn't Ann have said so? The doctor referenced was Dr. Tiebout, the same doctor that had treated Bill W. and Marty Mann in previous years. Bobbie's letters, the earliest being June 27, 1949, written while voluntarily staying at Blythewood, portray a woman who emotionally and physically had spent the previous couple of weeks stunned in silence.[457]

Bobbie was not immediately "discharged," as Bob P. asserted. Her position was declared "vacated" when the A.A. Board of Trustees met on July 25, 1949; roughly six weeks after her emotional breakdown. The minutes of that meeting reported the following motion:

> It was moved by Mr. S. and seconded by Mr. B. that
> owing to the illness of Mrs. Margaret B. that her office is
> declared vacated and that in appreciation of her valuable
> services she be paid 50% of one year's salary plus medical
> expenses incident to present illness not to exceed $2,000,
> to be effective as of August 1, 1949.[458]

If she had been "discharged" drunk, would the Board of Trustees have declared their "appreciation of her valuable services?"

A Medical Diagnosis and a Hospital Visit

Three days later, on July 28, Bobbie wrote her sister Ruth with concerns about Bobbie's physical health. She had some sort of medical diagnosis that was going to require a short hospitalization. She was 46 years old.

> I'm a little sicker than even I realized and had the unhappy
> news last Monday that I shall not be able to go back to work
> for at least six months – one doubtless compensation is that
> three people are being hired to replace me temporarily and
> do the work I did for too long. I was the goat who woke
> everyone up – fun!
>
> I have not told Pop that I am going into the hospital this
> afternoon for a slight operation. Naturally I'm scared pink
> because of the cancer background of the family. If all goes
> well, I shall be out in two days – this is just exploratory
> and the big job comes up later when my nerves and general
> health are better. Tried to have it done last Tuesday in
> the doctor's office but had myself a case of jitters so bad
> that the doctor stopped and said it had to be done under a
> general anesthetic . . .
>
> As I wrote, Pop knows little of the seriousness of my
> condition. He has enough on his mind and additional
> worry is more than I like to put on him. Anyhow there is
> a 99.44/100 chance that by Sunday I'll know the worst or
> the best.[459]

The results were not the worst, but that would not be learned for some months.

On August 22 Bobbie wrote her Uncle Gene[cliv] a letter concerning the distribution of some of her late mother's possessions. She offered to come to Cincinnati, if necessary, but also that her treatment with Dr. Tiebout had to be her first priority. In this letter her main concern centered on her psychiatric treatment. But did an underlying medical condition contribute to her need for treatment?

> I could run out for a weekend or in the middle of the week
> anytime but I do not want to break into my treatment
> for longer. The two weeks away when the doctor was on

[cliv]   Eugene Stanley "Stubbs" Sears (1882-1950) died on February 7, 1950 soon after Bobbie's January 22 letter (Ancestry.com).

vacation and I was at Waumbek set me back a little.[clv] Wish I simply had a good healthy germ which could be cured by penicillin, then put a *[illegible]* on the whole thing. But a breakdown is an illusive thing. I have plenty of good days which give me confidence to get back into the swing, then low spots some which seem to wipe out all progress. About the only permanent constructive thought I can keep is that one day I'll be in balance again but the "when" no one can say. My leave of absence terminates the first of the year and I am now having to face the fact that even then I shall not be able to work then.[clvi] The office could not go along without help and three people are being trained to do what I did. If they are on the spot and producing in six months, there may not be a place for me even if I am OK. Of course this is just the kind of thinking I'm not supposed to do but you tell me how to turn off my thinking!!! "Tain't" like a water faucet.[460]

According to this letter, not only was she not discharged, but she had also been granted a leave of absence that expired more than six months after her abrupt exit. Her every work-day treatment with Dr. Tiebout, which led to her return to her Manhattan apartment on July 12, only took place because he went on vacation. She continued seeing the psychiatrist for an unknown period. No decision had been determined regarding her future, but these letters seem to prove beyond any doubt that the door had not been slammed shut behind her by the Alcoholic Foundation because of her abrupt exit.

Bobbie provided a summarization of her medical bills during 1949 in another letter to Uncle Gene dated January 22, 1950. Here she seemed resigned to the idea that her days of working in a high-pressure job were over forever.

[clv]   Mount Waumbek, New Hampshire is roughly 360 miles north of Bobbie's apartment at 40 Fifth Avenue in New York City.

[clvi]   No Alcoholic Foundation document has been found to confirm that she was granted a six-month leave of absence. However, Ann L. wrote letters that corroborate Bobbie's statements.

I was able to list around $2508.97 in provable medical bills over what my Blue Cross plan took care of for early in that year I had used up my limit on the Plan. Incidentally that "trip" I wrote about in November was my last (I hope) hospital jaunt. While all that intensive treatment was going on I said nothing, even the children and Pop knew, or now know, much of it.[clvii] Now that the prognosis is better than good, there is no reason to say much but 1949 was one helluva year for me. I'm told the future looks bright for me as far as my health is concerned with only spaced check-ups. It is wonderful what science has done in so many serious diseases.

So far, I have no time set when I can get out and work again and I shall probably never be able to do a demanding job like I did before . . . Our Christmas was nice tho *[sic]*, of necessity quiet. I was so laid up with my back that one of my friends had to come in and cook our turkey.[461]

Did she have any kind of "serious disease," as her words may indicate? For what was she treated? There is no answer. In any case, her physical health concerns, as stated in her July 28 letter to Ruth, seemed at least temporarily resolved by November 1949. There is no specific description of what medical difficulties led her into the hospital. If any diagnosis of her condition is discovered, it might explain her final choice, but for now it has been lost from our view.

Bill's Recollections of Bobbie's Collapse

Bill was to reference Bobbie's collapse (without actually mentioning her name), when he wrote the *Twelve Concepts for World Service*, adopted by the 12th Annual General Service Conference on April 26, 1962 – roughly thirteen years after Bobbie left her job. The following are selected sentences from Concept XI, "rotation among paid staff workers," explaining why

---

[clvii]   Possibly this should read "even the children and Pop knew, or now know, not much of it."

rotation was introduced at Headquarters for staff members as well as a salary policy for staff members based on time served:

> But the basis for compensating all staff members is identical. The increases are based on time served.

> In the business world, such an arrangement would be unworkable. It would practically guarantee indifference and mediocrity, because the usual money and prestige incentives would be lacking. In our entire operating situation, this is the sole major departure from the structure of corporate business. Consequently there should be proved and compelling reasons for such a corporate heresy, and there are.

> One primary reason for the adoption of rotation and equal staff pay was the security and continuity of the office. We once had the conventional system of one highly paid staff member with assistants at much lower pay. Hers had been the principal voice in hiring them. Quite unconsciously, I'm certain, she engaged people who she felt would not be competitive with her. Meanwhile she kept a tight rein on all the important business of the place. A prodigy of wonderful work was done. But suddenly she collapsed, and shortly afterwards one of her assistants did the same. We were left with only one partly trained assistant who knew anything whatever about the total operation.

> Luckily a good A.A. friend of mine, a fine organizer, pitched in and helped to put the office in order. We saw that we had to install a paid staff that simply couldn't break down. Next time there might be no one around to give the necessary amount of time for its reorganization. Besides this breakdown had cost us much confidence out in the field—so much so that we must have lost $50,000 in three years of group contributions.[462]

Obviously, Bobbie was the "one highly paid staff member." But by 1962, could it be possible that Bill thought most A.A.s wouldn't recognize the "staff member" as Bobbie? No longer did he refer to her as National Secretary. Did Bill think he could write principles here without the personality of Bobbie being remembered by the Fellowship?

Bill then engaged in a kind of recollection that can prove unreliable when compared to written records. Not only was his memory vague in this matter, but it could also be considered judgmental, or worse. He asserted that Bobbie "had been the principal voice in hiring them [her subordinates]. Quite unconsciously, I'm certain, she engaged people who she felt would not be competitive with her." How could Bill be certain of this statement more than a dozen years after Bobbie's exit? His attendance at Headquarters was infrequent at best. It's highly doubtful he could have remembered most of the names of those who worked for Bobbie, much less have judged their competency. Charlotte had been extremely valuable to Bobbie and often she couldn't praise Charlotte enough.[463] Bill himself had praised Charlotte previously in 1947.[464] Bobbie spoke highly of Ann L., as becoming ready to be a regular correspondent. Virginia (Jinny) and Lucy were relatively new hires. In Bobbie's salary recommendations she described how she intended to rotate and train her staff so that they could effectively adjust staffing when someone was absent or resigned. To Bobbie her three employees had the potential, if not the experience. Bill's words seem uncharacteristically harsh and inaccurate.

Bill continued, "Meanwhile she kept a tight rein on all the important business of the place. A prodigy of wonderful work was done. But suddenly she collapsed, and shortly afterwards one of her assistants did the same. We were left with only one partly trained assistant who knew anything whatever about the total operation."

Bobbie did keep a tight rein on events for which she considered herself responsible. Yet, once again, Bobbie had trusted Charlotte implicitly. No tight reign was required with her. Charlotte was assigned area contacts that were her exclusive responsibility, which can be encountered routinely from mid-1946 until October 1948.[clviii] Then Bill referenced that Bobbie "suddenly collapsed." Note that he did not say "relapsed!" He did not say discharged! Bill followed with the assertion that "shortly afterwards one

---

[clviii]   No one to date has studied Charlotte's letters, which might approach a couple of thousand.

of her assistants did the same [collapsed]." That assistant was Charlotte, though the date of her final exit remains unclear. But even after Charlotte's return from Ohio and undeniable relapse, three assistants were left: Ann, Lucy, and Jinny. Bill remembered only one.

The August 3, 1949 A.A. Bulletin #7 included the names of Bobbie's three assistants in the reorganization announcement that followed her departure. Ann and Lucy reported to Senior General Secretary Marian M. who was "in direct charge of all public relations dealing with press, radio, films, doctors, members of the clergy etc." Virginia (Jinny), along with a new hire Polly, worked for a second Senior General Secretary Ruth B., who was responsible for maintaining contact with all A.A. groups nationally and internationally.[465] Ruth and her two assistants were mentioned in a September bulletin signed by Polly.[466] (She used her first and last name, ignoring the policy of anonymity in A.A. bulletins announced the previous year). Bill had claimed that we "were left with only one partly trained assistant who knew anything whatever about the total operation." Note that Bill omitted the addition of the two supervisory secretaries in the reorganization, both senior to Bobbie's assistants, who were acknowledged at the July 25, 1949 Trustees meeting. Thus, six people took the responsibilities formerly of the four when Bobbie was still in charge.

Nevertheless, the loss of both Bobbie and Charlotte was a big hit to Headquarters. They inarguably represented the vast majority of Headquarters' experience communicating with A.A. members throughout the world.

Bill's Harshest Accusation of All

Whatever was said before, the harshest accusation of all which appears in Bill's Concept XI writing, was the allegation that Bobbie's "breakdown had cost us much confidence out in the field—so much so that we must have lost $50,000 in three years of group contributions."[467] The significance of this accusation should not be overlooked – it's the only dollar figure in the entire *Twelve Concepts for World Services*. What evidence remains that her collapse "cost us much confidence out in the field?"

1948 was a good year financially for A.A. Headquarters: roughly $7,000 was added to the cash balance on hand by year end[468] and contributions were just above $66,000.

The financial records accessed regarding 1949 are not straightforward. They have been pieced together. The 1949 A.A. Bulletin #2 put the annual budget of $75,000 on page 1 and $76,050 on page 2.[469] The $75,000 budget amount is used on subsequent A.A. bulletins. An April 1950 Bulletin #4 reported that there was a $17,000 loss for 1949,[470] which suggests that contributions for 1949 were $58,000—down significantly from 1948. Could Bobbie be held responsible for this reduction in contributions? This loss was for a single year and not three, and Bobbie was absent for only a little more than the second half of that year.

The 1949 A.A. Bulletin #4 dated June 7th, 1949 listed contributions for the first five months as just under $25,000 which would have resulted in an annual amount of around $60,000, or down $6,000 from the previous year. This bulletin was likely the last Bobbie helped create. The rate of contributions did not drop for the balance of 1949 after Bobbie's exit – they remained consistent. Any immediate financial impact of Bobbie's departure is not revealed in the contribution figures.

Contributions for 1950 were $76,536, 1951 were $97,586,[471] and for 1952 were $106,195.[472] Though 1950 contributions were around 30% above those of 1949, there still was a $20,000 overall deficit for the year. Very likely the A.A. International Convention in Cleveland greatly increased expenses. The two-year deficit is therefore estimated to have been $37,000. The Alcoholic Foundation covered the 1950 loss by transferring $20,000 of Alcoholic Foundation funds (money collected from sales of the Big Book), to Headquarters funds, which were kept on the books separately. The 1951 contributions were up 27%, which made for a break-even year. The 1952 contributions were up 9%, but expenses actually dropped by $5,000 which allowed for a $13,000 increase in cash on hand.

Somehow Bill W. attributed a $50,000 contribution shortage over a three-year period to Bobbie's collapse. Which three years? 1949-1951? 1950-1952? He did not specify. If the years 1949-1951 were chosen, contributions went up from $58,000 to $97,586 or 68%. If the higher 1948 contribution figure ($66,000) was used in place of the 1949 amount, contributions were still up 47% over the four years. If the 1950-1952 numbers were used, contributions went up 38% over the three years. How did Bill W. attribute a $50,000 shortfall and "loss of confidence" to Bobbie's collapse? At the least, Bill's accusation is highly questionable. "Problems of money, property and prestige divert us from our primary purpose," as Tradition Six concludes. How unfortunate Bill included a specific dollar amount associated with Bobbie's departure from Headquarters in the *Twelve Concepts for World Services*. Bill, after all, mainly dealt with principles, but often relied upon his recollections, which were not always accurate— especially when it came to amounts. His tendency to exaggerate numbers or dollars has become practically a part of A.A. legend. As a concepts man, with his only footnoted work being *Alcoholics Anonymous Comes of Age*, his interest lay in the parable and not in the detail.

If at any time Bill's belief that she cost A.A. $50,000 ever reached Bobbie after her collapse, news of such an accusation likely would have been positively devastating. There is no evidence Bill made such an observation prior to him writing the Concepts in the early 1960's.

In any case, rotating staff positions at Headquarters has helped Alcoholics Anonymous consistently practice principles over personalities. One must consider that this wisdom was implemented in a thankless manner when it applied to Bobbie – and then was prone to misinterpretation as the years went by and memories faded. Could this episode be among the reasons her name and contributions have been all but forgotten?

Regardless, Bobbie's days as National Secretary were over. She would never return. Whatever flame had burned so brightly in her role as National Secretary was never to shine again. Curiously, a 10-line typed poem was included with Bobbie's personal papers, with the date of June 10, 1949 stamped on it — the Friday before she quit. The author is unknown. Despite her painful, abrupt departure from the Alcoholic Foundation, despite the opportunity to express bitterness or resentment about how her role was to be eliminated, in the years that followed, there is hardly any record of a negative message about anyone in the Fellowship except Bobbie herself! What she may have decided not to write, even in her private correspondence, may be among her most under-appreciated contributions to the future of Alcoholics Anonymous. Her final words she kept for herself as National Secretary were those contained in this little anonymous poem.

> If you see a tall fellow ahead of a crowd,
> A leader of men marching fearless and proud,
> And you know of a tale whose more telling aloud
> Would mean that his head must in anguish be bound,
> It's a pretty good plan to forget it.

If you know of a thing that will darken the joy
Of a man or a woman, a girl or a boy;
That will wipe out a smile, or the least way annoy
Or cause any gladness or brightness to cloy –
It's a pretty good plan to forget it.

- 246 -

Ironically, had she decided to speak negatively about Bill or Alcoholics Anonymous, she might be more well-known to A.A. members today.

Secret Preparations

pon quitting her job, she abruptly left her Fifth Avenue apartment in Manhattan and sought refuge at Blythewood in Stamford, Connecticut. Dr. Harry Tiebout had been medical director at Blythewood since 1935[473] and she was desperate to meet with him. He had treated both Marty Mann and Bill W. Bobbie may have had some interactions with "Dr. T." previously, though to what degree remains unclear. She was soon to report that though the doctor was no longer on the premises of Blythewood; he was located conveniently nearby in Greenwich, Connecticut so she could drive back and forth to his office. The doctor scheduled meetings for her once a working day for about four weeks.[clix] Blythewood served as a convenient hotel for her where her meals were prepared and where she felt safe and secure. She could come and go as she pleased.[474]

The day after she so abruptly left her job, A.A. Headquarters General Manager Hank G. wrote Bobbie a letter of gratitude. The letter provides ample evidence that Bobbie was not dismissed. Hank only had the best wishes for her. There was no hint of any alcoholic slip. The decision to quit her job was hers and hers alone!

> I couldn't leave my office tonight without squeezing in a few minutes for just a brief note. My hat is off to you – your decision took real guts, if I may put it bluntly. Your good friends are all with you to the limit. To illustrate, Mr. Harrison told me today he would like to come visit

---

[clix]   Bobbie's diary of dreams began while she was a patient of Dr. Tiebout. According to the diary, she left A.A. Headquarters on June 13, 1949 and she immediately went to Blythewood. Her first day home was July 12, 1949.

you. By all means, do permit him – he wants to so much. Lois, Thalia,[clx] Bill and I are going to the Events[clxi] this week end. Perhaps Thursday or Friday I might be able to visit with you a bit. Frankly I find it hard to write – your friendship has meant so much to me, and I want to help more than you realize. Believe me, Bobbie, if I repeat and repeat, get it off your chest to some one – this life should be and can be so happy and good. You deserve the best. May you have the serenity to accept the things you cannot change, courage to change the things you can, and the wisdom to know the difference.[475]

Bobbie's First Post-Resignation Letter

Bobbie wrote her first post-resignation letter on June 27 from Stamford, Connecticut to the Chairman of the A.A. Board of Trustees Leonard Harrison, who was mentioned in Hank G.'s letter of June 14. She wished to make amends for her quick exit.

Dear Mr. Harrison:

I believe you know I have wanted to write you for several weeks even before I came to Blythewood but it was an impossibility. I just couldn't. Today on this borrowed typewriter I seem to have found a medium through which I can express myself a little.

I'm sorry I left the office so abruptly and caused so many friends unhappiness and so much additional work. That sentence comes from my heart but is so inadequate. I cannot find the words to write that I feel.

No one could be more grateful than I to be here with Dr. Tiebout. I had hoped, and often prayed, to hang on until August and a vacation. But that would have been

---

[clx] Thalia remains an unknown person at this time.

[clxi] While the "Events" aren't known, June 14 was very close to A.A.'s 14th anniversary.

only a temporary solution to something which has been fundamentally wrong with me for years, probably long before I found AA. The compulsive, frantic activity which I misnamed "necessity" turned me into a machine which could not stop until it broke down in every way. No one ever made me, or even asked me to work as I did. I just couldn't help it and didn't know why. Out of this chaos will come something better than I have ever known and perhaps some day I can be truly useful, maybe for the first time in my life.

This is a poor excuse for what I want to say. The old, now meaningless, words are gone and it is too soon to expect a replacement. Thank you for understanding.[476]

Her description of her "compulsive, frantic activity" unmistakably represented part of her emotional disturbance. The evidence of workaholism was present even if she had never heard of the word. She "just couldn't help it and didn't know why." In addition, her tendency for self-condemnation is also exhibited when she stated that she had not been "truly useful" in the past. The huge contribution she had made to the success of Alcoholics Anonymous seemed to have vanished from her memory, leaving only a void. At least there seemed to be some vague optimism that "out of this chaos will come something better . . . " She seems to have disregarded just how much her letters and her presence meant to so many. Her lack of maintaining her own recovery face-to-face while National Secretary would, sadly, prove to have lethal consequences.

She repeated her self-condemnation in calling herself "dumb" when she wrote a letter to Tom B. of Ohio a few days later on July 1:

No one could be more grateful than I to be here and under Dr. Tiebout's care. The decision to come was one of the hardest I have ever made for I have never learned, I guess, how to give in. My job here is that and so much else – I need so desperately to be taught how to live quietly and to do everything without self-propelled determination, without a machine-like discipline. I look back and wonder how I could have been so dumb for others have told me those truths (you too) many times. I guess I was like the alky – everyone could see where he was headed except he himself.[477]

Then she went on to explain how she was benefitting from her time with Dr. Tiebout:

Dr. Tiebout is giving me deep analysis. God knows I've probably been headed for this from the time I was born and actively so for the past few years. I have my good days and the horrible ones. Analysis is no joke. Today is on the good side but it is only the second I've had in weeks. Fortunately I'm luckier than some. I have my car here, can go and come as I please. Dr. Tiebout is no longer connected with Blythewood but I came here instead of going another place or an Inn because it is fairly close to his office. Later when I get more rested I may go to the Pickwick Arms, a very good hotel in Greenwich. It seemed best for me to get out of all familiar surroundings completely and so far I have no desire to go home or back to anything. Have been to New York twice but only when I had to. The club is nearby and when I feel like it I go there to "sun". Not up to swimming yet but that will come.[478]

Odds and Ends

On July 6 she wrote some notes to herself titled "Odds and Ends Jotted Down or Thought From 7/1 to 7/6." These notes began with the following paragraphs:

One can't really be hurt from without – only from within – peace with oneself is the shield (ego word?). No shield needed if one is at peace. I have used "shields" against everything for too long – they in some form or another have been "my defenses" (defenses should not be necessary).

When I came to Dr. T. "in control" meant being able to face or take anything with synthetic props (probably ego-propelled). Sunday thought of being "in control" in opposite sense. "Control probably one of those words like "power, aggressiveness, must, devious, insidious" feel uncomfortable when I use them now. Beginning to get a glimmer that when I thought I was "in control before" I was really "out of control."

Drinking releases EGO completely. Want to learn why I drank recently – why I feel so little remorse – why I feel it unimportant (is this not facing it?) Should it matter more than it seems to now? If I am willing to tell all, is that enough?[479]

In her own words, Bobbie provided conclusive evidence that she did drink again, though not when or where or why or how much. As a matter of fact, she "wanted to learn why [she] drank recently." Thus, Bobbie inadvertently provided one more validation of the paragraph in *Alcoholics Anonymous* that deals with such matters (for the purpose of emphasis, "he" has been changed to "she"):

Once in a while she may tell the truth. And the truth, strange to say, is usually that she has no more idea why she took that first drink than you have. Some drinkers have excuses with which they are satisfied part of the time. But in their hearts they really do not know why they do it. Once this malady has a real hold, they are a baffled lot. There is the obsession that somehow, someday, they will beat the game. But they often suspect they are down for the count.[480]

Bobbie is an example that a slip after nine years of sobriety makes the slipper as baffled as someone who never stopped drinking but wanted to stop. She then made the following observation:

I have been the "iron woman" to people for so long, they all seem to expect the impossible now and I can't explain. I don't mind what they think but hate to disappoint them. Just can't help those panic reactions or can I in some other way? HOW? Tom B.'s letter brought this on and it was so evident at Bill and Lois', also with Hank and Burr.[481]

This final sentence suggests that sometime during Bobbie's stay at Blythewood she visited the home of Bill and Lois, less than twenty miles away. She also would have visited the home of General Manager Hank G. and his wife Burr, but she may have not been able to admit that she drank again since she could not "explain" her compulsion. She didn't want to disappoint them. If she didn't tell the truth to these people and the Fellowship she so deeply respected, she risked suffering the consequences of being "as sick as our secrets."

Bobbie and the Beginning of the Dream Diary

She returned to her Manhattan apartment on July 12. The first entry in her typed dream diary was written on July 13.[clxii] She never acknowledged if Dr. Tiebout suggested she keep such a diary, so it is possible she got the idea elsewhere. She would continue the diary for the next three and a half years. Her first recorded dream involved a visit to Headquarters, though the layout of the office wasn't as she remembered it.

> Passed into what I expected would be bookkeeping office
> but instead saw Mr. Chipman sitting at a very large desk.
> Tried to tell him how sorry I was I could not work but he
> smiled and did not answer.[482]

Interestingly enough, she wrote A. Leroy Chipman a letter of amends the very next day on July 14, 1949.

> Among my friends, you are one of whom I have thought
> many times. My sudden break from the office brought
> you much added work and responsibility. For this, I am
> sorrier than words can express and had I been capable
> of avoiding what happened, I would have. My complete
> collapse in every way was inevitable for I was trying to
> hold on by force, determination and will-power instead

[clxii]   Fortunately, she typed the Dream Diary. Her handwriting is mostly unreadable.

of living usefully with the fundamental beliefs given me through my association in AA. . . . I should like you to know that whether or not I return to our office, all of you may count on me to pass on to others whatever I learned while there which might be useful.[483]

On July 15, she wrote some entries that were possibly related to a visit with Dr. Tiebout. The good doctor had written about the alcoholic ego for years. Bobbie wrote these questions regarding her ego, which was often not her friend.

Does it ever die? Isn't it a real permanent part of everyone? – Is it ever killed off or just controlled into impotency?

How do some escape without having to crack-up in one way or another? – Does hereditary background and/or environment guide which way ego is to develop? – How did people like my mother-in-law, husband, brother-in-law and you[clxiii] escape being ego driven?

Do suicides kill themselves to destroy the ego?

If Dr. Tiebout answered any of these questions for Bobbie, she either forgot to write them down or the answers were lost.

Worldwide Praise for Bobbie

News of Bobbie's departure took some time to reach the Fellowship. The first out-of-state letter known to have been sent to Bobbie regarding her departure is dated June 28, 1949. The news was received with disbelief and loss – almost as if the spirits of the Fellowship had been somehow diminished. Letters eventually came from all over the world including New Zealand, India, Ireland, Australia and Argentina. These written tributes may have been as warm-hearted as for any A.A. still living. Many A.A.s loved their Bobbie, despite having never met her.

New Zealand, July 13, 1949:

[clxiii]   "You" meant Dr. Tiebout.

I have just had a letter from New York saying that you are off on extended leave. You have been overdoing it I expect and I want you to know that you will be in my prayers more than usual until I hear that you are back to your usual form.[484]

Australia, July 23, 1949:

I can realize that you and Charlotte and others in the office work under terrific mental strain. Frankly I couldn't do it, so to offset that there must be a happy medium . . . Remember one thing if we could ever be of any help do not hesitate to say so.[485]

India, July 28, 1949:

Your letter has been of very vital significance to me. It brought me words of a deep and yet practical piece of philosophy . . . How many times have I found muttering the very words you have said to me and what a solace and help they have been . . . Do write and tell me you are well and happy.[486]

Ireland, August 9, 1949:

I am sincerely grateful to you for all the kindnesses you showed both to me and to the struggling Dublin group. That we are no longer struggling is in very great part due to your help and encouragement and to your letters of advice.[487]

Australia, August 19, 1949:

It is with the deepest regret that I learned today, per 1949 A.A. Bulletin #7, that you are retiring on the grounds of ill health – You have worked so hard for others & have neglected yourself. The work you have done for AA's in the States & abroad will go on now – AA's remembering always with the deepest gratitude how much they owe you.

I myself owe everything to your encouragement, advice, & help. In the early days of AA Australia when we were so petulant & irritable, your kindliness & sympathy made us go on. When at first everything seemed to be so hopeless. When we did get on our feet & became arrogant, and when soon split asunder. Your wisdom steered our sinking tossed ship to a haven of rest once again.

I cannot express adequately my own feelings of gratitude to you. In the autumn of 1944 I did not know myself how desperate I was. Threatened with the loss of everything I valued. Now when I have regained everything and more I feel most humble.[488]

Springfield, Massachusetts, July 27, 1949:

When I first came into AA nearly five years ago, the cognomen[clxiv] "Bobbie" was then a by-word for AA lore. The then old-timers spoke almost reverently about her and to me she grew to be the epitome of AA's magnificence – almost a myth of the ultimate in AA ... Those of us who have had some contact with her appreciate more keenly and deeply the countless sacrifices she has donated in our stead – we also understand that her love for AA has paved her every thought and action with inspiration and encouragement for the sick alcoholic.[489]

Lincoln Park, Michigan, August 10, 1949:

Bobbie, these few lines is an indication of how true AA's are thinking every place and at this very moment. We feel so close though few of us have had the pleasure of meeting you. You have our love, our devotion, and our blessings. We will be with you always, right to the very end – May God spare and keep you.[490]

Detroit Michigan, August 11, 1949:

I am deeply moved at learning of your resignation as our national secretary . . . All old-timers should feel as I do, that you have played a most important role in AA, for you came in when we were comparatively small, and you had to meet the load of rapid expansion and guide us through it. I am appalled at the mere thought of how you weathered the storm . . . I have these letters always nearby and reread them many times during my last year of illness.[491]

Warwick, Rhode Island, August 12, 1949:

[clxiv] Cognomen - an extra personal name given to an ancient Roman citizen, functioning rather like a nickname and typically passed down from father to son.

At best words are but futile things, but I want to add my small tribute to those of hundreds of others. May a very fine and gracious lady have many years of happiness and peace in return for the joy and help she has given to her fellow men.[492]

Port Crane, New York, August 11, 1949:

I know that time after time reading your letters and talking with you has kept me sober. I've gone over and over your words and gained peace from your understanding and patience . . . You also have shown us that rules are silly and the desire to follow God's will is the only important step.[493]

Lexington, Kentucky, August 12, 1949:

I think you have left the office in pretty good shape and in pretty good hands. I just can't imagine, though, how much it will be without you steering things. Glad I'm not there, I'd miss you too much.[494]

Evanston, Illinois, August 15, 1949:

I feel privileged to have been one of those so closely associated with you in the days back when. We have both seen the growth in the group, which has at times appeared incredible. This, of course, has been much more noticeable to you because of your broader experience with AA all over the world. I should like to point out in this connection, that I for one feel that the contribution which you have made, and which has had so much bearing on the growth of the group and on the healthy state in which it now exists, can hardly be measured. I should also like to take the opportunity to express to you my most sincere appreciation for the incalculable assistance you have been, not only to many of us as individuals, but to AA as a whole. These contributions can be neither minimized nor forgotten.[495]

Detroit, Michigan, August 26, 1949:

Through all these critical and formulative years of Alcoholics Anonymous, no other single guiding heart and hand has contributed more to our welfare and progress than yours. From all this, too, you must have drawn an inner reward beyond measure. But I think, best of all, Our Father in Heaven must be smiling down on a little girl who took up the torch when the need was desperate and followed a guidance greater than her own. And, as just one of the many, I want you to know how grateful I am.[496]

San Francisco, California, September 7, 1949:

Of course, the main office will never seem the same to me, with you away. You will be greatly missed I know. But that job was a man killer & no wonder you need a good rest . . . And if you decide a trip to California would help, we'd certainly roll out a red carpet & get a brass band.[497]

Evanston, Illinois, October 5, 1949:

Take it easy my dear and always remember you have a place in the hearts of many that no one else can ever fill – I hope the future brings the peace and happiness we all desire and the courage to face the rough spots because we have something to live by that is priceless.[498]

Australia, December 17, 1949:

No one appreciates what you have done more than me in the Antipodes[clxv] do. You guided us through a very critical period, when at times we gave way to black despair. As one A.A. in Australia put it: "A.A. must have Divine guidance, otherwise how could it have survived what we tried to do with it." But thanks be to God. A.A. in Australia is now a very alive & well established movement. We survived the passage through the ultra enthusiastic stage when we wanted to repair everyone. By the grace of God we refused all financial offers & are now content to walk in poverty. Organization of a sort has become necessary because the movement is now nation wide with branches in many towns and all the States. But the means opportunities are not yet on land &

[clxv] "In geography, the antipode of any spot on Earth is the point on Earth's surface diametrically opposite to it. A pair of points antipodal to each other are situated such that a straight line connecting the two would pass through Earth's center. Antipodal points are as far away from each other as possible." Dr. M. considered New York to be the furthest point possible on the planet. (Wikipedia)

> we are content to wait until the Lord provides the means. Many
> of us have now been sober for three years or more and we have
> developed the serenity and peace of mind to cope with problems,
> that are inseparable from A.A. The problems no longer worry us;
> relapses by prominent A.A.s we accept with serenity; criticism
> often of a harsh kind leaves us unmoved. The solid nucleus of A.A.
> is here in Australia & with God's help, it will stay.[499]

Despite all these heartfelt words of praise and appreciation, Bobbie seemed incapable of warming up enough to recognize the written love being sent to her from all over the world. Other than Dr. Tiebout, no record has been found of any person in the Fellowship that functioned as a spiritual advisor or sponsor for the rest of her life. Bill W. was the only person known to have functioned somewhat like a sponsor, but those days were long past. Upon further examination, never in any of Bobbie's letters throughout the years, personal or professional, did she write about any kind of experience with personal sponsorship. There's no evidence of her actually doing a fourth step or fifth step, or for that matter, any other step besides the first one, the ninth, the eleventh, and the twelfth. While Bobbie provided so much backup for Bill, neither one of them authored wisdom on sponsoring individuals during these years.[clxvi] Her twelfth step activities were almost entirely associated with her work, but the rewards of a spiritual awakening never seemed to materialize. At a minimum, any remaining serenity seemed to vanish the moment alcohol once again touched her lips.

Most of the envelopes of the letters Bobbie received, which otherwise would have allowed us to track Bobbie's addresses after she left her job, have been lost. During the balance of 1949, she is mentioned as being in Connecticut and New Hampshire. How much time she spent at her Manhattan apartment at 40 Fifth Avenue is not clear, nor do we know how she filled her days while there. If she was going to A.A. meetings in this period, there's no evidence to prove it. Her daughters may have been

---

[clxvi] Bobbie wrote the following on January 11, 1947: "We do not have any material available on sponsorship here. However, both the Akron and Cleveland Ohio groups put out such pamphlets. If you will write them I am sure you could get copies." Bobbie to Ed of Sacramento, California, G.S.O., Box 35, R17, File V, p. 121.

staying with her during some of these times particularly before they got married – one in 1950 and the second in 1952.

Bobbie Wants To Set Things Right

Soon after her return to her apartment on Fifth Avenue, she wished to set things right with the office from which she had so abruptly departed. On July 14, 1949, she wrote the General Manager Hank G. who had written her words of support the day after she quit. She wrote with an idea for a new role for herself.

> When I phoned you yesterday about discussing certain things with you and Bill, I felt sure I was finally on the right track in trying to put together some of the pieces of the jigsaw puzzle which was my life as associated with the office. 24 hours and much thinking has made me surer that what I have in mind is right. But I would like your help, and Bill's if he feels up to it . . . I don't know whether it would be best to see you and Bill separately or together – you two decide that.[500]

What were the certain things she wished to discuss? Did she meet with these two men either together or separately? No one knows.

There was no mention of any meeting with Hank G. or Bill when she decided to draft a letter to the Alcoholic Foundation Trustee Leonard Harrison. He had written her good tidings in his own handwriting after her resignation in an undated personal letter. He wished her to "be ready to enjoy a new life. I sincerely hope you can in some way come to feel the genuinely warm good wishes that constantly flow out to you from your many admirers."[501] For reasons unexplained, Bobbie's papers include three previous type-written drafts of her response to him, which suggests it carried a great significance to Bobbie. Not only that, but the final draft also dated July 24 was presented to Mr. Harrison only after it received the approval of Dr. Tiebout. Here is the letter in full:

> Thank you for your letter which was forwarded to me after I left Blythewood. I had heard of your trouble with an infected foot and hope by now it is completely healed

and you can look forward to a restful and happy vacation in August.

Please believe in spite of contradictory actions I have always wanted above all else to do what is best for AA and our office. On this premise only, I should like to offer some temporary assistance if it will be useful.

My experience in the office should be available unless it is assumed it was worth nothing. It is not mine to keep but belongs to AA and were it possible to pass it along without the knowledge of anyone, I should be more content. Matters are coming up daily which must now be acted upon without the background necessary to make the difference between a good and the best solutions. Ann L———, if you agree, can play a part in the transferring of my experience on to others. She is loyal, trustworthy and has capabilities which few know as I do. Perhaps her unawareness of these is one of her greatest assets. If given the opportunity she could be used for the good of AA as a whole.

And, more specifically, perhaps I can help from behind the scenes writing some of the letters which I am told Charlotte has been doing but will be unable to continue doing much longer. If it will help bridge the change over, may I help in the following way; that such letters as given me to answer be signed by someone else, probably Ann L———. It is evident that such a plan could only be carried out if my part in it were known only to you and Ann. I could rough out letters which Ann could transmit quickly to the Autograph machine and edit in her own way if changes are indicated.

Dr. Tiebout will need be consulted as to whether he feels I should attempt this so, if you receive this letter it will be with his approval.[502]

The July 14 letter to Hank G. and this July 24 letter could not be more different. Bobbie first proposed a meeting with Hank G. and Bill to discuss a possible new arrangement for her. In the second letter, Bobbie proposed an arrangement between Leonard Harrison, Ann L., and herself wherein she would secretly assist Ann without the knowledge of the two men. Why were these letters so different? Hank and Bill had to have had already made firm commitments regarding how Headquarters would be staffed. This personnel plan was to be presented for the Trustees' approval the day after Bobbie's second letter. No contingency plan for Bobbie's return was recorded, so it is probable that Bobbie's suggestions were rejected.

Bobbie's astonishing sentence that her "experience in the office should be available unless it is assumed it was worth nothing" suggests a great deal of pain and hurt feelings if not bewilderment. She went on to say her experience at A.A. Headquarters "is not mine to keep but belongs to AA and were it possible to pass it along without the knowledge of anyone, I should be more content." That is a statement of principles before personalities. The fact that "her experience at A.A. Headquarters" did become all but forgotten by the vast majority of Alcoholics Anonymous adds a sad twist of irony.

The Trustees meeting held the next day on July 25, most likely before Mr. Harrison received Bobbie's letter, declared Bobbie's office position vacated and a new office arrangement. Leonard Harrison eventually responded to Bobbie's letter on August 18 in his own handwriting, for confidentiality, after he returned from his vacation indicating it was okay to contact Ann L.[503] However, there is no documented evidence that anything else resulted from Bobbie's letter.

Bobbie Writes Amends to Bill and Lois

On September 16, Bobbie thought it best to write an amends letter to Bill. She also included Lois:

> Last week, your message to me which Ann phoned Charlotte, and Charlotte told me was so indirect that all I could gleam from it was that you are still feeling badly. I am sorry, more than I can tell you and so wish you might find your way out of your darkness. I think of you often

and pray for you much. It is so much easier to pray for others than for one's own self.

Have you ever been able to understand how much I wish I could have avoided the pain caused you and Lois? It is beginning to come to me that these things cannot be explained in words but are only felt thru understanding. Because of my illness and the so little I now know of it, a small bit of the suffering you have gone thru is clearer to me. How I wish that there was something I could do to help but any such help, from the outside, only warms me temporarily and the answer to the "quiet" I long for only seems to come from way down deep within.

My regrets are many but they no longer haunt me nor can I feel any blame in the old sense; this and so many other feelings have been given me by our great and kind Dr. T. What a wonderful human being he is.

About eight years ago you opened the door to 30 Vesey Street and in so doing you gave me what might have been a useful life. Along the way, I took a detour and lost myself. I hope one day I can earn the right to do something so you will feel your faith in me was not completely misplaced.

Love to you and Lois.

Affectionately,

Bobbie[504]

One wonders: what was the "quiet" Bobbie longed for that seemed beyond her grasp? Were accusatory voices ringing in her ears? Was she lamenting the loss of her youth, when she appeared adorable, the center of attention dancing on stage? Back then she seemed to have a delightful future. While she stated she had many regrets, very little evidence has been discovered about what she thought those regrets were. While she left such things as a ninety-nine page dream diary behind, she left no record of taking a personal inventory or recording any conversations where she shared secrets with a sponsor or spiritual confidant. Except for Dr. Tiebout, it appears she rarely sought out anyone to soften painful memories or reduce fears that could decrease her anxiety.

Bill's Two 1949 Letters to Bobbie

Bill received Bobbie's amends letter and replied on September 27 with the words of a kind and caring gentleman with deep compassion for his former recovery partner. He thanked her for persevering in the past when he was all but immobilized by his mood swings, for which she always tried to protect him in her letters to the Fellowship.

> I have read and reread your note of ten days ago. Somehow it caused me to relive the really happy moments of those eight years gone by. This, I think, thanks to the news between your lines that your own illness is melting away. I'm specially grateful for the lift, these many weeks I have been too submerged to care much about going on again.
>
> You said you felt sorry you had caused Lois and me disturbance – so far as I'm concerned, that will always be quite the other way around. I cannot doubt that my own obstinate (yes, downright willful) illness hung like a millstone about your neck.
>
> But, like you, I hope I've come to the place of real regret and have departed the valley of remorse where no life is to be found; where I could breathe nothing but great clouds of my own perverse and inverted pride. God knows how long I've been learning too that self condemnation leads so subtly, but O so surely – to the condemnation of others. I often wish the word "blame" could be taken out of my feeling and speech forever. Greater responsibility, less blame. Then all would be quieter.
>
> I notice you put quotes around that word "quiet." That's just what I've been trying to do lately. Those familiar

sayings, "Be still and know that I am God" and "Lead Kindly Light" are becoming meaningful.

I suspect you are under the spell of slander as portrayed by Vincent Sheen *[sic]*.[clxvii] So am I. Though all that is far from where I am, it's great vista would draw me on. It must be so with all who read the book.

Yet I must tell you I cannot take the problems of the "AA old timers" too grimly for I think they have a constructive purpose. What, in our self pity, we call "disillusionment" with ourselves and others is really meant to be, I believe, naught but the beginning of a perfectly healthy deflation down to our own right size. When that has really happened we can't be overly disturbed by what we see in others. So long as we condemn, we haven't got down to size.

The Divine Paradox on this subject seems to be: The more we shrink the taller we grow. To believe this is real comfort; God is just, not all is shrinkage, Bobbie dear.

As you guess, I've greatly withdrawn from my usual rounds. Do not think I mean to retreat forever; it has been a venture in quietude I felt I must make or else. After a bit, I feel I shall be enabled to step back into the path of my more active obligations, whatever they prove to be. May God grant that I may willingly and gladly do so.

Typically, this message has said a lot about me though I trust you may also find here something about you – something truly helpful.

You know Bobbie, I have always looked up to you, your "illnesses" not withstanding. As a person of marvelous

---

[clxvii] Vincent Sheean wrote *Lead, Kindly, Light* published in 1949, a biography of Mahatma Gandhi who had been assassinated on January 30, 1948. Presumably Bill's reference to slander was in regards to Gandhi, who was often vehemently misrepresented and accused throughout his life.

inner integrity – something far more basic than I ever had. I want you to know how much I appreciate this great gift of yours; how you went all out to share it with me. Though I've learned not to expect too much of myself, you must know the high value I shall always set on your inspiration. Despite all your vicissitudes I know you still have that priceless quality. Hold fast to that assurance if you do. God will see you through.

One time (soon I hope) I would like to catch up with you on the path of progress.

Affectionately

Bill[505]

He focused on a key element of Bobbie's trauma—self-condemnation. Bobbie called herself "dumb" in the past. Her negative self-image may have dated all the way back to her dancing days when she may have visualized herself as too short to be a ballerina. Her psychological testing put her IQ in a class of relatively rare intelligence, so calling herself "dumb" was nonsense. Bill praised her very significant contributions to Alcoholics Anonymous and to himself. Nevertheless, she found her life empty and her virtues and talents without merit. Sober or not, alcoholics are not the only people on earth that make up stories about themselves and then fall for them, but some alcoholics may simply have more programming than most in making themselves miserable.

Bobbie received an unexpected gift from the Board of Trustees. They had previously awarded her $2,000 for medical expenses knowing that she had been at Blythewood and was likely to require additional treatment elsewhere. As a result of the October 24, 1949 Quarterly A.A. Trustees meeting, they awarded her an additional $3,750 as an outright gift.[506] The amount represented half of the requested annual salary amount she made the previous March. Once again, had Bobbie been discharged drunk, would the A.A. Trustees have gone out of their way to honor her in such a manner during a year when contributions had fallen, as Bill would assert years later, because of her departure?

Bill W., more than any single individual, knew of the accomplishments Bobbie had made during her seven and a quarter years as National Secretary. On December 20, 1949, he wrote a truly gracious letter to her. It clearly outlines how appreciative he was of her devotion to him personally as well as the superb dedication she devoted to the fellowship of Alcoholics Anonymous. There is no blame for anything; only praise.

> Christmas makes me want to say some things. Not new things, just old ones you mustn't ever forget.
>
> I want you to remember, since I am the only one who can have any real idea what your labor for AA meant to its infancy, just how much I appreciate and love you for that. And, though recent storms may have left you feeling unstrung and unfit, please always believe that you possess, down deep, the integrity and resource to meet any weather. That is a quality in you which has always inspired me – and still does. I am sure you are destined for a greater and happier usefulness than any you have ever known. Oh, Maggie dear, please believe that of yourself it can come so true. Then there is your capacity for devotion of which Lois and I and so many have been the continuous receivers for years, though in my case your unswerving loyalty was so often undeserved. It is deeply appreciated just the same.
>
> Also believe that pain can be, and usually is, the price and touchstone of progress.[clxviii] But I know it's hard to cling to <u>that</u> fact when suffering is intense and you feel done.
>
> God knows, that awful blackness which will not melt is bad enough but I am beginning to see that a bitterness which cannot yield must be worst of all. And, believe me, I now understand what must have been your feelings as you helplessly had to watch me stuck in the murk. If only neurosis could be more enjoyable.

[clxviii] The first person pronoun was omitted, which matches what Bill wrote.

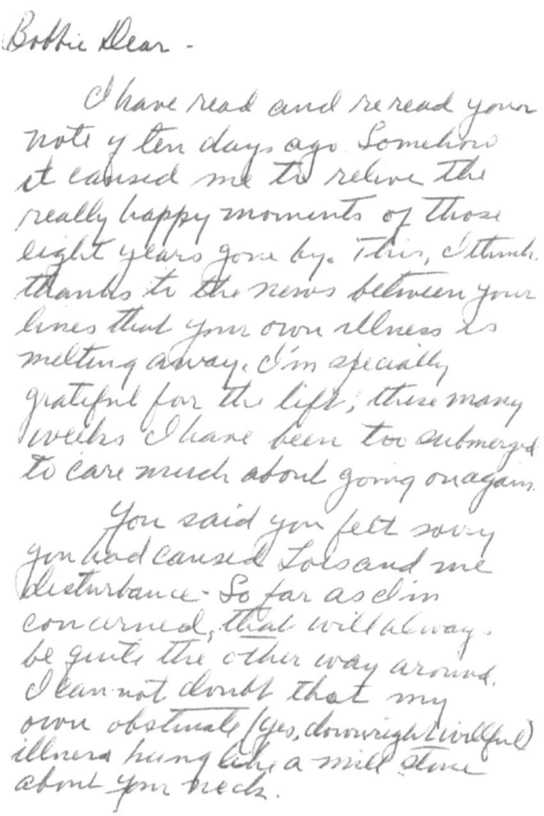

Bobbie Dear -

I have read and re read your note of ten days ago. Somehow it caused me to relive the really happy moments of those eight years gone by. This, I think, thanks to the news between your lines that your own illness is melting away. I'm specially grateful for the lift; these many weeks I have been too submerged to care much about going on again.

You said you felt sorry you had caused Lois and me disturbance - So far as I'm concerned, that will always be quite the other way around. I can not doubt that my own obstinate (yes, downright willful) illness hung like a mill stone about your neck.

FIGURE 23 - PAGE 1 OF BILL'S LETTER TO BOBBIE, SEPTEMBER 27, 1949

Now that my own transit down the Styx[clxix] seems to have passed me thru its last miserable cavern, I find myself unable to regret the experience, except as it affected others. Somehow I feel that great good might come out of it. If value can come out of alcoholism, then why not out of compulsive bitterness or depression? I am sure that it can, and so I want you to have the same surety. You say you know all these things. Of course you do. But when one is sick one forgets. At least I did. And I can remember how you used to remind me!

---

clxix In Greek mythology, Styx is a deity and a river that forms the boundary between Earth and the Underworld. (Wikipedia)

So we stand by, confident of your return to health, and to us. Come to Bedford Hills the moment you feel able.

Lois joins me in great affection.

Bill[507]

Bobbie's Mood Remains Dark

These warm-hearted messages from Bill, along with so many others expressing encouragement and thanks from the Fellowship to Bobbie, did not seem to illuminate the dark mood that continued to plague her. She sent out Christmas cards in 1949 to those who had written her earlier in the year, but the effort appeared simply obligatory. After the New Year celebrations, the ability to accurately track her activities diminishes since only a few letters exist that cover the next two years. We have little idea how Bobbie occupied her time or if she participated in Alcoholics Anonymous. The only letter known to have been written by Bobbie in 1950 is a rather dry inquiry to Dr. Leonard Strong involving personal financial matters.[508]

Bobbie was looking for work by May of 1950, according to the following reference letter Bill wrote for her on May 7.

To Whom It May Concern:

I highly recommend Margaret R. B—— to any who might think of engaging her. I have known Mrs. B—— for ten years, eight of which she was my principal assistant in the work of The Alcoholic Foundation of New York with which I have long been associated as a trustee. During these eight years, Mrs. B—— acted as executive secretary to the Foundation and very capably managed its busy office. Here she was charged with the immediate conduct of our public relations which required much contact with press and radio – sometimes pictures. She looked after the layout, printing and wholesale distribution of a large book and pamphlet literature. She directed our dozen employees well indeed, and she understands both office routine and accounting. I can add that Mrs. B—— is a person deservedly noted for her discretion, loyalty and unusual capacity for sustained work.

She was obliged to leave the Foundation a year ago because of her health which I believe is now quite restored. I shall be happy to supply further information, should that be desired.[509]

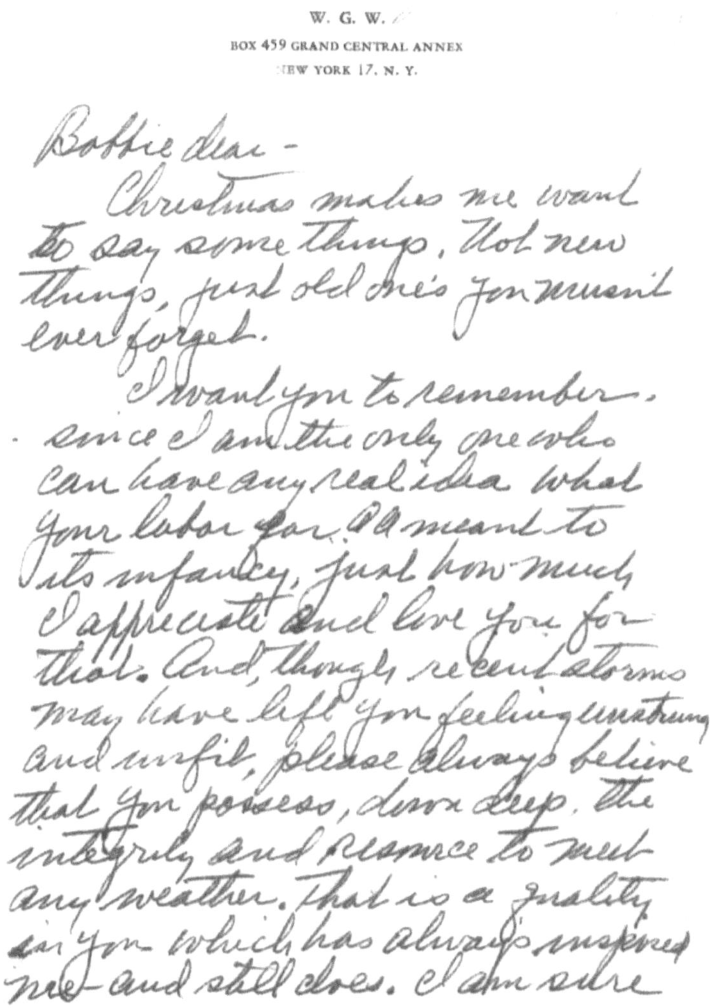

W. G. W.

BOX 459 GRAND CENTRAL ANNEX

NEW YORK 17, N. Y.

FIGURE 24 - PAGE 1 OF BILL'S DECEMBER 20, 1949 LETTER TO BOBBIE

Bobbie assisted in the production of the 1950 Hallmark[clxx] movie *One Too Many* produced by Kroger Babb in Hollywood. It's possible that Bill's letter helped land her the job of "Technical Advisor" along with a doctor for this film. The two had their names appear prominently right after the stars and costars were introduced.[clxxi] Her technical advice had to have involved alcoholism and Alcoholics

FIGURE 25 - *ONE TOO MANY* MOVIE CREDIT AS TECHNICAL ADVISOR

Anonymous. The movie featured a female concert pianist who denied her alcoholism until she ended up in a strait jacket in a psycho ward. The main character does get sober. As a current day review wrote, "It would be easy to dismiss this movie as dated, preachy and painfully ironic. It's no *Lost Weekend.*"[510]

By this time Bobbie adopted a new spelling of her nickname to be "Bobbe." The reasoning behind this change is not known. Here is how her name appeared in the credits of *One Too Many*.

[clxx]   Should not be confused with the Hallmark Hall of Fame or Hallmark Greeting Cards. The Hallmark name was chosen by Kroger Babb in 1945 to represent his production company.

[clxxi]   Her name and the doctor's appear at the 1 minute and 5 second mark of the film.

Bobbie's Visit to Akron, Ohio

Bobbie remained close enough to Alcoholics Anonymous to learn of Dr. Bob's death who died on November 16, 1950. She made the trip to Akron to attend his memorial service. Not all that surprisingly, she was accompanied by her long-time friend Dick S. Hers was the fourth signature on the first page of the 29-page guest book with his signature immediately following.

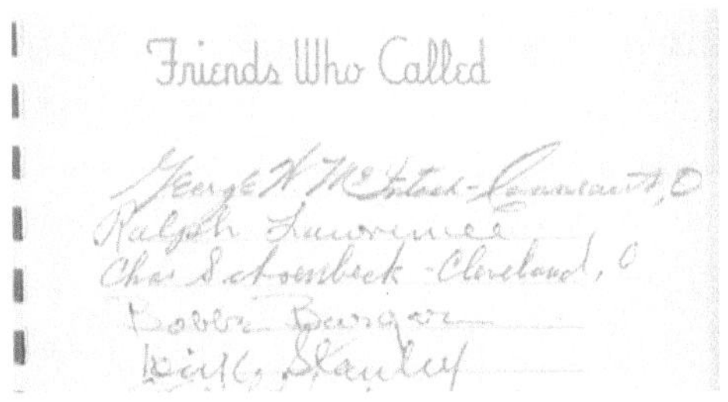

FIGURE 26 – "BOBBE'S" SIGNATURE ON DR. BOB'S MEMORIAL GUESTBOOK

Bill's Hand-written 1950 Christmas Letter

Bill's 1950 hand-written Christmas letter to Bobbie dated December 21 was short and directly to the point.

Bobbie Dear,

Never has there been a Christmas where old friends were such a cause for gratitude. And to none do I owe more than you those days we were together, when we helped fashion the shape of things to come, are set down in my book of the never-to-be forgotten. My endless thanks to you, dear Bobbie.

Should 1951 bring any cloud, may it soon be dispelled. And may I help you to do that. For now Merry Christmas dear partner.[511]

Bobbie's Dream Diary Main Themes

The subjects she reported dreaming about took on a certain repetitive nature, which by no means should be considered surprising. Some of her dreams were filled with romantic male figures of her past. Two names appeared fairly often from her first trips to Europe before she was married: Julio and Manalo. She dreamt her bedroom adventures with Julio were prone to have been interrupted by her mother. Donald Sawyer appeared on occasion in a professional capacity. She had multiple dreams of her deceased first husband, Norman, including a dream that she was remarrying him. Surprisingly, her second husband Shep appeared in a more favorable manner than might be expected. Dr. Tiebout occasionally made some sort of appearance or recommendation. Both parents were included from time to time. She remembered some big fights she had with her father. The male who appeared most often through her dream diary, though, was Bill W. Her feelings for him were undeniably strong. Sometimes her fondness for him was revealed, though he was never portrayed as being romantic with her. Other times she dreamt he pronounced very unfavorable judgments of her.

Bobbie's entries are marked by increasing anxiety. As more entries are made in the diary the more anxiety appears. Dark dreams dominated her nights: the kidnapping or deaths of her daughters, forced hospitalizations, executions, atomic bombs, false accusations, threats of violence from unknown or unseen sources, deaths of various people in bizarre circumstances, consequences for her drinking alcohol such as loss of memory or ending up in jail—all were among the diary entries. The fearsome subjects appeared in increasing frequency as time went by. She left nothing behind that gave any clue regarding any therapy or professional treatment she received after her visits to Dr. Tiebout, who appeared in her dreams, nor is any pattern of drinking revealed that she may have followed or how long her periods of sobriety may have been. She attended A.A. meetings on occasion while in California.[512] While early in the 1940s she mentioned the 24th Street Clubhouse on many occasions, her letters and notes examined never mentioned the popular 405 West 41st Clubhouse, which became the Manhattan Group's meeting place in 1944. She simply may have been too ashamed of her return to drinking to show her face at an A.A. meeting in New York.

Bobbie had men pursuing her upon entering Alcoholics Anonymous back in March 1940, which lasted around two years. However, upon becoming National Secretary, there is no record left of her dating anybody for very long. One conclusion can be reached from these dreams about men: they either involved Bill or someone who preceded him. With one exception[clxxii], there were no personal dreams of any male she met after she became Bill's trusted secretary. While she did have one dream in which Kroger's common-law wife Mildred Horn accused Bobbie of having an affair with him, the dream quickly went off to other subjects.

Lois Wilson appeared in the dreams on occasion, but usually with her husband. Charlotte L. often appeared with her husband Joe. Both of Bobbie's daughters were frequently included, sometimes in bizarre ways. A variety of former female office employees at A.A. Headquarters made their appearances suggesting that relationships among them were not always pleasant. Overall, other women were not the focus of most of her dreams.

Actions by Panel 1 of the General Service Conference

The first General Service Conference of Alcoholics Anonymous met in the spring of 1951. Among the actions taken at the conference resulted in this May 7, 1951 letter to Bobbie from Dr. Leonard Strong, Chairman of the A.A. Foundation.

> The initial meeting of the General Service Conference, so long in preparation, has come and gone. You would have been cheered by the high caliber of delegates and their grasp of the problems of the central office and of the Alcoholic Foundation. I am sure had this occurred during your tenure many problems would have seemed less pressing, as there is promise of a smoother future.
>
> As representatives of a cross section of Alcoholics Anonymous, they wished the Trustees of the Alcoholic Foundation to acknowledge their cognizance of their debt to you and to express their deep gratitude for your sage counsel, guidance and advice over your long years of service.

[clxxii] Kroger Babb, her boss in Hollywood in 1950 for the movie *One Too Many*.

On instruction of the Alcoholic Foundation and for Alcoholics Anonymous I convey to you their thanks and best wishes and add the assurances of my own pleasure at being so designated.[513]

The first General Service Conference wished to thank Bobbie for her service and voted unanimously for the Alcoholic Foundation to write this letter to her.[514] Unfortunately, very little of her 1951 correspondence is known to have survived, so there is no way to determine her reaction to this kind and well-deserved gesture.

Bobbie's Gun Removed by her Daughter

Bobbie was drinking sometime during the summer/fall 1951. Her son-in-law George wrote her a letter dated October 16 that documented, beyond all reasonable doubt, that she had been drinking in the presence of Gloria some months previously. To George, drinking was one thing – handling a gun while drinking was something else. George, in a very gentle but firm manner, wrote her on behalf of himself and his wife.

> In this matter of the gun however, I seemed to have stepped into the middle of something, more or less unwittingly, and now that I'm here, I will stay . . . I fully agree with Gloria's decision to remove it from the apartment last summer. As a matter of fact I have the gun now . . . You are so interested in your children's welfare that no sacrifice is too great for them; yet you persist in actions which are of no conceivable advantage to yourself and which cause your family untold hardship. Now don't get me wrong. I am not referring to your drinking or to any manifestation directly associated with it. The difficulty lies in those areas outside of the drinking problem . . . I understand that on two occasions you removed the gun from the desk drawer while you were drinking. Now it is dangerous enough to handle a wicked little automatic like this when you are sober; it is foolishness ten times compounded when you are drunk.[515]

Bobbie wrote a response to George dated October 21 which did not directly address her drinking. Most of the letter dealt with the terms involving the return of the gun to her safety deposit box.[clxxiii] She did admit one thing: "I'm ashamed to admit that [my affairs] are not in the most orderly state right now."[516] But then she made what remains the closest self-analysis she left behind:

> I would like to be a different person; I would like to be all
> that everyone expects of me. But this form of conceit, and
> I should know as I've tried unsuccessfully to practice it for
> almost fifty years, developed in me a conflict between two
> warring forces which never learned to live with or accept
> each other. If I had known years ago what I know today,
> much of the tragedy in my life could have been avoided.
> One of my major problems is to learn this now, which is
> not easy and cannot be done by just wishing it were so.
> I'm probably the only one who believes in my ultimate
> recovery – how could it be otherwise?[517]

No one knows how many people knew of Bobbie's drinking or its severity. We have no idea to what degree she was participating in Alcoholics Anonymous or any of her vacation locations. Regardless, help was still available to her through Bill and others had she asked for it. Possibly a geographical cure was visualized by Bobbie to help her regain her sobriety and self-esteem when she made at least two trips to Hollywood.

Some clues about her might be found using her own letters, written to others when she was National Secretary, regarding alcoholics who relapsed.

> I think we can all learn all there is to know about AA with
> or without slips. I once talked to a member who had her
> first slip after more than four years in AA. She explained it
> in one sentence that ran something like this. "I am entirely
> to blame, I let myself get too far away from the principles
> by which I want to live, there's no excuse for the slip and
> no one but myself is to blame". This girl threw herself into

---

[clxxiii] No evidence has been found to indicate that the gun was never returned to Bobbie.

AA immediately after her trouble and is one of our most valuable members.[518]

Yet, Bobbie hardly "threw herself into AA" after she left her job because A.A. for her had simply become a job. She acted as if isolated and powerless over her alcoholism. Further, there's this she wrote regarding herself and the potential for a slip back in March 1947:

> Personally I'm inclined to agree with you about slips. I know that if I ever drink again it will be deliberate. Actually the word slip was started in the early days. Why this word was chosen, I'm not sure. Again it doesn't seem too important which word we use – the important thing is the meaning we apply to it. I doubt that any member in AA very long believes a slip is an accident about which we can do nothing.[519]

These words come to mind that are occasionally heard in A.A. meetings today: "If one is left alone with a problem, this actually represents a conscious choice and is not an accident." Then there can be this wise observation regarding the shame left behind by a relapse: "There is no shame in asking for help. The real shame is not asking for help." Bobbie apparently had forgotten about the astute observations she had made over the years. However, she did not have access to the thousands of letters she had written for A.A. as National Secretary, nor did she have any desire to return to Headquarters to read any copies of them. If she had done so, she might have read some of her wisest words of all written when she had been National Secretary for only seven months: "Of course we never forget we are alcoholics and that we can slip back into the old way of thinking if we get careless."[520]

Bobbie Heads to Hollywood Once More

On February 13, 1952, Bill wrote this message to a Californian to assist Bobbie in finding work in or around Hollywood. The letter provides a glowing summary of the years Bobbie spent working for Alcoholics Anonymous.

Dear Chet,

I continue to have enjoyable recollections of our all-too-brief visits with each other. May good fortune bring us together more.

What I have to say this time is about Bobbie B. You don't know her, but you ought to. For Alcoholics Anonymous will never record the deeds of a more devoted servant to our cause than hers in our pioneering time. For several years in the fearsome time of A.A.'s adolescence, she was my principal associate at the Foundation Office. Few will ever comprehend what she did to make Alcoholics Anonymous what it is today in unity and in numbers. Two or three years ago, her health gave away under the strain.

I think I told you about my conflict with the Board of Trustees. She was caught badly in that wringer through no fault of her own. They didn't hire enough help for the office, and the assignment got too tough for anyone to manage. Belatedly, many of them, and many others, are realizing how much we are in her debt.

It so happens that she is now in Los Angeles. Knowing public relations as she does, being experienced in the dramatic arts, Hal Wallis has employed her as technical advisor on his movie version of the highly successful stage play, "Come Back, Little Sheba". Hal pretty much knows her worth as Bobbie and I once cooperated with him on another movie project that in the end fell through. Anyway, she's in your town.

So, I am bound to ask you this special favor. Will you see her? We are concerned about her future – that she be happily employed in what she would like to do – and can do. Maybe you have some connections or suggestions that could be of benefit. If so, Chet, you shall have my timeless thanks. And in any case, my gratitude for making her acquaintance.

Well understanding the vast activity that your life is, I shall not often ask anything of this sort. But this time, I'm presenting you with one of my finest friends, a most unusual person, and an opportunity to help and please me more than I can say.

Devotedly yours,

Bill[521]

Bill's letter may have had immediate results, but the timing as reported in her next letter may have been a coincidence. Bobbie wrote Helen B. of A.A. Headquarters on March 16 and relayed her experiences as an assistant to Hal Wallis in the production of the movie *Come Back, Little Sheba*. Burt Lancaster played the part of Doc Delaney, who struggles with alcoholism and causes severe trauma for his wife, played by Shirley Booth, because of his severe relapse after celebrating one year sober. Shirley Booth won a Best Actress Oscar and a Golden Globe for her role.[522] A three-minute scene of an A.A. meeting takes place near the beginning of the movie, for which Bobbie functioned as an advisor. Her words provided ample evidence that Bobbie, who had no desire to return to Headquarters, continued to maintain a friendly relationship with some of the employees who worked at the Foundation.[clxxiv] Excerpts from the letter follow:

> It was only natural that the meeting scene which runs about 3 minutes at the present stage be patterned after a meeting held here in this vicinity. I recognized the set immediately as being a miniature replica of the North Hollywood Group "club". This scene starts with a close-up of the "God grant me"[clxxv] prayer which if left as is will be

---

clxxiv   Helen B. was in contact with Bobbie as far back as March of 1946, when they exchanged letters. Helen was the secretary for the Boston Central Office. (*But, For the Grace of God.* Wally P., p. 58)

clxxv   The Serenity Prayer.

read completely by all who see the picture.[clxxvi] The camera pulls back from this shot, showing some of the members entering an already half filled meeting. Next is a shot of the leader opening the meeting (page 14 of the shooting script). Then the presentation of the "cakes" to those who are having "birthdays".[clxxvii] I can see where this may cause a yowl to some eastern and Midwestern groups but it is good A.A. as practiced here. Don't quote me, but from the membership figures in the current *Grapevine*, one might conclude that the Southern California Groups "have something". I happen to know from the sobriety angle that the No. Hollywood Groups have a very high record. Also from the picture viewpoint some "action" was needed to keep this scene from being just documentary and dull. The last shot shows "Doc" reading the 12 Steps in their entirety from the book, Alcoholics Anonymous (a "still" picture of this and other meeting scenes are being sent you for your records or any use to which you care to put them – exception being, they may not be reproduced in any manner. I explained they need not worry on this as it would be contrary to our Traditions to publicize the picture in any way). The meeting scene fades out with the reading of the last step. Here I shout "hurrah". I was apprehensive that perhaps someone would want to have a speaker give a "pitch" as they call it here . . . I like the way this meeting was handled and I hope all AAs will, too, when they view it.[523]

One can only wonder what Bobbie thought after she actually saw the movie, which she may have done in a theater back in New York. The scene featuring Burt's character reading the Twelve Steps out of the Big Book was cut. Her name does not appear anywhere on the credits, which might have been a second source of disappointment. One wonders if she was included in her temporary role as an advisor to Hal Wallis only as a

---

[clxxvi] The prayer is seen for about 12 seconds (9:56-10:08) in the movie.

[clxxvii] Four Cakes were lit by the meeting chair: one with four candles, one with three, two, and one. Burt Lancaster's character received the cake with one.

favor to Bill. Besides the brief period of advice regarding the accuracy of the three-minute scene of the A.A. meeting, she probably had nothing else productive to do:

> Actually my working hours on this motion picture have been few but most of my 8:30 AM to 7:00 PM hours have been spent at the studio. This picture is not primarily about Alcoholics Anonymous as you know – the AA part is incidental to the main theme of the story – but, for my money, this is as it should be. And I guess you all know that altho I'm working for Hal Wallis my heart is working overtime to see that our AA is "done right by"[524].

Her second letter dated March 16 takes on added significance because these two March letters are among the last that were found among her private papers. Regardless of a previous return to drinking, she reported to Bill that she was actively participating in A.A. at this time so she may have been sober for a while.

> Dear, dear Bill,
>
> I've just finished a letter to Helen B. giving her and all who are interested a bird's eye view of AA in COME BACK LITTLE SHEBA. I'm also sending her some "stills" from the meeting scene. One, I believe, you will like. It shows the main character, "Doc" (played by Burt Lancaster) holding the book, Alcoholics Anonymous, and reading the 12 Steps from it. If it shows up as well on the screen, everyone who sees the picture will see the title for some seconds. Please read my letter to Helen so I will not have to include that news in a letter to you. There's much other news to give you, some typewritten and some between the lines.
>
> Thank you for introducing me to Chet and Lorraine. How I've enjoyed the time spent with them. I called Chet on my first day here, then bumped into him that nite at the 6300 Club (is that a thriving spot!). My first Saturday I

> dined with them in their lovely home which I left, after
> hours of the best chatter, carrying a beautiful red camellia
> Chet stooped down and picked out of his garden on our
> way to my car. Last Tuesday, I attended his home meeting
> for beginners which he was leading and had the honor
> of reading the 12 Steps. Seriously, it meant a great deal
> to me – think it is the first time in all my good (and bad)
> years in AA that I've read them out loud. And, I liked it.
> I've been to five meetings since coming out here and wish
> I could have squeezed in more.[525]

Bobbie may have been on the other side of the country, but she was also aware that Bill was writing a book, which turned out to be *The Twelve Steps and Twelve Traditions*.

> I've only touched a small segment of AA in our big family
> but I'm sure hoping you are writing away at that book. The
> misconceptions and tales on early AA and pre-AA are
> fantastic. Picked up a honey of a one Dr. Bob, Catholicism
> and the 12 Steps. Will tell it to you – it is too long to write.
> I gave up trying to straighten this one out. The man who
> told it "knew for certain". It seems that time is the only
> teacher who can convince us <u>not to be so sure about which
> we are absolutely certain</u>. Like in everything, I'm learning
> that slowly and in the hard way . . . Love to you and Lois
> and, <u>keep writing that book</u>.[526]

Some very significant words written in this previous paragraph deserve repetition: "It seems that time is the only teacher who can convince us not to be so sure about which we are absolutely certain." The absence of a sponsor for Bobbie comes to mind, for there are techniques that can be used in Alcoholics Anonymous besides waiting for time to pass. Many an alcoholic has a story to tell upon entry into the program. Typically, only some of that story can be shared in a general way from the podium or during discussions with a group. As life happens, more can be revealed and self-understanding can change. The only way a current inventory can typically be fully shared is through a one-on-one, face-to-face encounter with a sponsor or a trusted personal resource of some kind. There remains no evidence that Bobbie ever had an intimate spiritual confidant besides Bill, and that had been years ago. Thus, Bobbie became certain about a story about herself and there was no one to talk her out of it. The consequences were tragic.

Very little else seemed to result from her trip to California. Once upon a time she had dreams of being an actress, but those days were long gone, too.

Sybil's Wedding

On June 28, 1952, Sybil married Robert Edwards. Bobbie had to have been significantly involved in helping arrange for both weddings and she had two years before for Gloria's ceremony. The wedding registry of the event includes the names of Bill and Dr. Tiebout and his wife. While Lois and Bill gave a wedding gift to Sybil, Lois' name does not appear on the wedding registry. Bobbie had to have returned from California for this second wedding as she had been in Hollywood.

Bobbie wrote the following to her daughter Gloria and her son-in-law George on February 12, 1953 regarding their third wedding anniversary upcoming in four months. The couple had been previously blessed with a daughter, Lauren, born the previous August. Bobbie's first grandchild was going to have a marked influence on her thinking about the future.

> Darlings –
>
> The enclosed is my June 16th remembrance for you. I had a hunch you would enjoy J.B.'s Body and can see no reason to wait for the proper date in June to get my gift for you. I do hope you'll enjoy it and I'll be glad to baby-sit at 22 Leewood that nite if I may.
>
> Love,
>
> Mommie[527]

Bobbie had written her last letter.

12

Quiet Achieved

Bobbie died by suicide on February 17, 1953. She was just 49 years old. The event was planned for some time and was no accident. Her occupation, according to her death certificate was "housewife,"[528] the role she never wanted. Not only had she found being a housewife unfulfilling, she hadn't been one since her divorce from Shep in 1937. Was it a coincidence that Bobbie's true love, her first husband Norman, had died twenty-four years before almost to the day?[529] Did she wish to rejoin her first husband, who had been so cruelly separated from her by pneumonia after less than four years of marriage?

Bobbie's son-in-law George, who was still alive as 2022 commenced, recalled how he found Bobbie's body at her apartment. He explained this event to two of his daughters in May of 2019.

> Basically, Gloria hadn't heard from her mom for a couple of days, and she wasn't answering her phone. So George went to her apt building. He had a key, but the doorman let him into her apt at 40 Fifth Avenue. George found her lying on her bed. He thinks she had died the night before. He found an empty bottle of sleeping pills. George's dad (Albert S.) was "desperate that no one know that she committed suicide so the obituary reflected that she died from natural causes."[clxxviii]

[clxxviii] The death certificate, signed by the medical examiner, read "I further certify from the investigation and (examination) that, in my opinion, death occurred on the date and hour stated above, and the causes of death were chronic cardio vascular disease."

> Official cause of death was chronic cardiovascular
> disease, but this was because George's dad (Albert S.)
> was insistent no one know that she committed suicide, so
> that her reputation would not be tarnished.[530]

Thus, family shame resulted from the suicide, which led to the desire for their reputations not to be "tarnished" by her final decision as well. But what was her reputation? Who was around Bobbie much in those last years of her life besides her two daughters and their husbands? Was she attending A.A. meetings in New York after her return from Hollywood? Had she continued drinking after Gloria had taken her gun away in mid-1951? When was her last drink? So many questions can be asked of which these are but a sample. Answers remain hard to come by, which may not be all that unusual for those left behind because of suicide.

If there ever was a close female friend or sponsor, that person, or people, remains a mystery. One likely candidate would have been Charlotte, but after her dismissal from A.A. Headquarters, she soon fell out of sight.[531] The only true close confidant known to influence Bobbie throughout her days as National Secretary was one person and one person only: Bill W. The memories of Bobbie's grandchildren were that both of Bobbie's daughters insisted that Bobbie was in love with Bill. Yet, as a married man and icon of Alcoholics Anonymous, he was obviously never a realistic match. Besides, Bill was probably idolized similarly by many women due to his charismatic personality and leadership capabilities. Though they appeared to be very close until 1944 when they stopped traveling together, the distance between them seemed to increase until Bobbie's collapse in 1949 removed the office as a place where they could see each other. Though Bill remained supportive, as his 1949 and 1950 letters to her prove, they rarely encountered each other after her departure. Bill and Lois were invited to Sybil's wedding on June 28, 1952, but only Bill signed the wedding register. Bobbie's visits to the home of Bill and Lois appear to have been exceedingly rare unlike Nell Wing[clxxix], who at times seemed to visit so often she practically lived there.

[clxxix] "So, during her decades of A.A. service, she was a regular weekend guest at Stepping Stones, Bill and Lois W.'s residence in Bedford Hills, New York—sometimes in a working capacity with Bill, but more often as a friend and surrogate daughter." Hunter, Jones, and Ziegler. *Women Pioneers in 12 Step Recovery*. Hazelden Foundation. ©1999, p. 91.

Then there was the poem found by Bobbie's body. George said he found this poem at her bedside when he discovered her: *The Hound of Heaven* by Francis Thompson (1859 to 1907), a 182 line poem.[532]

J.R.R. Tolkein said of the Francis Thompson poem that it was "one of the most profound expressions of mature spiritual experience" and declared that it had a profound influence on his own writing. In 1912, in one of the first major studies of the poem, John Francis O'Conor wrote this: "The name is strange, but when one reads the poem this strangeness disappears. The meaning is understood." In a eulogy after Thompson's death written by G. K. Chesterton, he simply concluded, "He was a great poet."[533] Richard Burton recorded this "haunting poem" using all the gifts of his voice.[534] What symbolism was she trying to leave behind by being found with this poem? Read the poem and come to your own conclusions.[clxxx]

Was suicide the only way Bobbie could achieve the "quiet" that seemed so elusive? As C. S. Lewis was to write some years later, "No noise is so emphatic as one you are trying not to listen to."[535] Did her loss of sobriety contribute to her hopelessness and eventual demise? When had been her last A.A. meeting? Was her choice to keep alcohol in her apartment after she got sober originally part of her undoing? When was her last conversation with anyone that could have functioned as a sponsor which might have influenced her to make a different choice? It's easy enough to pose the questions, but the answers remain out of reach.

A note was found by her side – a very short one. It seemed to have been rapidly scribbled in her handwriting immediately before her death, possibly even after she had taken the dosage of sleeping pills to end her life – an apology written to her first grandchild Lauren who had yet to experience her first birthday:

Darling –

I love you – please forgive me – I've got to do this. Tell Lauren when she grows up that I love her but can't face her.[536]

[clxxx] Selected verses of the poem were presented by Father Ed Dowling to the A.A. International in St. Louis in 1955. *Alcoholics Anonymous Comes of Age* p, 259-261.

Bobbie wrote that she couldn't face her grandchild. Was it because she was not going to be able to stay sober? Were her memories so filled with shame and defeat that she figured her presence would have somehow diminished Lauren's chances for a healthy future?

Bobbie's safety deposit box was opened a couple of weeks after her death. Proving it was a premeditated decision to take her own life, a message was found there expressing her wishes. She desired to have her daughters to have first choice of any of her possessions having confidence that they would divide things equitably. After that, she listed ten people for which she wished to receive some token to remember her by, which, interestingly enough, included Dr. Tiebout. Bill W. was given her collection of *A.A. Grapevines*. She did not desire a funeral and hoped to be cremated almost immediately. She concluded her remarks with, "You'll miss me (I hope you do) but for crying out loud, go on enjoying life to the fullest knowing that I'm O.K. and in spite of some trouble I've had a very wonderful life being your mother."[537]

Bill was to write the following tribute to Bobbie in the April 1953 *A.A. Grapevine*. His mention of her death by a heart ailment, while not true, was merely repeating what the family had announced as the cause of her death.

> MARGARET B., affectionately known throughout AA as "Bobbie," passed away in her sleep on February 17th of an unforeseen heart ailment.
>
> She had headed our A.A. General Service Office at New York in all the years of AA's adolescence—that exciting but fearsome period when no one could tell for sure whether our fledgling society would survive or not.
>
> Across her desk came thousands of pleas for help from individuals and hundreds from growing but anxious groups who wanted to be advised of the latest AA experience in meeting the problems that assailed them. It was out of this experience that AA's tradition was formed. And upon our tradition her devoted labor set a mark which will endure so long as God will have our society last.

> Her pioneering work has proved an inspiring precedent
> for every Intergroup and Foundation secretary, and her
> departure creates in the heart of each of her friends a void
> which can only be filled by the memory of what she left us
> and the assurance that her destiny is happy and secure.[538]

Bill truly wrote an eloquent tribute to her. But as the years passed by, has her mark endured "so long as God will have our society last?" Are A.A.s today relatively assured that her "destiny is happy and secure?" Unfortunately, for reasons that just now may be emerging, her name has been remembered rarely, except for those already interested in the 1940s.[539] These years haven't been explored very often in any great detail by many. To this day, many A.A.'s avoid Traditions meetings and discussions about their origins. But, understandably, over time, as a sense of gratitude begins to emerge, many A.A.s begin to wonder just how this Fellowship came about and who were intricately involved in the creation and growth of this spiritual phenomenon. Was Bobbie's suicide an embarrassment to Alcoholics Anonymous by those that knew she didn't die of a heart ailment? Was her onetime close relationship to Bill a potential source of scandal? There may have been only one man she dated after becoming close to the co-founder: Tom B. from Cleveland, Ohio, who wrote her at least two letters sporting the salutation "Dear Darling" in April 1943."[540] Prior to Bill, there was always some man pursuing her – even when she was in and out of sanitariums. Have any stereotypical prejudices against an alcoholic woman of that era persisted to this day? Did the fear of a "loose A.A. woman" or her suicide lead to a desire to hide her contributions despite Bill's tributes? Once again, the questions can be asked, but the answers are in short supply.[clxxxi] Hopefully more shall be revealed in the future that

---

[clxxxi] There are five books known to allege some kind of sexual impropriety by Bill W. through at least part of his life. The books are 1) *Getting Better Inside Alcoholics Anonymous* by Nan Robertson, ©1998. 2) *My Name is Bill* by Susan Cheever, ©2004. 3) *Bill W.* by Francis Hartigan, ©2000. 4) *Bill W. and Mr. W.* [anonymity required title shortened] by Matthew J. Raphael, ©2000. 5) *Dreaming: Hard Luck and Good Times in America*, By Carolyn See, ©1995. After careful checking of all five of these books, none of them mention Bobbie in any way. Could the five authors have missed such a story about Bobbie and Bill? The Raphael book assertion of "philandering" relies on two of the mentioned authors, See and Robertson, for sexual allegations

sheds more light on these questions. After all, the majority of her letters included in the G.S.O. Archives were not examined in preparation for this book because of time and financial constraints, not to mention the pandemic. Who knows what might be learned in the future about her? Even fewer letters written to her were examined. Some of her most significant challenges and contributions may yet be identified.

Her name appeared in a few A.A. publications after her death. Bill wrote a June 1955 *Grapevine* article titled "How AA's World Services Grew Part II." The article is classic Bill: strong on uplifting perceptions, weak on numeric accuracy. He wrote that Ruth had left in 1941, not 1942. Bobbie served as National Secretary for seven and a quarter years, not ten. Perhaps, however, the facts should not obscure the true value of the message:

> Leaving the imprint of her devotion upon our Society for all time, Ruth had left, in 1941 to be married. She was followed at the office by Bobbie B., one whose immense industry was to acquaint her with uncounted thousands of AAs during the next ten years. Hers was to be a signal service in the exciting time of AA's adolescence, when no one could be sure whether we could function or even hang together at all.[541]

against Bill, but without any specifics in the era Bobbie lived and without a primary source. The Francis Hartigan conducted a 1999 interview with Tom P. in which Tom expressed his opinions of Bill's alleged sexual guilt 47 years before. Tom himself was around 87 years old. Susan Cheever quoted the same Tom P., himself a divorcee, relying entirely, according to her endnotes, on Tom's oral history when he was probably older than he was for the Hartigan interview. What decades can do to alter memories. Nan Robertson made some sensational allegations about Bill's "womanizing" with the only woman specifically named being Helen W., who appeared on the scene when Bill was suffering from signs of emphysema at the age of 61 in 1956. Carolyn See wrote about her stepmother, a six-time divorcee, who claimed she could have been the "First Lady" of A.A., but mentioned no events or locations when any improper behavior took place. In the end, there is the absence of corroborating evidence in these allegations against Bill, which has led some prominent A.A. historians of recent times to reject the assertion that Bill was a philanderer.

Bill wrote in *Alcoholics Anonymous Comes of Age* that Bobbie had written "thousands of letters to struggling individuals and wobbly new groups [that] made all the difference during that time when it seemed very uncertain that A.A. could hang together at all."[542] Later in the same book he wrote:

> Bobbie's complete loyalty and devotion and her unbelievable energy and capacity for hard work were priceless helps during the confused and hazardous years which now lay ahead of us . . . Problems of every description poured in upon us, but by 1945 a considerable degree of order had come out of what had been a chaotic situation. On all sides the membership of our society asked for the experience and guidance of the New York office in solving their problems. Things finally began to run so smoothly that the average A.A. member has taken our world service record for granted. Until recently these Headquarters services were largely invisible to him. Nevertheless, this unseen activity has surely been responsible for much of our growth and unity.[543]

However, a most fitting tribute to Bobbie was written by Bill roughly five weeks after her death when he wrote a consoling message to Gloria:

> Dearest Gloria,
>
> This is to tell you how deeply I share the loss of your good mommy with you, and I also write to offer you every reassurance and possible help that I can.
>
> My first recollection is that of the tremendous debt of gratitude we all owe her. I think of the thousands she helped – those many who will never realize the unfailing devotion and love she gave them. Then there will be times – people like you and me who were close – who did better understand her magnificent spirit and her love for us. All this we are bound to appreciate more and more as time passes on. I know this will be as true for me as it

will for you. And my great regret will be that I failed to return in kind all that she gave me; that she never seemed to receive from life all that she put into it.

Yet I am sure you must share with me the comforting thought that her new life, a little way out of our sight and hearing, has only begun, and that it surely must be filled with bright promise. For no one that I have ever known could be more deserving.

If, at any time, you feel the need of anything that I can do for you, please call upon me instantly. Thus I shall be able to show the affection I bear for your mother and for you.

Devotedly,

Bill[544]

A Possible Fitting Conclusion

Upon reaching the conclusion of a biography, one might expect an answer to a most important question raised here. Why did she do it? "I've got to do this" was scribbled in her suicide note. A hypothesis has formed.

Roughly eight or nine years after Bobbie's death Bill wrote that her 1949 collapse "had cost us much confidence out in the field . . ."[545] By now it should be crystal clear that Bobbie knew a great deal about Bill that generally was not known to most A.A.s. Robert Thomsen's *Bill W.* biography written in 1975—four years after Bill's death—began to reveal some of what Bobbie already knew. Thomsen wrote about Bill's depressive episodes and the secret steps he took on his own behalf.

> For many Bill W. had become their spiritual mentor . . . It seemed inconceivable that their Bill, who'd been released from his obsession, had not by the same means been freed from every other difficulty and defeat . . . [They] simply did not want to believe that this man could on occasion be crippled by depressions and so utterly depleted by his own efforts to decipher their causes that he finally

would have to turn to an outsider for help. But this was the fact. Beginning in the summer of '44, twice a week Bill drove the fifteen miles from his home in Bedford Hills to Tiebout's office in Greenwich, Connecticut.[546]

Bobbie knew all of this! She knew intimate details of Bill's life more than two decades before most of Alcoholics Anonymous began to learn fragments of Bill's "behind the scenes" story. If Bobbie was to reveal the full breadth of her memories, how could she have ever shared her recollections without, in paraphrasing Bill's words, "costing us much confidence in the field?" She expected that whenever she was going to be in front of the membership, many questions addressed to her were going to be about Bill.[clxxxii] He was going to live for almost another two decades. By ending her life, she removed the possibility of being the source of confidential and personal information about a man she had protected and guarded for all her years as National Secretary. There is no record of her ever telling or writing her story. Few, if any, of her potentially sensitive memories of Bill were shared while he lived. Confidence in the field was a real concern of hers! As a possibly unintentional byproduct, she sacrificed her storytelling and was almost entirely forgotten. Her guaranteed silence continued protecting and guarding Bill. Was this the reason she wrote "I've got to do this?" Who can say? One thing is certain: learning about the personal sacrifices Bobbie and Bill made to help create Alcoholics Anonymous, which has saved the lives of so many, should bring nothing but increased gratitude for both.

In the words of Nell Wing, "I can't tell you the number of alcoholics – all over the world – who owe their sobriety to that special lady." Some who have read this biography may be in her debt more than they know if they learn how Bobbie may have helped start A.A. in their community or assisted someone high up in their sobriety tree. As more is revealed about her in years to come, then Bobbie, A.A.'s "fantastic communicator," will

---

[clxxxii] When Ruth Hock told her story on March 12, 1978 in Glendale, California, the majority of the talk was filled with references to Bill. Similarly, when Nell Wing gave a talk on August 17, 1992 in New York City, the majority of the talk was about her experiences with Bill. These talks are precisely ones that Bobbie probably felt she could not give. When she was touring with Bill in the early 1940s, most people wanted her to talk mainly about her experiences with him.

increasingly receive the gratitude she has deserved but has been denied for almost seventy years. Acknowledging her long overlooked contributions, which Panel 1 of the first A.A. General Service Conference wished us to remember in 1951 without them actually knowing the full breadth of her contributions, is long overdue. This biography of Bobbie is not an ending. It is a beginning.

FIGURE 27 - THE MOST FAMOUS PICTURE OF BOBBIE

APPENDIX

The Empty Jug, June 1946, Vol. 2, No. 8, page 1. This newspaper column included in full for purposes of documenting the accusations made by Carl K. about Bobbie and Bill.

An Open Letter to Subscribers, Members of A.A.[clxxxiii]

Since its inception some twenty-one months ago, THE EMPTY JUG, because of its defiance and vigorously expressed convictions, has met with the disfavor of the New York office.

Of eleven letters of criticism that have been received by the editor of THE EMPTY JUG, nine of them have come from the New York office.

We have been wrist-slapped for our stand on anonymity, but we still don't like it, and we are able to withstand the accusations that we are going in for personal glorification.

We have been scolded for our statement that "atheists are fools and idiots," but in that assertion we do not back-track an inch. We believe in God as the Supreme Being and as our Creator, and we do not apologetically refer to Him as "the man upstairs."

We have been denounced for our attacks on the liquor industry, but we could still turn a machine gun on the whole kaboodle with no more compunction than we would have exterminating a nest of snakes.

And in every instance, the New York office has blamed us because WE TOOK SIDES AT ALL.

Members of Alcoholics Anonymous, they smugly inform us, "do not take sides on anything, do not argue, do not enter controversies."

[clxxxiii] Reprinted from *The Empty Jug*, pages 1- 2, June 1946, Vol 2, Number 8. If ever there was an example of the need for the Twelve Traditions, this polemic article epitomizes the consequences of how an alcoholic can behave without them.

There is nothing in THE TWELVE STEPS that says whether a member of AA should argue or not in print or out.

There is nothing in THE TWELVE STEPS that says a member of AA has to be a fence-straddler, in print or out.

There is nothing in THE TWELVE STEPS that says a member of AA has to submerge his identity in a program of namby-pamby, wishy-washy, middle-of-the-road tactics on questions affecting his life and the lives of persons he loves.

THE TWELVE STEPS are the principles or precepts of AA. We have followed them to the best of our ability for the two years we have been in the organization, and we shall continue to practice them to the best of our ability.

Everything else pertaining to A.A. is METHOD and to adopt methods which fit our conscience and our convictions, we do not find it necessary to accept those issued by the New York office as being acts of Providence which we are supposed to swallow as if they were so many pills. We have tried this a good while and a number of times we have had acute indigestion.

The Alcoholic Foundation is made up of seven persons, all of whom have the typically-New York notion that the Garden of Eden and the Throne of God are both located on Manhattan Island.

Why isn't Cleveland represented on the Foundation? Or Chicago? Or Los Angeles? Or New Orleans? Or Memphis?

Not that such an adjustment of the personnel of the Foundation would alter the weight of the repercussions that will come in response to this open letter, but it would give a more equitable interpretation in the overall picture of A.A. in the United States.

In all probability THE EMPTY JUG will be "ex-communicated" for the statement of policy we are about to make, but there is one thing about it—nobody will have any misgivings about where THE EMPTY JUG STANDS.

WE WILL FIGHT LIQUOR AS LIQUOR.

The other day a young man of about twenty-five came to the door of our office. He was hunting a lawyer who has the adjoining office. He had a beard of several days growth. A tousle-headed baby girl was lying across his right shoulder. Behind him were two other children, a little boy about eight and a little girl about six. The expressions of fright and bewilderment on their little faces were terrible, like that of a puppy driven into a corner by the snarls of a bloodthirsty beast.

The lawyer was out and we told the young man his office hours were uncertain.

The young man stood there. Tears came into his eyes. "I'm sorry," he said, "but I haven't slept for four nights. My wife has been drunk for three weeks. I couldn't leave the children at home with her. I love her, but there's nothing to do but get a divorce. That's why I went with a lawyer."

IF ONLY ONE PERSON—ONLY ONE—OUT OF 135 MILLION PEOPLE SHOULD GET DRUNK AND CAUSE THAT MISERY, THAT TORMENT, THAT HELL IN THE HEARTS OF INNOCENT BABIES, THERE IS NO JUSTIFICATION WHATEVER FOR LIQUOR.

THE EMPTY JUG MAKES THAT FLAT STATEMENT . . . AND IT WILL CONTINUE TO MAKE IT.

THE EMPTY JUG WILL MAKE ANOTHER STATEMENT – THAT THERE IS IN THIS COUNTRY TODAY A DEFINITE AND POWERFUL CONSPIRACY TO DEBAUCH AMERICA.

The conspirators are the head men in the liquor industry, the head men in Hollywood, the head men in radio, the head men in Tin Pan Alley. The head men in some publishing houses—and it would be interesting to see how often a big stockholder could be found in all five classifications.

Fantastic? Let's see?

The motion picture industry will tell you that the kind of pictures it makes is determined by what the people want. At the liquor industry's own figures, there are about 50 million people in the United States who drink in some form or other.

THAT LEAVES 85 MILLION WHO DO NOT DRINK, BUT MORE THAN 90 PERCENT OF THE MOTION PICTURES HAVE DRINKING SCENES IN WHICH DRINKING IS GLORIFIED AS A NECESSARY AND PLEASURABLE PART OF LIVING.

The other evening we saw a picture "Cluny Brown" featuring Charles Boyer and Jennifer Jones. Miss Jones played the part of Cluny Brown, an unusual English domestic.

Some ten minutes was devoted to the occasion of Cluny Brown taking her first cocktail. After she had taken it, she stretched herself out, languorously and seductively, on the sofa and talked about the "wonderful Persian cat feeling" she had.

No motion picture, with the exception of "The Lost Week-end," which was a herring dragged across the trail, gives anything but the exciting and glamourous part of drinking.

Because of the picture "Cluny Brown" alone, hundreds of youngsters will take that first drink . . . and many of them, in a few short years, will be able to look back upon lives of destitution, heartaches and despair.

If only one life is wrecked because of that picture, Ernst Lubitsch, who produced it, is as definitely a murderer as the worst killer that ever breathed.

And what part does Tin Pan Alley play?

A couple of current song hits are "Shoo Fly-Fly and Apple Pan Dowdy" and "I'm a Big Girl Now."

Both songs are "suggestive" and that is their entire purpose.

In radio the majority of plays mention drinking in some manner.

Drinking and lax morals go together. Liquor is an aphrodisiac.

Excessive drinking and excessive laxity of morals will debauch America all right. Don't worry about that. Not if it is allowed to continue as it is now going.

Decadent France will be child's play compared to the things that will happen in this country.

The other evening we stopped for a late dinner at one of the better drive-in restaurants in Memphis. We counted five tables with liquor bottles on them and SEATED AT EACH OF THE TABLES WERE SCHOOL KIDS. There wasn't a boy or girl over sixteen, and all of them were drinking. All of them were "being smart." All of them were practicing "gracious living."

If only one of those girls, through laxity in the beginning because of drunkenness, becomes a prostitute—if only one of those boys sends his life hurling down the path of disgrace and futility—you FENCE STRADDLERS can thank the insidious influences that you are allowing to exist in the name of tolerance.

The liquor manufacturers will tell you that they don't like alcoholics – that they create a disturbance in decent drinking places.

Don't let 'em kid you!

They wish everybody was an alcoholic. They wish this country was full of human derelicts.

THAT THIS IS THE LONG-TERM PURPOSE OF THESE CONSPIRATORS—MAKERS OF THIS COUNTRY A NATION OF

HUMAN DERELICTS SO THEY WILL HAVE COMPLETE CONTROL OF THE GOVERNMENT.

If there is not a conspiracy of this kind, kindly tell us why all the forces we have depicted so consistently use their power to destroy the finer things of life?

THE CROWD OF SHEEP

It is our opinion that virtually every person starts drinking because he or she thinks it is cute and smart.

It is our opinion that the majority of social drinkers do their drinking for identically the same reasons, because they think it is cute and smart—although the adult technique is more blasé—and because they want to pretend to be something they are not.

Happily we have lost all desire to be more of a jackass than we are naturally, and we have abandoned all intentions of ever again following a crowd of people in which artificiality and hypocrisy are the chief traits.

Furthermore, we know that any person who drinks enough whiskey will become an alcoholic—but little or much, we see no justification for liquor whatever.

INCONSISTENCY OF THE NEW YORK OFFICE

Glibly and of the drop of a hat the New York office will start its harangue about never taking sides on any question. At the same time it will lean over backwards to keep from hurting the feelings of the liquor interests, but will speak with contempt and derision of W.C.T.U.

Why is this? Well, we'd like to know, too.

We do not care especially for the W.C.T.U.—its methods need streamlining—but we do know its members are honest and sincere, its purpose is constructive, and we will take W.C.T.U. one thousand to one over the designing snakes who control the liquor industry.

OUR VOTE OF CONFIDENCE

THE EMPTY JUG has been given a vote of confidence by the Chattanooga Group of Alcoholics Anonymous. This does not mean that the members of the Chattanooga Group will always agree with the editorials of THE EMPTY JUG, but it does mean that they are convinced of the sincerity of the editors of the paper and grant them the right to express their opinions of good A.A.s under sponsorship of the group.

ANY SUBSCRIBERS NOT WISHING TO HAVE THE EMPTY JUG CONTINUED DUE TO THE PAPER'S FUTURE POLICY, JUST STATED, CAN GET A FULL REFUND OF THE SUBSCRIPTION PRICE, REGARDLESS OF WHEN THE SUBSCRIPTION WAS ENTERED, BY JUST WRITING THE OFFICE AT 204 JAMES BUILDING, CHATTANOOGA, TENNESSEE.

Bobbie on the Wet-Dry Controversy

May 5, 1944

Dear Gerry [Denver, Colorado]:

That is an interesting story. And we think it is just fine that the industry of liquor realizes our worth. Fact is they are all for the alcoholics but the alkies are the ones that prohibitionists use as the bad example to bolster their cause. I don't know of any bartenders or liquor dealers who don't go for AA – they do not like to sell to alcoholics as it hurts their business – they only want the controlled drinkers as customers. However, we must watch our step not to in any way be allied with, implications or otherwise, the liquor people. As you know, nationally our policy is to sit on the middle of the fence and not offend either the drys *[sic]* or the wets. We can do this because controversy on the subject can keep people away and some alkies could die if kept out of AA. If we showed a leaning to siding with the distillers, then the ministers and other prohibitionists would keep their people away from us and if we go "dry" (heaven forbid – and that is my personal opinion) then the alkies themselves would keep away as they all hate anything that smells of blue nosing.[clxxxiv] So on controversial matters we take no sides. You may come

---

[clxxxiv] Blue nosing: a puritanical person, a prude.

up against some criticism from the more or less straight laced people that you are accepting polluted money. I wouldn't let that worry you but I would be sure to explain to those liquor people that although you appreciate the contributions that you cannot as a group let any strings be tied to it. Recently the Research Council on Problems of Alcohol has gotten in a little Dutch because many of their donations are from people like Schenley, Walker and Calvert. I am going over this with you in case something pops up that you do not foresee.

I do hope you get to see those two swell groups in Chicago and Detroit. Best to everyone.

Sincerely,

Bobbie

GSO, Box 36, R18, File D, p. 59

Letter from Leonard Strong, May 14, 1951

Mrs. Margaret B——

70 Fifth Avenue[clxxxv]

New York, N.Y.

Dear Mrs. B——:

The initial meeting of the General Service Conference, so long in preparation, has come and gone. You would have been cheered by the high caliber of delegates and their grasp of the problems of the central office and of the Alcoholic Foundation. I am sure had this occurred during your tenure many problems would have seemed less pressing, so there is promise of a smoother future.

[clxxxv] Her actual address was 40 Fifth Avenue.

As representatives of a cross section of Alcoholics Anonymous, they wished the Trustees of the Alcoholic Foundation to acknowledge their cognizance of their debt to you and to express their deep gratitude for your sage counsel, guidance and advice over your long years of service.

On instruction of the Alcoholic Foundation and for Alcoholics Anonymous I convey to you their thanks and best wishes and add the assurances of my own pleasure at being so designated.

Sincerely yours,

Leonard V. Strong, Jr.

Source: The Bobbie Family Collection

Bobbie's Big Book Signed by "Bill"

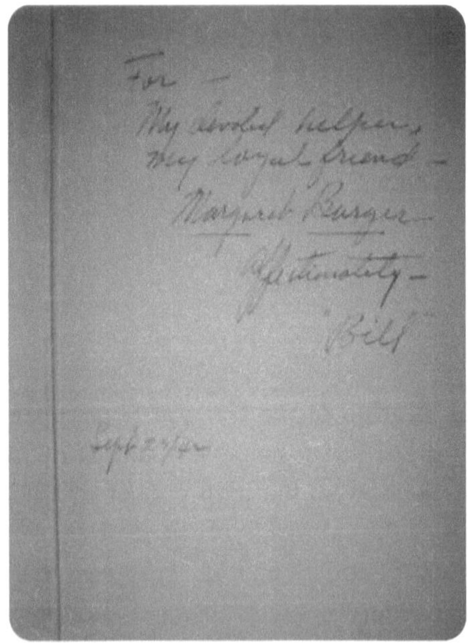

FIGURE 28 - BOBBIE'S BIG BOOK SIGNED BY BILL

ENDNOTES

[1]   www.Silkworth.net, Chapter 11 – The General Service Conferences, "This Conference, held April 23-27, 1958, voted to change the name of A.A.'s 'General Headquarters' to "General Service Office,' more accurately conveying its position in the service structure and its function."

[2]   Email from Lauren W. dated 10/14/2019.

[3]   Email from Lauren W. dated 10/14/2019.

[4]   Bobbie scored 130 on the Bellevue Adult Intelligence Scale in 1945. This may have qualified her as being 1 of 180, which would result in her being more intelligent than most of the people she encountered. Following chart from https://en.wikipedia.org/wiki/IQ_classification:

Current Wechsler (WAIS–IV, WPPSI–IV) IQ
Classification

IQ Range ("deviation IQ")	IQ Classification
130 and above	Very Superior
120–129	Superior
110–119	High Average
90–109	Average
80–89	Low Average
70–79	Borderline
69 and below	Extremely Low

[5]   *Yonkers Statesman*, Yonkers, New York, July 27, 1922, p. 10.

[6]   Two letters were found from a "Julio." One used stationary that carried the heading of "Villa Mendichka" (a villa located in Urrugne, area Boyeiex, in the department of Pyrenees-Anlantiques). It may have been written from the south of France but mailed from Venezuela. A second letter was mailed from Bairritz in southwestern France on the ocean. In any case, this gentleman seemed in every way to be one of her admirers, if not a lover. He may have

been wealthy. He appears multiple times in Bobbie's dream diaries in an affectionate role.

[7]   *The Yonkers Herald*, Yonkers, New York, September 23, 1923, p. 3.

[8]   *The Brooklyn Daily Eagle*, Brooklyn, New York, March 11, 1924, p. 11.

[9]   *The Yonkers Herald*, Yonkers, New York, January 17, 1925, p. 6.

[10] Norman Chapman Burger to Bobbie dated 9/13/1921, The Bobbie Family Collection.

[11] *The Yonkers Herald*, Yonkers, New York, June 18, 1925, p. 8.

[12] Norman Chapman Burger to Bobbie dated 12/11/1925, The Bobbie Family Collection.

[13] Ibid.

[14] *Brooklyn Daily Eagle*, Brooklyn, New York, February 19, 1929, p. 24.

[15] Shep to Bobbie, not dated, "Thursday – 12:15" with stationery carrying the heading of "George LaMonte & Son, 61 Broadway, New York." The Bobbie Family Collection.

[16] Envelope of a letter to Bobbie from Shep, March 21, 1932, The Bobbie Family Collection.

[17] Kathryn Murray with Betty Hannah Hoffman. 1960. *My Husband, Arthur Murray*. Curtis Publishing Company, Inc. Simon and Schuster, Inc. Famous names on pages 90-91 include marriages of dance instructors of both sexes to people such as Cornelius Whitney Vanderbilt, Burgess Meredith, Neva Patterson and others. Arthur Murray had customers among the very wealthy including the Rockefellers and Vanderbilts.

[18] Shep to Bobbie, March 21, 1932, The Bobbie Family Collection.

[19] Columbia University, College of Physicians and Surgeons, Department of Psychiatry, 722 West 168th St., New York, cover letter dated June 23, 1945: "Dear Mrs. B: In accordance with the permission which you recently granted, I have had the medical history of your life, as you gave it to Dr. L.R. Sillman, abstracted and camouflaged. A carbon copy of that abstract is attached for your information and approval. Will you read it over and edit it if necessary? If you feel that you can grant permission for the publication of this history, will you sign the permission below? We hope to publish this history together with some twenty others in the Quarterly Journal of Studies on Alcohol. The editor of that journal is saving space for these histories in the September and December, 1945 issues. Therefore, we would appreciate an early reply." It is not known if she approved the publication of her psychological profile.

[20] Shep to Bobbie, February 29, 1936, The Bobbie Family Collection.

[21] John Gillette Roberts (Pop) to Bobbie, March 3, 1936, The Bobbie Family Collection.

[22] In 1998, *The New York Times* published an article on the history of the Hartford Retreat for the Insane. : "In the 1930's, under the leadership of Dr. Charles Burlingame, came expansion and promotion. The hospital decided

to market itself as a refuge for the wealthy. 'It was the turning point,' says Bruce Clouette, the museum's other main historian. 'This established the institute as an elite, country club sort of place.' But along with millionaires and movie stars, the institute continued to take state-assisted patients." The institute was renamed "Institute for Living" and continues today. https://www.nytimes.com/1998/09/20/nyregion/the-view-from-hartford-the-history-of-insanity-shameful-to-treatable.html.

[23] Shep to Bobbie, June 17, 1936, The Bobbie Family Collection. Shep wrote Dr. Burlingame directly, as mentioned in this letter.
"A video, taken from a 1930's promotional film by the Hartford photographer George E. Meyers, reflects the slick image Dr. Burlingame wanted to project. With demonstrations of equipment, sports and fashion shows, it was almost an early infomercial for staff and patient alike." https://www.nytimes.com/1998/09/20/nyregion/the-view-from-hartford-the-history-of-insanity-shameful-to-treatable.html.

[24] Shep to Bobbie, June 10, 1936, The Bobbie Family Collection. Date approximate derived from the date of the Republican National Convention, which was held in Cleveland that year.

[25] https://en.wikipedia.org/wiki/Henry_Luce.

[26] Shep to Bobbie, June 17, 1936, The Bobbie Family Collection.

[27] Memorandum re Margaret S., Lawyer Leslie Nichols, Cleveland, Ohio, February 8, 1937, The Bobbie Family Collection.

[28] Ibid., p. 3.

[29] Shep to Bobbie, August 30, 1936, The Bobbie Family Collection. The date is approximate; other documents determined this date, not written on the letter.

[30] Shep to Bobbie, November 23, 1936, The Bobbie Family Collection.

[31] Shep to John Gillette Roberts (Pop), November 27, 1936, The Bobbie Family Collection.

[32] Shep to John Gillette Roberts (Pop), December 6, 1936, The Bobbie Family Collection.

[33] Shep to Bobbie, December 28, 1936, The Bobbie Family Collection.

[34] Shep to Bobbie, January 9, 1937, The Bobbie Family Collection.

[35] Memorandum re. Margaret S., Lawyer Leslie Nichols, Cleveland, Ohio, January 26, 1937, The Bobbie Family Collection.

[36] Columbia University, College of Physicians and Surgeons, Department of Psychiatry, 722 West 168th St., New York; Bobbie's Psychological Profile, The Bobbie Family Collection.

[37] Ibid.

[38] https://patch.com/connecticut/stamford/stamford-hall-new-englands-largest-private-sanitarium/. The facility closed in 1965.

[39] *Mrs. Marty Mann, The First Lady of Alcoholics Anonymous*, Sally Brown & David R. Brown, Hazelden, Center City, Minnesota, 25012-0178, ©2001, p. 127.

[40] Mac to Bobbie, February 3, 1940, The Bobbie Family Collection.

[41] Bobbie to Lois Wilson, March 14, 1940, The General Service Office Archives, Box 46, R22, File NY B, p. 15, 16.

[42] Ruth Hock to Bobbie, March 18, 1940, The General Service Office Archives, Box 46, R22, File NY B, p. 17.

[43] *Pass It On: The Story of Bill Wilson and How the AA Message Reached the World*, Alcoholics Anonymous World Services, Inc., ©1984, p. 235.

[44] *A.A. Grapevine*, June 1959, *The World's First Clubhouse for Drunks!*, https://www.aagrapevine.org/magazine/1959/jun/worlds-first-clubhouse-drunks.

[45] Mac to Bobbie, June 24, 1940, The Bobbie Family Collection.

[46] *Pass It On*, Alcoholics Anonymous World Services, Inc., ©1984, p. 317.

[47] Mac to Bobbie, October 8, 1940, The Bobbie Family Collection.

[48] Lois' Diary, October 10, 1940.

[49] Mac to Bobbie, October 11, 1940, The Bobbie Family Collection.

[50] Mac to Bobbie, October 17, 1940, The Bobbie Family Collection.

[51] Mac to Bobbie, October 25, 1940, The Bobbie Family Collection.

[52] Mac to Bobbie, November 20, 1940, The Bobbie Family Collection.

[53] https://en.wikipedia.org/wiki/Sloane_House_YMCA.

[54] Mac to Bobbie, November 22, 1940, The Bobbie Family Collection.

[55] Mac to Bobbie, November 29, 1940, The Bobbie Family Collection.

[56] Dick S. to Bobbie, May 5, 1941, The Bobbie Family Collection.

[57] Dick S. to Bobbie, May 19, 1942, The Bobbie Family Collection.

[58] Kaufmann, Kevin, "Rigorous Honesty: A Cultural History of Alcoholics Anonymous 1935-1960" (2011). *Dissertations*. 73., https://ecommons.luc.edu/luc_diss/73, p. 160.

[59] Bobbie to John P. from, January 1, 1943, General Service Office Archives, Box 34, R16, File Cal B., California General, p. 46. "I seldom get up to go to the club at 24th street as all my time is spent down here now. However I do know Don V. and Ida P. very well (she followed me as secretary up there in 1941 and will give them your messages next time I see them. Don is very busy in a big job with WPB and we only see him for a minute at a time. He is flying all over the country and is unable to get to meetings. Bill and I do talk to him on the phone occasionally." Also, from the May 1945 *Grapevine*: "Since we're on the subject of women and their work, we must mention, at least in passing, the splendid and consistent work of Bobby *[sic]* B., five years in A.A. Though Bobby *[sic]* works—and how! —here in Manhattan, she is perhaps even better known to the thousands with whom she corresponds all over the country, in her capacity as National Secretary of the Central (A.A.) Office in New York, since 1942. Before that she was secretary of the

Manhattan Group, and before that, as Bobby *[sic]* herself puts it, 'I was just a drunk.'"

60 According to Bill's 1955 talk regarding the history of A.A. in Manhattan (http://www.minnesotarecovery.info/literature/Manhattan.htm, History of the Start of AA in New York City), there were 6,000 inquiries that resulted from the Alexander article. According to A.A. Bulletin #3 published on 6/30/41 signed by Ruth Hock, there were 4,400 responses since the Alexander article composed of 2,325 SEP (*Saturday Evening Post*) letters along with an additional 2,075 received for other matters. Even at the lower figure, A.A. Headquarters was pumping out at least 50 responses every working day among their other responsibilities. However, none of Bobbie's writings for the Foundation have been identified that carry a date earlier than February 16, 1942. Her original letter to Lois asking to attend an A.A. meeting at Steinway Hall was dated March 14, 1940.

61 *Grateful To Have Been There*, Nell Wing, Hazelden Foundation, ©1992, 1998, p. 167-168. Also from "Service Material from the GSO, ORIGIN OF THE SERENITY PRAYER: A HISTORICAL PAPER, "Some fifteen years later, reminiscing about this event, Ruth Hock Crecelius, our first nonalcoholic secretary, said: 'It is a fact that Jack C. appeared at the office (30 Vesey St., Manhattan) one morning for a chat and during the course of which he showed me the obituary notice with 'Serenity Prayer.' I was as much impressed with it as he was and asked him to leave it with me so that I could copy and use it in our letters to the groups and loners. At this same time, Bobbie B. who was also terrifically impressed with it undoubtedly used it in her work with the many she contacted daily at the 24th Street Clubhouse. Horace C. had the idea of printing it on cards and paid for the first printing."
Robert Thomsen contradicts much of this account. On page 292 of *Bill W.*, he claims the prayer was received by Ruth while she was still working in Newark, New Jersey, which dates the event before or during March 1940.

62 Many of Dick's letters are difficult to date. He did not place a date on most of them, only the day of the week and sometimes the time. The only way to date any of his writing is by the postmark on its envelope, but many of those envelopes have been lost. The majority of his correspondence in The Bobbie Family Collection date from April or May of 1941.

63 Dick S. to Bobbie, April 7, 1941, The Bobbie Family Connection [37/102].

64 Dick S. to Bobbie, date est. April 1941, The Bobbie Family Collection [67-70/102].

65 Dick S. to Bobbie, est. mid-1941 from proximity with other letters with postmarks, The Bobbie Family Collection.

66 Dick S. to Bobbie, est. late April 1941, The Bobbie Family Collection, from a PDF, page 28/102.

67 Ibid., 33/102.

68   John Richard Stanley Family Tree, Born April 8, 1893. (Ancestry.com)

69   Dick S. to Bobbie, est. late April 1941, The Bobbie Family Collection [97/102].

70   Dick S. to Bobbie, May 5, 1941, The Bobbie Family Collection [18-19/32].

71   Bobbie to K.L. of Sacramento, CA, July 30, 1942, General Service Office Archives, Box 35, R17, File V, p. 29.

72   Bobbie to Mr. J of Wheeling, WV, February 18, 1942, West Virginia Archives (G.S.O. markings were not recorded by West Virginia).

73   *Alcoholics Anonymous Comes of Age.* Alcoholics Anonymous Publishing, Inc., p. 196. 1957.

74   Bobbie to Columbus A.A., February 27, 1942, General Service Office Archives, Box 50, R23, File Ohio P.1, p. 25.

75   Bobbie to Mr. W., February 27, 1942, General Service Office Archives, Box 50, R23, File Ohio P.1, p. 26.

76   Bobbie to Mr. S., February 27, 1942, General Service Office Archives, Box 50, R23, File Ohio P.1, p. 27.

77   *Alcoholics Anonymous*, Alcoholics Anonymous World Services Inc., 4th Edition, ©1939, 1955, 1976, 2001, p. 565.

78   Bobbie to Mr. W., March 9, 1942, General Service Office Archives, Box 50, R23, File Ohio P. 1, p. 33.

79   Bobbie to Art B. of Buffalo, NY, March 10, 1942, General Service Office Archives, Box 47, R22, File NY H, p. 64. Art would become a significant part of Atlanta A.A.

80   Bobbie to Art B. of Buffalo, NY, April 10, 1942, General Service Office Archives, Box 47, R22, File NY H., p. 70.

81   A.A. Bulletin dated March 20, 1942 provided to all A.A. groups signed by Bobbie, though inevitably Bill W. must have assisted on the creation of this message.

82   Ibid., p. 3.

83   Bobbie to James G., San Diego, CA, March 25, 1942, General Service Office Archives, Box 34, R16, File Cal. B., California General, p. 38.

84   A.A. Bulletin dated May 5, 1942, provided to all A.A. groups signed by Bobbie.

85   *Grapevine*, June 1944, Vol 1, No. 1, P.O. General Service Office Archives, Box 328, Grand Central Annex, New York 17, New York.

86   Bobbie to Mr. L. R. of San Quentin, May 15, 1942, General Service Office Archives, Box 36, R17, File HH, p. 7.

87   Bobbie to Warren T. of Richmond, CA, August 10, 1944, General Service Office Archives, Box 35, R17, File S, p. 54, 55.

88   Bobbie to Warden Sanford of Atlanta Federal Prison, November 25, 1944, GSSA.

89   Bobbie to Bill of San Quentin, November 21, 1945, General Service Office Archives, Box 36, R17, File HH, p. 73.

90 Bobbie to Warren T. of Richmond, CA, April 9, 1943, General Service Office Archives, Box 35, R17, File S, p. 8.

91 Bobbie to Rod of San Francisco, August 2, 1943, General Service Office Archives, Box 36, R17, File AA.2, p. 174.

92 Bobbie to Lon M. of San Quentin, February 29, 1944, General Service Office Archives, Box 36, R17, File HH, p. 31.

93 Bobbie to Mr. W. of Columbus, Ohio April 9, 1942, General Service Office Archives, Box 50, R23, File Ohio P.1, p. 53.

94 Bobbie to Mr. B. of Columbus, Ohio, April 27, 1942, General Service Office Archives, Box 50, R23, File Ohio P.1, p. 58.

95 *Alcoholics Anonymous*, Alcoholics Anonymous World Services, Inc., Fourth Edition, ©2001, p. xiii.

96 Bobbie to Bob of Atlanta, October 20, 1943, Georgia State Archives, G.S.O. markings not available

97 Bobbie to Bill of San Diego, July 30, 1942, General Service Office Archives, Box 35, R17, File Y.1, p. 27.

98 Bobbie to Arnold of Buffalo, September 11, 1942, General Service Office Archives, Box 47, R22, File NY H, p. 81.

99 Bobbie to Brad of Stockton, CA, October 1, 1942, General Service Office Archives, Box 35, R17, File V, p. 36.

100 Bobbie to Fay of Los Angeles, CA, September 25, 1942, General Service Office Archives, Box 35, R17, File I.1, p 154, 154a.

101 Bobbie to Dick S. of Akron, November 20, 1942, General Service Office Archives, Box 49, R23, File Ohio – C.1, p. 39.

102 Bobbie to Bill H. of Cleveland, November 27, 1942, General Service Office Archives, Box 50, R23, File Ohio O.10, p. 12.

103 Bobbie to Ray H. from San Francisco, October 15, 1942, General Service Office Archives, Box 36, R17, File AA.2, p. 155.

104 Bobbie to Ray H. from San Francisco, November 19, 1942, General Service Office Archives, Box 36, R17, File AA.2, p. 157.

105 *Mrs. Marty Mann, The First Lady of Alcoholics Anonymous*, Sally Brown & David R. Brown, Hazelden, Center City, Minnesota, 25012-0178, ©2001, p. 116. "A single woman in AA was vulnerable to inappropriate attention by AA men and also perceived as a threat by the wives of men in AA." Also: *Slaying The Dragon*, William White, First Edition, Chestnut Health Systems/ Lighthouse Institute, Bloomington, Illinois, 61701, ©1998, pages 158-159: "To manage this potential disruption during A.A.'s early years, women and men sat on different sides of A.A. meeting rooms and the first women seeking help were often sponsored, not by A.A. members, but by their wives. As more single and divorced women entered A.A., friction between these women and the wives of A.A. men increased. This led to the creation of "closed

meetings," attended only by alcoholics, in addition to "open meetings," which were open to all."

[106] Bobbie to Beatrice J. of Hartford, Connecticut, General Service Office Archives, Box 37, R18, File G, p. 46.

[107] https://en.wikipedia.org/wiki/Battle_of_the_Atlantic

[108] Alcoholics Anonymous 1939-42, Archives of the General Service Board of Alcoholics Anonymous, p. 38.

[109] Bobbie to Dick S. of Akron, Ohio, July 10, 1942, General Service Office Archives, Box 49, R23 File Ohio – C.1, p. 33.

[110] Bobbie to John P. of California, January 5, 1943, General Service Office Archives, Box 34, R16, File Cal B., California General, p. 46.

[111] *Alcoholics Anonymous*, Alcoholics Anonymous World Services, Inc., ©1939, 1955. 1976. 2001, p. 19.

[112] Dick S. of Akron to Bobbie, May 19, 1942. Bobbie Family Collection.

[113] Columbia University, Collection of Physicians and Surgeons, Department of Psychiatry, June 23, 1945. Profile created for the purpose of sharing it anonymously in the *Quarterly Journal of Studies on Alcohol* (JSAD.COM). From the original pages provided to Bobbie for her approval, not from the publication. It was scheduled to appear sometime in the latter half of 1945.

[114] Bobbie to Warren T, Richmond, CA, June 3, 1943, General Service Office Archives, Box 35, R17, File S, p. 16.

[115] Bobbie to Warren T, Richmond, CA, May 8, 1944, General Service Office Archives, Box 35, R17, File S, p. 32 or up to 38.

[116] Selected words from Tradition Six, *Alcoholics Anonymous*, Alcoholics Anonymous World Services, Inc., ©1939, 1955, 1976, 2001, p. 562.

[117] Bobbie to Warren T., Richmond, CA, July 10, 1944, General Service Office Archives, Box 35, R17, File S, p. 43.

[118] *DuPont: From the Banks of the Brandywine to Miracles of Science*, Adrian Kinnane, "To DuPont Employees – Past Present and Future," ©2002, E.I. du Pont de Nemours and Company, Wilmington, Delaware, 189898, p. 143.

[119] Bobbie to Warren T., Richmond, CA, May 24, 1944, General Service Office Archives, Box 35, R17, File S, p. 39, 39a.

[120] Bobbie to Warren T., April 25, 1949, General Service Office Archives, Box 36, R17, File AA.3, p. 34, 34a.

[121] Bobbie to Red of Hartford, Connecticut, January 5, 1943, General Service Office Archives, Box 37, R18, File G. p. 48.

[122] Bobbie to Red of Hartford, Connecticut, January 22, 1943, General Service Office Archives, Box 37, R18, File G, p. 52.

[123] Bobbie to Red of Hartford, Connecticut, January 26, 1943, General Service Office Archives, Box 34, R18, File G, p. 53.

[124] Bobbie to Scotty in Cincinnati, Ohio, January 29, 1943, General Service Office Archives, Box 49, R23, File Ohio – N, p. 34.

125 Bobbie to Warren T. of Richmond, California, February 12, 1943, General Service Office Archives, Box 35, R17, File S, p. 4.

126 Bobbie to Wally G. of Akron, Ohio, March 2, 1943, General Service Office Archives, Box 49, R23, File Ohio – C.1, p. 41.

127 Bobbie to Bill B. of San Diego, California, March 3, 1943, General Service Office Archives, Box 35, R17, File Y.1, p. 27.

128 Bobbie to Dale A. from Seattle, Washington, March 8, 1943, N.A.B.A. Archives, Atlanta, GA, G.S.O. markings missing.

129 A.A. Bulletin, April 15, 1943, signed by Margaret R. B., distributed to all active groups—about 225 at the time.

130 Bobbie to Esther E., April 18, 1943, Texas Archives, from a photograph.

131 Bobbie to Esther E., August 6, 1943, Texas Archives, from a photograph.

132 Ibid.

133 Bobbie to Esther E., September 21, 1943, Texas Archives, from a photograph.

134 Bobbie to Esther E., October 20, 1943, Texas Archives, from a photograph.

135 Bobbie to Bill of the Miles Avenue Group of Cleveland, Ohio, April 22, 1943, General Service Office Archives, Box 50, R23, File Ohio O.19, p.17.

136 Bobbie to Ed from Buffalo, New York, June 23, 1943, General Service Office Archives, Box 47, R22, File NY H, p. 100.

137 Bobbie to Dr. Stephen Smith of Columbia, Missouri, November 16, 1943, Box 44, R21, File Mo. C, p. 81 (Area 38 Archives).

138 Bobbie to Rod from San Francisco, CA, July 6, 1943, General Service Office Archives, Box 36, R17, File AA.2, p. 170.

139 Bobbie to Wally G. of Akron, Ohio, July 10, 1943, General Service Office Archives, Box 49, R23, File Ohio – C.1, p. 45.

140 Bobbie to Warren T. of Richmond, California, July 12, 1943, General Service Office Archives, Box 35, R17, File S, p. 26.

141 A.A. Bulletin to all members, September 29, 1943.

142 Bobbie to Dr. Stephen Smith of Columbia, Missouri, September 15, 1943, Box 44 R 21, File Mo. C, p. 73 (Area 38 Archives).

143 Bobbie to Dr. Stephen Smith of Columbia, Missouri, April 14, 1942, Box 44, R 21, File Mo. C, p. 21, (Area 38 Archives).

144 Bobbie to Dr. Stephen Smith of Columbia, Missouri, June 9, 1942, Box 44, R21, File Mo. C, p. 27, (Area 38 Archives).

145 Bobbie to Dr. Stephen Smith of Columbia, Missouri, July 23, 1942, Box 44, R21, File Mo. C., p. 36, (Area 38 Archives).

146 Dr. Stephen Smith of Columbia, Missouri to Bobbie, April 14, 1943, Box 44, R21, File Mo. C., p. 61, (Area 38 Archives).

147 Bobbie to Dr. Stephen Smith of Columbia, Missouri, April 30, 1943, Box 44, R21, File Mo. C., p. 64, (Area 38 Archives).

148 Bill W. to Dr. Stephen Smith of Columbia, Missouri, July 1, 1943, Box 44, R21, File Mo. C., p. 71 (Area 38 Archives).

149   Bobbie to Dr. Stephen Smith of Columbia, Missouri, November 16, 1943, Box 44, R21, File Mo. C., p.81 (Area 38 Archives).

150   Bobbie to Dr. Bob, September 30, 1943, General Service Office Archives, copy available has catalogue absent.

151   Bobbie to Evan of San Diego, California, November 2, 1943, General Service Office Archives, Box 35, R17, File Y.1, p. 38.

152   Bobbie to Art B. of Atlanta, GA, July 30, 1943, GSSA Archives, G.S.O. ID missing: "Think the way to handle the Negro question is as you suggested. Let the members help them from their own Groups. It is the only and best way for both sides. Boy, I hope you get one going and start the ball going for other Groups."

153   Bobbie to Bill H. of Cleveland, October 5, 1943, General Service Office Archives, Box 50, R23, File Ohio O.19, p. 23.

154   "We do not have a colored group anywhere and the problem is popping up more each day. I do know in Pittsburgh they have accepted one colored member and I suggest you write and ask them just how the situation is handled there. Most groups feel that colored members cannot be mixed in with our groups for the simple reason we would lose many white members for every colored we helped, therefore, "the greatest good for the greatest number" must prevail. However, I do know that many of us feel the colored race has its right to A.A. just as much as we. So we more or less decided that when we get such inquiries we can ask single colored prospects to attend one meeting as an observer, after that some of the older members of the group might offer to help these people establish their own group in their own vicinity. However, I do think you can get some valuable advice from Pittsburgh, so write. D. Walter S. . ., Pittsburgh; he is the secretary there and I know he will be glad to tell you just what they have done with this problem." Bobbie to Pauline of Pittsburgh, October 26, 1944, General Service Office Archives, Box 49, R23, File Ohio –N, p. 53.

155   William White. *Slaying The Dragon, The History of Addiction Treatment and Recovery in America*. Chesnut Health Systems, ©1998, 2014, P. 159, Edition 1; p. 207-208, Edition 2.

156   Sally Brown & David R. Brown. *Mrs. Marty Mann, The First Lady of Alcoholics Anonymous*. Hazelden. Center City, Minnesota, 25012-0178. ©2001. p. 116.

157   Glenn F. Chesnut. *Heroes of Early Black AA, Their Stories and Their Messages*. Hindsfoot Foundation. San Francisco & South Bend. ©2017, p. 3.

158   Ibid, p. 15.

159   From Bobbie to Ed in Cleveland, June 1, 1945, General Service Office Archives, Box 49, R23, File Ohio – N, p.55.

160   *Alcoholics Anonymous*, Alcoholics Anonymous World Services, Inc., Fourth Edition, ©1939, 1955, 1976, 2001, p. 28.

161 Bobbie to Mrs. McKey of Valdosta, GA, January 30, 1946, G.S.S.A. Archives.

162 Bobbie to Wayne of Atlanta, GA, March 28, 1947, G.S.S.A. Archives.

163 Bobbie to Joe in Cincinnati, July 8, 1947, General Service Office Archives, Box 49, R23, File Ohio – N, p. 78.

164 Atlanta Central Office Meeting Schedules in the mid-1960's still listed "Colored Groups" separately from the balance of other A.A. meetings.

165 *Benign Anarchy, Alcoholics Anonymous in Ireland*, Shane Butler, Trinity College Dublin, Irish Academic Press, Dublin, Portland OR, ©2010, p. 64-68.

166 Ibid, p. 68.

167 Ibid. p. 70-71.

168 Bobbie to Olive of Los Angeles, CA, General Service Office Archives, Box 34, R17, File H1 California North, P40-41.

169 Bobbie to "Dear Secretary," June 25, 1947, G.S.O. assumed.

170 Ibid.

171 *But, For the Grace of God*, Wally P., The Bishop of Books, Wheeling, West Virginia, ©1995, p. 102-103.

172 Ibid, p. 138.

173 "Women Alcoholics Have a Tougher Fight," by Marty M., May 1945, *Grapevine*, PO Box 1980, Grand Central Station, New York, NY.

174 Bobbie to Art B. of Buffalo, NY, October 14, 1942, General Service Office Archives, Box 47, R22, File NY H, p. 85.

175 Bobbie to Esther in Dallas, November 13, 1943, Dallas Archives, G.S.O. information not recorded.

176 *Central Bulletin*, Cleveland, Ohio, June, 1945, Vol. III-No. 9, p. 2.

177 "Women's Meetings," by Grace O., October 1946, *Grapevine*, PO Box 1980, Grand Central Station, New York, NY.

178 Bobbie to Bill of Cincinnati, Ohio, General Service Office Archives, Box 49, R23 File Ohio – N, p. 46.

179 Bobbie to Dick S. of Akron, Ohio, General Service Office Archives, Box 49, R23 File Ohio – C.1, p. 33.

180 Bobbie to Dale of Seattle, WA, December 7, 1944, NABA Archives.

181 Bobbie to Vic of Sacramento, CA, January 11, 1944, General Service Office Archives, Box 35, R17, File V, p. 79.

182 Dr. M. did not consider himself an alcoholic at this time. He would later to join the fellowship, thus, the requirement for anonymity is being followed.

183 *Alcoholics Anonymous, The Australian Experience*, Commemorative Edition, The General Service Board of Alcoholics Anonymous, Australia, ©1995, p. xvi.

184 Bobbie to Dr. M., February 2, 1943, *One to Another*, p. 43, The General Service Board of Alcoholics Anonymous Australia, ©2014.

[185] *Medicine Looks at Alcoholics Anonymous*, today included in "Three Talks To Medical Societies" by Bill W., pamphlet P-6, Alcoholics Anonymous World Services, Inc., not dated, pages 27-28.

[186] The following is adapted from pages 27 and 28 of *Three Talks to Medical Societies*. The intent is to compare Bill W.'s words presented in May 1944 to those Bobbie wrote on May 4th, 1943 in a letter to Dr. M. almost a year earlier. Both wrote five ways medicine differs from religion in treating alcoholics. In both, religion and medicine were on the same lines, which isn't possible to show here as written. Instead, the presentation is vertical, with Bill W.'s (BW) writing directly compared to Bobbie's (BB). The 1944 pamphlet stated: "Let's compare briefly what in a general way medicine and religion tell the alcoholic." Bobbie's answers of a year earlier resemble Bill's but vary sometimes.

1. BW Medicine Says:	The alcoholic needs a personality change.
1. BB Medicine:	Personality Change
1. BW Religion Says:	The alcoholic needs a change of heart, a spiritual awakening
1. BB Religion:	Spiritual awakening, conversion etc
2. BW Medicine Says:	The patient ought to be analyzed and should make a full and honest mental catharsis.
2. BB Medicine:	Analysis and Catharsis
2. BW Religion Says:	The alcoholic should make examination of the "conscience: and a confession — or a moral inventory and a frank discussion.
2. BB Religion:	Moral Inventory plus honest discussions or confessions.
3. BW Medicine Says:	Serious "personality defects" must be eliminated through accurate self-knowledge and realistic readjustment to life.
3. BB Medicine:	Adjustment by re-education, self-discipline and self-understanding, unselfishness – to cure self-centeredness.
3. BW Religion Says:	Character defects (sins) can be eliminated by acquiring more honesty, humility, unselfishness, tolerance, generosity, love, etc.
3. BB Religion:	Religion adjusts by recommending the virtues – honesty, humility, tolerance.

4. BW Medicine Says:	The alcoholic neurotic retreats from life, is a picture of anxiety and abnormal self-concern; he withdraws from the "herd."
4. BB Medicine:	Doctor says we must get back into "The Herd."
4. BW Religion Says:	The alcoholic's basic trouble is self-centeredness. Filled with fear and self-seeking, he has forgotten the "Brotherhood of Man."
4. BB Religion:	Preacher says we forget "Brotherhood of Man."
5. BW Medicine Says:	The alcoholic must find "a new compelling interest in life" must "get back into the herd." Should find an interesting occupation, should join clubs, social activities, political parties, or discover hobbies to take the place of alcohol.
5. BB Medicine Says:	Doctor says we must find a "new compelling interest" – hobbies, politics, clubs, change employment, sex relations, etc.

[187] *One to Another*, p. 50, letter dated July 13, 1944.

[188] *One to Another*, p. 52.

[189] From Alcoholics Anonymous, New York, NY, "Markings, Your Archives Newsletter," Vol 34, No. 3, Winter 2014/2015: "At the same time, Dr. Tiebout remained active in his field, and continued to publish academic articles on A.A. and the treatment of alcoholism. His first such article, published in 1944 in *The American Journal of Psychiatry*, was titled "Therapeutic Mechanism of Alcoholics Anonymous." This article served as an introduction to the A.A. program of recovery, and explained A.A. to the scientific and medical communities. It demonstrated the importance of ego reduction to the alcoholic, and made it clear that a religious awakening contributed to the recovery of the early A.A. members. The concept of "surrender" is repeatedly emphasized by Dr. Tiebout in this and other articles, meaning that the individual must become totally willing to accept their own powerlessness and the need for help from a greater power. However, Tiebout is careful to emphasize that the alcoholic must surrender fully, rather than simply comply with the wishes of a therapist. He believed that there could be no compromise with the ego, which could always reassert itself and lead to drinking once again."

[190] *One To Another*, p. 55.

[191] Ibid., p. 57.

[192] Ibid., p. 58, 59. No letter to Rex by Bobbie found in the book.

[193] Ibid., p. 59.

[194] Ibid., p. 61.

195 Did she have to have approval from the Trustees or Bill W. to send these six copies to Australia? The cost would be $15 for the six books plus a substantial postage charge. While her job title was secretary, sending six books to Australia without approval suggests she was more an executive than a secretary.

196 *One To Another*, p. 66.

197 Ibid., p. 66-67.

198 Ibid., p. 70. Note that Bobbie had used this phrase seven months earlier in letters dated 3/27/1945 to New Haven, Connecticut and 3/30/1945 to San Francisco. Both letters involved radio broadcasts. The strategy was to have others outside of A.A. provide favorable publicity rather than A.A. members providing it. Thus, she was knowledgeable of "attraction rather than promotion" no less than thirteen months prior to its introduction to the Fellowship.

199 Ibid., p. 71. Claiming "eleven years of experience" dates approximately from Bill's sobriety date. While this might be a rather minor exaggeration, doesn't Bobbie here resemble Bill through stretching numbers?

200 Ibid., p. 68.

201 Ibid., p. 73.

202 Ibid., p. 73-74.

203 Ibid., p. 76.

204 Ibid., p. 76.

205 Ibid., p. 78-79.

206 Ibid., p. 83.

207 Ibid., p. 84.

208 Ibid., p. 94.

209 Ibid., p. 95.

210 Ibid., p. 96.

211 Ibid., p. 97.

212 Ibid., p. 103.

213 Ibid., p. 108.

214 Ibid., p. 110.

215 Ibid., p. 111.

216 Ibid., p. 113.

217 Ibid., p. 119.

218 Ibid., p. 120.

219 Ibid., p. 130.

220 Ibid., p. 138.

221 Ibid., p. 142-143.

222 Ibid., p. 154.

223 Ibid., p. 161.

224 Ibid., p. 162.

225 Ibid., p. 165.

226 Ibid., p. 176.

227 *The Empty Jug,* Volume 2, Number 6, March, 1946, page 1.

228 Bobbie to Jimmy, 7/22/1946, Chattanooga, TN, Box 52, R24, File Tenn C, p. 43. Jimmy succeeded Carl as the new secretary of the Chattanooga Group: "I grew to know him very well during our almost two years of correspondence." General Service Office Archives, G.S.S.A., ID missing.

229 Carl K. from Chattanooga, TN, to Bobbie B., August 22, 1944, General Service Office Archives, GSSA, ID missing.

230 Bobbie to Carl K., September 1, 1944. A.A. Headquarters did not appear to know of any Chattanooga meetings until November 12, 1943, when Bobbie acknowledged the receipt of a letter from Chattanooga announcing that a group had been formed there. General Service Office Archives, GSSA, ID missing.

231 Carl K. to Bobbie B., September 22, 1944, General Service Office Archives, G.S.S.A., ID missing.

232 Bobbie to Carl K, September 26, 1944, General Service Office Archives, Box 52, R24, File Tenn C, p.11.

233 Carl K. to Bobbie, November 26, 1944, General Service Office Archives, Box 52, R24, File Tenn C, p. 17.

234 Carl K. to Bobbie, March 18, 1945, General Service Office Archives, Box 52, R24, File Tenn C, p. 18-21.

235 Ibid., p. 21, note the reference to Bobbie's last letter, which is missing.

236 Bobbie to Carl K., March 22, 1945, General Service Office Archives, Box 52, R24, File Tenn C, p. 22, 22a.

237 Carl to Bobbie, April 20, 1945 (est. date), General Service Office Archives, G.S.S.A., catalogue information missing.

238 Carl to Bobbie, July 18, 1945, General Service Office Archives, G.S.S.A., catalogue information missing, most likely author error.

239 "The *Grapevine* Adopted As National Periodical, Will Be Made Larger. Beginning with the December issue, four more pages will be added to the *Grapevine* to allow for additional features, and letters and contributing articles from A.A.s throughout the country. The enlargement is in line with the adoptions of the *Grapevine* as the national A.A. periodical as announced in the recent letter from Bill W. to the secretaries of the more than 600 A.A. groups" (The *Grapevine*, Vol II, No. 6, November 1945, p. 1).

240 Carl K. to Bill W., est. date October 15, 1945, page 2 only, G.S.O. Archives, G.S.S.A., catalogue markings missing.

241 Bill W. to Carl K., October 23, 1945, G.S.O. Archives, Box 52, R24, Tenn C, p. 36, 37.

242 *The Empty Jug,* Chattanooga Group of Alcoholics Anonymous, Chattanooga, Tennessee, October 1945, Volume 2, No. 2, p. 2.

243 Bill W. to Carl K., November 14, 1945, General Service Office Archives, Box 52, R24, Tenn C, p. 38, 39, 40.

244 Bill W. to Rev. Sam D., November 14, 1945, General Service Office Archives, Box 39, R19, File GA H, p. 12, 13 (Macon).

245 Bill W. to Rev. Sam D., November 14, 1945, General Service Office Archives, Box 39, R19, File GA H, p. 12, 13 (Macon).

246 Rev. Sam D. to Bill W. November 24, 1945, General Service Office Archives, Box 39, R19, File GA H, p. 12, 13 (Macon).

247 *The Empty Jug*, Chattanooga Group of Alcoholics Anonymous, Chattanooga, Tennessee, March 1946, Volume 2, No. 6, p. 1.

248 Ibid., p. 2.

249 Bobbie to Rev. Sam D., April 10, 1946, General Service Office Archives, G.S.S.A., Catalogue markings missing.

250 Rev. Sam D. to Bobbie, April 13, 1946, General Service Office Archives, Box 39, R19, GA H, p. 17, G.S.S.A.

251 Rev. Sam D. to Carl K., April 13, 1946, General Service Office Archives, Box 39, R19, GA H, p. 14, 15, G.S.S.A.

252 Carl K. telegram to Rev. Sam D., April 15, 1946, General Service Office Archives, Box 39, R19, GA H, p. 23, G.S.S.A.

253 Bobbie to Rev. Sam D., April 17, 1946, General Service Office Archives, Box 39, R19, File GA H, p. 21, G.S.S.A.

254 Bobbie to Rev. Sam D., April 24, 1946, General Service Office Archives, Box 39, R19, File GA H, p. 24, G.S.S.A.

255 Rev. Sam D. to Bill W., June 26, 1946, General Service Office Archives, Box 39, R19, GA H, p. 35, G.S.S.A.

256 *The Empty Jug*, Chattanooga Group of Alcoholics Anonymous, Chattanooga, Tennessee, June 1946, Volume 2, No. 8, p. 1-2.

257 Rev. Sam D. to Carl K., copied to Bobbie, July 5, 1946, General Service Office Archives, Box 39, R19, GA H, p. 37, G.S.S.A.

258 Rev. Sam D. to Bobbie, July 11, 1946, General Service Office Archives, Box 39, R19, GA H, p. 38, G.S.S.A.

259 Rev. Sam D. to Bobbie, July 16, 1946, General Service Office Archives, Box 39, R19, GA H, p. 41-42, G.S.S.A.

260 Bobbie to Rev. Sam D., July 15, 1946, General Service Office Archives, Box 39, R19, File GA H, p. 40, G.S.S.A.

261 Bill W. to Rev. Sam D., July 26, 1946, General Service Office Archives, Box 39, R19, File GA H, p. 44, G.S.S.A.

262 *Twelve Steps and Twelve Traditions, The Grapevine* and Alcoholics Anonymous Publishing. New York, N.Y, 1952, 1953, p. 187.

263 "Why Alcoholics Anonymous is Anonymous." *Language of The Heart, The Grapevine*, Inc., PO Box 1980, Grand Central Station, New York, NY 10163-1980. 1988, p. 213, January 1955.

264 Bobbie to Jimmy, August 7, 1946, General Service Office Archives, Box 52, R24, File Tenn C, p. 45.

265 "This Matter of Fear." *Language of The Heart, The Grapevine*, Inc. PO Box 1980, Grand Central Station, New York, NY, 10163-1980. 1988. p. 267-268, January 1962.

266 Bobbie to Fay of Los Angeles, CA, April 17, 1942, General Service Office Archives, Box 35, R17, File I1, p. 142.

267 Bobbie to Sam of Atlanta, GA, June 24, 1942, General Service Office Archives, Box 39, R19, File GA C, p. 40.

268 Bobbie to Bob of Atlanta, GA, July 8, 1942, General Service Office Archives, Box 39, R19, File GA.C, p. 42.

269 Bobbie to Dick S. of Akron, Ohio, November 20, 1942, General Service Office Archives, Box 49, R23, File Ohio – C.1, p. 39.

270 Bobbie to Ray of San Francisco, CA, February 17, 1943, General Service Office Archives, Box 36, R17, AA.2, p. 162.

271 Bobbie to Dan, from Seattle, Washington, November 12, 1943, General Service Office Archives, information missing.

272 Bobbie to Frank of Los Angeles, California, March 17, 1944, General Service Office Archives, Box 35, R17, File I.1, p. 181.

273 Bobbie to Phil LaV., LA Central Office, January 26. 1945, General Service Office Archives, Box 35, R17, I.2, pP. 4-5.

274 *Time Magazine*, March 5, 1945.
https://www.a-1associates.com/aa/MAGAZINES/aaonradio.htm.

275 Bobbie to Titus A. Frazee, Executive Director, California Temperance Federation, Los Angeles, CA, March 20, 1945, General Service Office Archives, Box 34, R16, File Cal A., p. 76, California Inquiries.

276 *Twelve Steps and Twelve Traditions, The Grapevine*, Inc. and Alcoholics Anonymous World Services. 1952, 1953, 1981. p. 155.

277 Bobbie to Ed, New Haven, CT, March 27, 1945, General Service Office Archives, Box 37, R18, File L, p. 44.

278 *Twelve Steps and Twelve Traditions, The Grapevine*, Inc. and Alcoholics Anonymous World Services. 1952, 1953, 1981. p. 180.

279 Bobbie to Tom of San Francisco, CA, March 30, 1945, General Service Office Archives, Box 36, R17, File AA.2, p. 235.

280 Bobbie to Dave, Colorado Springs, Colorado, January 3, 1946, General Service Office Archives, Box 36, R18, File C, p. 18.

281 Bobbie to Buck, Albany, NY, May 23, 1946, General Service Office Archives, Box 46, R22, File NY C, p. 30.

282 Bobbie to Harry of Cleveland, Ohio, December 22, 1948, General Service Office Archives, Box 49, R23, File Ohio O.1, p. 176.

283 https://en.wikipedia.org/wiki/The_March_of_Time

284 Dialogue comes from the YouTube: https://www.youtube.com/watch?v=6cxacjuPMT0. (Wikipedia)

285 Bobbie to John of Atlanta, July 17, 1946, Georgia Archives, General Service Office Archives, catalogue markings missing. (Some text has been omitted to maintain anonymity).

286 Hollywood. Oct. 8, by Louella Parsons, Motion Picture Editor International News Service, copied from The Democrat and Chronicle of Rochester, New York.

287 Bobbie to Crawford of Cleveland, Ohio, February 14, 1949, General Service Office Archives, Box 49, R23, File Ohio – O, p. 38-39.

288 Charlotte L. to Bobbie, October 1946, The Bobbie Family Collection.

289 Taken from Alcoholics Anonymous, Cleveland: https://www.aacle.org/my-name-is-and-im-an-alcoholic/. Box 459. 2012.

290 Big Book Sponsorship: https://bigbooksponsorship.org/articles-alcoholism-addiction-12-step-program-recovery/fellowship/aa-meeting-introduce/. Underline in the original.

291 The Alcoholic Foundation Bulletin dated June 5, 1947 signed by Bobbie and her colleague Charlotte.

292 Bobbie to Ray of San Francisco, CA, November 17, 1943, General Service Office Archives, Box 36, R17, File AA.2, p. 210.

293 Bobbie to Ray of San Francisco, CA, November 17, 1943, General Service Office Archives, Box 36, R17, File AA.2, p. 197.

294 Bobbie to Ray, August 11, 1942, From the General Service Office Archives, Box 36, R17, File AA.2, p. 153.

295 Bobbie to Wally G. of Akron, Ohio, October 29, 1942, General Service Office Archives, Box 49, R23, File Ohio – C.1, p. 38.

296 Bobbie to Charles L. of Savannah, GA, November 16, 1942, General Service Office Archives, Box 39, R19, File GA I, p. 2.

297 Bobbie to Bill H. of Cleveland, November 17, 1942, General Service Office Archives, Box 50, R23, File Ohio O.19, p. 10.

298 Bobbie to Tom of the Buffalo Group, November 19, 1942, General Service Office Archives, Box 47, R22, File NY, p. 90.

299 Bobbie to Red, January 26, 1943, General Service Office Archives, Box 37, R18, File G, p. 53. Bobbie to Luke, February 2, 1943, General Service Office Archives, Box 49, R23, File Ohio – K, p. 11.

300 Seven letters from 1942 collected from the G.S.O. mention the handbook project. The earliest one was on May 5: "They will probably give us ideas for paragraphs in the handbook. We are looking for questions just as much as solutions to spring-board our thinking apparatus into action." (From the General Service Office Archives, Box 46, R22, File NY E, p. 51). On March 3, 1943, Bobbie wrote the following regarding the handbook project: "The handbook is progressing slowly. I doubt very much that we will finish even

the rough draft for several months. This kind of writing must be checked and rechecked very carefully inasmuch as it is a compilation of the experience of all of our groups. As to price, I haven't the slightest idea. That will depend upon the amount of copy and cost of material at the time of printing." (General Service Office Archives, Box 49, R23, File Ohio – C.1, p. 41). While a "Handbook for the Secretary" was published in 1949, to what degree this earlier effort contributed to the 1949 product is unknown. In any case, the letters document that Bill and Bobbie often worked on the project together.

301 *One To Another*, General Service Board of Alcoholics Anonymous, ©2014, Bobbie to Dr. M. of Sydney Australia, February 2, 1943, p. 42-43.

302 Bobbie to Wally G., March 2, 1943, General Service Office Archives, Box 49, R23 File Ohio – C.1, p. 41.

303 Bobbie to Bill B., March 3, 1943, General Service Office Archives, Box 35, R17, m Y.1, p. 27.

304 Bobbie to Wally G. of Akron, Ohio, March 28, 1944, General Service Office Archives, Box 49, R23 File Ohio – C.1, p. 54.

305 W.T.S. of the Charleston Group to Bobbie, March 22, 1943, from the West Virginia A.A. Archives: "We have invited the Parkersburg Group (14 members) and the Columbus Group (hope many of them can come) and have many interested parties who will be here. Incidentally, we have invited the sponsor of the Group (March 15, 1949), Irwin M. ex-Cleveland member who is now in Baltimore, Md. Could go on and on but will save some of the conversation for March 27, 28, & 29th. We do want you and Bill to know that we appreciate your making this visit and hope that while we can hardly supply material for a book, we believe you both need a little relaxation and a change of scenery and it will benefit us."

306 Bobbie to the Charleston Group, West Virginia, April 1, 1943 (Most likely from the General Service Office Archives, however, no references are recorded).

307 Bobbie to Dave D., May 13, 1943, General Service Office Archives, Box 35, R17, File M, P. 10.

308 Bill W. to Bobbie, June 1, 1943, The Bobbie Family Collection.

309 Bobbie to Beth and Ben, June 5, 1943, General Service Office Archives, Box 34, R16, File Cal B., California General, p. 50.

310 Dr. Stephen Smith of Columbia, Missouri to Bobbie, Box 44, R21, File Mo. C., p. 70 (From Area 38 Archives).

311 Bobbie to Dr. Stephen Smith, Box 44, R21, File Mo. C., p. 69 (Area 38 Archives).

312 *The American Weekly* articles are reproduced in Alcoholics Anonymous 1943, The Archives of the General Service Board of Alcoholics Anonymous, pp. 34-35, 38-39, 40-41.

313   Bobbie to Evelyn in Tennessee, August 12, 1943, General Service Office Archives, Box 52, R24, File Tenn G, p. 26.

314   Shepard Spink to John Gillette Roberts, December 6, 1936, The Bobbie Family Collection.

315   Bill W. from the commuter train to Bobbie, August 13, 1944, The Bobbie Family Collection.

316   Bobbie to Dale from Seattle, October 20, 1943, General Service Office Archives, catalogue markings missing.

317   Bobbie to Dr. Stephen Smith, November 16, 1943, Box 44, R21, File Mo. C, p. 81 (Area 38 Archives).

318   Bobbie provided a detailed, scheduled itinerary in advance of the trip. There may be some side-trips within this itinerary that are unscheduled or missing. The train reservations predominantly determined this list, which Bobbie apparently mailed to various groups. There was no date on the itinerary itself. "Bill's itinerary, Leaving NYC on October 24, through Chicago, arriving in Denver on October 27, leave Denver on October 29, overnight in Williams on October 30, leaving Williams on November 1, arriving LA on November 2. Three weeks in LA. Leaving on 11/23, arriving SF on 11/24. Leave SF on 12/4, arrive Portland on 12/5. Leave Portland 12/6, arrive Seattle 12/6. Leave Seattle 12/7, Arrive San Diego 12/8. Leave San Diego on 1/3, arrive LA 1/3. Leave LA 1/3 arrive Tucson Jan. 4. Leave Tucson Jan 7, Arrive Houston Jan 8. Side trip to New Orleans Jan 12. Leave Houston Jan 14, Arrive Dallas Jan 14, Leave Dallas Jan 15, Arrive Little Rock Jan 15. Leave Little Rock Jan 19, through to NYC." From the General Service Office Archives, Box 36, R17, File AA.2, p. 186.

319   *Pass It On*, Alcoholics Anonymous World Services, Inc., New York, New York, 1984, pp. 286-291. The reference to Omaha, Nebraska is from *Lois Remembers*, p. 143.

320   Bill W. from Denver, Colorado to Bobbie, October 29, 1943, The Bobbie Family Collection.

321   *Lois Remembers*, Lois W., Al-Anon Family Group Headquarters, Inc., ©1979, p. 143.

322   *Pass It On*, Alcoholics Anonymous World Services, Inc., New York, New York, 1984, p. 287.

323   Bobbie to Frank, November 3, 1943, General Service Office Archives, Box 34, R16, File Cal E., California Chino Prison, p. 4.

324   Lois W. *Lois Remembers*. Al-Anon Family Group Headquarters, Inc., 1979, p. 143.

325   Bill W. from San Francisco to Bobbie, November 27, 1943, The Bobbie Family Collection.

326   Bill W. from San Francisco to Bobbie, December 2, 1943, The Bobbie Family Collection.

327 Bobbie to Victor M., September 23, 1943, General Service Office Archives, Box 35, R17, File V, p. 62.

328 *Pass It On*, Alcoholics Anonymous World Services, Inc., New York, New York, 1984, p. 286.

329 Bobbie to Ray of California, December 2, 1943, General Service Office Archives, Box 36, R17, File AA.2, p. 211.

330 *Pass It On*, Alcoholics Anonymous World Services, Inc., New York, New York, 1984, p. 290.

331 Letter to the Fellowship from Bill W., January 11, 1944, General Service Office Archives, Box 49, R23, File Ohio O.2, p. 42.

332 Bobbie to Chuck of Denver, CO, December 1, 1943, General Service Office Archives, Box 36, R18, File D, p. 53.

333 Bobbie to Ray of San Francisco, CA, December 2, 1943, General Service Office Archives, Box 36, R17, File AA.2, p. 211.

334 Jay D. Moore. *Alcoholics Anonymous and the Rockefeller Connection*, Shut Up and Get in the Car Publishing, P.O., Box 30032, Albuquerque, NM, 87190. August, 2015. p. 307.

335 Lois W. *Lois Remembers*, Al-Anon Family Group Headquarters, Inc. 1979. p. 143.

336 Bobbie to C.W. of Portland Oregon, March 15, 1944 (est. date), General Service Office Archives, catalogue information missing.

337 Bobbie to Bern of Knoxville, Tennessee, May 1, 1944, From the General Service Office Archives, Box 52, R24, File Tenn G., p. 36. "I am very disappointed that I won't be with Bill and Lois as originally planned but the work here has gotten so heavy Bill and I cannot be away at the same time. Please note the new address when you write us – we've moved to larger offices in the Grand Central area."

338 Fulton Oursler (January 22, 1893 – May 24, 1952) was an American journalist, playwright, editor and author. In July 1944, in the second *Grapevine* ever published, he was to write the charming article "Charming Is the Word for Alcoholics." Fulton's second wife was Grace Perkins, a writer. Several of her novels were made into films. Oursler published the novel *The Greatest Story Ever Told* in 1949. This is the couple to which Bill must have been referring.

339 Bill W. from the commuter train to Bobbie, April 11, 1944, The Bobbie Family Collection. Pass It On dedicates Chapter Sixteen to Bill's interests in "persistent fascinations and involvements with psychic phenomena," which led to so-called "spook" nights.

340 Mel B. *My Search for Bill W.* Hazelden, Center City, Minnesota, 55012. 2000, p. 22. In addition, *Pass It On* includes this sentence on p. 293: "Now, scarcely five years later [in 1943], he was plunged into an abyss of such bleakness and negativity as to make him suicidal."

[341] Robert Thomsen. *Bill W.* Hazelden, Center City, Minnesota, 55012-0176. 1975, p. 299.

[342] Francis Hartigan. *Bill W.* Thomas Dunne Books. St. Martins Press, 175 Fifth Avenue, New York, NY, 10010. 2000. p. 166-167. Hartigan has the year as 1945 when the meetings began with Dr. Weekes. However, *The Soul of Sponsorship* by Robert Fitzgerald, S.J., Hazelden, Center City Minnesota, ©1995, has Bill starting visiting Dr. Weekes in 1947. In addition, an explanation for Bill as Mr. A.A. and Bill as simply a human with needs is provided on p. 44 in a letter Bill wrote: "[The doctor's] thesis is that my position in AA has become inconsistent with my needs as an individual. Highly satisfactory to live one's life for others, it cannot be anything but disastrous to live one's life for others as those others think it should be lived. One has, for better or worse, to choose his own life. The extent to which the AA movement and individuals in it determine my choices is really astonishing. Things which are primary to me (even for the good of AA) are unfulfilled. I'm constantly diverted to secondary or even useless activities by AAs whose demands seem to them primary, but are not really so. So we have the person of Mr. Anonymous in conflict with Bill W——. To me, this is more than an interesting speculation—it's homely good sense."

[343] *Pass It On.* Alcoholics Anonymous World Services, Inc. 1984. p. 292-303.

[344] Nell Wing. *Grateful To Have Been There.* Hazelden Foundation. Center City, Minnesota, 55012-0176. 1992. p. 37.

[345] Evidence is only circumstantial that parental duties required Bobbie to miss the trip. Her daughters were teenagers by this time.

[346]

Year	%Chg	TTL A.A. Groups
1944		325
1945	72%	560
1946	79%	1,000
1947	65%	1,650
1948	21%	2,000
1949	34%	2,685
1950	31%	3,527
1951	26%	4.432

Chart shows percentage growth of A.A. by year starting in 1944. No other year in A.A. history after 1951 had a comparable growth rate higher than 14%. Source: 2013-00-00-Apps-1-Group-and-Member-counts.pdf c/o Arthur S., used with permission.

[347] Bobbie to Bill H., June 30, 1944, General Service Office Archives, Box 50, R23, File Ohio O.19, p. 28.

348 Bobbie to Joe of the Cleveland Group, July 25, 1944, General Service Office Archives, Box 49, R23, File Ohio O.1, p. 168.

349 Bobbie to Albert Scott, August 9, 1944, General Service Office Archives, Box 25, R17, I.6, p. 6.

350 Bobbie to Henry L. S., August 15, 1944, General Service Office Archives, Box 50, R23, O.8, p. 26.

351 Bobbie to Mr. L., August 15, 1944, General Service Office Archives, Box 35, R17, File Y.1, p. 45.

352 Bobbie to Tim, August 23, 1944, General Service Office Archives, Box 47, R22, File NY H, p. 133.

353 Bobbie to Curley, September 1, 1944, General Service Office Archives, Box 47, R22, File NY H, p. 135.

354 Bobbie to Frank, November 15, 1944, General Service Office Archives, Box 49, R23 File Ohio – K, p. 19.

355 Bobbie to Ed in Birmingham, May 2, 1945, General Service Office Archives, Box 34, R16, File Ala B., p. 14: "And now about the invitation for me to visit Birmingham. I can't tell you how much I appreciate the kindness and thoughtfulness back of it and wish I might accept without reservations. Unfortunately, with Bill on the inactive list because of his health, more and more of the work of this office is falling on my shoulders. Until we get more help and an assistant to take over while I am away, I shall have to stick very close to home plate. But please won't you give me a rain check on the invitation. And I do thank everyone who had a part in inviting me to visit with you. I am sorry to end on this- negative note. I wish I might have –said "yes", hop the train and been with you in the very near future."

356 Bobbie to Barry of Minneapolis, Minnesota, November 11, 1944, Box 44, R21, File Minn. G.1, p.8.

357 *Cleveland Central Bulletin*, December 1944.

358 *Alcoholics Anonymous Comes of Age*. A.A. World Services, Inc. p. 208.

359 Nell Wing. *Grateful to Have Been There*. Hazelden, Center City, Minneapolis, 55012-0176. p. 22.

360 Robert Thomsen. *Bill W.* Hazelden. Center City, Minnesota, 55012-0176. 1975. p. 281.

361 Bobbie memo to the groups, February 12, 1945, General Service Office Archives, catalogue markings missing.

362 Bobbie to Warren T. of Richmond, CA, May 3, 1945, General Service Office Archives, Box 35, R17, File S, p. 69, 69a.

363 Bill W. to Leonard Harrison, May 2, 1945, full text 3877 words, source confidential.

364 Ernest Kurtz. *Not God*. Hazelden. Center City, Minnesota, 55012. 1979, Chapter V "Attaining Maturity" p. 111.

365   Bobbie to Warren T. of Richmond, CA, May 3, 1945, General Service Office Archives, Box 35, R17, File S, p. 69, 69a: "Also, perhaps you haven't heard that Bill, on doctor's orders, has been inactive in this office for almost a year. He became so rundown and exhausted that it was necessary for him to think of his health first. Inasmuch as he gave all his time to us for ten years I guess we will have to agree now that he does deserve a good rest."

366   Bobbie to Fred, October 3, 1945, Atlanta, GA, G.S.S.A., From the General Service Office Archives, catalogue markings absent: "Suppose you will attend the meeting Monday [October 8] at Birmingham. How I wish Bill, Lois and I could make it. When science finds a way for a person to be in two places at the same time, I'll take to the road again. Right now with Bill inactive it is necessary for me to be right behind this desk."

367   Bobbie to Web, December 18, 1945, G.S.S.A. Archives, Macon, GA, General Service Office Archives, catalogue markings illegible.

368   Bobbie to Vic, February 1, 1946, General Service Office Archives, Box 35, R17, File V, p. 115.

369   Bobbie to Sterling, February 26, 1946, General Service Office Archives, Box 35, R17, I.6, p. 17.

370   Bill W. to Bobbie, February 27, 1946, The Bobbie Family Collection.

371   Bobbie to George, April 11, 1946, General Service Office Archives, Box 36, R17, File AA.2, p. 267.

372   According to Ancestry.com, Charlotte was born on January 9, 1916, making her twelve years younger than Bobbie. She lived in Hocking, Ohio, according to the 1930 census, which is 50 miles southeast of Columbus, Ohio. She was in Logan, Ohio in 1935, just seven miles from Hocking. She married in 1937. Just 16 months later she married a second time. In 1939, she resided in Columbus, Ohio. The date of her third marriage is not known. She was married to a Joe T. by 1949, though while working with Bobbie, she seemed to keep her maiden name. She lived until March 27, 1987 and died in Warrenton, Virginia.

373   Charlotte L. to Bobbie, October 1946, The Bobbie Family Collection, written while Bobbie was in California.

374   Ernest Kurtz. *Not God*. Hazelden. Center City, Minnesota, 55012. 1979. p. 350.

375   Charlotte to Luke, August 9, 1946, General Service Office Archives, Box 49, R23 File Ohio – K, p. 25. Charlotte also documents that she started work with Bobbie in April and that she joined A.A. in Cleveland about five years ago.

376   Bill W. To Rev. Sam D., July 25, 1946, General Service Office Archives, Box 39, R19, File GA H, p. 44.

377   Ernest Kurtz. *Not God*. Hazelden. Center City, Minnesota, 55012. 1979. p. 120, 351, Bill W. to Bobbie dated September 17, 1946.

378   *Pass It on*, p. 326-327.

379   *Lois Remembers*, p. 149.

380 Bobbie to Warren T. of Richmond, CA, October 1, 1948, General Service Office Archives, Box 35, R17, File S, p. 85.

381 Christmas Bulletin dated December 5, 1946, printed on a lovely piece of Christmas stationary with a candle in the upper left-hand corner along with holly and poinsettia leaves.

382 Bobbie to Gay, January 13, 1948, General Service Office Archives, Box 35, R17, File J, p. 13-13a.

383 Ibid., p. 13-13a.

384 http://area83aa.org/docs/archives/83Mar2018.pdf.

385 Bobbie to Rev. Sam D., April 14, 1948, General Service Office Archives, Found at the GSSA, catalogue markings missing.

386 Bobbie to Elizabeth, May 4, 1948, General Service Office Archives, Box 35, R17, File Y.2, p. 5.

387 *Lubbock Morning Avalanche*, Lubbock, Texas, 17 April 1948, page 1, "Story of How Alcoholics Anonymous Had Aided Hundreds Over Nation Related At Meeting Here," Subtitle "AA Sectional Convention to Conclude Today."

388 *St. Louis Star Times*, St. Louis, Missouri, April 23, 1948, page 12, "Many Alcoholics Described as Persons of Great Ability." Selected from the article: "The nation's alcoholics were praised here today as being usually men or women of great intelligence and skill and extremely ambitions people. The praise came from Bill W., an eastern broker and co-founder of Alcoholics Anonymous . . ."

389 Bobbie to Harold, May 7, 1948, General Service Office Archives, Box 36, R18, File D, p. 96.

390 Bobbie to Jim, June 4, 1948, General Service Office Archives, Box 47, R22, File NY H.1, p. 26.

391 *The Austin American*, Austin, Texas, "At Least 800 Expected Here for AA Parley," June 16, 1948, page 13.

392 *New Press*, Fort Myers, Florida, "Co-Founder of Alcoholics Anonymous Says 'We're [All a] Bunch of Screwballs,'" September 4, 1948, page 1.

393 *Des Moines Tribune*, Des Moines, Iowa, October 23, 1948, Page 1. This page 1 article contains a very unusual quote from Bill regarding his length of time sober. Taken directly from the article: "Not How Old – How Long Dry! A.A.'s Quick With Answer Here at Convention." by Lillian McLaughlin. Ask Bill, the former Wall Street broker who was one of the founders of Alcoholics Anonymous, how old he is—and he'll have to stop to think. 'Let's see now,' he says,' then remembers, '53!' But ask him how long he's been 'dry,' and the answer whips right back in a split second. 'Thirteen years—on Nov. 4 it'll be 14!'" From most every other source, Bill's correct answer should have been December 11, 1934 when he checked in for the last time into Towns Hospital.

394 *Star Tribune*, Minneapolis, Minnesota, October 24, 1948, page 20.

395 Bobbie to Central Group A.A.s, January 27, 1949, General Service Office Archives, Box 34, R16, File Ark E-1, p. 9.

396 Frank Amos to Bobbie, February 4, 1949, The Bobby Family Collection.

397 Bobbie to Harold, April 13, 1949, General Service Office Archives, Box 36, R18, File D, P. 113-113a.

398 "Growth of Alcoholics Anonymous Described as Group Meets Here." May 23, 1949. *The Gazette* (Montreal, Quebec, Canada).

399 *Dr. Bob and the Good Oldtimers,* A.A. World Services Inc., New York, New York, 1980, p. 202: "Dorothy S. informed the New York Office that a committee of seven—five men and two women—was functioning in the Cleveland area. In addition to being the first central committee, this is said to be the first example of rotation in A.A., since one man and one woman dropped of each month to be replaced by the next in line according to seniority. Bill W. gave Al G., the first chairman, credit for setting up the principle of rotation in A.A., either in the fall of 1939 or upon the later establishment of a more formalized central committee. "Up to that time, all of our affairs had been in charge of the ultra-oldtimers, and we naturally supposed it would always be that way," said Bill."

Also: *A Narrative Timeline of AA History*, Accumulated and Edited by Arthur S, Arlington, TX, Version 2014-03-01, p. 41: "**1941** - August, Clarence S, founder of AA in Cleveland, joined with Abby G and other Cleveland members to help start AA's first Central Office. Bill W also credits the Cleveland Central Office with introducing the principle of rotation to A.A."

400 Bobbie to Ray, December 9, 1942, General Service Office Archives, Box 36, R17, File AA.2, p. 159.

401 Bobbie to Tex, June 23, 1943, General Service Office Archives, Box 36, R17, File II, p. 29.

402 Bobbie to Dale in Seattle, January 19, 1943, General Service Office Archives, catalogue markings missing, Found in N.A.B.A. Archives in Atlanta.

403 Bobbie to Carl K, March 22, 1945, General Service Office Archives, Box 52, R24, File Tenn C, p. 22-22a.

404 Bobbie to Frank, November 22, 1943, General Service Office Archives, Box 34, R16, File Ariz B., p. 2. "The little exception is the use of Bill's name. He is as anonymous in print (when we can control it) as any one else. He prefers it this way and says we are stronger in publicizing the A.A. principles than personalities." Here she has written a close facsimile to the ending of Tradition Twelve more than two and a half years before they were published in the *Grapevine* in April 1946.

405 *Language of the Heart, The Grapevine*, Inc., PO Box 1980, Grand Central Station, New York, New York, 10163-1980. "How A A's World Services Grew Part II," p.154.

406 *Twelve Steps and Twelve Traditions*, Copyright 1952, 1953 by *The Grapevine*, Inc., and Alcoholics Anonymous Publishing, Sixteenth printing, p. 191-192.

407 The $20,000 figure written by Bobbie in a letter to Mrs. Herbert M, January 15, 1946, General Service Office Archives, Box 34, R16, File Cal. A., p. 122.

408 Bob P. *Alcoholics Anonymous World History*, General Manager, G.S.O., 1975-1984 (Some may refer to this history as the *Manuscript of AA World History*), p. 150. Note: there is an online PDF available of the Bob P. history, but the page numbers of the PDF do not match the hardcopy referred to here. Nell Wing in *Grateful to Have Been There* wrote on page 33 that by 1949 "we had six A.A. staff gals and fourteen other employees."

409 *Our A.A. General Service Center, The Alcoholic Foundation of Yesterday, Today and Tomorrow,* by Bill, Part 1, "The Alcoholic Foundation of Yesterday," April 8, 1947, Page 21.

410 *Our A.A. General Service Center, The Alcoholic Foundation of Yesterday, Today and Tomorrow,* by Bill, Part 2, "The Alcoholic Foundation of Today," April 8, 1947, Page 4.

411 Ibid., p. 7.

412 Ibid., p. 8-9.

413 *Our A.A. General Service Center, The Alcoholic Foundation of Yesterday, Today and Tomorrow,* by Bill, Part 2, "The Alcoholic Foundation of Today," April 8, 1947, Page 9: "All this was done by a staff of twelve people – three alcoholics and nine "nons". It cost the A.A. Groups about $36,000, still averaging a dollar a member for 1946, a year of steeply rising expenses."

414 Nell Wing. *Grateful to Have Been There, My 42 Years with Bill and Lois and the Evolution of Alcoholics Anonymous*, Second Edition. Hazelden, Center City, Minnesota, 55012-0176. p. 15.

415 Ibid., p. 20.

416 Ibid., p. 15.

417 "Traditions Stressed in Memphis Talk," *Language of the Heart, The A.A. Grapevine*, Inc., PO Box 1980, Grand Central Station, New York, New York, 10163-1980. October 1947. p. 67.

418 "Why Can't We Join AA, Too," *Language of the Heart, The A.A. Grapevine*, Inc., PO Box 1980, Grand Central Station, New York, New York, 10163-1980. October 1947. p. 108.

419 "Tradition Two," *Language of the Heart, The AA Grapevine*, Inc., PO Box 1980, Grand Central Station, New York, New York, 10163-1980. January 1948. p. 78.

420 Arthur S. *A Narrative Timeline of AA History*, Public Version. 2014. Pg 49 of 134.

421 Tom Y. to Bobbie B., April 20, 1948, The Bobbie Daughter's Collection.

422 Tom Y. to Bill W., April 20, 1948, The Bobbie Daughter's Collection.

423 *AA History Lovers*, Message 8194.

[424] For a summary of the history of the A.A. Grapevine: *A Guide to the A.A. Grapevine, The Story of the International Journals of Alcoholics Anonymous and a Workbook for Grapevine and La Vina Representatives*, The A.A. Grapevine, Inc., 475 Riverside Drive, New York, New York 10115, ©2004, Appendix I, p. 54-58.

[425] Bobbie to Tom Y., April 22, 1948, The Bobbie Daughter's Collection.

[426] General Headquarters, PO Box 459, Grand Central Annex, New York 17, NY, May 14, 1948, TO ALL MEMBERS.

[427] Bulletin dated November 10, 1948: "Our Charlotte L., one of the General Office Staff Secretaries, has gone upon a long leave of absence which may prove permanent. She goes with her husband, Joe T., to Ohio where they have both made business connections of much promise."

[428] Bobbie to Charlotte L., September 16, 1948, The Bobbie Daughter's Collection.

[429] Cleveland Central Bulletin, December 1948, p. 3.

[430] Bobbie to Art of Binghamton, NY, February 14, 1949, General Service Office Archives, Box 46, R22, File NY E.1, p. 14.

[431] PROPOSED MATTERS FOR DISCUSSION AND APPROVAL AT THE MEETING OF THE FINANCE COMMITTEE OF THE ALCOHOLIC FOUNDATION, INC. MARCH 3, 1949. SUBMITTED BY MARGARET R. B., The Bobbie Daughter's Collection. Note: Names have been altered from a title (Miss or Mrs.) followed by a last name to first name, last initial to ensure anonymity even if they were not alcoholics.

[432] AA History of General Service, Margaret B., 1942-1949, Oklahoma Archives Committee, May 1990: From Page 3, Minutes of the Regular Quarterly Meeting of the Board of Trustees of The Alcoholic Foundation, July 25, 1949: "It was moved by Mr. Amos, seconded by Mrs. Birrell that Mrs. Marion M. be offered the position of Senior General Secretary of the General Service Headquarters at a salary of $400 per month, effective August 1, 1949, and Mrs. Ruth B. be offered the position of General Secretary at $400 per month; both on a temporary basis for six months, to be continued if mutually agreeable.

Mrs. M. to be Senior Secretary for the period of one year, at which time the seniority will be rotated and so successively at yearly intervals, subject to change at the discretion of the General Service Committee.

Motion was carried.

Messrs. Harrison and Kerr voting nay.

It was moved by Mr. Amos, seconded by Mr. Stanley that as of August 1st the Secretarial Staff be composed of:

Ann L. at a salary of $325 per month
Virginia T. $300
Polly F. $300
Lucy P. $250

Motion was carried.

Mr. Kerr voting nay.

[Note: Names of secretaries have been altered from a title (Miss or Mrs.) followed by a last name to first name, last initial to ensure anonymity, even if they weren't alcoholics. Trustees names have been left alone.]

[433] PROPOSED MATTERS FOR DISCUSSION AND APPROVAL AT THE MEETING OF THE FINANCE COMMITTEE OF THE ALCOHOLIC FOUNDATION, INC. MARCH 3, 1949. SUBMITTED BY MARGARET R. B., The Bobbie Daughter's Collection. Note: Names have been altered from a title (Miss or Mrs.) followed by a last name to first name, last initial to ensure anonymity even if they were not alcoholics.

[434] From Works Publishing Inc., Present Officers and Directors, 1948, "The directors of Works Publishing, Inc. also function as the General Service Committee." Five names are listed as current directors one of which is Bobbie's along with Leonard V. Harrison. This appears to be a ballot to elect the next group of directors.

[435] The February 7, 1949 bulletin provided details of the 1949 budget, which totaled $76,000, or $1,000 more than stated in later bulletins. There is no explanation for this difference. Salaries are listed here at $50,000, or about two-thirds of the entire Headquarters budget for 1949.

[436] *Alcoholics Anonymous Comes of Age.* Alcoholics Anonymous Publishing, Inc., (now known as A.A. World Services, Inc.). USA. 1980. pp. 211-212.

[437] Esther E. from Dallas, Texas to Bobbie, May 29, 1949 (Note, the letter itself was just marked "Sunday," but the date derived from the date it was received at Headquarters, June 1, 1949, which, coincidentally, matched the day Anne died.)

[438] The Gazette, Montreal, Quebec, Canada, Monday, May 23, 1949, p. 3.

[439] Lucy P. to Art C., May 24, 1949, General Service Office Archives, Box 46, R22, File NY E.1, p. 16.

[440] The Gazette, Montreal, Quebec, Canada, Wednesday, May 25, 1949, p. 15.

[441] Dick S. to Bobbie, mid-April 1941, The Bobbie Family Collection: "You are simply tired, Bobbie. You've been under a pretty stiff strain – you know – you take this work seriously – and have been dealing with sick, sensitive people.

The best of us, only on the way to recovery. Knowing full well that actually, will never catch up with it."

442   Dick S. to Bobbie, May 19, 1942, The Bobbie Family Collection: "Don't over do – oh hell, what's the use of arguing with a nit wit – I have, for a year now – and you do over do – and in doing it weaken yourself – we must as you say do everything you <u>can</u>, but you should also do it as <u>nice</u> as you can – and that don't mean in an overtired condition."

443   Esther E. to Bobbie, May 29, 1949, The Bobbie Family Collection. The first paragraph of the letter reads as follows: "Honey – Did I have a thrill last Saturday night! Dr. Bob and Anne came to see me!! We'd had a gang out all day. It was about 8:30 – Frank was in his pajamas reading. I was barefoot, in shorts writing to mama. Was so excited I never could find my shoes the whole time they were here!! Well Dr. Bob said he was so glad he got to see so much of me!! They were here for a week with Bob & Betty – resting – Anne wasn't well – and still isn't – young Bob talked to his Dad today & Anne is under an oxygen tent. Some sort of virus."

444   Bobbie to Ebby T., June 1, 1949, The Bobbie Family Collection.

445   Bobbie to Clarence P., June 6, 1949, The Bobbie Daughter's Collection.

446   General Service Headquarters, Alcoholics Anonymous, 1949, Bulletin #5, June 7, 1949.

447   Fiona Dodd. *The Authors*. 2012. p. 174.

448   Bob P. *Alcoholics Anonymous World History*, A.A., General Manager, G.S.O., 1975-1984, "Manuscript of AA World History." 1985. p. 150 of hardcopy. A PDF exists, but the page numbers are different. These words appear on p. 164-165 of that PDF.

449   Bulletin dated November 10, 1948: "Our Charlotte L., one of the General Office Staff Secretaries, has gone upon a long leave of absence which may prove permanent. She goes with her husband, Joe T., to Ohio where they have both made business connections of much promise."

450   Joe T. (husband of Charlotte L.) to Bobbie, July 8 or 15, 1949, The Bobbie Family Collection.

451   Charlotte L. to Bobbie, July 18, 1949, The Bobbie Family Collection.

452   Charlotte L. to Bobbie, "Friday," assumed to be written while Bobbie was staying at Blythewood, The Bobbie Family Collection.

453   Bobbie's "Dream" folder, page 98, June 28, 1949, from Blythewood: "Stayed alone quietly thinking of "silver platter" (from interview), then to [Dr. Tiebout's] article on "surrender". What was my act of surrender? Was it my complete collapse on June 13th at 6:30 preceeding *[sic]* call to Dr. T.? Know and felt I could not go on. Put up every resistance but nothing clicked – mustered every force by which I have lived – THERE WAS NO WAY OUT. Blindly reached for help. It was not help for drinking (am I ducking this?) or

anything I could put a name to – just could not go on on *[sic]* my own. Outside reasons influences (reasons) meant nothing."

454   Marty M. *AA Grapevine*, "Women Alcoholics Have a Tougher Fight." May 1945.

455   From Bobbie's "Dream" folder, page 98, written on or about June 28, 1949 from Blythewood.

456   Ann L. to Harold, June 27, 1949, General Service Office Archives, Box 36, R18, File D, p. 116.

457   Bobbie to Tom B. of Atlanta and Bobbie to Tom B. of New York, July 1, 1949, The Bobbie Family Collection.

458   AA History of General Service, Margaret B., 1942-1949, Oklahoma Archives Committee, May 1990: Page 2, Minutes of the Regular Quarterly Meeting of the Board of Trustees of The Alcoholic Foundation, July 25, 1949.

459   Bobbie to her sister Ruth, July 28, 1949, The Bobbie Family Collection.

460   Bobbie to Uncle Gene, August 22, 1949, The Bobbie Family Collection.

461   Bobbie to Uncle Gene, January 22, 1950, The Bobbie Family Collection.

462   Bill W. *Twelve Concepts for World Service, 2005-2006 Edition.* Alcoholics Anonymous World Services, Inc. 475 Riverside Drive, New York, NY, 10115. 3. Rotation among paid staff workers, p. 58-59.

463   Samples of Bobbie's praise for Charlotte:

September 18, 1946: "I am so happy you have been to the Asheville, N.C. meeting for there you will meet Charlotte L., my very able co-worker. She will bring you closer to our office in her talks for I understand she has been asked to speak on these matters."

April 9, 1948: "Your letter of April 6th addressed to Bill, has come to my attention. During Bill's travels, he asks that Charlotte or I open all his mail and acknowledge it. He will have your letter when he returns about May 1st and will write you himself then."

August 19, 1948. "What a joy and pleasure your letters are, not only to me but to Charlotte. She will be writing you one of these days, but not immediately. Charlotte is a true alcoholic and like all of us can give very good advice, about "Easy Does It" to others, but she seldom applies it to herself. Two or three weeks of too much work finally got her down, and she had a slight upset stomach. She's been out now for a couple of days but called me a little while ago to say she would be in and back to work. I did my best to persuade her to stay in bed one more day but with no success. I do very much want you to know Charlotte – she is not only a lovely person to look at, but has one of the sweetest dispositions I know. Her one fault is in not taking care of herself but perhaps we can attribute that to youth. You see, she is just a youngster and one of the lucky ones who found AA about 7 years ago at the age of 25. Her husband is also an AA member and a darling – together they make what I believe may be called a perfect couple."

464 Bill W. *Our A.A. General Service Center, The Alcoholic Foundation of Yesterday, Today and Tomorrow,* Part 1, "The Alcoholic Foundation of Yesterday." April 8, 1947. Page 21.

465 General Service Headquarters, Alcoholics Anonymous, 1949 Bulletin #7, August 3, 1949.

466 A Letter to All A.A. Members, September 1949, signed by Polly F.

467 Bill W. *The A.A. Service Manual, Combined with Twelve Concepts for World Service.* Alcoholics Anonymous World Services, Inc. 475 Riverside Drive, New York, N.Y., 10115. p. 56.

468 The Alcoholic Foundation Inc., A.A. Group Contributions for General Headquarters Expenses, Statement of Cash Receipts and Disbursements, Year Ended December 31, 1948, dated February 17, 1949. Beginning Cash Balance: $2,319.38. Ending Cash Balance: $9,256.20. Total Contributions: $66,065.86.

469 General Service Headquarters, Alcoholics Anonymous, 1949 Bulletin #2, February 7, 1949.

470 General Headquarters, Alcoholics Anonymous, 1950 Bulletin #4, April 1950.

471 1950 and 1951 figures from Financial Statements of The Alcoholic Foundation and Subsidiaries, Exhibit A-1.

472 1952 figures from The Alcoholic Foundation, Inc. Statement of Income, Expenses, and Principal of Funds, Years Ended December 31, 1952 and 1951, Exhibit C of Appendix I, p. 38.

473 https://en.wikipedia.org/wiki/Harry_Tiebout.

474 Bobbie to Tom B. of Ohio dated July 1, 1949; Letter from Bobbie to Tom B. of Atlanta dated July 1, 1949.

475 General Manager Hank G. to Bobbie, June 14, 1949, The Bobbie Family Collection.

476 Bobbie to Leonard Harrison, June 27, 1949, The Bobbie Family Collection.

477 Bobbie to Tom B. of Ohio, July 1, 1949, The Bobbie Family Collection.

478 Ibid.

479 Dream diary entry dated July 6, 1949, The Bobbie Family Collection. Note: The dream diary was copied and sent to me in the reverse order in which it was written. There are 99 pages copied in the diary. These entries were found on page 97 of 99, which means they were at the beginning of the diary.

480 *Alcoholics Anonymous,* Alcoholics Anonymous World Services, Inc., ©1939, 1955, 1976, 2001, p. 23.

481 Dream diary entry dated July 6, 1949, The Bobbie Family Collection, p. 97.

482 Dream Diary entry dated July 13, 1949, The Bobbie Family Collection.

483 Bobbie to A. Leroy Chipman, July 14, 1949, The Bobbie Family Collection.

484 Ian to Bobbie, July 13, 1949, The Bobbie Family Collection.

485 Jack to Bobbie, July 23, 1949, The Bobbie Family Collection.

486 D.D.S. to Bobbie, July 28, 1949, The Bobbie Family Collection.

487 Major S.O. to Bobbie, August 9, 1949, The Bobbie Family Collection.

488 Dr. M. to Bobbie, August 19, 1949, The Bobbie Family Collection.

489 Larry to Ann L., July 27, 1949, The Bobbie Family Collection.

490 Sam M. to Bobbie, August 10, 1949, The Bobbie Family Collection.

491 Sarah K. to Bobbie, August 11, 1949, The Bobbie Family Collection.

492 Bill S. to Bobbie, August 12, 1949, The Bobbie Family Collection.

493 Sally and Ted B. to Bobbie, August 11, 1949, The Bobbie Family Collection.

494 Susan to Bobbie, August 12, 1949, The Bobbie Family Collection.

495 C.W.S. to Bobbie, (signed Bill S.), August 15, 1949, The Bobbie Family Collection.

496 George to Bobbie, August 26, 1949, The Bobbie Family Collection.

497 Margaret to Bobbie, September 7, 1949, The Bobbie Family Collection.

498 Dorothy to Bobbie, October 5, 1949, The Bobbie Family Collection.

499 Dr. M. to Bobbie, December 17, 1949, The Bobbie Family Collection.

500 Bobbie to Hank G., July 14, 1949, The Bobbie Family Collection.

501 Leonard Harrison to Bobbie, undated, The Bobbie Family Collection. The letter bears the heading "Leonard V. Harrison, 109 East 22nd Street, New York City."

502 Bobbie to Leonard Harrison, July 24, 1949, The Bobbie Family Collection.

503 Leonard V. Harrison to Bobbie, August 18, 1949, The Bobbie Family Collection.

504 Bobbie to Bill W., September 16, 1949, The Bobbie Family Collection.

505 Bill W. to Bobbie, September 27, 1949, The Bobbie Family Collection.

506 Dr. Leonard Strong, Secretary, The Alcoholic Foundation, to Bobbie, November 2, 1949, The Bobbie Family Collection.

507 Bill W. to Bobbie, December 20, 1949, The Bobbie Family Collection.

508 Bobbie to Dr. Leonard Strong, January 18, 1950, The Bobbie Family Collection.

509 Letter to Whom It May Concern written by Bill W., May 7, 1950, The Bobbie Family Collection (Alcoholic Foundation Letterhead).

510 Movie review from IMDb.com: https://www.imdb.com/title/tt0042808.

511 Bill W. to Bobbie, December 21, 1950, The . From the Bobbie Family Collection.

512 Bobbie to Bill W., March 16, 1952, The Bobbie Family Collection.

513 Dr. Leonard Strong to Bobbie, May 14, 1951, The Bobbie Family Collection (Alcoholic Foundation Letterhead).

514 https://www.aagrapevine.org/magazine/1951/jun/conference-report, June 1951 "It was also unanimously resolved that the Conference go on formal record, by letter, as declaring its deep appreciation to Bobbie B. for her years of faithful service as Secretary of AA General Headquarters and the General Service Office."

515 George Singer to Bobbie, October 16, 1951, The Bobbie Family Collection.

[516] Bobbie to George Singer, October 21, 1951, The From the Bobbie Family Collection.

[517] Ibid.

[518] Bobbie to Art of Danbury, Connecticut, General Service Office Archives, Box 37, R18, File E. p. 4.

[519] Bobbie to Jack of Tucson, Arizona, General Service Office Archives, Box 34, R16, File Ariz D., p. 12-13, March 10, 1947.

[520] Bobbie to Harry of Jamestown, NY, General Service Office Archives, Box 47, R22, File NY T, p. 11, October 14, 1942.

[521] Bill W. to Chet, February 13, 1952, The Bobbie Family Collection.

[522] https://en.wikipedia.org/wiki/Shirley_Booth.

[523] Bobbie to Helen B. of Headquarters, March 16, 1952, The Bobbie Family Collection.

[524] Ibid., p. 2.

[525] Bobbie to Bill W., March 16, 1952, The Bobbie Family Collection.

[526] Ibid, p. 2.

[527] Bobbie to Gloria and George Singer, February 12, 1953, The Bobbie Family Collection.

[528] City of New York, Department of Health, Bureau of Records and Statistics, Manhattan, February 25, 1953. #56-53-104210.

[529] The obituary of Bobbie's husband appeared in the Brooklyn *Daily Eagle*, Brooklyn, New York, on February 19, 1929 with a date of death of February 18.

[530] Note from Lauren W., Bobbie's grandchild, regarding conversation she had with her father on May 13, 2019. The Bobbie Family Collection. (Note the slight modification changing "Dad" to "George.")

[531] According to Ancestry.com, Charlotte lived until March 27, 1987 and died in Warrenton, Virginia on March 27, 1987. Her participation in A.A. after her New York experiences in 1949 aren't known.

[532] Note from Lauren W., grandchild of Bobbie, regarding conversation she had with her father on May 13, 2019. From the Bobbie Family Collection.

[533] Oxvision Films, July 31, 2019, The Hound of Heaven – The Story of Francis Thompson, https://www.youtube.com/watch?v=oN0iq1yzrTk.

[534] "Richard Burton reads the haunting poem 'The Hound of Heaven' by Francis Thompson," https://www.youtube.com/watch?v=gToj6SLWz8Q.

[535] C. S. Lewis. *Letters to Malcom, Chiefly on Prayer*. 1964, 1963. Harper Collins, p. 28

[536] From Bobbie to her first granddaughter Lauren, February 17, 1953, an excerpt from her suicide note, found by her bedside by her son-in-law. The Bobbie Family Collection.

[537] Bobbie's estate, handwritten note found in safe deposit box at the Chase Safe Co.,

March 1, 1953
To Sybil, Gloria, George & Bob –

This is the note mentioned in my will to cover special gifts to friends.
$100.00 to Mary L. A.

After Sybil and Gloria have divided my effects and each has chosen what she
wishes (amicably I hope and know) please choose (or let each friend choose)
something of mine for the following friends.

Charlotte L. T.
Ann M.
Ruth D.
Virginia B.
Virginia S.
Elizabeth A.
Marie E.
Tom B.
Dr. T.

(This will take some thought but I'd like him to have something of mine).
Anyone else I have forgotten.

I didn't list you, George and Bob, because in reality you are "in" this on this
through your wives.

Please give my complete set of *AA Grapevine* issues to Bill W. The almost
extinct copies (first 5 years) are in a box in top shelf of linen closet – others
in book shelves.

If neither Sybil or George want my tea set, offer first to Virginia & Bill B.,
then dispose of as you wish or to one of the above mentioned friends, perhaps
Charlotte.

Sybil & Gloria – divide jewelry, furs, etc. between yourselves, that is what
is not in box marked Sybil & Gloria. I make no division myself knowing you
will both bend over backwards to give each other the best break. There is
plenty for your both.

Please return gun and ship it to Ruth and Johnny D.

I hope you'll take your ½ share of my small life insurance policy and do something silly, different or exciting with it, something you wouldn't do otherwise – like a luxurious vacation cruise or trip. Think it will stretch to a short one for each of you and your husbands.

I would honestly not like a funeral. Perhaps the four of you will be with me to the cremation (as soon as law allows – can be in few hours) and my ashes to go to Brooklyn with your father – ask Uncle Bill about this. Anyone who want to remember me with flowers, please substitute check to cancer fund – you girls can give me a few red roses or gladiolas.

The above (all this note to the four of you) are my wishes <u>if you agree</u>. Don't want to impose any set promises or demands – you who are left should make all final decisions as you think best.

You'll miss me (I hope you do) but for crying out loud, go on enjoying life to its fullest knowing that I'm O.K. and in spite of some trouble I've had a very wonderful life being your mother.

Mommie
Bobbe

My safe deposit box is now at Chase – West 14th Street Branch. Savings account at Bowery (42nd St.). All insurance or life policies either in the box or my file home.

In book case (outside girl's room door) is a multilith copy of an AA book. It's very valuable as there were only about 50 printed. Today there are only a few known copies. If George doesn't want it sent it to Ray H. in San Francisco. Get address from Bill W. Also advise on value if George keeps it.

[538] *A.A. Grapevine*, April 1953, P.O. Box 1980, Grand Central Station, New York, NY, 10163-1980

[539] Even a book published in 1999 by three authors (who will remain nameless) that was intended to document significant female contributors to A.A. did not include a chapter on Bobbie. They did for both Ruth and Nell. Though Bobbie was an alcoholic, and Nell and Ruth weren't, the one mention Bobbie did receive broke her anonymity and did so by misspelling her last name (p. 93). They referred to Bobbie as just a staff member. They claimed that it was Bobbie that introduced Nell to Bill W., while Nell's biography reported that it was Charlotte L., who was Bobbie's assistant, that actually did the introduction. They didn't mention that Nell was hired to be Charlotte L.'s

assistant and that her first role was mainly to be a receptionist. Instead, they immediately elevated her importance. They insisted that Nell was involved in answering inquiries resulting from *The Lost Weekend*, despite the fact that the movie premiered 15 months (November 16, 1945 according to the Arthur S. Timeline) before Nell was hired on March 3, 1947. The controversy resulting from Marty Mann and the NCEA letter took place in September 1946—a half year before Nell was hired. As the only source quoted by these three authors was Nell Wing's biography *Grateful To Have Been There*, they on occasion misrepresented Nell's words and invented some of their own.

[540]   Tom B. from Cleveland, Ohio to Bobbie. One letter is dated April 13, 1943. The other is undated, but appears to have been written around the same time. The Bobbie Family Collection.

[541]   *Language of the Heart*, "How AA's World Services Great Part II, Copyright ©1988 by the *A.A. Grapevine*, Inc., PO Box 1980, Grand Central Station, New York, NY, 10163-1980, p. 152

[542]   *Alcoholics Anonymous Comes of Age*, 1957, 1985 by Alcoholics Anonymous Publishing Inc., New York, NY, p. 16.

[543]   Ibid, pp. 196, 198.

[544]   Bill W. to Gloria Singer, March 30, 1953, The Bobbie Family Collection.

[545]   Bill W. *The A.A. Service Manual, Combined with Twelve Concepts for World Service*. Alcoholics Anonymous World Services, Inc., 475 Riverside Drive, New York, N.Y., 10115. p. 56.

[546]   Robert Thomsen. *Bill W.* Harper & Row, Publishers, Inc., 10 East 53rd St., New York, N.Y., 10022. p, 334.

INDEX

I

I Am an Alcoholic 160
    RKO 15 short film 160
I Am An Alcoholic 161
I'll Cry Tomorrow 18
Illinois, Chicago 32, 33, 35, 51, 65, 78, 88, 91, 158, 170, 171, 177, 202, 211, 213, 299
    Formation of 2nd black A.A. group 88
Illinois, Evanston 256, 257
I'm a Big Girl Now 296
India 253, 254
Iowa 154
Iowa, Des Moines 155, 212, 213
Ireland 92, 93, 253, 254
Ireland, Dublin 92

J

Jack C. 32
Jackson, Charles 148
Jellinek, E. M. 70, 155
Jenn
    From California 156
Jews 42, 104
Jim S. of Washington D.C. 87
Joe L. 223, 224
    Charlotte's husband 273
John Barleycorn 76
Jones, Jennifer 295
Julio 272

K

Kaiser Shipyards 47, 64, 65, 66, 67, 68, 180
    Only Company Openly Employing an A.A. 64
Kansas City Times 172
Keith and Orpheum Circuit 158
Kennedy, Dr. Foster 55, 150
Kentucky, Lexington 256

Kentucky, Louisville 183, 185
Killinger, Barbara, Ph.D 236
King School Group 79
Kinnane, Adrian 67
Kissing Time 4
KPASS radio 152
KRJ Radio 149
    Egregious A.A. historical errors 149
KRNT Radio Theater 155
Kurtz, Ernest 200

L

Laird, Landon 172
Lancaster, Burt 278, 280
Lane, Clem 74
Language of the Heart 67, 73, 185
Language Of The Heart 32
Lauren W. 285
    Bobbie's grandchild 282
Lewis, C. S. 285
Liberty Magazine 56, 99
Link, Henry C. 82
Liquor company executives compared to a nest of snakes
    Criticism by Carl K. 139
Liquor industry 134, 139, 152, 293, 295, 297
Liquor's quit us! 173
Little, Rich 158
Lois Remembers 32, 183, 207
Lombardi, Kate Stone 26
Lombardo, Guy 25
LOOK Magazine 195
Lorraine
    Wife of Chet 280
Louisiana, New Orleans 181
Loyola University 32
Lubitsch, Ernst 296
Luce, Clara Booth
    Wife of Henry Luce 16